A CIVIC SURVEY AND PLAN
FOR THE
CITY AND ROYAL BURGH OF EDINBURGH

A CIVIC
SURVEY & PLAN

FOR THE

CITY & ROYAL BURGH

OF

EDINBURGH

PREPARED FOR THE

TOWN COUNCIL

BY

PATRICK ABERCROMBIE, LL.D.

AND

DEREK PLUMSTEAD, A.R.I.B.A.

OLIVER AND BOYD
EDINBURGH: TWEEDDALE COURT
LONDON: 98 GREAT RUSSELL STREET, W.C.
1949

FIRST PUBLISHED 1949

COPYRIGHT

Printed in Great Britain by
MCLAGAN AND CUMMING LIMITED, EDINBURGH

FOREWORD

by THE RIGHT HON. SIR ANDREW H. A. MURRAY, O.B.E., J.P.

Lord Provost of the City of Edinburgh

THE life, the happiness, and the usefulness of the citizen is influenced by many factors and not the least of them is environment. The buildings and their architecture, the open spaces, the roads, and the railways provide the daily environment. They exert an influence on the outlook of man. They can add or detract from human happiness. They can promote or retard efficiency. The importance of Town Planning cannot therefore be overstressed, and accordingly I welcome the Advisory Report presented by Sir Patrick Abercrombie and Mr. Derek Plumstead in their respective capacities as Consultant and Town Planning Officer. Prepared on the instructions of the Town Council, the Report should prove to be an indispensable aid in connection with the statutory obligations placed upon the Edinburgh Corporation by the Town and Country Planning (Scotland) Act, 1947.

We are all entitled to our own views and ideas, but personally I hope there will never be any general desire to increase in any substantial degree either the acreage or the population of the City of Edinburgh. Within our present limits there is ample scope for experiment and for the expansions, rearrangements, and developments which are necessary to our wellbeing. The overcrowded areas must be ironed out to give more living space and to provide healthier and better housing conditions and facilities. Industry where presently cramped and badly situated must be adjusted and given breathing space for development. Transport must be planned to give an efficient service and to meet the needs of all sections of the community. Buildings outworn in their usefulness and forms of architecture that are ugly and without merit must yield their place to new ideas and new conceptions.

During the war years we had of necessity to adapt and to make do. Such an arrangement was costly and irksome. We look forward, however, to a future when we can plan with confidence and in accordance with contemporary and fundamental principles which have progressively found acceptance in all parts of the country. In that planning which must precede building, if we are to develop in an ordered fashion, we must be bold and seek only that solution which will give the best final result. Present planning must be related to an ultimate objective to be attained in the years ahead.

This is no time for passive indifference. The opportunity is ours to-day to employ our gifts to the benefit of our heirs and successors and towards the provision of a better and happier community. I am sure that the Advisory Report with its implications, with the facilities it unfolds and the opportunities it suggests, will command the interest and the attention of all who would seek to enrich a goodly heritage by the noblest contributions of our own generation.

City Chambers
Edinburgh

Lord Provost

PREFACE

TO accept the responsibility of preparing a plan for the future of a City of such history, tradition and learning as Edinburgh seemed daring in the extreme especially as only one of us knew the city and the other carried but the dimmest recollections of a previous visit. In spite of this, however, we welcomed the opportunity of working together again for the third time on city planning. Even a lack of local knowledge has at the outset the advantage that fresh thought and conception can be brought to bear upon the problems as they are found. To discover such a city as a visitor is exciting enough but with the help of contemporary civic survey technique, the study of its character becomes more enthralling as each part of the economic and social structure is unfolded.

Edinburgh is the home of the Civic Survey. The first was launched some thirty years ago by Sir Patrick Geddes but his method was different from the fact finding science leading to a Plan that has developed in recent years. The opportunity had arrived to use a new technique where fact finding and planning are contiguous operations. In any case a fresh survey was required to obtain essential data to meet contemporary conceptions of a very different kind from those of thirty years ago. For instance, between the wars there was the garden city movement and the conception of civic design evolving a new comprehension of unified building groups: there followed the idea of community planning as a counter to the " housing scheme " and when related to communications the precinct principle was evolved.

The results of bomb devastation led to a tremendous impetus being given to crystalising these original thoughts as they are interpreted in planning reports. These reports it is hoped have led the public to a greater understanding of the complexities and scope of town and country planning. The authorities whose cities had escaped devastation rightly realised that the inherent problems were similar to those of the bombed towns and that the biggest stumbling block to solutions was the old bogey of compensation. The new Act removes that obstacle and redevelopment of outmoded areas is now well within the combined resources of central and local authorities.

This report consists of the Civic Survey and the Plan as two essential features set side by side portraying their respective pictures as a whole. The plan contains a set of suggestions in a logically related composition incorporating all the present and future requirements of the city both statutory and otherwise. It is an advisory plan which may be incorporated as a whole or in part in the first statutory development plan under the new 1947 Act. In substance it is the same advisory plan which had been prepared and submitted in outline to the Town Council in October, 1947. This report goes a stage further and elaborates its proposals in some detail and explains its contents.

The Plan and Survey were prepared during the period of office of Lord Provost Sir John Falconer and its submission terminated a period of happy association with a Civic Head who showed a keen and friendly interest in our work. This Report has been prepared during the term of office of the present Lord Provost the Right Hon. Sir Andrew Murray, to whom we are indebted for a similar happy association.

Mr. Macartney, the former city engineer, who was originally nominated to prepare the advisory plan with us resigned his appointment in the early stages to take the Chair of Municipal Engineering and Town Planning at Alexandria : he, therefore, cannot be held responsible for the proposals particularly those relating to traffic contained in the Report.

How all embracing is town planning is revealed in the civic survey where the interest of every Corporation Department fulfilling an important part in city administration is involved. Consultations were held from time to time and we are indebted to the heads of these departments for their help : to the Town Clerk for the important data from which the Clyde Report was compiled and for his kindly help in administrative matters and to the City Chamberlain for the financial aspects of pre-war projects. In the considerable field-work from which the results of the social aspect of the survey were compiled and correlated our thanks go to the Medical Officer of Health and to the Chief Sanitary Inspector and to Mr. Robertson and his team of inspectors and enumerators, (120 or more), for the organised visits to some 123,000 dwellings within the city confines : to the City Architect for the valuable housing records of the inter-war years, to the City Engineer for his assistance in the traffic census and for placing at our disposal the Dean of Guild Court records of building activities. Without the willing co-operation of the City Assessor and his department the industrial aspect of the survey could not have been so comprehensive. For the true position of recreational facilities in Edinburgh we have to thank the Director of Parks for the data that led to the conclusions in the open spaces section : to the Police and Transport departments for their contributions concerning the communications of the city. The police superintendant's Conference on various suggestions for road improvements was encouraging in its constructive criticism.

The Corporation has a tremendous task in modernising its design of schools in accordance with the new Education Act. We are indebted to the Corporation Education Department and to the Scottish Education Department for their guidance.

Mr. Macrae, the former City Architect has contributed Chapter Two (The Historical Review) and we wish to thank him for this important part of the Civic Survey and for the exacting work that lies behind it.

Our task, however, could not be completed without consultations with representative organisations in the city. Serious oversights would have been found in the plan if no account had been taken of the future requirements of British Railways to meet changing demands upon their facilities : the Leith Dock Commission and their programme for doubling the Dock area could not be overlooked : the Edinburgh and Leith Chambers of Commerce had information to impart as did various Government departments : the University afforded the opportunity of working out with their Architect, Dr. Holden, their original scheme for George Square : the Merchant Company and other private schools, National Playing Fields Association, the Rights of Way Society, and others gave material help.

Finally we wish to acknowledge the contributions made by those concerned with the preparation of the report. The rapid and constantly changing scene on the " planning front " created unsettled conditions for staffing and special thanks are due to those who stood the whole course from the beginning. We wish to thank our Spanish friend, Mr. Alfonzo Martinez, for his speedy assistance in producing attractive perspectives of some of the projects. To Messrs. Graham, Flett, P. Lawson, Bennett, Brien, Davidson, Comfort, and to those who gave assistance for part of the time that is Messrs. Mackenzie, W. Lawson, Jack, Wood, and Wight and to those in the modelling section, Messrs. Sunter, Peden, Callan, and Main : to Miss Hogg and Miss Watson for the secretarial work : to Mr. Robertson of the Royal Institute of British Architects library for the index—all of whom contributed in their several ways to the preparation of this report we wish to express our appreciation of the work they have done.

Upon the excellence of presentation depends a proper understanding of the contents and in this we are pleased to acknowledge the results of the willing efforts of the printing trade : to Messrs. McLagan & Cumming of Edinburgh under the direction of Mr. Tom Curr ; to Messrs. Gilchrist Brothers of Leeds, and to Messrs. Vincent Brooks of London, all of whom undertook the difficult lithograph work of the folding maps and the illustrations. Messrs. McLagan & Cumming and Messrs. Gilchrist Brothers carried out the half tone and line block illustrations requiring highest quality in this technique of printing, while Messrs. Henderson & Bisset have solved the complex problem of binding the volume. No one could have contributed more to the art of typography than Messrs. Oliver & Boyd, the publishers. Their setting out of the title pages, contents and index is an essential feature upon which depends the ease of access to the book.

This book but marks the end of the first stage on the road to improvement in the living environment. Everything concerning the City's future still depends upon the action taken in future years. May the reader therefore be the more diligent and free to express constructive criticism whether at home or oversea.

The following are responsible for the finely composed photographs :—
Aerofilms Ltd. : P. 19, 26, 27, 28, 36, 37, 38, 39, 40, 41, 68, 69, 70, 73, 74, 75, 83, 84, 85, 86, 87, 88, 89, 95, 96, 97, 98, 110, 111, 112.
H. Wylie Esq., P. 1. L. T. Swiecicki Esq., P. 20. J. T. Knight Esq., P. 21, 42. R. Martin Esq., P. 14, 13. E. J. MacRae Esq., P. 16. R. E. Scott Esq., P. 8. Miss J. Cottingham, P. 31. G. R. Anderson Esq., P. 25. Reproduced from Oliver and Boyd's "Georgian Edinburgh," by Walter Scott Esq., P. 81, 71, 72. J. S. Spence Esq., P. 43, 44. H. Maclucas Esq., P. 45, 17. J. Downie Esq., P. 46. H. Percy Esq., P. 47. T. E. Taylor Esq., P. 18. W. T. Spiers Esq., P. 54. Reproduced from "Edinburgh" in Ward Lock's Fair Britain Series, P. 60, 61. F. C. Diener Esq., P. 51. F. G. Sykes Esq., P. 55. J. Laurence Tweedie Esq., P. 53. J. B. Shearlaw Esq., P. 52.

INTRODUCTION

by SIR JOHN IRELAND FALCONER, L.L.D.,

Lord Provost of the City of Edinburgh 1945—1948

ONE cannot be said to plan the city of Edinburgh. The City is already there. It has grown through the centuries as necessity has required and permitted. It is extraordinary to find how harmonious and effective that growth has been. Like a natural plant it has evolved. But evolution in nature differs from the direction of man, who alters conditions to meet the designs of the living mind. The advances of progress dictate the requirements of the modern town. Traffic, convenience, health, recreation have all taken on new aspects which together influence the appeal and convenience of a city as a place of residence and work. In providing for the future of an existing town, and especially Edinburgh, one has also to harmonize with the needs of the present the rich legacy which has come down to us from the past, the like of which belongs to no other city.

This plan deals with the growth of a living city and can only be tentative. It shows certain suggestions. Like all such proposals it remains in the realm of suggestion until some action is taken, but it at least gives material which may help to mould opinion. The Corporation have had placed before them the data upon which to build. They have engaged planners of distinction to lend their experience. This is the third city to which the planners' have brought their combined talent. They have given us this plan. I feel sure that what they have produced will be found an invaluable stimulus to future progress. It is put forward as a guide for consideration, discussion, criticism, amendment, and adoption of such part of it as is considered suitable.

The future of this City concerns not merely us, as its present citizens, but our successors, and very many sons and daughters of Scotland all over the world who hold it enshrined in their hearts. It is, therefore, a trust which calls for our most careful consideration.

John I Falconer

CONTENTS

xi

ILLUSTRATIONS

FOLDING MAPS

PLATES

ILLUSTRATIONS : PLATES

ILLUSTRATIONS IN THE TEXT

LIST OF TABLES

PREAMBLE

A Plan for Edinburgh must needs be a hazardous undertaking : there can be few cities towards which the inhabitants display a fiercer loyalty or deeper affection, feelings which have existed in the past and which persist to-day. Even its blemishes are venerated and there is no more endearing term than that which recalls the pollution of its atmosphere. The planner who dares to propose improvements must go warily and whatever he proposes he must expect sharp and informed criticism and even abuse. But fortunately the city's astonishing topography, which with the enrichment of its historic buildings, makes it one of the romantic cities of the world, curbs the exuberance of the reformer, who can use none of the clichés of civic art : Edinburgh binds the designer to her rock-bound site.

Nevertheless no capital City can remain static and even if there were no faults of the past to correct, there would still be the changes of the present to provide for, especially urgent in their impact upon an ancient and venerated shrine. One or two of these changes may be briefly alluded to, well-known though they are : the increased development of a near-by coalfield : the mounting volume of traffic, both local and through, along streets laid out for a less hurried age : a recent and incoherent suburban sprawl, requiring rationalisation for neighbourly life : a new conception of living standards in the old quarters : a desire for a more regular distribution of open space, especially for games : an adequate diversification of industry : the accommodation for a festival : these and other needs are clamouring for treatment as a whole and not each one in a separate compartment, whether of ministry or office. It is the great task of the present to provide for these pressing needs, while at the same time having full regard to the past.

A report upon planning proposals makes no attempt at a general description of the place concerned; this would be especially foolish or foolhardy of a town such as Edinburgh which has an unsurpassed literature, both incidental and direct, including the mighty names of Scott, Cockburn and Stevenson : nor should it pose as a guide book; many of these have been produced, one quite recently and with admirable subjectivity by Mr. Scott-Moncrieff. A survey, by the greatest of modern civic analysts, Patrick Geddes, is also in existence at the Outlook Tower—a pioneer work in urban research.

But without trespassing on these hallowed studies, the planner must seek some precision of background for his proposals, he must show that his apparent rashness is based upon solid knowledge, gathered for his own particular purpose. He has been fortunate that a precise and learned study of old Edinburgh, mediaeval and renaissance, has been recently made by Mr. E. J. MacRae, with this immediate object of the background of reconstruction in view. These historic surveys already published, have been summarised here and brought down to the less attractive but equally important nineteenth century. Other surveys have been expressly undertaken : in the first instance, a plan showing, according to a detailed classification, the exact use to which every square yard of land within the city's boundary is put : a sort of illuminated ordnance map which, taken by itself with its factual limitation, is indeed illuminating. This and other surveys follow, of course, the normal practice in civic

diagnosis : housing, industry, shops, traffic, open spaces, etc. It was felt that an extremely detailed social survey was required owing to the sharp juxtaposition of different types of residence and densities and the difficulty of distinguishing them from the map only : this must be one of the most complete social surveys carried out in any town in recent years, and the opportunity was taken of obtaining useful information for the medical and education officers. Another direction in which the survey has been carried into detail, was that of the trends of industrial expansion or contraction. In the recreational survey a special feature has been made of the football grounds, and their accessibility to and frequency of use made by the clubs.

In addition to the fund of information about the city already available (supplemented, as just remarked, by these ad hoc surveys) the city has for long received suggestions for its improvement : indeed at one time it seemed that every proposal had already been forestalled : it only required some co-ordination of these brilliant, miscellaneous and sometimes contradictory remedies and developments. It would appear that every practising architect and engineer had made his contribution and every technical student had added his dream-project. Finally and most fortunate for the producers of this plan, there is the Clyde Report, the work of three distinguished laymen, whose knowledge of their city is personal and intense and who have made a series of recommendations which, though not embodied in a plan, yet form a coherent program which has been largely followed in the plan herewith presented. In the technical working out of these intricate and interrelated proposals the planners have perhaps gone further than the Clyde Report envisaged : but generally it will be found that the results are a logical detailed development of the general premises of the Advisory Committee.

With this background of knowledge made accessible by survey and with these pregnant ideas put forward by eminent minds, the planner approaches his task with due humility, but also with a certain degree of confidence. The different aspects of the plan which has now been prepared, are given in some detail and under different headings in the Report which follows : the aspects must be assembled in the mind into a mental master-plan to create the whole picture of the future Edinburgh. In this preamble some of the salient features are extracted in order to give a general indication of its contents, rather than a logical sequence of its component parts.

The first aspect to be considered is that of population. The ultimate size of the city is not strictly a matter falling to the local planner to determine : it should be a question of national direction : the size of the capital in proportion to the anticipated population of Scotland. But there is the regional growth, here a foretellable quantity (as concerning the Lothian coalfield). It has accordingly been decided between the planners concerned (like everything else at this stage subject to ministerial confirmation) that the direct colliery growth shall be kept distinct from Edinburgh by means of a cut-off of unbuilt upon land; it is being planned distinctly (though, of course, conjointly) by Sir Frank Mears, the regional consultant. Edinburgh will re-act indirectly, but considerably to this regional increase of population.

This greatest source of new growth being accordingly handled regionally, there is no need to provide for a considerable increase of Edinburgh proper: the figure of *453,000 'resident' population has been taken as a working assumption.

The other principal conclusions arrived at as a result of the social survey are that the reduction of certain patches of very high density can be obtained by regrouping within the city bounds: there is no need for the creation of an external satellite or New Town to take the overspill of the denser parts. Indeed the limits of built-up Edinburgh, as proposed, fall well within the municipal boundary, allowing for its own encirclement of open space except at one part where the green belt must lie wholly without it. This civic green belt will however merge into the regional open spaces and the Pentland National park whose northern tip is within the city.

It is natural in a Capital City to jump from these outermost areas to the centre where is congregated an interlocked mass of varied problems, concerned with traffic, government, office and shopping activities, monumental buildings, national amenities and humble homes. It is indeed difficult to summarise the description of central planning given in Chapter 7. The general aim has been to preserve the outward aspect of this ancient city whose lineaments are familiar throughout the world: to this end the most drastic of the practical road improvements have been threaded through, as it were, the existing structure, passing in many places underground and leaving the superstructure unaffected. Engineering expenses it is believed, will be less than those required for widening and demolishment. The triple-decker road to Princes Street, the eastern connection with Leith Walk: the central connection via the Mound and North Bridge to the Pleasance (joining the valley-crossing from Leith Walk) and finally the western emergence from Princes Street with a wide loop round the Meadows to join the Pleasance route to the south—this group of inter-related road proposals is the solution offered for central Edinburgh's traffic problem. They are also closely related to the removal of the main Waverley Station, and the linking of a local electrified railway: the northern valley thus recovers its full degree of amenity, if not its original loch. The proposed combined railway station, set slightly further back than the Caledonian, from Princes Street, requires detailed study, but it is believed to be feasible, without injury to the Meadows.

The Royal Mile asks for a close integration of historic and architectural treatment with sharply defined zoning: the Lawnmarket and High Street reserved for administrative, central community and commercial buildings and the Canongate redeveloped for residential purposes. There will be some conflict between historic preservation and living conditions, but this can be resolved: there is also an industrial element, which conflicts and which it is suggested must ultimately be eliminated. In special, the surroundings of Holyrood should be made worthy of the Royal Burgh. The retention and enlargement of housing in this quarter will make a real neighbourhood, closely linked with the rebuilt St. Leonards and Pleasance.

The chief feature in the New Town, the lay-out of which is inevitably untouched, being one of the principal examples of renaissance planning of the world, is the great front of Princes Street. Relieved of its through traffic, the problem here is twofold, after the predominent zoning for shops and hotels, is determined. It is assumed that rebuilding is

★—'Resident' population refers to the total number of persons for whom housing accommodation has either been provided or is required in the proposals. The total population includes not only the resident population but those living in hotels, institutions, etc.

inevitable—there are less than half a dozen frontages that could claim preservation; the two questions then are the architectural treatment desirable and the amount of floor space required, affecting the height of buildings. The report is as much against a precise uniformity (the original conception) as it is against an unbounded licence of individual caprice. Princes Street is perhaps the outstanding example in Great Britain of the need for the imposition of control of civic architecture, for which as yet no hint of guidance has been made under the 1947 Act.

The principle of "Precinctal Planning" which runs through the whole scheme for the city, affecting and protecting equally homes, industries, shops, community groups, open spaces, etc. has several well-marked exemplars in central Edinburgh, in some cases only the affirmation of what already exists but which has not escaped invasion. The University quarter with its closely related Hospital and other educational buildings such as Heriot's School has been determined before this plan was presented: it fits into the central scheme and completes ideas and proposals which have been long advocated by Geddes, Mears, the Clyde Report and others, and was nobly begun by Adam.

If the Academic quarter is an old idea, the Festival Centre is new—indeed not yet created, but urgently called for by the new role which Edinburgh has assumed with such world-wide acclamation. The Usher Hall is naturally the focal point of music: but the Festival is of an even wider appeal and it has been felt that the city is large enough to hold two centres, at approximately either end of Princes Street: the other centre accordingly has been located near St. James' Square where a complete remodelling (dictated partly by the central traffic complex) is proposed between the top of Leith Walk and the Register House. Midway between these two Festival precincts lies the Festival Club in the centre of George Street (the old Assembly rooms): there are thus three interconnecting routes; the dignified quiet George Street, the busy shopping Princes Street, the landscape beauty of Princes Street Gardens and the rocky base of the Castle.

The recreation spaces of the central area of a city, should be the climax of the whole park system: this is very much the case in Edinburgh where Arthur's Seat dominates the scene and poses its bare volcanic crags next the Royal Palace: other and equally emphatic focal points are the Castle Rock and Calton Hill. These salient natural features are balanced by the Princes Street Gardens and the numerous squares of the New Town. The Water of Leith, developed as a parkway, provides a link radiating from the centre at Dean Bridge to the Forth at Leith and to the Pentland Hills in the south. The completion of the recreation space system for the remainder of the municipal area, consists in supplementing the impressive acreage of golf courses and hill tops, by distributed play grounds and smaller parks to meet the needs of community grouping.

The encircling green belt has already been alluded to: this includes a narrow but precious coastal strip from Granton to Cramond, and stretches out to the Pentland National Park. A green belt need not be wholly in public ownership and may include farmlands and here should embrace Dalmeny and other lands outside the boundary.

Housing and industry are two studies of paramount importance: they are both comprehended under Zoning Proposals which both delimit areas, and impose restrictions of density and type of use. The residential zones are further affected by the principle of Community Grouping which should permeate not only the new areas but the existing built up city, with its regrouped and reduced population.

The Plan can at this stage do no more than suggest the areas of these communities and indicate their centres : detailed and continuous planning must be forthcoming to achieve this essential aspect of city redevelopment, applying the standards of population, density, recreation spaces, schools provision, church, social centres, shops, etc. The Educational system is shown interpenetrating the residential areas, with its own hierarchy leading from the Nursery school to the University.

Industry is given great prominence in the Clyde Report : this may seem remarkable in a city which is not primarily industrial. But it is certain that the activities of a Capital City, with its obvious role of administrative, educational, business, shopping, cultural and recreational prominence, must also include a solid core of industry which must be given every facility to flourish. Not necessarily to expand greatly : it will be found on examination that the industrially employed population in proportion to the whole, represents nearly the national average; this might well be maintained as the target and attention given to rendering the industries themselves as efficient as possible. This will entail a consider-able amount of removal, for those capable of it, to more convenient sites in close relation to but distinct from residential areas. New industrial estates, one in process of formation, should be located and the chief existing industrial areas, Leith, Dalry and Gorgie, remodelled for greater efficiency.

The road planning of the central area has been briefly alluded to. The general system proposed for the whole area, related to regional and national requirements has been planned so that traffic may reach its destination without invading the precincts into which the city's activities are grouped. Broadly speaking, the main radial system uses new routes in preference to the widening of existing roads : a new grid of main roads is superimposed upon or tunnelled under the existing system, based not upon a single central point or area, but upon the east-to-west axis of Princes Street (itself a reflection of the central ridge from the Castle to Holyrood).

Perhaps the most important single radial proposed is the approach road from the south east : for this a completely new route is possible, avoiding all riparian building and the severing of communities : it runs parallel to the old Innocent railway beneath Arthur's Seat and past Duddingston to con-nect up with the Ministry of Transport's route east of Musselburgh. The normal pattern of ring roads to distribute the radial traffic must be modified to conform to Edinburgh's topography : the central ' ring ' has for its northern section the straight line of the lower level Princes Street; it then loops west round the Castle rock and east under the ridge of Canongate to unite near the southeast corner of the Meadows. An Outer Ring Road could not be justified on the existing destination census, as there is only a small amount of through traffic : but as a long term policy it will probably be required when the coalfields are fully developed.

These, then, are some of the main features of this Plan for Edinburgh with its Centre, its industrial Port of Leith, its sea-side satellite at Portobello, its close-in communities and its surrounding villages. It is planned to consist of a coherent civic unity, framed in its green belt and so distinct from industrial central Scotland on the west, and the growing Lothian coalfield on the east : on the north it has nature's boundary of the Firth and on the south the Pentland Hills.

The Plan has been described as over-bold and presented at an inopportune time : it is true that it endeavours to look ahead for fifty years and should be therefore regarded not as a set piece of design but as the basis for a programme of work. It is also true that these are difficult times and that no great building or engineering operations are being under-taken at the moment. But two successful Festivals have proved that Edinburgh's courage is undimmed and that she will seize the first chance that is given to her to show that she can also lead the world in Civic Design. If this study is of some value for her future, the labour and thought which have been expended upon it will not have been in vain.

AIMS OF CIVIC SURVEY AND PLAN

PURPOSE.

A SURVEY is required to provide up-to-date information about the problems in the city : to anticipate development which will seek to establish solutions whether or not there is a plan. It is better to guide future development by means of a development plan showing all that can be anticipated than hope for the best by leaving it to follow an unguided course. It is the lack of such guidance that lead to the 'laissez faire' results of the past that we all regret to-day and hope to avoid in future and indeed correct.

TRENDS.

IMPORTANCE is attached to the past trends of human activities whether they are economic, as in the industrial field, or whether they are social, as may be reflected in the community life of the home and its environment. In some measure we have to be prophets in planning for the immediate and more remote future, so that it is necessary to consider past trends with those of the present—the present being more indicative of the immediate future, while past trends considered together with those of the present, can give a lead for the more remote future. By way of illustration, attention is drawn in the report to the traffic problems of the roads. Thirty years or so ago, traffic was nothing compared with what it is to-day and, over a pre-war ten-year period, doubled itself. The present traffic is, despite restrictions and shortages of new cars, almost as much as the highest in pre-war and experts agree it will again double itself in ten years time. The plans must clearly allow for this foreseeable trend.

COMPLETE PICTURE.

FROM the mass of data obtained, and illustrated in the form of maps the Planning Scheme may emerge as a logical sequel marrying what is best from the old, with what is considered best for the future. The chapters describe the facts that may be read from these maps ; and a special effort has been made to present the information in a way that is at once attractive and easy in the visual sense to comprehend. This should, therefore, encourage their study and eliminate that natural aversion to the dry-as-dust statistical table. The broad picture they portray while satisfying the first glance, requires close examination to absorb the figures and facts which are either quoted in the Legend and appendix, or on the maps themselves.

HISTORICAL BACKGROUND.

HISTORICAL buildings and features of the city offer a fine heritage. They reflect the traditional character of the periods in the city's historical development. The best and most interesting have been surveyed and recorded so that development proposals may avoid, if possible, demolition. Where a conflict of interest between the historical and future development arises the relative values of each may be justly weighed in the balance.

CRAMOND

CRAMOND

CRAMOND BRIDGE

CRAMOND
BRIDGE

DAVIDSON

BARNTON

TURNHOUSE

CORSTORPHINE

CORSTORPHINE

GOGAR LOCH

SIGHTHILL

JUNIPER
GREEN

CURRIE

SCALE   ¾   ½   ¼   0   ½   1   1½

MAP I

SURVEY OF HISTORICAL EDINBURGH

This historical section illustrates the growth of the City. From early nuclei, Edinburgh remained of small area through the Middle Ages but of gradually increasing density until after the middle of the eighteenth century, when new communications for transport linked the City with the vacant ground to the north.

An exodus of the professional class took place first to the south at George Square, and soon after to the north, where the formal spaciousness of the New Town from Princes Street to Queen Street gave a new setting to their dwellings. This was succeeded by large extensions of open planning to the north, west and east.

The Industrial Era brought a large unplanned increase of building and population only exceeded by the intensive development of the available sites during the inter-war period of the present century. Various extensions of the City Boundaries, the last in 1920, incorporated large rural areas giving the City its present extent of 50 square miles.

This Map indicates the remaining fragments of the works of these succeeding centuries, and is intended to serve as a guide and a safeguard against indescriminate redevelopment.

PLATE I

KIRKWOOD'S PLAN & ELEVATION OF THE NEW TOWN

This record of 1819 of Craig's scheme shows pictorially the elevations of the street facades. Princes Street was infinitely more pleasing than the present-day disorder, though there is monotony in the standard height of its buildings. The scheme, planned in 1766, materialised from public initiative of the Corporation. Following the Renaissance mode, George Street is made the main feature with two formal Garden squares at each end. Princes Street, planned originally for dwellings, has become almost entirely commercial, leaving very little of the original structures, and has become the most important street. Without an amended architectural scheme these changes become unco-ordinated and untidy. A solution in outline is shown on Plate No. XXXI, from which good architecture can be achieved in co-operation with developers. The present layout can still substantially serve contemporary needs as it has for 150 years, but future land use should adhere to the zoning proposals.

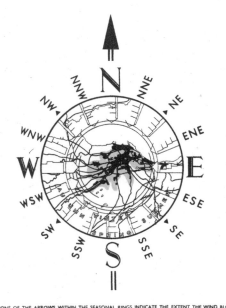

THE PORTIONS OF THE ARROWS WITHIN THE SEASONAL RINGS INDICATE THE EXTENT THE WIND BLOWS AS A PROPORTION OF THE PREVAILING WEST WIND IN SUMMER.
THE LENGTH OF THE ARROWHEADS WITHIN THE ANNUAL RINGS INDICATES THE EXTENT AS AN ANNUAL TOTAL.

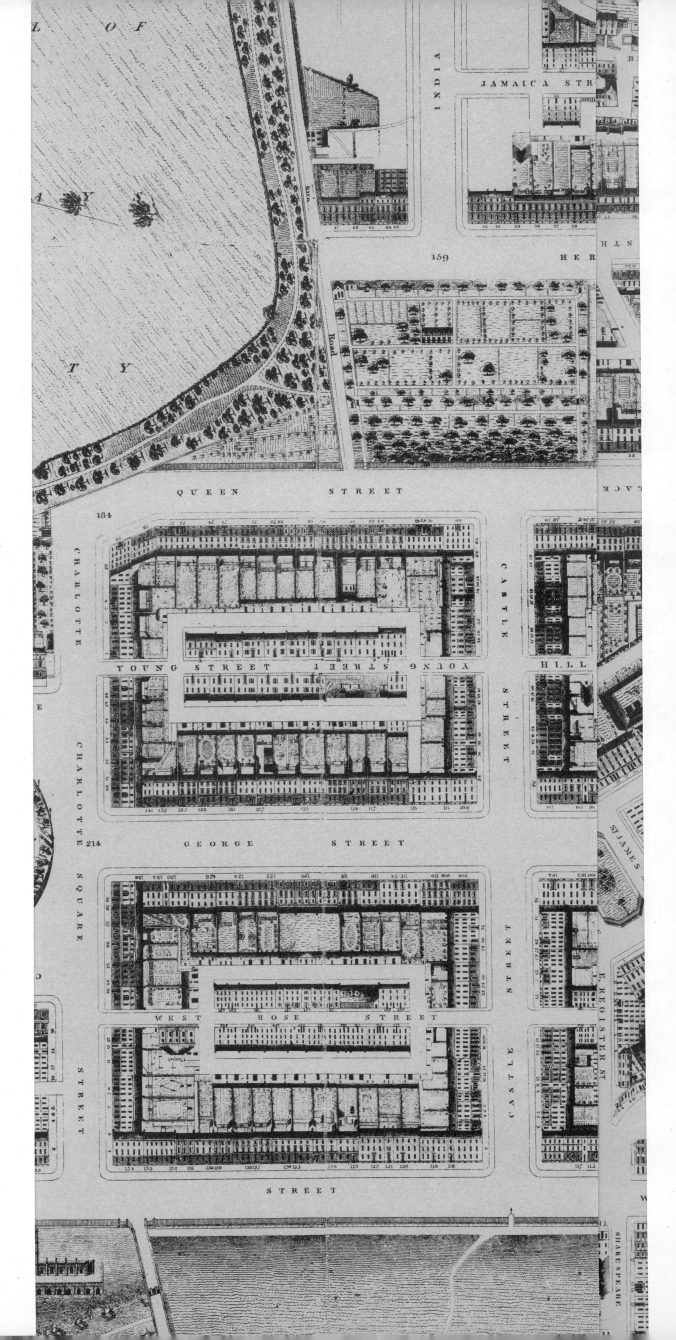

PLATE II

SURVEY
OF
ANN STREET

GENERAL NOTES

The outside and party walls, chimney stacks and skews are of stone, the roofs of slate, the balcony railings of cast iron, and the windows of wood. All interior staircases are of stone.

The only differences which are not represented are the modern dormer windows of Numbers 4, 6, 8, 16, 18, 24, 40 and 42, the modern Mansard Roof on Number 12 and the low garden walls and railings.

The Elevation of the West Side is the same as that of the East Side with these minor exceptions : The window spacing in the South End Block differs slightly ; in the Centre Block the pilaster capitals have no " egg and dart " enrichment and there is a small circular " eye " in the pediment ; the only balconies are at the First Floor windows of Number 13. And there are variations in fanlight and front door design.

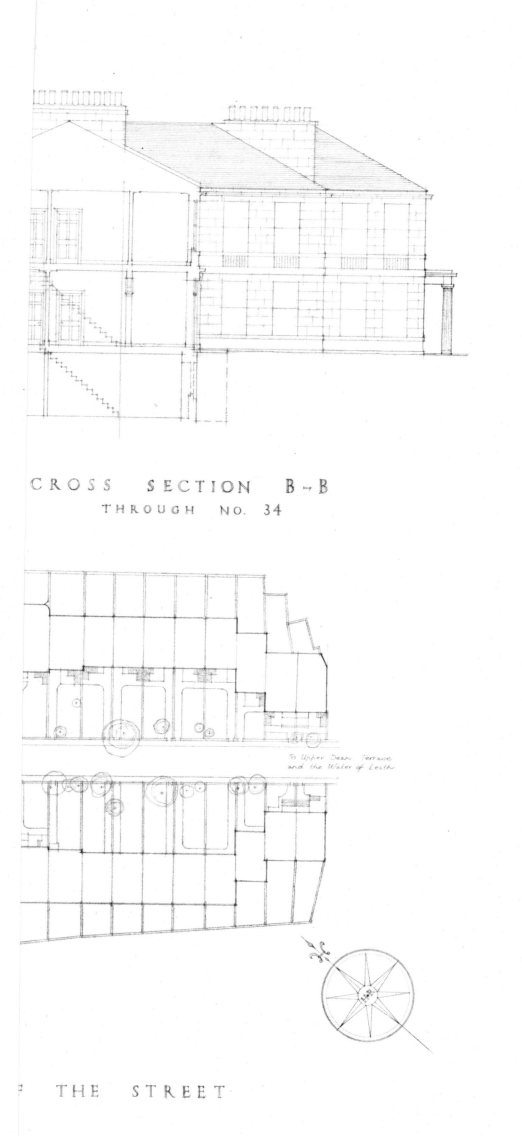

CROSS SECTION B–B
THROUGH No. 34

To Upper Dean Terrace
and the Water of Leith

THE STREET

CHAPTER ONE

HISTORICAL REVIEW

By E. J. MACRAE, F.R.I.B.A.

*This chapter has been written independently and its inclusion does not necessarily indicate
the writer's agreement with the conclusions or recommendations in the main report.*

" Amid much confused and imperfect recollection of picturesque groups of ancient buildings and magnificent assemblages of elegant modern ones, I carried away with me two vividly different ideas—first results, as a painter might perhaps say, of a " fresh eye," which no after survey has served to freshen or intensify. I felt that I had seen, not one, but two cities—a city of the past and of the present—set down side by side, as if for purposes of comparison, with a picturesque valley drawn like a deep score between them, to mark off the line of division."

Hugh Miller—Mason, Geologist, Author—on his first view of Edinburgh in 1824.

THE CITY AND ROYAL BURGH OF EDINBURGH

INTRODUCTION. Edinburgh's diversity of interest as a city is due partly to its natural setting and partly to its evolution during some nine centuries of development. From a Town Planning point of view its interest is that, at two great periods at least, it had a plan.

For convenience the following historical description of Edinburgh has been divided into five periods, beginning with its early history up to Robert the Bruce's Charter of 1329, followed by mediaeval times culminating in the Reformation; then its growth for two centuries under the influence of the Early Renaissance while still confined within its ancient boundaries; the flowering of classical culture for 75 years in Georgian days; and finally the modern development during the last 120 years from the spread of mechanised industry to the present day when the boundaries enclose some fifty square miles with many acres of rural character. At the end of each period a description of Edinburgh is given.

The first five of the nine centuries except for one important break had an almost continuous background of border warfare, the very borderline itself changing from time to time. Edinburgh and the Lothians were part of England until 1018. After that the border, fiercely contested, often overrun for years, once extended southwards to the Tees, remained as before until the Union of the Crowns of England and Scotland in 1603. In these struggles four Scots rulers were killed and three taken prisoner. This border warfare naturally involved destruction of buildings and of burghal records.

Physically, the origin and growth of the city were affected by several volcanic intrusions in the form of abrupt hills from 400 to 800 feet high shaped by the west-to-east flow of the ice in the Pleistocene age and all showing their steep escarpment to the west and tailing off eastward. The most westerly of this group, with a mile long ridge, had near its lower end a hill at each side with converging valleys between where the softer material had been eroded. This ridge with its cliff on the west became the site of the fort which led to the formation of Edinburgh. From one of the other two hills Henry VIII'S armies in mid-16th century viewed the burgh they were ordered to destroy and their reconnaissance has given us the earliest reliable sketch of it (see plate no. III). On this same hill the Greek revivalists of the early 19th century, forcing a resemblance to the Acropolis, erected their monu-ments and introduced modern Athens. The position and form of these hills is clearly shewn in the plan dated 1763 on page 11.

The military sketch referred to above is dated 1544 and every hundred years since then an important plan of the city has appeared—Gordon of Rothiemay's most useful picture of 1647; the first real plan, executed for the Town Council by William Edgar in 1742; the first Ordnance Survey of 1851 and now the new Town Planners' Plan of 1947. For the parts of the surrounding country absorbed in Greater Edinburgh John Laurie's Survey of Edinburghshire in 1763 is the most useful.

Edinburgh up to 1329.

In the second century A.D. the Romans occupied Inveresk a few miles to the East and Cramond a few miles to the West of Edinburgh, but the position of the road between these points is uncertain and practically no visible evidence of the occupation remains within even the present extended city boundary outside of museums. In the interval before 1000 A.D. very little is known of Edinburgh. Even the origin of the name is obscure. The fortress on the crag with the King's seat existed in early centuries and gradually houses were built within the enclosure. Later, leaving an open area in front of the castle for protection, a small hamlet grew up on the Castlehill before the burgh itself was planned.

The year 1018 is important. Then the Lothians ceased to be part of England as the result of the victory of Malcolm II King of the Scots over Northumbria at Carham. In 1076 Malcolm Canmore married Saxon Margaret who had sought refuge in Edinburgh Castle after the Norman Conquest and their daughter Matilda was married to King Henry I of England. Norman influence, already attested by the little chapel in the Castle probably built before the death of Margaret in 1093, increased as David I married the widow of a Norman baron and gave much land and many offices to Anglo-Normans. In spite of this infiltration from the South, the determination of Scotland not to give up the area from Forth to Tweed is one of the marked features of the succeeding centuries and directly affected the history of Edinburgh.

In effect the Celtic forces from the North who drove the Anglo-Saxons southward in 1018 and added for all time the

Lothians to Scotland, were soon after displaced by Anglo-Saxons and Normans from the South who came not forcibly but by invitation. It was during these changing times that the burgh of Edinburgh came into being.

Our first authentic record of the Burgh of Edinburgh is inferential. In the charter granted by David I early in the 12th century to the Abbey of Holyrood he gives from the rent of his burgh of Edwinesburgh an annual grant, a toft or plot of ground and half of the fat, tallow and hides of the slaughters of the burgh, showing that Edinburgh had been for some time established as a King's burgh. The Charter also gave Holyrood ground for a burgh between Abbey and Edinburgh. This became the Canongate, a separate burgh until modern times and never walled, but geographically part of Edinburgh which thus had the Castle on the high ground to the west and its Royal Abbey and later palace at the foot of the slope.

Edinburgh was laid out on a definite plan with its 100 feet wide street in the centre of the ridge (Lawnmarket and High Street of later days) with plots of garden ground behind the houses stretching up and down the slopes on either side, an annual payment being paid to the King, the origin of Scots ' Feu.' The remarkable systematised Burgh Laws of Scotland, Edinburgh being then one of the four Southern Scots burghs, mention the arrangement of a house with a toft of a rood of land. These old quarter acre plots can still be clearly traced from present boundaries. These were contributing factors in the Plan. The Canongate was laid out on similar lines, many of its gardens being still shown on 19th century maps ; one is still there.

The Castle was the origin of the first burgh and it is still roughly the geographical centre of the extended city.

In 1166 the pique of the Scots King William the Lion because of his unrequited services to the English King in France led to an alliance between Scotland and France, which was renewed in 1295 and lasted until the Reformation. This alliance had an important bearing on Edinburgh and its port of Leith which had its beginnings when Edinburgh came into being. During most of the 13th Century Scotland was at peace with England and the burgh of Edinburgh developed rapidly during the long reigns of Alexander I and II, a period of peace not to be experienced again until near the end of the 16th century. The reign of Edward I and his desire to annex Scotland strengthened the Franco-Scottish bond. The English occupied Edinburgh Castle. Then followed the rise of Wallace and Bruce and the liberation of Scotland, when Scots independence was recognised in the Treaty of Northampton in 1328. Such was the background of Edinburgh as it grew from a hill fort to a King's Burgh.

Edinburgh in 1329.

In 1329, for the first time for centuries, the Castle rock had no castle, its defences having been removed by Bruce so that it could not be held by the enemy. Edinburgh was an unwalled burgh with its small houses on its High Street from Lawnmarket to Netherbow backed by their gardens, interrupted by the ancient church of St. Giles. A stream ran down the valley on each side of the ridge. Below the Castle rock to the northwest was the church of St. Cuthbert's, already in being at the time of the 12th century charter to Holyrood. To the south and west of the castle rock were the King's gardens, orchards and farm. South of the stream and path in the south valley the Black Friars had their monastery, then decorated with hangings of Edward II captured at Bannockburn. Beside the monastery garden was the church of Our Lady of St. Mary in the Fields. Beyond on south and north

was still the forest of Drumselch, the name remaining from the Celtic period (the ridge of hunting).

Outside the Town the Canongate was being built on. Merchant Guilds of merchants, (who did not work with their own hands) together with craftsmen were all burgesses recognised by the 12th century Burgh Laws, their work being connected with the simple necessities of food and clothing : the craftsmen were also the beginnings of the Incorporations of Crafts of later years. From the burgesses, men who held, originally direct from the King a plot of ground, the local Government was chosen.

EDINBURGH 1329—1560.

From Bruce's Charter to the Reformation.

Edinburgh's Charter granted by Robert the Bruce on 28th May, 1329, in the last year of his life, is the earliest which has survived, and is a confirmation of earlier charters. " We have confirmed to the burgesses of our burgh of Edinburgh the aforesaid our burgh of Edinburgh, together with the port of Lethe the mills and the rest their pertinents." This led to an awkward relationship between Edinburgh and its port of Leith, about two miles away, which continued until the incorporation of Leith in the extended city of Edinburgh 600 years later.

In 1329 Edinburgh, impoverished by the previous wars, was about to enter another period as devastating. This lasted until the Reformation and prompted the organised defence of the first city wall, built halfway down the southern slope and roughly parallel to the High Street. The stream in the marsh to the north was dammed to form for four centuries the protective moat of the North Loch. The year 1385 saw the severe destruction of the Burgh and its church by Richard II. Again and again the refortified Castle was occupied by the English, once for many years. Gradually factors, including its geographical position, made Edinburgh the Capital of Scotland. At Holyrood in 1503 James IV married Margaret Tudor, sister of Henry VIII. Again Scots Independence was officially recognised and prospects of peace seemed hopeful, but ten years later, James upholding the alliance with France when Henry had entered on a league against her, marched a large army collected from all Scotland against England and there followed the disaster of Flodden in 1513. The Provost of Edinburgh with his Council and the flower of Edinburgh's manhood fought on that field from which few returned.

For Edinburgh one of the direct consequences of Flodden was the defensive City wall built after 1513. This wall, starting from the Castle, extended southwards and taking in the monastic suburbs to the south, returned northwards towards the Nor Loch. (See plan of Edinburgh in 1763 on page 11).

The wall with its controlled gates (ports) at suitable points was actually not effective in keeping out invaders, gunpowder being now at their disposal; but the wall had the definite effect of restricting Edinburgh to its limits for 250 years and for still another century there resulted the excessive overcrowding which is still being dealt with to-day.

Edinburgh suffered further and worse devastation due to Henry VIII's anger at the refusal of the Scots to betroth the infant Scots Queen Mary to his son, preferring the French heir apparent. This is expressed in his directions to the Earl of Hertford in 1544 " beate down and over throwe the Castle, sack Holyroodhouse and as many towns and villages about Edinburgh as ye may conveniently do . . . . . Lyte and burne and subverte it and all the rest, putting man, woman and childe to fire and sworde without exception where any resistance shall be made against you." Hertford's destruction in 1544 and as Protector Somerset in 1547, of Edinburgh and

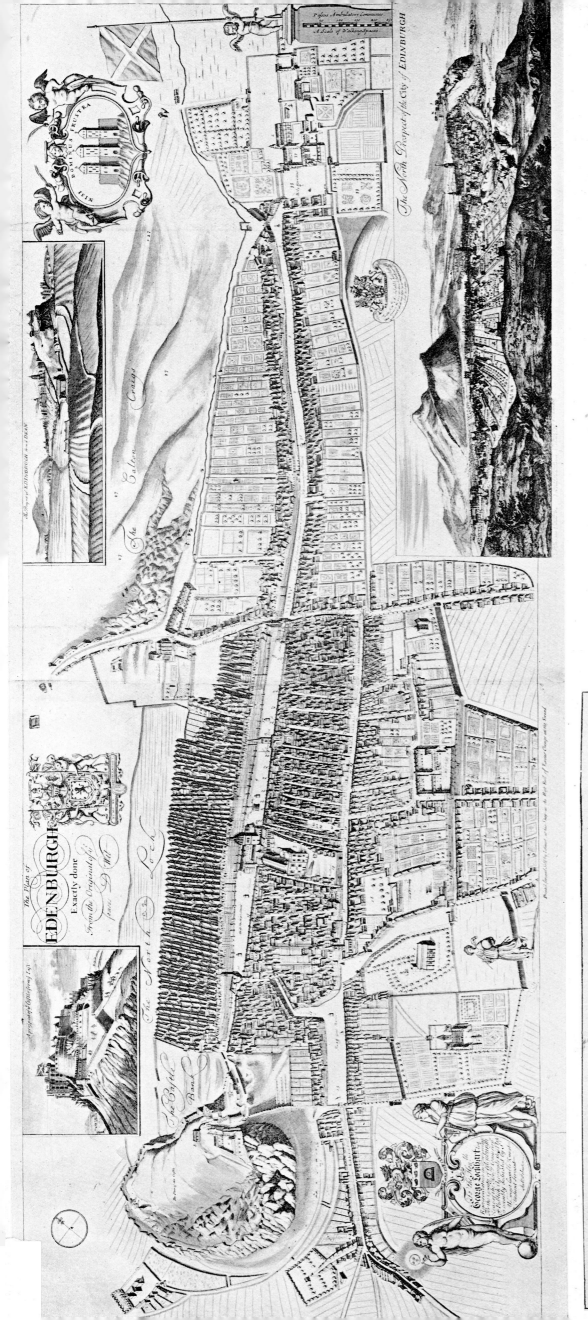

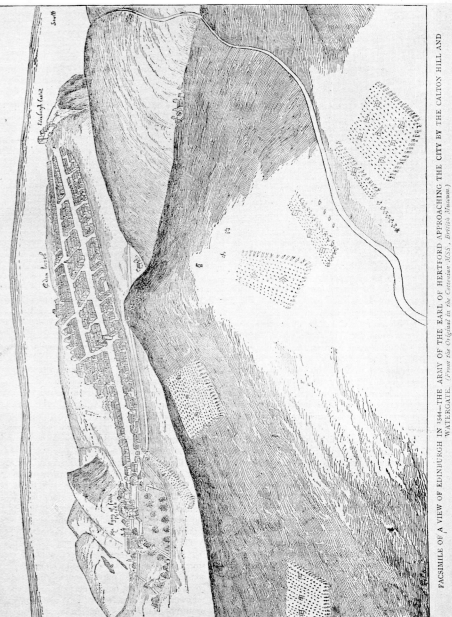

PLATE III

1. *Edinburgh at the time of 1647 is shown here in Rothiemay's Plan (prepared under Commission of the Town Council) built upon a ridge with a fortified cliff. The sketch at the bottom right shows physical features of several volcanic intrusions consisting of abrupt hills some 400 to 800 feet high. It is a walled and moated Burgh showing the Flodden Wall built after 1514 descending southwards from the Castle and embracing the suburbs before returning northwards to the Nor Loch and separating Edinburgh from the Canongate Burgh. Clustered tenements are shown built partly upon the original garden plots in overcrowded profusion. Wynds or closes in between and running down the steeply sloping sides of the ridge connect with the single main street running the length of the ridge now known as the "Royal Mile."*

2. *The Earl of Hertford's military sketch of 1544 shows Edinburgh far less intensively built-up than its successor 100 years later as seen above in Rothiemay's record.*

FACSIMILE OF A VIEW OF EDINBURGH IN 1544—THE ARMY OF THE EARL OF HERTFORD APPROACHING THE CITY BY THE CALTON HILL AND WATERGATE. *Prepared from the Original in the Cottonian MSS., British Museum*

PLATE IV

Hollar's prospect of Edinburgh in 1670 confirms the same overcrowding within the fortifications. The Canongate Burgh, however, still retained spacious gardens being outside the walled town. The rugged features of Salisbury Crags appear in the foreground to the south-east while the Firth of Forth is seen in the hinterland to the north.

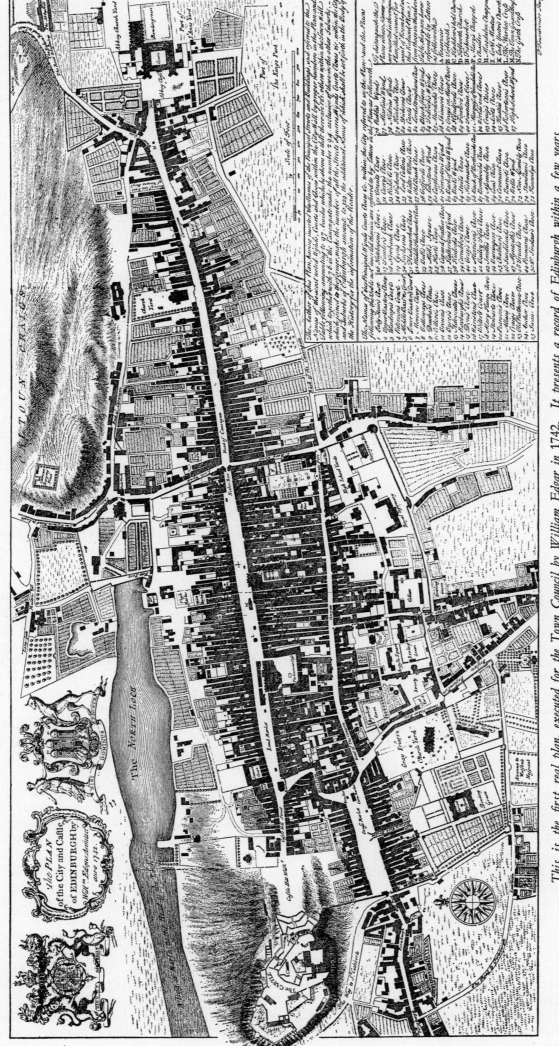

This is the first real plan, executed for the Town Council by William Edgar in 1742. It presents a record of Edinburgh within a few years of the "break out" from the confines of the fortified town to the suburbs of George Square and the New Town. It shows little difference to the mass congestion of Rothiemay's time in 1647. Note how little of the back gardens of the Canongate were built on at this time as compared with the walled town of Edinburgh on either side of the High Street; and compared with to-day where the Breweries now dominate the Palace of Holyrood House.

the villages and mansions near (most of these now part of Greater Edinburgh) was thorough and there is little surviving before these dates; but the battle of Pinkie in 1547 was the last between the two countries.

During all this period of wars and sackings and troubles, the Renaissance was working out along with the struggle between Catholicism and Protestantism. The Port of Leith figures prominently in this struggle when Mary of Lorraine, the Queen Regent, had her palace in Leith. In 1559 French soldiers assisted her in building fortifications round the town of Leith against the Protestant Scots Lords of the Congregation assisted by English troops with their ships. This wall with its nine bastions and a perimeter of a mile and a quarter was a solid defence but had a short life, for after the Reformation settlement, some five years after it had been completed, Edinburgh insisted on the departure of the French and the removal of the portion of the wall next Edinburgh. The remainder disappeared gradually and no trace of it is left now except some of the names of the ports. This was the end of the Franco-Scottish Alliance which had no meaning after Protestantism was established in Scotland and in view of the approaching Union of the Crowns of England and Scotland.

Edinburgh about 1560.

It is interesting to glance at Edinburgh as it was just before 1560, a walled and moated burgh and full of mediaeval colour and life.

Roads everywhere were still primitive. The main street ran east from the Castle and was continued beyond the wall through the High Street of the Canongate to Holyroodhouse, while the only through north and south traffic was outside the city wall. Wynds ran down the slopes to the valley and up again on the other side. Gardens were being built on. The ceremonial approach was by the West Port through the Grassmarket and up the West Bow, the Upper Bow having a gradient of 1 in 5. Most of the houses had still thatched roofs. The jousting ground at the Barras, west of the Grassmarket, laid out by the English occupiers some two and a quarter centuries before, with its attendant chapel, was still complete though no longer used for tournaments. The later tournament ground of Greenside adjoining the church of the Carmelite Friars was being used for open air plays. Two miles out in the forest to the south was a hospital for segregation and treatment during plague adjoining the chapel of St. Roque, 'patron of Pestilences,' and its cemetery was used along with local temporary cleansing stations on each outbreak.

Inhabitants were reminded of justice by the branks at the Mercat Cross and the stocks at the Canongate Tolbooth, while grisly heads could be seen " upon a prick at the highest stone of the Gavell of the Tolbooth towards the publick street." The cross of St. John stood in the street at the head of the Canongate. The Canongate had its own cross and at the foot of the street was the Girth Cross which had to be touched by those who fled from justice at the boundary of the sanctuary of the Holyrood Abbey precincts.

Along the Water of Leith a mile away was a chain of waterdriven mills with little communities growing round them, at this time chiefly for grinding meal for the burgh. Many of these mills were already several hundred years old.

Goods of all kinds were displayed in the 'Markets' at points in the wide High street, Cowgate and Grassmarket. The Merchant Guild had gradually become more important, but the crafts were now in Incorporations, each holding a seal of Cause from the Town Council, with a convener not yet officially recognised. A Convener of Trades is at present a member of the Town Council. Up to this date, however, the crafts were not represented on the Town Council as the Merchant Guild was. Defensive armour became important and building became less primitive, so incorporated crafts had now included armourers, wrights and masons, hammermen. Surgeons were still incorporated with barbers.

In the year 1559 great changes took place following the organised destruction of buildings of the Roman Catholic Church, and the clearing of the sites of the monastic foundations, changes which were to lead to important new uses of the land. Ecclesiastical architecture, apart from the Parish and Collegiate Churches, was practically obliterated. Even these churches were " cleansed " of their fittings, coloured glass and decoration. The pre-Reformation stained glass now remaining in Edinburgh can be held in one hand. Edinburgh had to make a new beginning after the destruction by Henry VIII's emissaries and the Reformation.

Of the period ending in 1560 there are not many buildings surviving except the following :— parts of the Castle, the ruined nave of Holyrood Abbey and the north-west portion of the Palace; the tower and crown of St. Giles, and most of the interior; a rebuilt portion of the splendid church of the Holy Trinity and its altar piece diptych dating from 1470; the chapel of the Hospital of Mary Magdalene in the Cowgate whose patrons were the Incorporation of Hammermen, changed over at the Reformation to the services of the Reformed Church; a few houses in the Royal Mile; the remains of some half dozen castles and towers in the extended city which include Merchiston Castle where John Napier, inventor of logarithms, was born in 1550, and parts of five village churches; but the whole mediaeval pattern and plan of the Old Town is still unchanged.

1560—1750 POST-REFORMATION.

Like some other ancient towns emerging from mediaevalism but loth to leave their established boundaries, Edinburgh remained within its defensive walls with only one small extension until about the middle of the 18th century— a century and a half after the Union of the Crowns of England and Scotland in 1603 had made defences meaningless. We read that the walls of 1513 were still being repaired and kept in order. This had been formerly done " to resiste and withstand the ennemi without and to apprehende and retaine malefactors within " but at the end of this period it was chiefly for the prevention of smuggling which was rife following the new customs provisions of the Union of Parliaments of 1707. Actually the Telfer wall, a formidable battlemented structure, enclosing extensions on which Heriot's Hospital was built, was only begun in 1620. A section of this in the Vennel is still complete.

Though the area of the city remained static for this long period, conditions within the city walls were rapidly changing in two respects, first, in intensity of population and housing and, second, in the re-allocation of the large open area to the south cleared of its Religious Houses after the Reformation.

As to the population, the process, begun earlier, of building on the closes or garden spaces behind the original houses down the slopes from the ridge continued until of each plot only a narrow path (now called a close) was left at right angles to the main street, and on the remainder of the gardens houses were built. As the population increased, the houses on the main frontage were rebuilt as tenements or " lands " of several storeys and these, as well as the houses in the closes, rapidly increased in height until there were continuous tenements which had in an extreme case as many as a dozen storeys. This intensive building, shown on Gordon of Rothemay's picture of 1647 and accentuated later, raised questions of public health owing to the difficulty of applying even rudimentary sanitation in a continuously built area without waterborne drainage. Fevers and plague were endemic and leprosy was common. Outbreaks of the Pestilence occurred with awful severity at intervals until 1645. In the latter year 2,736 people died of plague in the small town of Leith. Energetic and ruthless measures to deal with plague became a matter of routine—segregation, organised disinfection of clothing and summary execution of people concealing infection.

Problems arose also as to the structural safety of the lofty tenements and havoc was wrought by the frequent fires. For example in 1624 Parliament forbade the use of thatch and ordered roofs of new houses to be of slates, or tiles, or lead and it is easy to understand an Act of the Scots Parliament of 1698, " taking into consideration the great danger the " Edinburghers were exposed to by the excessive height of " their houses both in respect of fire and falling, they enacted " that no building to be erected in the city thereafter shall " exceed five storeys in height, the front wall at the ground " storey to be three feet in thickness . . . ." The tenement of several storeys became a fixed feature of life in the Old Town and gave a set in this direction when two centuries

tively large areas formerly occupied by the Religious Houses on the southern suburbs beyond the Cowgate. Within two years of the Reformation the Town Council asked Mary, Queen of Scots, for these lands for educational and other useful purposes. The loss of the monasteries which had been the chief source of relief to the sick and the poor, and of education, made all these problems acute. The deliverance is worth quoting : " for laik of provisioun to supporte " thame quilks ar indeid puir, that their miserabil estait " being under the Hands of God, and veseit be him be " seikness, aige and utherwis they, quilks baith be the Law " of God and Nature oucht to be helpit . . . . . . And siclyke " it is nocht unknawin to your Heines that the common order " quhairby men attains to serve the Common Weill of their " Cuntrie, cumis be letteris, lerning and Sciences quilks " cannocht be obtenit bot be lerning at scules . . . . . ; the " remeid of baith, the quilks we doute nocht, bot be the " erecting of Hospitals to sustene the Puir : and by planting " the scules to bring up the Youth." In due time the pleading was successful. On the largest site, that of Blackfriars were begun in 1578 the High School, in 1635 Lady Yester's Church, in 1697 the Surgeon's Hall and in 1738 the Royal Infirmary. On the site of Kirk o' Field, the scene of the

This drawing illustrates the last phase of building in the Canongate. The five storey 18th century tenements are continuous on the frontage and there are at three points the beginnings of tenement building at right angles to the frontage as " back-lands " built on the original gardens. In the centre is the gable of one of the two storey cottages which were there before the tenements. At the extreme right is the end of a small mansion house entering from the close at some distance from the front street.

later the rapid growth of population in the Industrial Age had to be housed. In the Old Town the social life in these tenements was arranged on intimate lines. Gradations of society were made vertically, all classes entering by one door and passing each other on the turnpike stair, the lowest and uppermost storeys of each tenement housing the poorer families. This had at least the advantage that each class was familiar with the mode of life of all the others.

The second problem was the re-allocation of the compara-

puzzling murder of Darnley, was begun in 1581 the "tounis Colledge " the only Scots University not founded before the Reformation and therefore started under civic, rather than ecclesiastical, patronage. One effect of this start was that it came more under the effect of the Renaissance and from the first stress was placed on its higher standard in the Humanities. As to the Greyfriars' Site " the situatioun thairof being " sumquhat distant from owre Town " the Council asked for this " to make ane buriall-place to burie and eird the Personnis

" deceased thairin, sua that thairthrow the air within owre said " Town may be the mair pure and clene." This was almost immediately granted and the burial ground of Greyfriars now contains monuments shewing the evolution of post-Reformation architecture for over 300 years, with the remains of many of the greatest men of the time, including Regent Morton (buried in the felons' quarter) and George Buchanan, prince of Latinists. On this site the Town Council erected a church in 1612 and by addition a second in 1720.

One interesting venture of the Town should be mentioned as it affected the remainder of this re-allocated land, the open ground between Kirk o' Field and Greyfriars. The name " Society " still survives to mark the establishment there in 1597 of the " Fellowship and Society of Brewers of Ale and Beer in Edinburgh," a commercial Incorporation promoted by the Town Council. Water was led from the south (or Borough) Loch in leaden pipes, pumped up by a windmill which gives its name to a street near George Square. On this site also was an important quarry. On this, and the adjoining area, have been built the science and art museum and the Heriot-Watt College. On the open space, west of Greyfriars, the Merchant Hospital and further west George Heriot's Hospital were built. On the site of the monasteries and adjoining ground therefore—the only area of the city not occupied by dwellings—there came to be built this extraordinary range of institutions dealing with the social needs and culture of the community.

Of the troublous life of Mary Stuart who entered Edinburgh as Queen in 1561 until she left the city for ever in 1567, six years of eventful and dramatic history centred round Edinburgh, its palace and its Castle. The Union of the Crowns under James VI in 1603, while withdrawing the Court from Holyroodhouse and adversely affecting business for a time, confirmed the cessation of warfare with England and led to a state of peace which had a good deal to do with the rise of the new distinctive Scots domestic architecture of the early 17th century, whose L-shaped houses with crow-stepped gables and dormer windows had such a naive perfection of proportion unencumbered by defensive features. Good examples in the extended city are Gogar, Peffermill and Stenhousemill. In the Old Town of this period are town houses like Moray House and Acheson House and tenements like Gladstone's Land, while the public buildings include the old Parliament Hall and Heriot's Hospital, the most important building of its time in Scotland, illustrated on plate no. VI The long struggle of the Covenant, the " Invasioun of the English " during the Commonwealth and the contest between Presbyterianism and Episcopacy all centred round Edinburgh. The Union of Parliaments in 1707 removed to London the seat of Parliament which had been in Scotland for centuries and was a severe blow to the capital of Scotland. The opening up of the Highlands by military roads after the rising of 1715 had its effect on the Jacobite rising under Prince Charles Edward Stewart in 1745 and eventually removed the fear of an Highland invasion, and in the end had the effect of providing peace and security, new opportunities for trade and the preparation of the way for the Golden Age which began after the middle of the 18th century. Trades were still in close Incorporations regulated by very restrictive legislature only removed in 1846. Towards the end of the period under review these numbered fourteen and dealt with Clothing (skinners, furriers, waulkers, websters, tailors, cordiners and bonnetmakers; Food (fleshers and baxters); crafts and building (wrights and masons, goldsmiths, hammermen); surgeons and barbers, dissociated in 1722. Of these Incorporations the Tailors' Hall of the Cowgate is still preserved, as is Candlemakers' Hall in Candlemaker Row.

In the Canongate are two " lands " belonging to the Cordiners (or shoemakers) with the coats of arms of their Incorporation. Several other coats of arms of various trades are built into modern buildings through the Town. From time to time the Town Council, sometimes because of outside suggestion, arranged for foreign craftsmen to come over to give training in new uses of the crafts. At the beginning of the 17th century an envoy was sent to " Ingland " (where many Flemish weavers had settled) and the " Law Cuntreys for the " hame-bringing of Flemyngs and utheris for making of " broad claithe . . . . . . and uther stuffis sic as is maid in " Flanderis of our Scottis woll " to instruct master weavers and contracts were later entered into with them. A village specially built for French weavers in 1730 has given its name to Picardy Place, off Leith Street.

Water supply was largely from public and private wells and from the South Loch : but in 1674 water was brought in lead pipes from Comiston, three miles away.

Edinburgh in 1750.

In area Edinburgh was generally as in 1560 but was more closely built on. The Canongate had houses on the frontages but most of the gardens behind the houses were still complete except at the head of the Canongate next Edinburgh. Outside the city wall ribbon development was taking place on the coaching roads to the south at Potterrow, Bristo and the Pleasance. Off the Grassmarket the suburb of Wester Portsburgh was established. The mediaeval city still occupied the Ridge and ran down to the valleys. North to south communications were still outside the city walls. The principal gates were the Netherbow Port and West Port, the latter leading to the town by the West Bow. The walls were still complete. Frontages had been varied by the building of Milne's Court (1690) and James' Court (1725) and the first modern square, Argyll Square, had just been built off the present Chambers Street. St. Giles still had in front of it on the High Street the Luckenbooths, a range of high buildings forming a fashionable shopping centre with the Tolbooth in line with them to the west. Edinburgh's oldest statue of lead of Charles II erected in 1685, stood in the Parliament Close near the picturesque Jacobean Parliament Hall. The Castle had its palace and Half Moon Battery. Holyroodhouse had its new palace, the Abbey had disappeared, its abbey church was a ruin, but a new parish church had been built in the Canongate.

To the north was the Trinity College church with its hospital.

1750—1825 THE GEORGIAN AWAKENING.

To a stranger in Princes Street to-day the first impression is of a monumental city. He sees this broad street with an Acropolis at the end; on one side the street is open to the sun with a view over a valley to the Castle Crag and the silhouette of the Old Town upon the ridge. Then he sees the delicate harmony of Charlotte Square, George Street linking it with St. Andrew Square; further north are Heriot Row, Great King Street, Royal Circus, Drummond Place, and further west Moray Place—all open, orderly, imposing.

It is necessary to say something about this New Town, its provenance and its history. In every respect this production of George the Third's reign is the antithesis of the Old Town with its narrow closes herring-boned on the backbone of the ridge and built for defence. Here everything is open and spacious. It is the visible expression of Edinburgh's Golden Age, built up during a period of some two or three generations. Starting at a time when not a single street had been built for hundreds of years, whole streets graced with classic facades were to appear over a large area in rapid succession.

The New Town had its origin in the Renaissance, the reaction from mediaevalism and its outlook, the realisation of the inherent dignity of man as brought out by the study of the humanities. Classical culture led to a study of the architecture of Greece and Rome, and quite appropriately two architectural monographs of importance, both by Scotsmen, had just been published, one on the antiquities of Athens, the other on the last phase of the architecture of the Roman Empire.

This classical outlook dominated the minds of a group of men whose deliberations were to determine Edinburgh's development for centuries. In 1752 the Convention of Royal Burghs, a body continuing an institution as old as Edinburgh itself, appointed a Commission which reported on the development of Edinburgh and urged the building of a Royal Exchange and the extension of the city to the north with a connecting bridge across the valley. One of their number was George Drummond, Commissioner of Excise, six times Lord Provost, whose balanced enthusiasm was behind the new movement.

The arguments made for a New Town are interesting. " There is no risk of the Old Town being deserted, as people of fortune and of certain rank will probably choose to build upon the fine fields to the north and south of the Town, but men of profession and business of every kind will still incline to live in the neighbourhood of the Exchange, of the Courts of Justice and other places of public resort . . . . . Enormous cities are sometimes attended with real disadvantage such as vicious luxury, a general depravation of manners and a loose or neglected police; but let us boldly enlarge Edinburgh to the utmost. As it is not the seat of Government it can never become a centre of luxury and vice." The moral argument, with the apparent non-sequitur of the last sentence, is one which would not occur to the 20th century planner; but it is no doubt explained by the approach of those accustomed to local government, and the outcome was a New Town built by a Town Council.

Before this could take place, a far-seeing architect, James Brown, acquired ground to the south and built as a speculation George Square, and to this spacious Square with its simple and effective elevations on a domestic scale was the first large exodus of the élite from the Old Town, a galaxy

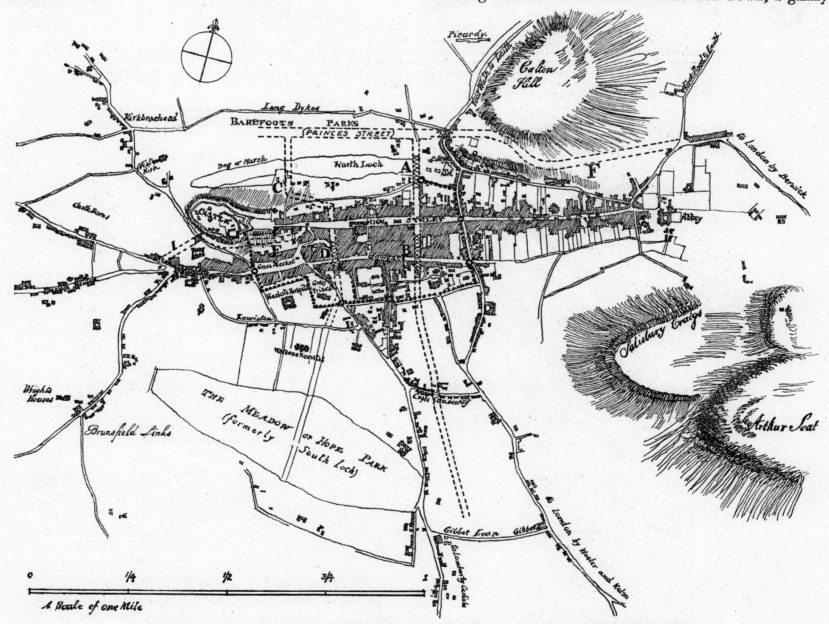

This Map, based on one by James Craig of 1763, shows Edinburgh just before the Georgian Expansion. The City wall, begun in 1513, is shown in a heavy dotted line with black circles for the principal Gates. The only road from north to south is seen outside the City boundary. High Level roads begun in the reigns of George III and George IV are lettered and marked with chain lines, crosses marking the viaducts and bridges.

A. *North Bridge, opened for traffic* 1772.   B. *South Bridge, opened for traffic* 1788.
C. *The " Earthen Mound " opened for traffic about* 1830.   D. *George IV Bridge, opened for traffic* 1836.
E. *Western Approach (Johnston Terrace)* 1836.   F. *Regent Bridge and Road,* 1819.

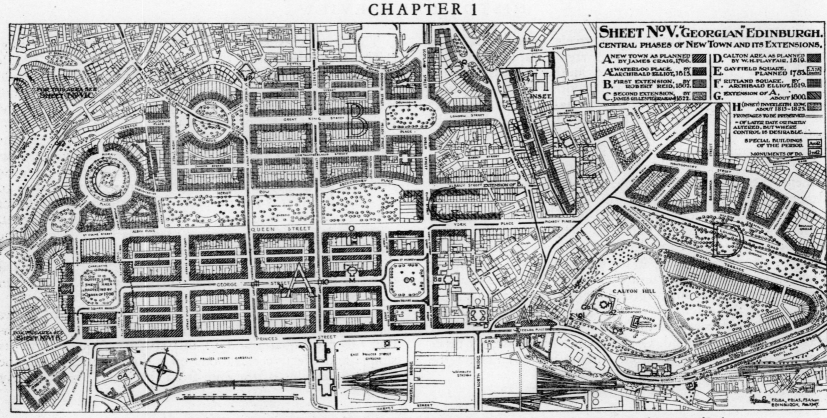

The detail plans on this page illustrate the extent of Edinburgh's heritage of Georgian Planning, the geographical disposition of which is seen on folding map No. 1. The work, carried out in stages over a period of sixty to seventy years, commenced with George Square in 1765 (on sheet No. VI plan A) and followed by Craig's New Town in 1766 (on sheet No. V plan A). The middle of the 18th century saw building expansion in both England and Scotland but it was in Scotland where these great schemes materialised at the instigation of public enterprise. The problems of rebuilding today, envisaged in the Plan, will call for a similar boldness of public initiative.

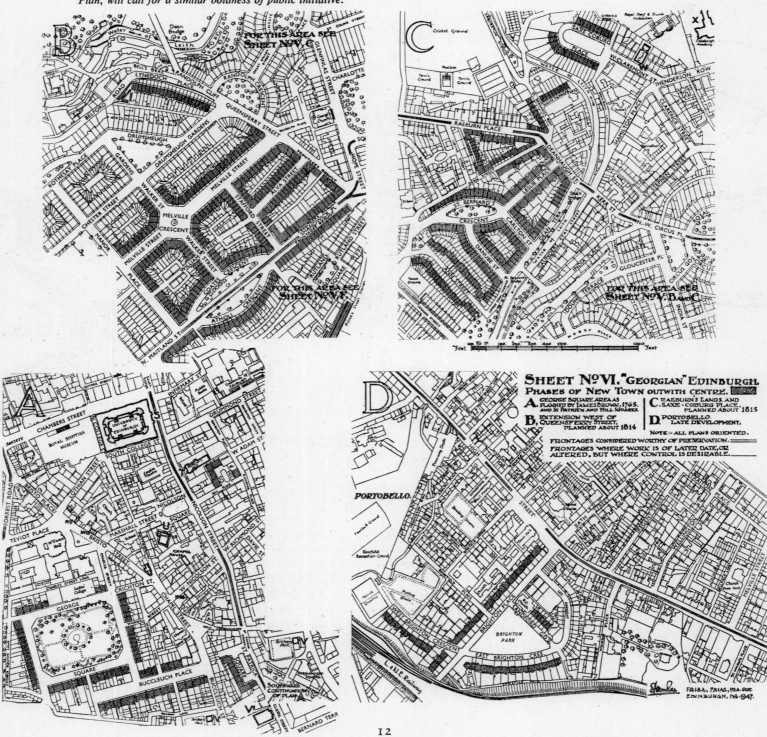

Aerial view of George Square [p. 19]

This is a pre-war view of " South Side " of the Old Town at a time when the St. Leonard's slum redevelopment scheme was in the clearance stage. The main thoroughfare passing through the centre of the picture is Nicolson Street connecting with " North Bridge " in the top right. George Square laid out in 1765 and representing the first departure from the Old Town is seen in the middle left. The Old Town may be traced by the built-up ridge running across the top of the picture from the Castle (top left) to the right of the picture. Most of the property seen here is ripe for redevelopment.

Grassmarket [p. 20]

The eastern end of the Grassmarket lies in the foreground with the Castle towering in the background. The vertical emphasis and " crow stepped " gables are typical of the old town buildings.

St. Giles at Night [p. 21]

The premier church of the capital, St. Giles, stands out boldly in this night view setting in the old High Street. The " crown " steeple, typical in Scotland, is seldom seen south of the Border. The " Tron " Church clock gleams from further down the High Street and the rest of this Royal Mile stretches on into the distance.

PLATE V

Ann Street, N.-E. Side [p. 14]

This is the north-east side of Ann Street showing a section of its incomparable architecture of the Georgian era designed by Sir Henry Raeburn on his own land. Seldom is Georgian architecture seen with so much variety in the facade composition offering dwellings of varying size to suit individual requirements. The building lines vary from no garden forecourt to deep forecourts achieving a happy blend between the " garden city " density to the higher one of the town house.

Ann Street [p. 13]

A closer view of the dominant feature of the Ann Street facade shows the unusual feature of a central pilaster on a gable front. Note also how the street lamps were originally provided in the design of the railings.

Heriot's School [p. 15]

Heriot's School originally a hospital built in the post-Reformation period of 1560-1750 is a fine heritage of Scottish architecture and except for the french turrets may be likened to the Elizabethan buildings of England.

An early prototype of the Corporation Coat of Arms carved in stone. [p. 16]

PLATE VI

of talent of the professions and arts seldom before gathered into a small area.

For the New Town proposed by the Commission, communications had first to be arranged across the valley. In the middle of the 18th century roads were still very primitive. Arthur Young writing on his six months' tour through the north of England in 1770 said, " I advise all who travel on any business but absolute necessity to avoid all journey further North than Newcastle. Until better management is produced I would advise all travellers to consider this country a sea and as soon think of diving into the ocean as venturing into such detestable roads." People were not transport-minded and in Edinburgh itself they put up with poor streets of bad gradients; but once the principle of high level transport was introduced progress became rapid. The connecting bridge over the valley to the ' New Town ' was actually begun in 1763 though, owing to mishaps, it was not opened till some nine years later. About twenty years later the Mound, erected from the excavations of the New Town, had formed a second connection from north to south and in 1788 the South Bridge was opened. Regent Bridge in 1819, George IV Bridge and Johnston Terrace in 1836, and the Dean Bridge in 1832, completed the connections, all of these being engineering works of considerable magnitude. These gave at the end of the period under review new conditions for travel with the consequent opening up of trade. (See Plan page 11).

In spite of opposition, the project of a New Town was pursued by the Town Council and, after a public competition and the acquisition of the land in 1766, the scheme of the 27-year old James Craig was put in hand in the following year. In the " Caledonian Mercury " of 1766 the basis of the competition is announced as " for preventing the inconvenience and disadvantages which arise from varying buildings without regard to any order or regularity." So far, in England such developments had been on private estates. The new feature of Edinburgh's scheme was its local government origin.

some of this later work, but shortly after its end the Town Council, after an abortive competition, invited W. H. Playfair to plan the area from the Calton Hill to Leith and of this the southern portion was carried out with its incomparable Regent and Royal Terraces, the northern part having been made impossible by railway developments. Concurrently the lands of Sir Henry Raeburn were developed on very individual lines and Ann Street, nearly finished at his death in 1823, has proved to be one of the most interesting of all, the frontages being recessed to form gardens. By the kindness of Mr. R. Scott Morton, A.R.I.B.A., drawings and photographs are shewn on plate nos. II & VI.

By the end of the period Edinburgh had a group of able architects, all familiar with the new style, while a school of building craftsmen, never surpassed at any period, used to advantage the splendid native sandstones. The elevations of the first streets were controlled simply by limitations of each frontage and the use of stone from named quarries; but Robert Adam in his design for Charlotte Square in 1791 (see illustration below) treated each side of the Square as one complete design, and this method was adopted in subsequent street designs with careful control in the feuing conditions which successfully produced complete frontages based on a design for the whole, though built in individual plots by many builders.

Along with the street frontages, many public buildings and monuments belong to this period, including the Register House and the Old University, the only public buildings designed by Robert Adam. The Greek Revival, as elsewhere, occurred as the culmination of the classic phase, but its vogue, with one or two notable exceptions, was limited to the decade 1822–32.

It is significant that many of the new buildings of this age had a cultural and social use—the University, Royal High School, Edinburgh Academy, John Watson's School, the Assembly Rooms, the Royal Institution and the City Observatory. Other public buildings are the Royal Exchange (now City Chambers); the Register House; Banks and

The original manuscript drawing of Robert Adam, Architect, 1791 for East Side of Charlotte Square.

Craig's work comprised only the layout of the first large parallelogram between Princes Street and Queen Street, with its three level streets running east to west, George Street in the centre being terminated by a square at each end. In 1802 an extension to the north was planned by Robert Reid, then only 26 years old, who also designed most of the elevations of the streets, from Heriot Row northward to Fettes Row, and from Church Lane eastward to Bellevue Crescent. The third stage was the masterly planning by James Gillespie in 1822 of the oddly shaped site left at the west where Craig's and Reid's plans terminated. This gap represented ground belonging to the Earl of Moray, and on it Moray Place and Ainslie Place were built. The Peninsular War had delayed

Insurance Offices; the Leith Trinity House, Customs House, and National Bank of Scotland. To this period also belong the following churches—St. Andrew's; St. George's; St. Mary's, Bellevue; Broughton Place; St. Stephen's, and others.

This great example of Georgian planning has permanently enriched Edinburgh with its extensive use of the Grand Manner. In the two first phases the weakness of its planning is in the fundamental conception of a static self-contained community of one class and blindness to differences of level, the requirements of transport and of commerce. Actually after nearly 200 years the original intention of the first scheme has been lost and the former aristocratic community has become a great commercial centre. The fine houses in the new streets place the family on the principal floors with servants in basement and attics, compared with the layers of different families similarly disposed in social levels in tenements of the Old Town; but the result of the sudden exodus of the families occupying the larger houses in the High Street and Canongate was to initiate sub-division with a too intensive use of the old tenements remaining.

So far only the physical development of the New Town has been described. It remains to mention the social and cultural life which this made possible and conversely the spirit which fostered it.

During this period the country was free from pre-occupation with civil warfare and the religious controversies which had so seriously affected peace during the preceding centuries. Apart from the threat of Napoleonic invasion which disturbed the life of Edinburgh, as of all the country, there was nothing to affect the long overdue period of peace which made this the steady, comfortable, intellectual period it was. The keynote of society was elegance, whether in dress, the dance, social recreation or buildings and furniture. The tempo of life was the easy speed of horse-drawn vehicles. This was reflected in the dignified orderliness of society and the literature of the Golden Age. Naturally, the adjustments of life to the new were revolutionary in their social implications. In the characteristic words of Lord Cockburn, "It was the rise of the New Town that obliterated our old peculiarities with the greatest rapidity and effect. It not only changed our scenes and habits of life but, by the mere inundation of modern population broke up and, as was then thought, vulgarised our prescriptive gentilities."

It is impossible to overrate the importance of Edinburgh as a literary and cultural centre at this time. The earlier years saw David Hume's philosophical works, James Boswell's Life of Johnson, and Adam Smith's Wealth of Nations, all immortal works, and in belles-lettres, history, criticism, philosophy, theology, a succession of great writers followed. In the later years the Romanticism of Sir Walter Scott and the importance of the critical essays in the Edinburgh Review and Blackwood's Magazine created a new literary centre. One has only to examine Raeburn's portrait gallery of contemporary people, which like Lord Cockburn's Memorials makes the period live, to get a cross section of the life of the time.

Edinburgh's predominance in literature resulted in general well-being and trade improvement. Books required printing and publishing and paper-making and paper-making machinery. One of the earliest of the large engineering firms in Edinburgh of to-day began in 1821 as makers of paper-making machinery. As roads improved and four coaching routes to London were used, coach-making (an earlier industry) and leather works became important in Edinburgh. Glass works, timber mills, shipbuilding were among the industries which rose during this period.

EDINBURGH 1825—1947.

This period is remarkable at first for the application of science rather than of art to life and industry and for the exploitation of the rapidly increasing population, with neglect of ideals in housing and health, and later for the awakening of the social conscience.

During this time the official area of the city increased by stages from less than one square mile to fifty. By 1825 the Georgian effort in building had nearly spent itself and an interval of about 50 years occurred before street frontages

were planned in the Grand Manner again. These, however, north of the Dean Bridge and of Haymarket, lacked the quiet dignity of the earlier phases.

In the third quarter of the 19th century most of Edinburgh's best stone-built villa suburbs and some of its worst tenement streets were built. The most intensive industrial housing was in the last quarter of the century.

The introduction of steam power was a revolutionary force. Mills and works now steam-driven produced vast increases of output. There was less interest in architectural design. In Edinburgh the absence of the earlier developments in textile factories which occurred elsewhere delayed the Industrial Revolution. The earlier mills of all kinds serving the Old Town had of necessity originated on rivers large enough to give water power, and for these mechanical energy was usually added on the old sites, both for milling of grain and for paper making. By 1770 the Carron Company had their own iron mills on the river at Cramond. Large engineering works began gradually, but most of the large works, including the great engineering and rubber works for which Edinburgh is famous began or were extended on a large scale only after the advent of the railways. Printing had its beginnings in Edinburgh in 1507 when James IV granted a charter to Walter Chapman and Andrew Millar " to furnish and bring home a prent (press) with expert men to use same for imprinting books." Edinburgh remained an important literary centre, hence the growing need for the printing, binding and publishing of books and the making of machines for paper-making, all of which are still important industries. Brewing had been carried out in various parts of the Old Town from earliest times. The absence of an enclosing wall in the Canongate allowed the gardens there to remain and these open spaces were taken advantage of when the breweries attached to their local wells in the valley extended, with the result that they have now dominated the south side of the Canongate.

Shipbuilding began early in Leith and its vicinity. The port of Newhaven, half a mile away, made history in the beginning of the 16th century when the " Great " Michael—the largest warship afloat—was built. In Leith shipbuilding is an important industry, and it has the credit of having built in 1837 in a yard now working for three centuries, the " Sirius," the first British steam ship to cross the Atlantic.

The period from 1825 to 1947 covers the complete evolution of modern transport. The Union canal was opened in 1822 but even earlier Edinburgh was seriously considering the application of canalisation to its local traffic. On Kirkwood's splendid plan of 1817 (see plate I) are shown these proposals, which not unnaturally came to nothing, as the hills and valleys rendered this type of transport unsuitable. With the help of Telford and Macadam roads improved to suit the speed of improved horse-drawn vehicles, the 3 inch broad wheels prescribed by law for the earlier soft roads being no longer necessary. Just before the development of railway transport, the possibilities of speed in canal passenger traffic and in horse-drawn coaches had been explored to the physical limit. In 1834 reporters left by mail coach after a banquet in Edinburgh at midnight on a Monday and the " Times " printed in London with an account of the banquet was sold in Edinburgh on the afternoon of Friday of the same week, and just before the development of the Railways one could travel the 45 miles from Edinburgh to Glasgow by canal in 5 hours in horse-drawn boats.

Edinburgh's first colliery railway, partly horse-drawn and partly pulled by rope up the steep hill from Duddingston to St. Leonards, carried passengers in 1834. The Edinburgh and

Newhaven Railway was opened in 1842. The North British Railway was connected from Edinburgh to Glasgow in the same year and in 1846 the Edinburgh and Berwick Railway was connected to London. With the improvements in transport, commerce and industry were put on a new footing.

Awakening of the Social Conscience.

In the 1860's Edinburgh's housing problem was one of the Old Town and its immediate extensions where subdivision of large houses followed the exodus of the wealthier families to the New Town. The decay of buildings and the absence of

associated with railway sidings and large industrial works. Along with these areas of intensive tenemental housing there was introduced an innovation, when for the first time streets of separate houses set in large gardens and separated by stone boundary walls were built, now forming the pleasant villa suburbs of Merchiston, Churchill, Grange, and Mayfield, practically taking up the whole area of the ancient Burgh Muir. Trinity and other villa areas were built to the north about the same time. The southern extensions of the southern suburbs and the development of the lands of Warrender followed about the end of the century.

FIG. 1

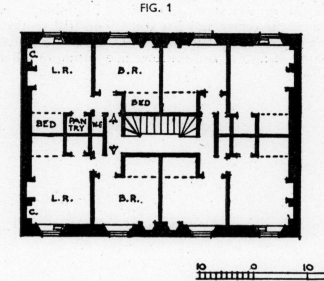

FIG. 2

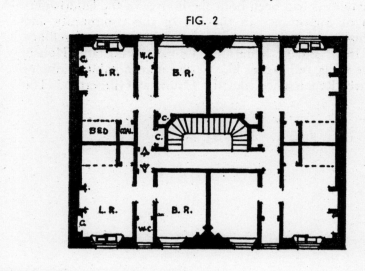

elementary sanitary provisions were added to the congestion of the central part in which over large areas some 80% of the total space was covered by high buildings. Conditions were aggravated by not replacing houses demolished to make room for railways, public buildings and churches. These conditions were described in journalistic and private surveys and in the great report of 1865 by Dr. Littlejohn, medical officer of health, who made bold recommendations. Following this the large Improvement Schemes of 1867 during Sir William Chambers' Lord Provostship and costing nearly £300,000 were carried out. Narrow wynds were opened out into streets—St. Mary's Street and Blackfriars Street— and new streets formed including Lady Lawson Street, Chambers Street, Market Street, Cranston Street and Jeffrey Street. New tenements were built on the frontages. Water-borne drainage was introduced and water supplies increased. A side light on the condition of working-class houses of the time is given by the publication in 1860 of a Report recommending a scheme for ideal houses worked out by a " Committee of the Working Classes of Edinburgh." A copy of their plan is shewn in fig. 1 for tenements of four storeys, each house having two rooms with bed recesses and of back to back planning, with internal stairs and primitive sanitation in the dark centre of the building, but with substantial stone and brick construction. Unfortunately this became the prototype—modified as to the sanitary provisions, but building depth increased thus worsening the internal lighting and ventilation—of thousands of substantial tenements built in the large industrial housing areas in the last decades of the century as in fig. 2.

Before about 1875 there were no new large areas of industrial housing, the initial increase of the population in the Industrial Age being taken up in the southern extensions of the Old Town and in Leith, and by ribbon development on old roads leading outwards. After this date the large new areas of industrial housing sprang up unrelieved by open spaces or softened by amenities, and these were closely

After the Boer War of 1899—1901 house-building declined. A certain number of houses were erected by the city under the Housing Act of 1890, embodying the ideals of the time, houses of one or two small rooms with sink in living room window and sanitary conveniences shared.

By 1919 the situation was that, owing to the reduction of speculative building, the arrears due to war and the cumulative disrepair of many years, the housing position was serious. When building began again under the 1919 Housing Act, ideals had completely changed and under this great Charter the principle was laid down that in state housing the size of house should be related to the size of the family and that the convenience of plan and provision of sanitation, light and open space should be directly based on human needs.

While Edinburgh's new housing areas kept up a reasonable density by the use of the utilitarian but ungainly hybrid of two-storey flatted houses along with three-storey tenements of modern plan, the new estates, even those for dispossessed persons, had an openness of layout like the villas of the previous century. In the urgent need for accommodation all available land within reach was used, but owing to financial stress, some of the accessories like full community provisions and recreation areas proportioned to the population were not available and all architectural treatment was starved. Some idea of the migration of population during the interwar years may be gained from the fact that new houses under all auspices were built for about one third of the whole population on an aggregate area of some seven square miles.

In 1920 Edinburgh extended its boundaries, nearly trebling its area and adding some 33 square miles. This was achieved by taking in a belt from three-quarters of a mile to four and a half miles wide of rural area with its villages on the periphery, including open country up to the ridge of the Pentland Hills, thus giving the city control of the marginal belt. At the same time the ancient port of Leith became part of the Greater City. The villages include some of character and of historical interest such as Newhaven with a tradition of fishing of at least five centuries; Cramond once a Roman station with its port and manor house and 15th century tower and its picturesque group of old houses rising up from the River Almond; Duddingston and its loch, once the site of a crannog, its Norman church, the manse of James Thomson the painter and the prehistoric cultivation terraces on the hillside; the tiny hamlet of Swanston on the slopes of the Pentlands, its thatched cottages beside the stream and village green and the former laird's house adjoining, all set in a wooded background.

Edinburgh had been so long the centre of civic and national government with its University and College of Justice that in these environs had been built the houses of the landowners and men of importance in the life of the community and these remain as monuments—early 17th century dwellings like the Inch, Pilrig, Peffermill, Gogar, Brunstane House, Stenhouse Mills, old castles like Craigmillar, notable examples of the early Renaissance like the Drum at Gilmerton. The position of the existing old buildings, old villages, castles, mansions and churches, in the whole of the extended area which still remain as records of the past centuries, is shewn on the folding map No. 1.

After some nine centuries of growth Edinburgh in 1948 is a city of nearly half a million people, extended radially outwards from its ancient centre and its 18th century overflow, with suburbs and a fringe of open country, a sea front of nearly ten miles and a populated area with all gradations of intensity from the congested centre to open country. There is a fine set of civic services including the Talla water supply from a reservoir 38 miles away. While still preeminent in education and culture, Edinburgh is a great commercial centre and has some industrial works of world wide importance; but there still remains its mystic background of history and romance in a setting of hill and valley and sea.

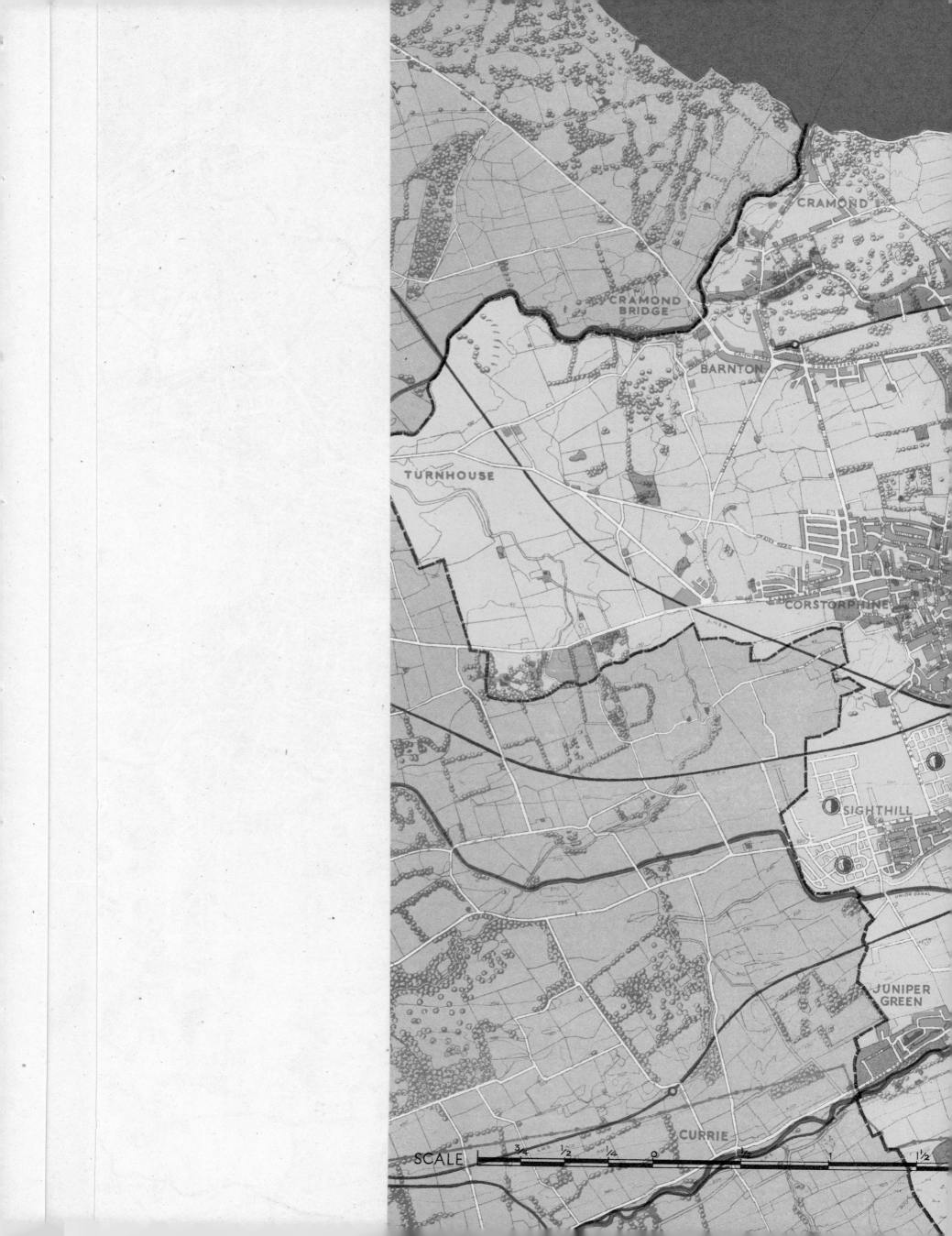

CRAMOND

CRAMOND
BRIDGE

BARNTON

TURNHOUSE

CORSTORPHINE

SIGHTHILL

JUNIPER
GREEN

CURRIE

SCALE   ¾   ½   ¼   0   ½   1   1½

MAP 2

SURVEY of INTER-WAR DEVELOPMENT

With the extent of inter-war property development shown on this Map in yellow and grey representing development prior to 1918, an idea of the amount of development possible over a period of twenty-two years is obtained. The Table in the Appendix gives various details as to quantities and money spent on all forms of building development. The peak period is in the middle " 30's " when £3 millions a year was reached by all forms of enterprise—public and private. The " self-contained house " of the three-apartment type predominated at an average cost of £500.

For such an enormous sum as £38 millions to be spent in twenty-two years of development without the co-ordinated influence of a town plan is a fact worthy of serious consideration. Much of our problems are attributed to that omission. The Map shows in yellow an expansion of this ancient City almost doubling it in size, yet how many would have scoffed if it had been anticipated or allowed for on a plan ? The Plan for Edinburgh does no more than make good this omission and correct where possible past errors : realization in point of time is of secondary importance to good development, but the important fact to grasp is that guidance from a plan costs no more, if as much, as to build indiscriminately without one. Surely a plan is an indispensable necessity.

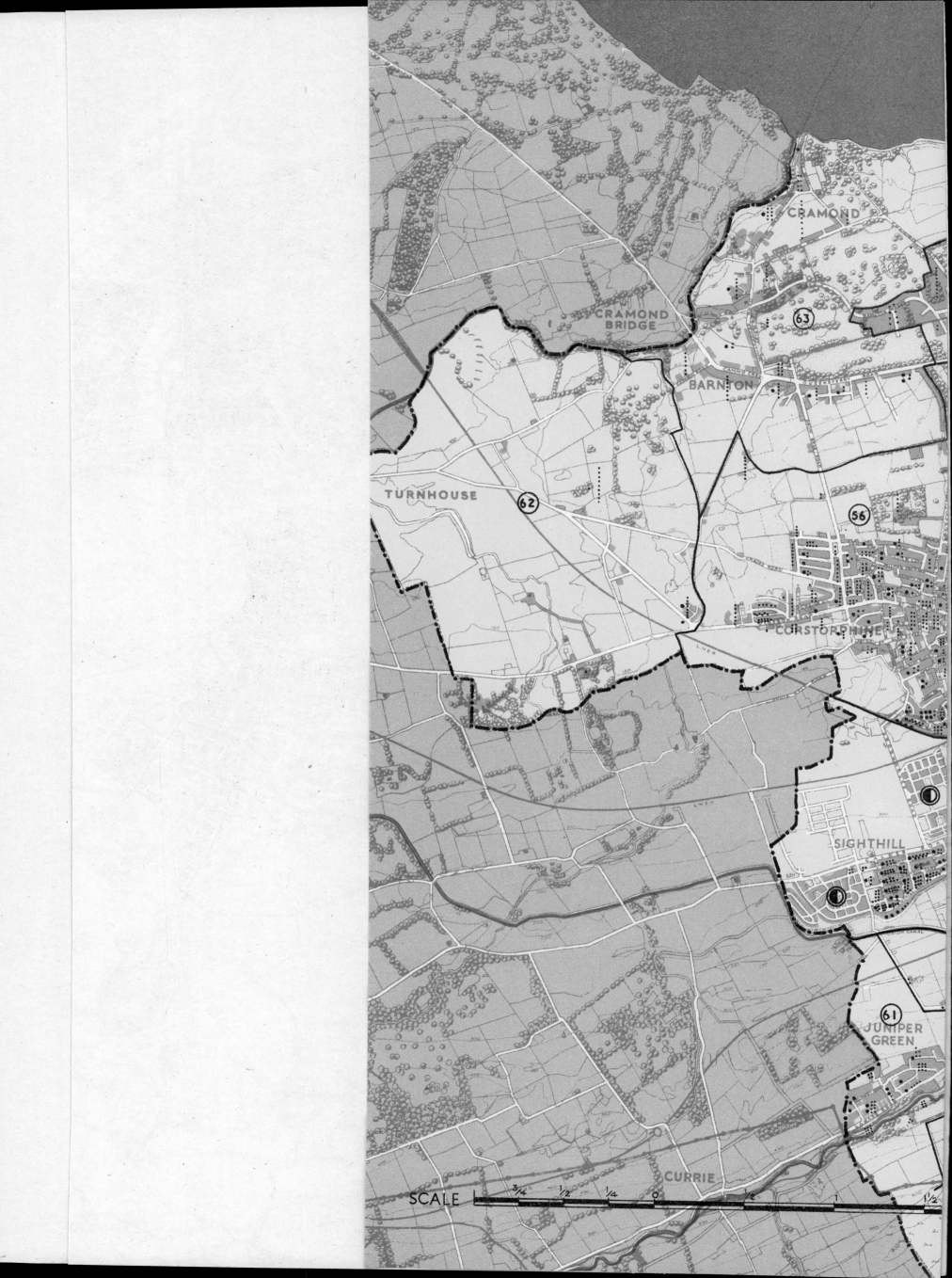

CRAMOND

CRAMOND
BRIDGE

63

BARNTON

TURNHOUSE
62

56

CORSTORPHINE

SIGHTHILL

61

JUNIPER
GREEN

CURRIE

SCALE   3/4   1/2   1/4   0   1/2   1   1½

MAP 3

SURVEY of POPULATION DISTRIBUTION

Before a planned distribution of the population could be started this survey of existing distribution had to be prepared to find where unnecessary and unhealthy concentrations occur. The old habit of huddling together in overcrowded profusion finds its origin in traditional defence inherent in medieval days, and fostered in recent generations by the industrial revolution. There is evidence to prove that large proportions of the breadwinners in the densely populated districts do not work there, and could quite easily decentralize to make more room for those that do. Planned dispersal to relieve overcrowding of both industry and population forms the policy in the Plan.

The totals of black dots show the population for the unit area of the " block " described in the chapter and the table in the appendix gives the population total for the unit area of the Social Survey District. For clarity the congested central areas of the City have the ' block ' area boundaries outlined in black while, for the less congested parts, reliance is placed upon the outline of the white roads to define the block boundaries.

CRAMOND

63

CRAMOND
BRIDGE

BARNTON

TURNHOUSE

62

56

CORSTORPHINE

SIGHTHILL

JUNIPER
GREEN

61

CURRIE

SCALE   ¾   ½   ¼   0   ½   1   1½

MAP 4

SURVEY OF POPULATION DENSITY

The Social Survey was conducted in detail and results were obtained from 119,724 dwellings. It has been possible to map the results for small areas known as the " block," that is, property containing a number of persons living on a known area occupied by dwellings. This is an advantage as the " block " often shows very bad conditions which would otherwise be lost where the density is assessed over a larger area of net residential property : for instance, though several districts show 200-400 persons per acre density, the map indicates several blocks of 700 and 800 and more persons per acre.

When these densities are related to the maximum proposed in the various zones of the Plan, a quick estimate may be made to assess overcrowding and show where re-development to the proposed maximum should first begin.

Generally it may be said that Edinburgh presents districts with very marked and contrasting densities within the same locality.

SCALE

MAP 5

SURVEY of POPULATION in FAMILY SIZES

Illustrating graphically the distribution of the population in family sizes for each survey district an overall picture is obtained of the kind of accommodation required to meet their needs. In any planned decentralization either to relieve overcrowding or to make way for industrial or other non-residential development, the appropriate proportions of dwellings sizes necessary to accommodate the decentralised population should be assessed. By correlating the results of the social survey as illustrated on this Map and on that showing dwelling sizes an assessment of a balanced distribution of dwelling types in any community can be obtained. The superimposed Tables give the totals of families for each size in the range from which interesting and useful comparisons may be drawn.

CRAMOND

CRAMOND
BRIDGE

BARNTON

TURNHOUSE

CORSTORPHINE

SIGHTHILL

JUNIPER
GREEN

CURRIE

SCALE   ³/₄   ½   ¼   0   ½   1   1½

MAP 6

SURVEY of DISTRIBUTION of DWELLING SIZES

The Social Survey covered many aspects of daily life in both the home and the factory or office. This Map illustrates graphically for each district of the City indicated by black boundary lines the distribution of dwellings in terms of their sizes. Reading this together with the Map giving a " Survey of Population in Family Sizes," an assessment may be obtained of the extent of overcrowding due to cramped and other sub-standard conditions based upon the Department of Health standards. An assessment can also be made of the number of dwelling sizes as a proportion of the total required in any proposed reconstruction to accommodate a balanced community of all family sizes. For instance, a predominance of one kind of dwelling in a population district should coincide with a corresponding predominance of family sizes appropriate for that type of dwelling. Any excessive predominance of a dwelling size in relation to the norm should be corrected wherever possible.

Differing slightly from the Population Density Map for clear illustration the information presented covers larger unit areas consisting of several blocks of built-up property. Each unit of the population district whose reference number appears in the circle, quotes this information in small data panels—the top row of figures indicates the dwelling sizes, and the bottom row their totals, and the row immediately above its percentages of all dwellings. For example, Unit Area 1B of the High Street District shows a predominance of 2-apartment dwellings totalling 567, representing 53% of all dwellings in the area.

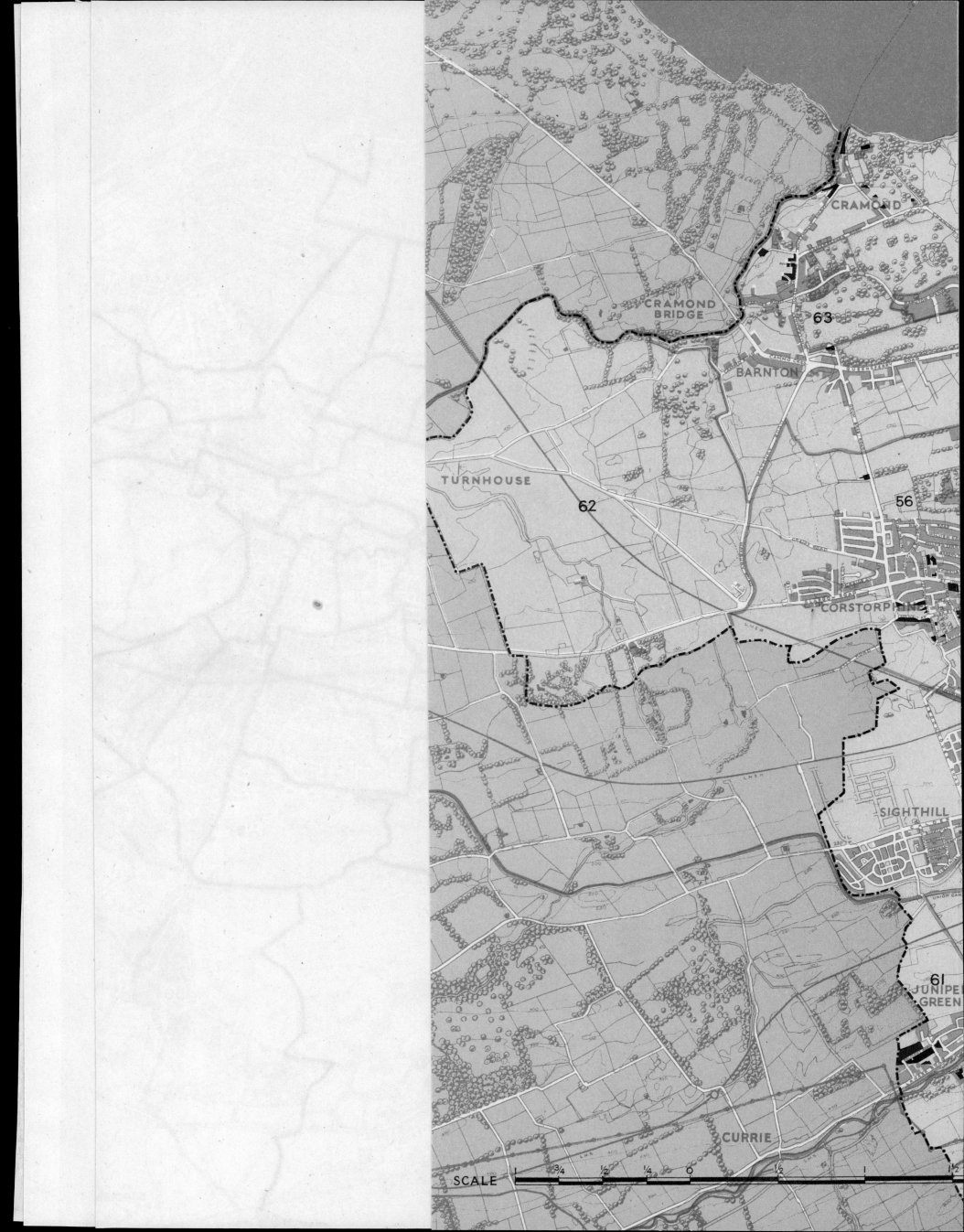

CRAMOND

CRAMOND
BRIDGE

63

CAMMO CRES

BARNTON

QUEENSFERRY ROAD

TURNHOUSE

62

56

CORSTORPHINE

LNER

SIGHTHILL

61

JUNIPER
GREEN

UNION CANAL

CURRIE

LNER

SCALE   1   ¾   ½   ¼   0   ½   1

CONDITION of DWELLINGS

This Map shows the Net Residential Areas coloured in two tones of grey according to the condition of fitness of the dwellings within them. The standard of fitness is determined according to the extent the dwellings contain normal present-day sanitary facilities. The dark grey colour does not indicate the exact location of the substandard dwellings but shows within a particular social survey block the percentage of dwellings which are sub-standard. The prevailing sanitary conditions for the 123,265 houses, and the factors that determine them are enumerated in the explanatory table in the chapter. The Plan takes into account these factors along with others in determining which areas are ripe for redevelopment.

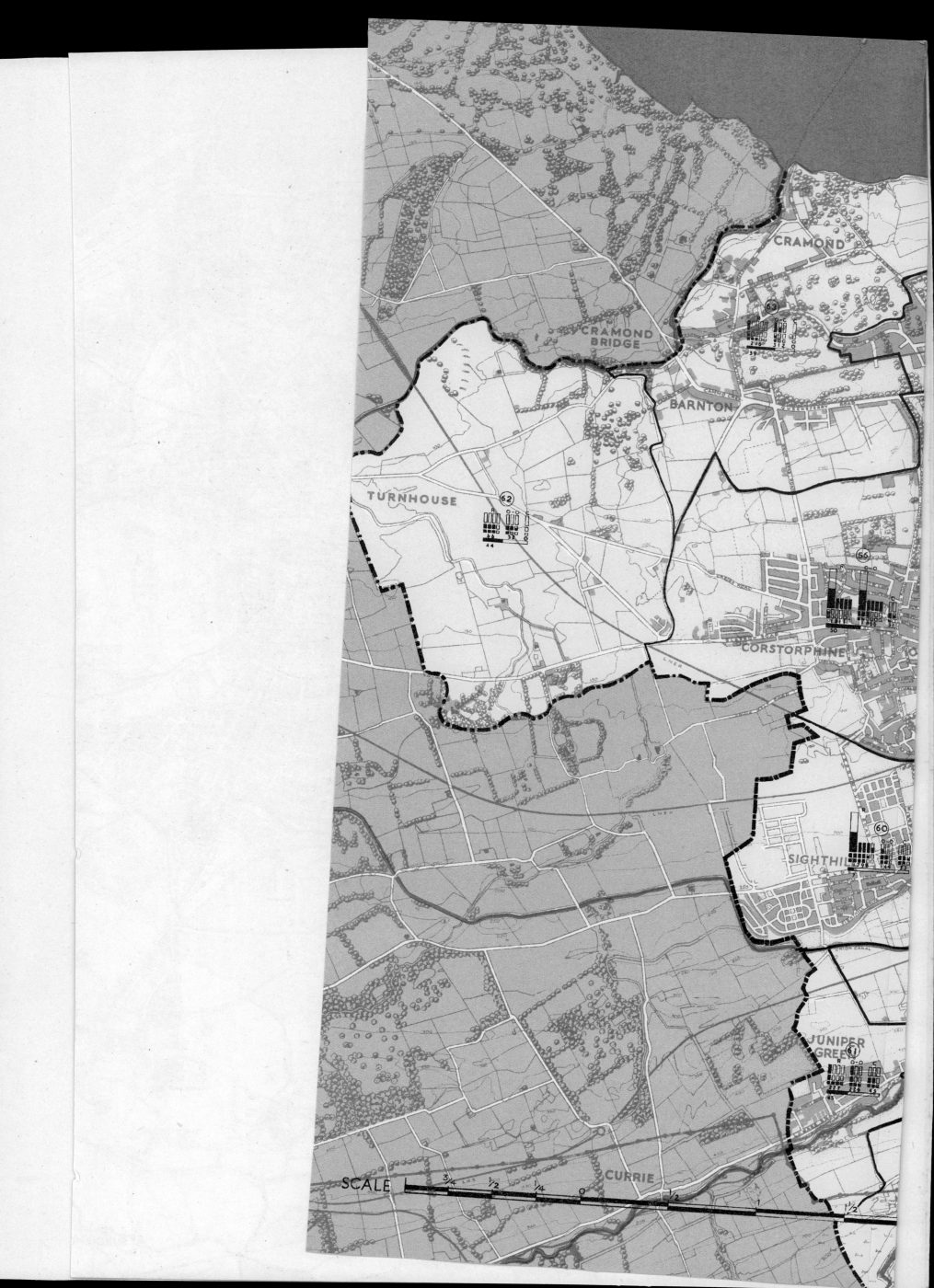

CRAMOND

CRAMOND
BRIDGE

BARNTON

TURNHOUSE

62

CORSTORPHINE

56

SIGHTHILL

60

JUNIPER
GREEN

CURRIE

SCALE 3/4 1/2 1/4 0 1/2 1 1 1/2

MAP 8

SURVEY OF DWELLING OWNERSHIP

Three types of ownership of dwellings are shown : Rented, Owner Occupier and Corporation. These are given in symbols and in actual numbers for each Survey district. In addition, a percentage of owner occupier dwellings is shown. It will be seen that in some of the older districts, e.g., Dalry, there is a heavy preponderance of Rented dwellings and very few Corporation dwellings. The effect of the Corporation Housing Schemes is, on the other hand, seen in such districts as Craigentinny, Granton and Craigmillar. The highest percentage of owner occupied dwellings are found in Blackhall, Braids and Fairmilehead, Craiglockhart and Kingsknowe.

The older areas containing the preponderance of Rented dwellings when compared with other housing surveys will be found to suggest either decentralization or replacing by Corporation houses.

PART I

CHAPTER TWO

THE CIVIC SURVEY

INTRODUCTION. Before a development plan for the future orderly development of a city can be prepared there must be made an initial survey setting out the many factors and problems to be considered. This requirement is no different in principle from the building contractor's need for details of the locality in which he intends to develop his housing estate ; or, to take a more recent analogy, the engineers knowledge of the catchment areas before constructing the various hydro-electric plants in the Highlands. In principle, a civic survey is just as essential for the logical planning of the city's future. A foundation of supporting facts must be obtained to answer a number of questions concerning the natural formation of the ground, the social and economic conditions of the citizens, the transport and civic services and of the private organisations which contribute to the city's life.

The many important problems that must be considered in such a survey are assembled in the form of maps, diagrams and tables. Some of these problems need not be studied in detail, but a full account of the facts together with the conclusions resolved from them, is essential for the proper explanation and understanding of the development plan as a whole.

To portray these essential facts of present day conditions the survey must include the uses and condition of land and property, the distribution of the people and dwellings, their occupations and places of work and play, and means and condition of communication.

To achieve this for Edinburgh the following surveys were undertaken :—

1. The Use of land and property.
2. Inter war development : immigration and emigration.
3. Social Survey of: (a) Population distribution.
   (b) Population density.
   (c) Distribution of family sizes.
   (d) do. dwelling sizes.
   (e) do. of dwelling condition
   (f) do. of ownership of those dwellings.
   (g) do. of the occupied bread-winners and their place of work.
4. Industrial Survey (a) Distribution of types of industries.
   (b) Analysis of trends of development.
5. Recreation Spaces.
6. Schools.
7. Communications : Roads and Railways.
8. Shop Distribution.

CONCLUSION.

1.—LAND USE SURVEY

During 1946 the use of all properties of the city was recorded and analysed upon coloured maps to a scale of 1/2500. From them a comprehensive picture of the whole city is obtained while technically they provide an important registry of industry, housing, communication, commerce, open spaces, schools and public buildings, including the most important buildings of historic and architectural interest. Though only a guide this is an essential first step in collating the other facets of the civic survey.

The Survey is detailed to the extent that it shows all ground level uses in their multifarious categories and in certain cases it shows the predominant use of the upper storeys of the buildings : as for example, tenements of four storeys or more in height are shown in deep red with a strip of black to indicate a ground floor use of shops. An indication of density is also given by the deep red for tenements of three and more storeys in height, the orange for two storied dwellings, and the orange with deep red cross hatching for the single storied dwellings. This indication of density had, of course, to be supplemented from the social survey statistics on population distribution to give the actual densities of distribution.

The intermingling of industry and crowded houses is strikingly revealed, as in many other towns and cities, and, like these other cities, Edinburgh will need to prevent not only a continuance of, but actively to remedy this mal-distribution. Leith has become much more industrialised in so far as it now has more ground space occupied by industry. Its total area is 1,309 acres and to-day there are 522 acres or 40% of the total area occupied by industrial concerns, leaving 327.42 acres, or 25% for net housing and 459.5 acres, or 35% for commercial or other use.

Another development already known, though its extent may not be appreciated, is the westward expansion of business, commerce and administration, spreading through the residential areas of Melville Street, Drumsheugh Gardens and even into the crescents beyond Palmerston Place. To what extent should this be permitted, if at all ?

From these first pointers, investigations have been made under their respective headings, such as the open space survey, to confirm, adjust and reassess these indications by broad analytical studies. What, for instance, is the extent of overcrowding indicated by the close development of three or four storey tenements ? Another: is Edinburgh really so well off for open spaces as the 12 acres per 1,000 population overall standard indicates ? Such questions can only be answered by detailed analysis. The results compared with the proposals will give the extent and nature of the change intended.

2.—INTER WAR DEVELOPMENT

This survey brings out the amount of building development of all kinds that took place between the two wars and represents the collective efforts of public and private enterprise.

Interesting and useful data may be extracted concerning the financial outlay involved during this 22 year period (1918—1939) : the movement of population resulting from it, the extent of property that may have to be retained in the scheme and the influence such property casts upon the proposals. These are described in the chapter on Realisation where they can more appropriately be explained in their true significance. Those who doubt the financial practicability of planning schemes will find the facts illuminating.

Population Movement.

From the population statistics supplied by the Registrar General for Scotland, together with the results of this Inter-war development survey, it is possible to show that not only could the whole of the estimated 20,244 families deemed to be living in overcrowded conditions in the 1935 Housing Act Survey have been rehoused in a modern environment, but also, more than half those living in areas of bad living standards generally.

These population statistics which are fully tabulated in Appendix 1 clearly indicated that emigration from the city (amounting to some 36,619 persons between 1918 and 1924) fell off to 48 persons in 1928 and ceased in 1929 and given place to immigration from outside. Examination of the records of building activity shows very little new house building up to 1924, but it steadily increased from 1926 onwards, particularly in the 1930's. Since there was little or no emigration during the remaining inter-war period of 1924 to 1939, when the vast majority of houses were built, there were only two sources from which the population occupying them came : that is immigrants from outside totalling 22,809 persons and those from out of the old parts of the city. This conclusion is supported from a correlated

calculation of the Registrar General's statistics and those of the Social Survey of 1946.

The population in the old part of the town in 1924, was 392,837 resident persons, and in 1946, for the same parts the population had dropped to 291,749 persons indicating a total decentralisation of 101,088 persons. Since there were 139,107 persons estimated as living in the 43,471 dwellings built by 1939, and, since not more than 22,809 could have been immigrants, at least 116,298 must have come from the old parts of the city (the grey areas on map No. 2).

To what extent could this development have relieved bad living conditions ? and to what extent did it do so ? The Corporation built some 15,142 dwellings during this 22 year period, but, approximately 6,000 were built under the slum clearance Acts, rehousing an estimated overcrowded population of 18,200 persons, or, 16% of the 116,298 persons known to have been rehoused. Yet the Housing Act Survey clearly indicated 20,244 families or roughly 64,780 persons as requiring reasonable living conditions while to-day there are at least 262,778 persons living in Gorgie and Dalry, St. Leonards, Leith and other districts under three or more of the following forms of living conditions :—excess number of houses per acre, mix up of homes with industry, sanitary sub-standard or unfit dwellings, too small dwellings for size of family. Though there is often only one of these forms of living conditions prevailing in individual areas, there are many instances of more than one form prevailing in the same area, and an indication of this geographically may be

LOCATION OF SUB-STANDARD LIVING AREAS.

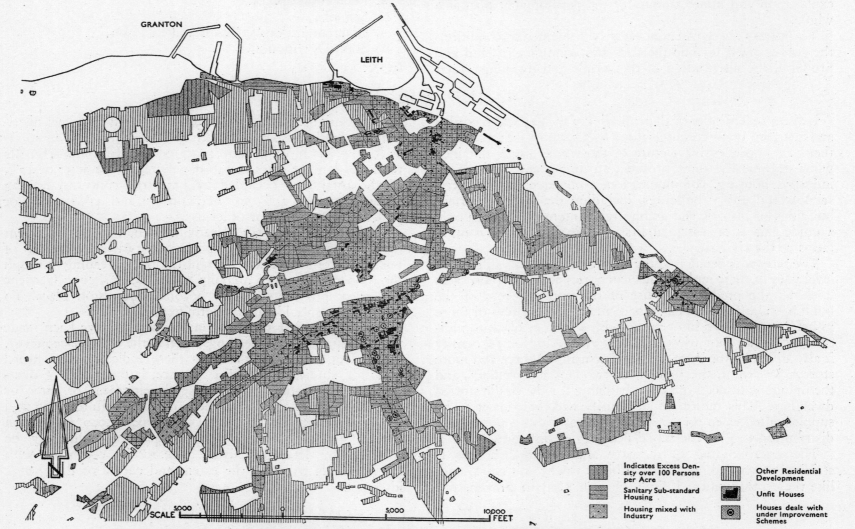

The four kinds of sub-standard living conditions mentioned above are seen in this diagram to coincide in many places. Experience teaches that one condition leads to another until complete deterioration occurs. Industry often seeks to establish itself in outmoded areas and hastens the process of 'blight.' No family can exist healthily in an atmosphere of smoke, grime and noise. Overcrowding the land reduces the access of light and air for and recreation space among the homes : bad internal planning as reflected in the lack of sanitary accommodation prevents cleanliness. Such conditions are too great a burden for the family and result in malnutrition, ill-health, disease and child delinquency.

Greenside Housing [p. 32]

New Housing in Gifford Park to replace condemned dwellings before the war [p. 77]

[P. 32]. *A view from Calton Hill of Greenside housing. This is where some of those who live in the sub-standard and overcrowded dwellings of the City. Approximately one third of the 1946 resident population live in such dwellings. Are they to remain indefinitely while new comers to the City occupy new houses now being built? Many of those known to be sharing dwellings with their "in laws" live in such conditions as these.*

[P. 33]. *Another view of Greenside where industry is seen in the foreground intermingled with these houses: an example of where the coincidence of the three kinds of substandard living conditions occur and shown in their geographical extent on diagram on page 18. The area in the Plan is scheduled for early clearance and zoned for commercial development and not housing partly because modern community development is impossible in such a small compact area.*

Greenside Housing [p. 33]

Leith Housing [p. 34]

A typical example of housing conditions in Leith. Some twenty to thirty thousand people live in such parts of Leith. This property lies at the back of Couper Street where slum clearance has been partially begun.

Broad Wynd [p. 35]

Derelict industrial property in the Broad Wynd, Leith. The street network of this old part of Leith is preserved but the zoning proposals recommend a much less intensive use of the property and confines the new use of property to commercial offices.

PLATE VII

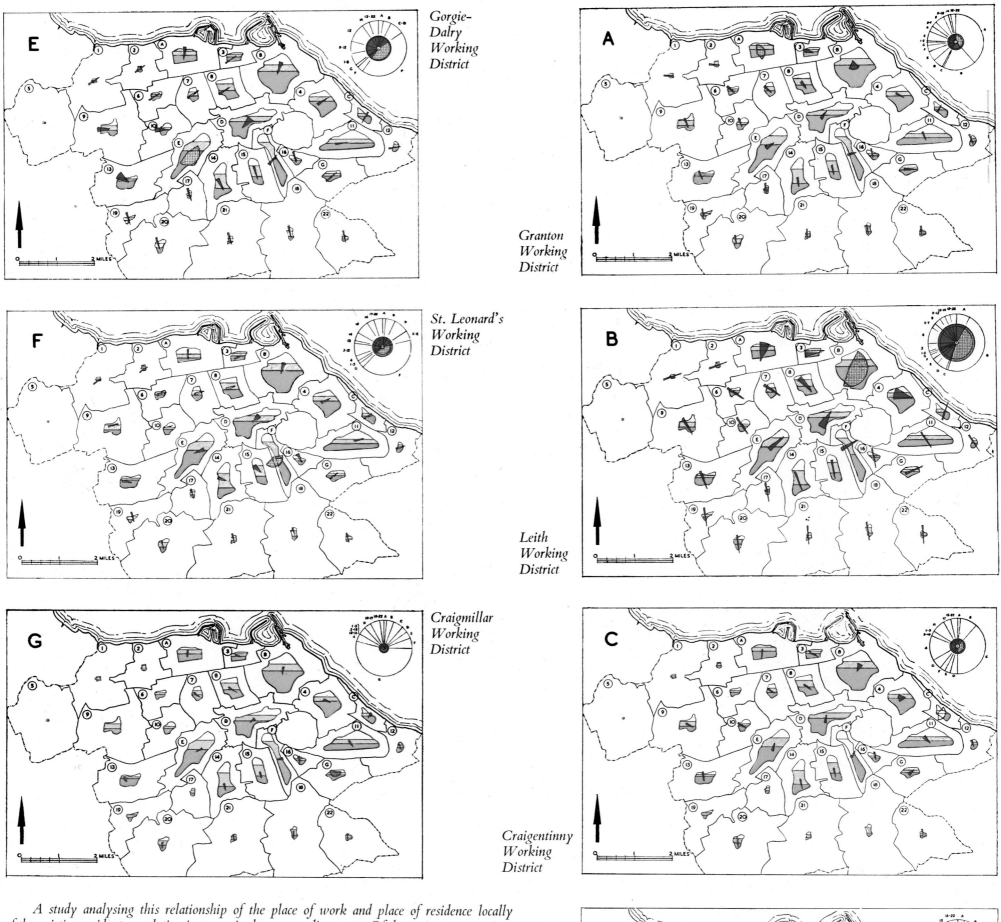

Gorgie-Dalry Working District

Granton Working District

St. Leonard's Working District

Leith Working District

Craigmillar Working District

Craigentinny Working District

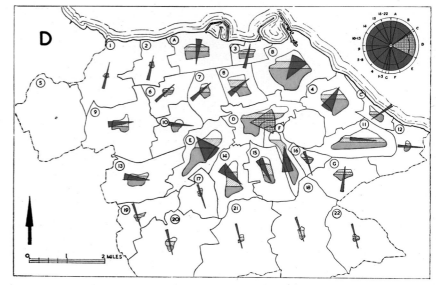

Central Area Working District

A study analysing this relationship of the place of work and place of residence locally of the existing resident population is set out in these seven diagrams. Of the answers to questions obtained at the time of the Social Survey in 1946 some 77,293 "breadwinners" (principal wage earners) have been accounted for in this facet of the Civic Survey. The seven diagrams represent seven working districts outlined geographically and lettered collectively from A–G and each showing the boundaries of the 22 residential localities containing one or more of the Social Survey Districts.

The irregular grey shapes show the proportions of all the residents in each working district who are either industrial "breadwinners" (solid grey colour), non-industrial "breadwinners" (grey hatched colour), and other '' breadwinners."

The distributed red wedge shapes (segments of a circle) indicate geographically where the "breadwinners" reside who work in one of the working districts. The larger the wedge the larger the number of "breadwinners." Those living in the same district as they work are represented by the red cross hatched wedge. The red circle on the top right hand of each diagram shows all these wedges to the same scale brought together as segments of a circle. The figures and letters beside each segment identify them.

The diagrams, therefore, show graphically or visually, the predominating occupation of all "breadwinners" in every part of the City and also what proportion live and work in the same area, and which are the other principal residing areas. Following this, the extent of travelling to and from the home and workplace can be assessed. The actual numbers are quoted in the Table in Appendix I.

PLATE VIII

appreciated in the diagram below. Estimates of the total population living in these areas under these various conditions are summarised in Appendix 1.

The records clearly show, therefore, that had there been a system of priorities controlling building development during this inter-war period, a much greater contribution than the 16% of the number rehoused could have been made to the relief of overcrowding. In fact, if all the 116,298 persons who had moved into new houses had been drawn from those living in bad housing areas, not only would those

in the worst areas (64,780 persons in 1935) have been provided for but also the majority living in overcrowded and out of date housing. Since the war the provision of new homes has still not been related to redevolopment thus worsening the position.

Further, if some reasonable form of control could be adopted to this end, a more definite estimate of time for realising the population redistribution proposals could be made. These facts have been taken into account in the redistribution proposals for population.

3.—SOCIAL SURVEY. POPULATION AND DWELLINGS

INTRODUCTION. This Social Survey mainly represents the human side of the story and the facts obtained can be specifically and scientifically related to the plan that follows. In some respects the Survey may be claimed to be unique in the manner in which the different aspects are presented for use in contemporary planning technique.

The survey was principally undertaken to obtain technical data in the form of statistics, from which to guide our research into the need for and extent of a redistribution of the existing population as might be found necessary to eliminate overcrowding and unhealthy conditions of the kind mentioned above. The results, in harmony with the other aspects of the survey, would assist in determining a satisfactory optimum size of population and, therefore, of the city in the Plan and these again could then be related to that for the Region. The distribution of the family sizes was also regarded as important as a determinant in the design of homes required for the redistribution of the population.

It should also be recorded that this survey not only gives the essential data but brings to light the extent of overcrowding as reflected by the high net densities. There is all the evidence of poverty, disease and bad diet which inevitably accompanies overcrowding in the lower income group areas.

The reason for basing the " Condition of Dwellings " part of the Social Survey upon the extent of the sanitary facilities found in the dwellings was that these generally give a concrete indication of the condition of squalor or otherwise. The results certainly support this contention as in the majority of cases the dwellings indicated as being sub-standard owing to the lack of the normal sanitary facilities of the separate W.C., sink, and bathroom, etc., approximate geographically with the dwellings which are so sub-standard as to be practically unfit for human habitation.

Further support is given by the coincidence of the dark grey areas on the " Condition of Dwellings " map with the high densities of the Population Density map : indeed medical surveys of such areas have long since these enlightened days proved that it is the imposition of drudgery and strain upon the housewife created by these conditions of overcrowding, lack of sunlight and absence of proper and adequate sanitation that leads to malnutrition, bad health and disease.

Geographically the city was sub-divided into 63 districts of well-known localities the centres of which are often the original nucleii of an old village or hamlet. Though now absorbed into the present mass of built up areas of the city these villages are sometimes still apparent as in the case of the Dean Village. Such centres give a valuable indication of where to seek a suitable neighbourhood centre in the Plan.

All the six maps illustrating the results are based upon the boundaries of these social survey districts and indicate the *net residential areas in each case. With the exception of the

★—A net residential area is the curtilage of a site including the depth of a building plot of land measured from the centre line of the road to the back of the garden and the frontage of the site.

family and dwelling sizes maps the information is given at " block level " : that is the small area of property surrounded by such physical features as roads, railways, river, etc. The number of dwellings in the block will obviously vary by the size of the block and the density of the dwellings. In the case of the family and dwelling sizes maps the information had to be given for larger unit areas consisting of several blocks. This was necessary as the tables were required to show the range of family and dwelling sizes and the tables would be too large for the smaller unit area for the scale of map necessary. By presenting the information in the other four cases for such small unit areas as the block fair estimates can be obtained. For example, a truer picture is obtained for density of population distribution where the high spots would, in an area as large as the Ward, be glossed over and lost. The striking differences in density between adjacent blocks of residential property would not have been apparent and the population redistribution estimates in the plan less reliable.

TABLE 1.

EXISTING RESIDENT POPULATION : NUMBER OF FAMILIES IN CITY

No. of Persons in Family	Percentage of total of Private Families	Total Private Families	Percentage of Population in Private Families	Population in Private Families
	Per cent		Per cent	
1	11·48	15,684	3·58	15,684
2	27·01	36,899	16·87	73,798
3	25·60	34,970	23·98	104,910
4	18·00	24,590	22·48	98,360
5	9·36	12,782	14·61	63,910
6	4·43	6,044	8·29	36,264
7	2·10	2,873	4·60	20,111
8	1·04	1,426	2·61	11,408
9	0·53	729	1·50	6,561
10	0·27	365	0·83	3,650
11	0·098	133	0·33	1,463
12	0·036	49	0·13	588
13	0·022	30	0·09	390
14	0·013	17	0·05	238
15	0·005	7	0·02	105
16 and over	0·006	8	0·03	128
Total number of Private Families	136,606		Total Population in private Families	437,568

Average Family size 3·2 persons per family

the six maps illustrating the material are as follows :—

(a) The existing distribution of the population in numbers of persons.

(b) The existing density of distribution in terms of the number of persons per net residential acre.

(c) For the same population its distribution in family sizes.

(d) Distribution of dwelling sizes.

(e) Distribution of the various conditions of those dwellings from the point of view of sanitation.

(f) Distribution of ownership of those dwellings.

(g) Distribution of occupied breadwinners and their place of work.

3. [a] POPULATION DISTRIBUTION.

This map is invaluable in assessing where the existing concentrations of population are and their total extent. Just as the Density Map shows the sharp contrasts of population density per acre for this unit area of the " block " so this map shows the large and small population groupings. These two bear out the first impression gained from the Land Utilisation Map where it shows the distribution of the high blocks of tenements in close juxtaposition with bungalows and two storey dwellings. By means of the black dots it is possible to assess the numbers of persons living in any one block area. An overall picture of this existing distribution of population is also at once visible to the eye from the black concentration or thinning out of the dots.

3. [b] POPULATION DENSITY.

For the same districts this map shows the existing density of distribution of the population on these net residential areas and again it is possible to assess individual densities for the block unit areas and to derive an overall picture concerning densities for the whole city. Here it is of interest to note the low density of the bungalow development of 16 persons per acre at Craigleith and of Merchiston property of 7 persons per acre compared with 100 persons per acre at Marchmont. All these areas are approximately the same distance from the West End. These sharp contrasts are too great for large areas situated approximately the same distance from the centre of the city.

3. [c] DISTRIBUTION OF FAMILY SIZES.

Here the population is shown distributed in these 63 survey districts in family sizes so that, any small reconstruction suggested (to relieve overcrowding for instance), the accommodation required for the population affected by it can be readily assessed. It is important to note that the main cause of overcrowding is not only the result of too small dwellings for the size of family, but also where the numbers of persons per unit area of land are too numerous for the available space about the dwellings. See photograph of Greenside on plate No. VII. In addition, the dwellings themselves are frequently too crowded together to permit adequate light and air for healthy living. Overcrowding caused by too large a family for too small a dwelling as the figures in the tables clearly show is an equally important factor. For instance, the Pleasance district, 5a, has only 1,641 one and two person families for 2,384 one and two apartment dwellings. Since these dwellings are all occupied there must be some of the larger families having to live in one and two apartment dwellings. This is in fact known to be the case.

3. [d] DISTRIBUTION OF DWELLING SIZES.

It is manifestly important, therefore, to find out the distribution of dwelling sizes throughout the city in order to correlate the findings with those for distribution of family size. In any reconstruction and development schemes that take place in the immediate and more distant future the appropriate proportion of house types can be determined to meet the redistribution requirements of the various sized families to be accommodated in accordance with the minimum standards that should be adopted. The minimum standards laid down in the Old 1935 Housing Act of Scotland served merely as a palliative to urgent cases of overcrowding in terms of size of family or numbers of persons and of sex of persons—all related to size of dwellings. These, however, were quite inadequate to deal with the problem of rehousing the densely populated areas. A new standard is suggested in chapter 3 of the " Plan."

Another feature of interest to be obtained from this survey is the existing distribution of the various income groups throughout the city indicated by the sizes of dwelling types to be found in these areas. For instance, Murrayfield has a predominance of 7 to 10 size of dwelling whereas the Pleasance or the Canongate has a definite predominance of the 2 apartment dwelling. The Department of Health's regulation, which still prevails, requires local authorities to build almost entirely four and five apartment sized dwellings, but the Department might with the help of the new facts put forward in the Plan, permit a greater variety of development and a less arbitrary distribution. This regulation was made as a corrective to the inter-war development excess of two and three apartment dwellings already indicated in 5a and again seen in districts 31b (Niddrie Mains) and 39a (West Pilton). Now that it is possible to assess the proportion of dwelling sizes required to meet the needs of the population planned for in any part of the city, a fresh directive from the Department should be given.

3. [e] DISTRIBUTION OF DWELLING CONDITIONS.

As the preceding map gives the distribution of dwelling sizes, this map for the same dwellings gives their condition. There are three categories, the sanitary fit ones (shown in light grey), the sub-standard (shown in dark grey), and the completely unfit for human habitation. The 'unfits', which are 6,924 in number, are not distinguished. The two tones of colour together indicate again the net residential areas. The information here is given for the block unit area of land. The amount of dark grey for any one block shows the proportion of the total dwellings in the block which are either unfit or substandard and does not indicate geographically the exact disposition of the buildings themselves that are fit or unfit, unless the whole block itself is within one of these categories. The tabulated results in the Appendix show that out of a total of 123,265 dwellings in the city, 76,923 had modern sanitary conditions. This means that more than one third the total are in varying degrees of sub-standard and unhealthy conditions. Such areas as Leith, Gorgie, Dalry and the Pleasance have a definite predominance of sub-standard and in the case of Leith two-thirds are in the sub-standard and unfit categories. There should, therefore, be no difficulty in getting any of these areas scheduled as " Redevelopment Areas " within the meaning of the Act and with as high a priority as prevailing economic conditions will permit. Comparison with the density map shows the coincidence of the sub-standard areas with the high density areas already referred to.

3. [f] DISTRIBUTION OF OWNERSHIPS OF THOSE DWELLINGS.

This map is of more general interest. It either confirms or dispels certain ideas concerning the extent of renting of property in certain population areas. Leith, for example shows quite a definite predominance of rented buildings as opposed to Corporation owned dwellings. It is of interest to note that it is only the new housing areas which show any real tendency for the owner-occupier type of dwelling as may be seen in district 55. Corporation owned property also is to be found mainly on the out-skirts of the city as in the case of districts 45 and 31.

3. [g] PLACE OF WORK—RESIDENCE SURVEY.

A study of the conditions of living would not be complete without an analysis of the geographical disposition of the home and the place of work.

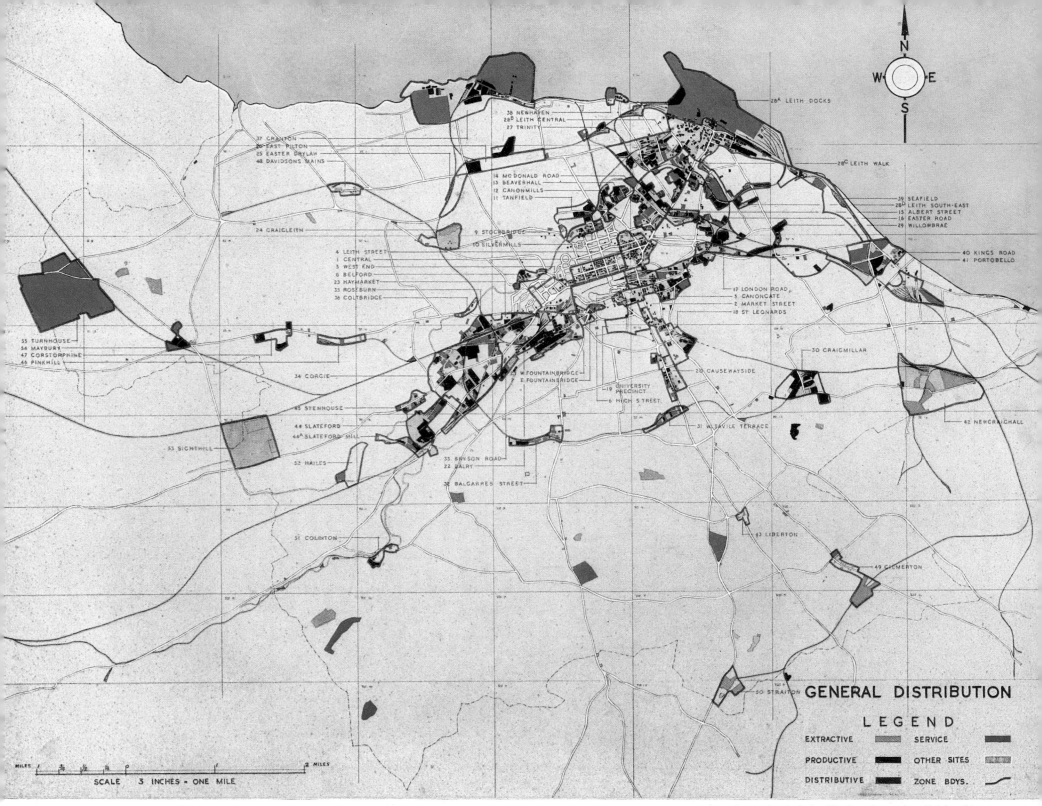

GENERAL DISTRIBUTION

LEGEND

EXTRACTIVE		SERVICE	
PRODUCTIVE		OTHER SITES	
DISTRIBUTIVE		ZONE BDYS.	

SCALE   3 INCHES = ONE MILE

Three Maps illustrate the geographical distribution of industry in the City under the titles : (1) "General Distribution"; (2) "Offensive Uses"; and (3) "Mobility". They show the present scattering of industry throughout the City. The areas in which industry predominates are named, with reference numbers to Table XXII, in Appendix III.

  1. The Map above shows broadly the nature of industries in each group, i.e. :—

Extractive includes Mining, Quarrying, Brickmaking, etc.;
Productive includes all the manufacturing Industries;
Distributive includes Wholesale Dealing, Warehousing or Storage;
Service includes Building and allied trades, Transport and all public services, Laundry and Motor Vehicle Servicing.

Bonnington

Bonnington

View of existing industry mixed with housing at Bonnington. The railway in foreground is seldom used to-day and is redundant in the proposals.

[p. 2]

Another view of Bonnington showing existing housing south of high level railway in a predominantly residential locality as distinct from a predominance of industry to north side of railway.

[p. 7]

PLATE IX

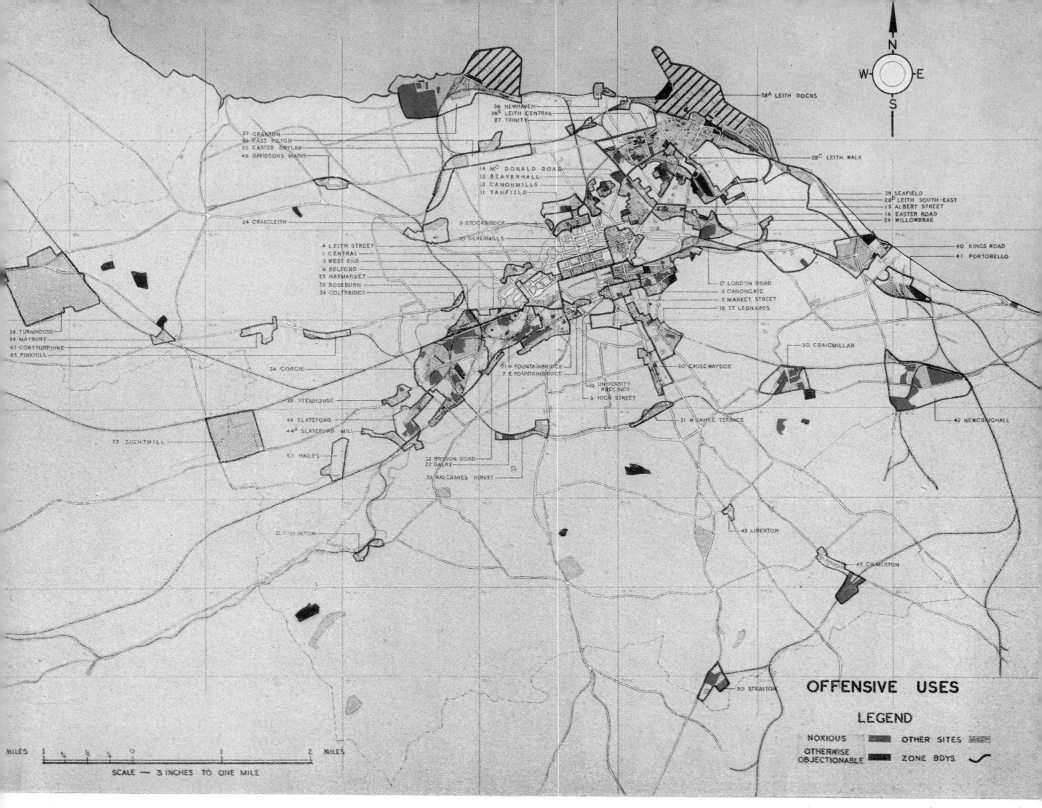

OFFENSIVE USES

LEGEND

NOXIOUS ▓ OTHER SITES ▨
OTHERWISE OBJECTIONABLE ▓ ZONE BDYS. ∿

MILES 1 ½ ¼ 0 1 2 MILES

SCALE — 3 INCHES TO ONE MILE

Map labels:

38 NEWHAVEN
28ᴮ LEITH CENTRAL
27 TRINITY
28ᴬ LEITH DOCKS

37 GRANTON
36 EAST PILTON
25 EASTER DRYLAW
48 DAVIDSONS MAINS

14 MC DONALD ROAD
13 BEAVERHALL
12 CANONMILLS
11 TANFIELD

28ᶜ LEITH WALK

24 CRAICLEITH

9 STOCKBRIDGE
10 SILVERMILLS

39 SEAFIELD
28ᴰ LEITH SOUTH-EAST
15 ALBERT STREET
16 EASTER ROAD
29 WILLOWBRAE

4 LEITH STREET
1 CENTRAL
5 WEST END
6 BELFORD
23 HAYMARKET
35 ROSEBURN
36 COLTBRIDGE

40 KINGS ROAD
41 PORTOBELLO

17 LONDON ROAD
3 CANONGATE
2 MARKET STREET
18 ST LEONARDS

58 TURNHOUSE
34 MAYBURY
47 CORSTORPHINE
46 PINKHILL

21 W FOUNTAINBRIDGE
7 E FOUNTAINBRIDGE

19 UNIVERSITY PRECINCT
6 HIGH STREET

20 CAUSEWAYSIDE

30 CRAIGMILLAR

34 CORCIE

45 STENHOUSE

51 W SAVILE TERRACE

42 NEWCRAIGHALL

53 SIGHTHILL

46 SLATEFORD
44 SLATEFORD MILL

52 HAILES

11 BRYSON ROAD
22 DALRY
32 BALCARRES STREET

43 LIBERTON

49 GILMERTON

51 COLINTON

50 STRAITON

2. Noxious or Objectionable Industries. By reason of the nuisance they cause, certain types of factory should be well separated or screened from residential areas and even from the non-noxious industries. It is necessary to find out where these factories occur. Re-grouping is essential to protect the areas in which people will live and work, from Noxious Industries which produce fumes or excessive noise or traffic or have, by their nature, unavoidably dirty or unpleasant surroundings. Their present location and extent will be a guide in formulating the proposals.

Dalry

Goods Yard, Haymarket

Part of Dalry industrial area with the Pentlands in the background. [p. 5]

Goods Yard, Haymarket in an area predominantly industrial. [p. 6]

PLATE X

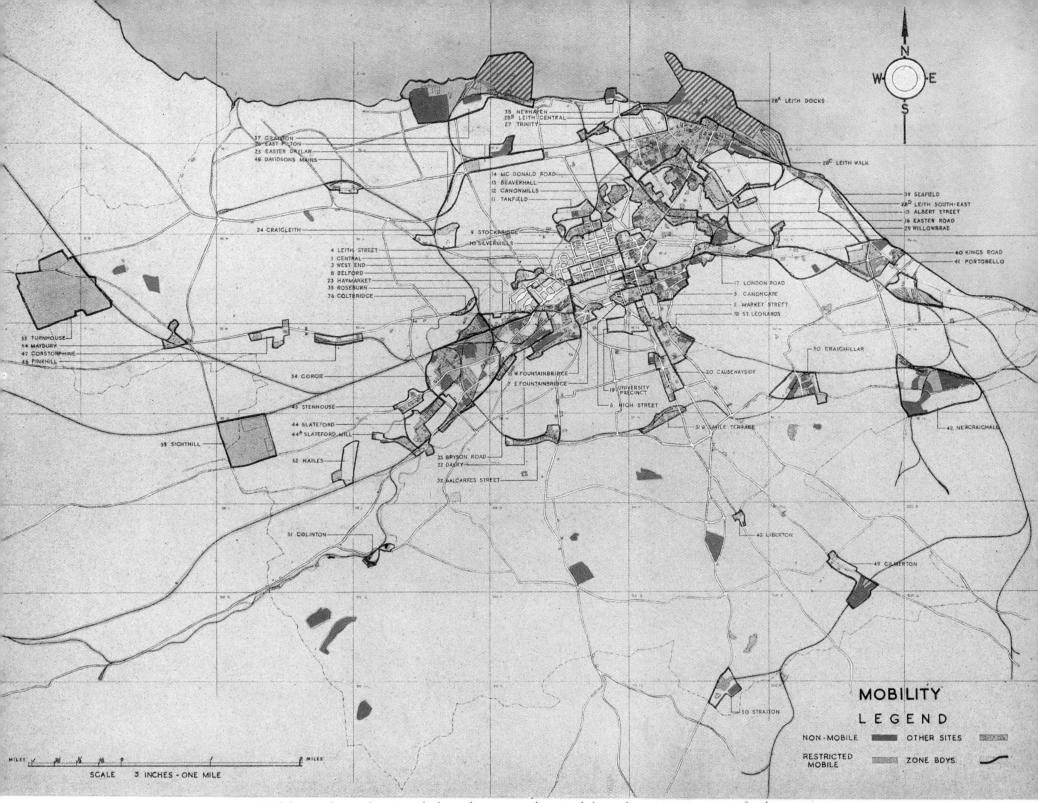

MOBILITY

LEGEND

| NON-MOBILE | | OTHER SITES | |
| RESTRICTED MOBILE | | ZONE BDYS. | |

SCALE   3 INCHES · ONE MILE

3. *Mobility applies to factories which can be more easily moved than others. It is important for the re-grouping proposals to know where these are located. Conversely the heavy industries have equipment that cannot be readily dismantled and re-erected. Similarly, industries are tied to a particular site or locality by :—*

(a) The nature of their work or raw material ;   (b) Special requirements of transport or other services ;
(c) The need to be near other factories which serve them or are served by them.

Mobile Industries include factories or workshops not "tied" or "heavy" and are generally of the "light" type.

Dalry   *Dalry*

Dalry. If the tenements in the background could be removed the heavy industries in foreground could have less cramped and awkward sites.

[p. 3]

Dalry industrial area showing close proximity of housing in background to existing industries in foreground.

[p. 4]   PLATE XI

*Evening at
Newhaven*

   The old fishing harbour at
Newhaven adjacent to Leith Docks
has a beautiful setting. Granton
Gasometer which looms in the
background would be a less sombre
object if painted in a cheerful
colour. This is important for such a
dominant landmark. The harbour
can be retained as a yachting
harbour since its fishing industry is
now mostly transferred to Granton
harbour.   [p. 8]

*A view of
Leith Docks.*
[p. 10]

*Another view of
Leith Dock ex-
tension area with
the New Break-
water in position.*
[p. 12]

*New Breakwater,
Leith.*

   A view of the
New Breakwater, Leith
Docks, enclosing future
reclamation for dock
extension. A total of
34 acres of new building
space gives about 50%
increase in dockside
building area, while the
water area would be
increased by about
100%.   [p. 11]

*Leith
Docks*
[p. 9]

PLATE XII

Here an attempt has been made to portray the occupational character of the locality and the extent of travelling between home and place of work. The geographical distribution of the blackcoated and industrial workers is shown in terms of " breadwinners " and the extent they predominate in any one of the 63 districts. The amount of travelling is apparent from the geographical location of the place of work relative to the home of the " breadwinner ". It is an important economic aspect of social life. The extent of mal-distribution of the working population indicated is invaluable as a guide to the detailed and planned redistribution of the overcrowded population that follows in Part II of the report.

CONCLUSION.

Overcrowding and bad housing conditions presents the most urgent problem arising out of this survey. Any new housing development should, therefore, be carried out almost entirely for the relief of these conditions. Though the open space survey shows that there still remains half the city area as open land by no means all can or should be built upon. It is for the plan to show how much of this will be required to satisfy this urgent problem. There is little doubt, however, that any development encouraging new immigrants to the city should be restricted to avoid land being used that is urgently required for the existing residents living in overcrowded and unhealthy conditions.

4.—INDUSTRIAL SURVEY.

INTRODUCTION. The main value of the industrial survey rests in the presentation of the relevant characteristics, and, their degree of importance to the city and the country as a whole. They may then also be considered in their true relative position with the other aspects of city planning. Much of the findings will probably be familiar to many of the citizens of Edinburgh though the extent that Edinburgh's industry plays in its town life and of the country may not. From a town planning point of view it is important to know what influence industry has upon the communications system, upon the public services (road, rail and teaching services for instance) rendered necessary by the presence of industry and in attracting ancillary activities into the city. This influence will have a direct bearing upon the general policy to be pursued as regards the extent to which Edinburgh should be industrialised.

In order that adequate information might be obtained concerning the existing distribution of industry and of the natural prosperity trends bearing upon zoning, this survey was undertaken to show, first, the location of industry and, second, the extent of expansion or contraction in its prosperity and then the extent of industrialisation as measured in terms of industrial insured persons and of Gross Annual Value. Finally an investigation was made into the distribution of the industrial and other workers of all classes to determine where mal-distribution exists.

For the Survey of distribution four broad headings were taken as a convenient classification. Further investigation was then made to find out which of the industries might be considered mobile in the sense that they may, for one reason or another, be more easily moved to another location than others. This would have a bearing upon the determination of the proposed industrial zones and the extent of possible redistribution of industry.

An investigation was also made to indicate the noxious types of industries or trades and their localities, as their siting at the detailed planning stage will require to be considered in relation to the residential communities.

For the trends in industry, Gross Annual Value was selected to indicate the matured kind of changes affecting the heritable parts of industrial property. These changes are likely to influence site areas.

The measure of existing industrialisation is found in the proportion of the present industrial insured population of the total city population. A comparison of this proportion with that for the country as a whole and for two well known industrial cities, Manchester and Glasgow, completes the picture. A trend in this important aspect is also found from these statements over the 17 year period 1929-1946.

A review of the existing conditions of the industrial worker was made and the existing average worker density Index (that is, the number of workers per floor area) was obtained, so that when improvement took place in any modern development or redevelopment, adequate space in the zones to be planned could be allowed for.

The investigation into the present distribution of the industrial and non-industrial population was possible from the results of the Social Survey. This was of importance to obtain a clear idea of the extent of unnecessary travelling that has become an unfortunate feature of every-day life : and more important still the extent of overcrowding caused by too many people trying to live near their work on too little ground area. There is a case for the regrouping of industry and redistribution of the population to avoid excessive travelling on the one hand and overcrowding on the other.

The result of this industrial survey gives the extent of normal industrialisation in Edinburgh and provides essential data necessary to determine the extent to which industrialisation should be encouraged having regard to the results from the other parts of the Civic Survey.

The Present Distribution of Industry.

There are some 56 existing industrial groups which arise from the Survey, each containing a variety of industries. Their types are indicated here as a broad classification in order, first, to give an over-all picture in its geographical significance. The diagrams on Plate Nos. IX, X, XI, show these classifications, but their sub-divisions may be seen analysed in appendix 3.

TRENDS IN INDUSTRY.

Edinburgh's Industrial Population as an Indication of Industrialisation.

The table below shows by comparison with Great Britain, Manchester and Glasgow, Edinburgh's industrial position. This is only one of the means of determining the degree of industrialisation of a city and may be indicated from the proportion of its total population engaged directly in industrial activities. The social survey produced results including all ' breadwinners,' insured and non-insured, engaged in these activities. These figures, however, cannot be compared with other cities owing to the fact that figures elsewhere only quote the insured worker. The industrial population index figures are, therefore, quoted only as including the insured worker. In the appendix other comparisons with other cities and for Great Britain are also stated on the same basis.

COMPARATIVE RELATIONSHIPS OF
TOTAL POPULATIONS AND INDUSTRIAL POPULATIONS

Table II

	Year 1932			
	Edin.	Man.	Glas.	G.–B.
1. Total Population (Thous.)	447·8	766·4	1,088·5	(45,000)
2. Indl. Population (Thous.)	84·5	283·3	277·4	9,304·5
3. (2) as percentage of (1)	18·9	36·9	25·4	20·7
4. Industrial Index	0·917	1·788	1·232	1·0
5. Industrial Importance (i.e. Indl. Population in percentages)	0·91%	3·05 %	3·00%	100%
	Year 1938			
1. Total Population (Thous.)	469·4	751·4	1,126·0	(46,200)
2. Indl. Population (Thous.)	(94·3)	252·8	306·8	10,750·0
3. (2) as percentage of (1)	20·1	33·7	27·3	23·3
4. Industrial Index	0·863	1·445	1·170	1·0
5. Industrial Importance (i.e. Indl. Population in percentages)	0·88%	2·36%	2·86%	100%
	Year 1946			
1. Total Population (Thous.)	459·4	623·5	1,050·0	(47,400)
2. Indl. Population (Thous.)	90·1	222·6	300·0	9,613·6
3. (2) as percentage of (1)	19·6	35·7	28·6	20·3
4. Industrial Index	0·965	1·757	1·406	1·0
5. Industrial Importance (i.e. Indl. Population in percentages)	0·94%	2·32%	3·12%	100%

Note—Figures in brackets are Interpolated.

The industrial survey also included a research into the question of mal-distribution of the industrial population under the heading " Place of work in relation to the home." This has been discussed previously under section 3 (g) and has an important bearing upon industrial redistribution in the proposals of the Plan.

Taking the research into the industrial population in its appropriate order, a study of Table II above, which quotes the proportions of the industrial insured workers in the total population, shows the trends from 1932 to 1946 as indicating very little change. The proportions in 1932 being 18·9% and 20·1% in 1938.

Next, by comparison with the two well known industrial cities, Glasgow and Manchester and with Great Britain, Table II shows Edinburgh with an industrial insured worker proportion of 18·9% in 1932 or approximately half the Manchester proportion of 36·9% or three quarters of the Glasgow proportion of 25·4% and slightly below that for Great Britain. In 1946 these relative proportions were much the same. This conclusion is supported by the figures quoted in the index figures where, both in 1932 and 1946, the comparison shows Manchester as being approximately 1·8 times as industrial as Edinburgh whose industrial importance relative to Great Britain remained about the same in 1946 as it did in 1932.

An interesting trend in the industrial population index for Edinburgh shows a 4·3% drop between 1929-38 but a sharper increase of 6·5% over 1929 in 1946. This drop is due to the number of insured persons engaged in industry in Great Britain rising during the 1929-39 period, by 17·6% against a population increase of 4·5% while the Edinburgh insured industrial worker rose only by 16·8% against a population increase of 8·4%. In short, Edinburgh's industrial employ-

ment did not expand at the same rate as the industrial employment for the country as a whole. The sharper rise is due to Edinburgh, for the first time, increasing its industrial employment twice as rapidly relative to its total population (i.e. 12% over 1929 as compared with 5·6% for the total population) as the industrial employment for Great Britain relative to the country's total population (i.e. 6% over 1929 as compared with 6·8% for the total population). With Edinburgh's houses used to capacity in these days this can indicate a trend for greater industrialisation. Though small at present it might well increase.

In conclusion it may fairly be stated that Edinburgh is not an " Industrial City " as her share of the country's industrial population is slightly below the average for the country and well below that of the two well known industrial cities of Manchester and Glasgow.

On the other hand the very small tendency to industrialisation in terms of the proportion of industrial workers to the total population, though less than the tendency over the whole country, has commenced a small upward trend. This is probably due to the war-time impetus to the industrial development as measured in terms of G.A.V.

Though the impending developments in the Lothian Coalfields will tend to encourage considerably such a trend this should not be permitted for the reasons stated in the proposals.

Trends in expansion or contraction of industrial use of land.

What has been happening to industry in recent years and in what direction may one anticipate future activity ? Those are the two important points to be considered : no plan can adequately provide space in the zones set aside for industrial use without knowing something of what to anticipate. The population trends have broadly indicated one facet of this but what of the material ones of factory sites, acreages and prosperity ?

Gross Annual Value as a reflection of space changes in real estate.

The heritable parts of a factory are real estate and from time to time expansion or contraction of the estate occurs which results from a matured change in prosperity sometimes affecting ground space needs. Gross annual value reflects such changes of site space from which estimates can be made for industrial requirements in the proposed zones. Increases in gross annual value may, for example, represent an extra wing to a building or an entirely new off-shoot from the parent factory while decreases often represent a vacation of premises or the conversion of factory space into non industrial use. These examples are typical and indicate a trend of industrial needs.

The measure of these changes is found in the Gross Annual Value returns of the City Assessor. It has been selected as the basis of research into these industrial trends for the following reasons :—

The Valuation Roll includes all firms in the City.

It registers any change in a trade of the city affecting its total in number.

It records any extension or construction in the use of the heritable parts of the premises.

It records any general reassessment or devaluation granted to a particular trade as in the case of the shipbuilding and engineering trade during the early '30's.

Although it is based upon rents long leases do not necessarily bar the possibility of reassessment when the heritable parts are altered.

DISTRIBUTION OF FOOTBALL PITCHES
IN PUBLIC PARKS

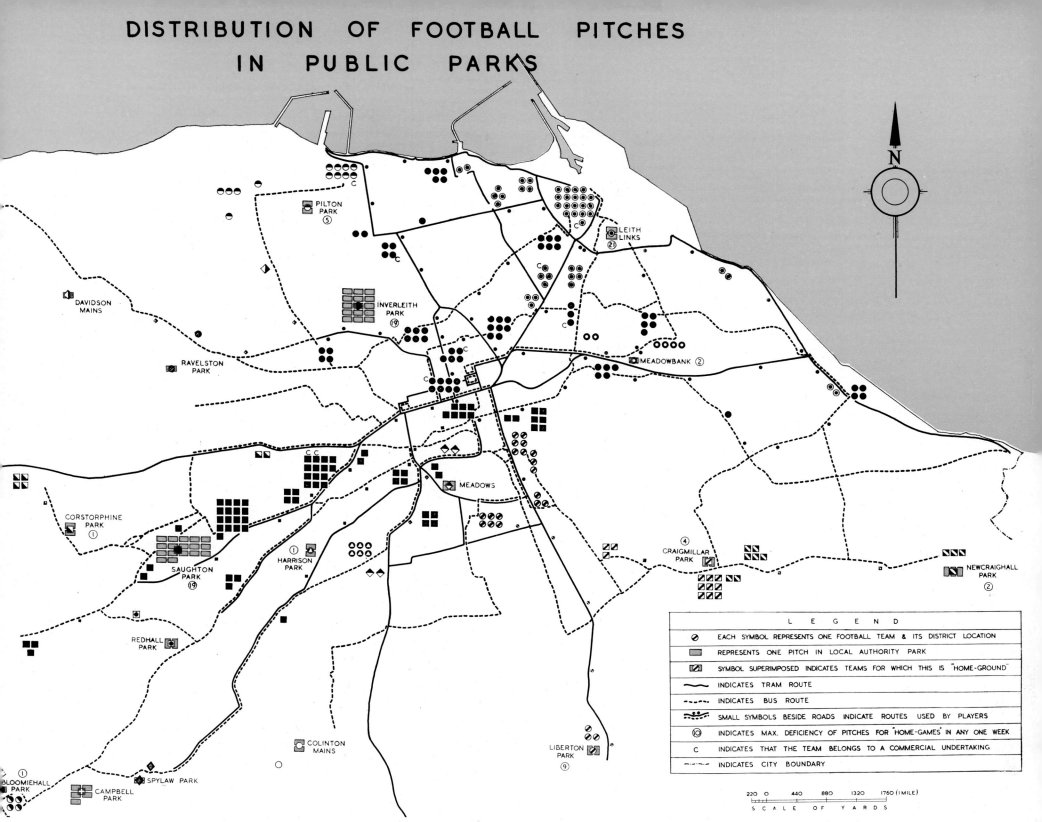

LEGEND

⊘	EACH SYMBOL REPRESENTS ONE FOOTBALL TEAM & ITS DISTRICT LOCATION
▢	REPRESENTS ONE PITCH IN LOCAL AUTHORITY PARK
▨	SYMBOL SUPERIMPOSED INDICATES TEAMS FOR WHICH THIS IS "HOME-GROUND"
∿	INDICATES TRAM ROUTE
---	INDICATES BUS ROUTE
••••	SMALL SYMBOLS BESIDE ROADS INDICATE ROUTES USED BY PLAYERS
⑩	INDICATES MAX. DEFICIENCY OF PITCHES FOR "HOME-GAMES" IN ANY ONE WEEK
C	INDICATES THAT THE TEAM BELONGS TO A COMMERCIAL UNDERTAKING
-·-·-	INDICATES CITY BOUNDARY

SCALE OF YARDS
220 0 440 880 1320 1760 (1 MILE)

PLATE XIII

TABLE SHOWING USE OF FOOTBALL PITCHES IN PUBLIC PARKS FOR TWO CONSECUTIVE WEEKS A & B

NAME OF PARK.	Symbols for Parks and Relative Teams.	Number of Teams using each Park as Home Ground. (Local)	(Com'l.)	Number of Teams with Home Ground Beyond own District.	Number of Games possible or Pitches available. A	B	Number of Home Games Required. A	B	Deficiency in Pitches due to Bad Distribution of Parks. A	B	Surplus of Pitches due to Bad Distribution of Parks. A	B	Number of Home Games Possible.
PILTON	⊘	12	1	—	2	2	6	7	4	5	—	—	1 IN 3 WEEKS.
LIBERTON	⊘	21	—	18	2	2	10	11	8	9	—	—	1 IN 5 WEEKS.
LEITH LINKS	⊙	43	2	4	2	2	22	23	20	21	—	—	1 IN 11 WEEKS.
DAVIDSON'S MAINS	◇	—	1	—	1	1	1	1	—	—	—	1	—
RAVELSTON	⊘	1	—	—	1	1	1	1	—	—	—	1	—
CORSTORPHINE	◩	6	—	2	2	2	3	3	1	1	—	—	1 IN 2 WEEKS.
SPYLAW	◈	1	—	—	1	1	1	1	—	—	—	1	—
HARRISON	◧	6	—	—	2	2	3	3	1	1	—	—	1 IN 2 WEEKS.
SAUGHTON	▪	70	2	25	17	17	36	36	19	19	—	—	1 IN 2 WEEKS.
REDHALL	⊡	1	—	—	2	2	1	—	—	—	1	2	2 IN 1 WEEK.
BLOOMIEHALL	◕	4	—	—	1	1	2	2	1	1	—	—	1 IN 2 WEEKS.
CAMPBELL	⊞	—	—	—	5	5	—	—	—	—	5	5	NO HOME TEAM.
COLINTON MAINS	○	1	—	—	2	2	1	—	—	—	1	2	2 IN 1 WEEK.
MEADOWS	◆	4	—	2	2	2	2	2	—	—	—	—	1 EACH WEEK.
MEADOWBANK	◉	6	—	—	1	1	3	3	2	2	—	—	1 IN 3 WEEKS.
CRAIGMILLAR	▨	12	—	—	2	2	6	6	4	4	—	—	1 IN 3 WEEKS.
NEW CRAIGHALL	◪	10	—	7	3	3	5	5	2	2	—	—	1 IN 2 WEEKS.
INVERLEITH	⊛	62	5	32	15	15	33	34	18	19	—	—	1 IN 2 WEEKS.
TOTALS		262	10	90	63	63	136	135	80	84	7	12	
BY COMBINING TWO WEEKS, TOTALS ARE					126		271		164		19		
AVERAGE WEEKLY FIGURES AFTER ALLOWING FOR SURPLUS PITCHES BEING IN FULL USE					63		136		73		—		

APPROXIMATE NUMBER OF PERSONS WHO PLAY FOOTBALL ON PUBLIC PARKS ON SATURDAY — 3,000. REPRESENTING 0·64% OF TOTAL POPULATION.

SURVEY OF FOOTBALL FACILITIES.

This diagram together with its tabulated data illustrates the present acute shortages of playing facilities. Football teams in some cases can only play once in 5 to 10 weeks on their home grounds while others can only play once a fortnight. If all the available public pitches were pooled as home grounds to even out the demand no one team could play more than once a fortnight and many only once in 3 weeks.

Apart from this general deficiency there is mal-distribution as instanced by teams in St. Leonard's having to share Liberton Park as a home ground and the Canongate teams sharing Saughton Park while 5 pitches at Campbell Park are hardly ever used. The worst case is Leith Links where teams can only play at home once in 11 weeks.

Water of Leith, Randolph Cliff [p. 29]

Playing Fields [p. 30]

[p. 76]

Cramond Island [p. 31]

[P. 31]. *A view of Cramond Island from above the foreshore develop-ment scheme. Edinburgh has ample recreation space for parkland of this kind having a standard of 3·5 acres for every 1,000 population as compared with a minimum of 4 acres per 1,000 as the acknowledged need.*

[P. 29]. *This superb gorge in the midst of the City is one of the finest gifts of nature to the constantly changing scene. Though over-wooded (see Plate XLVIII for comparison) this part of the Water of Leith offers an attractive retreat for the summer evening stroll. For the many thousands who pass daily over the Dean Bridge this aspect could be fully appreciated if the high parapet wall could be lowered. Suicide risks resulting in too intimate an embrace could surely be safe-guarded by replacing the upper portion by a railing.*

[P. 30]. *Here is a playing field used to capacity. Despite Edinburgh's apparent wealth of open space there is a definite paucity of public playing field space. There is only 1 acre for every 1,000 population as compared with the minimum acknowledged need of 4 acres per 1,000.*

[P. 76]. *Backs of Craigmillar Housing showing how the intervening ground between the buildings becomes down-trodden when there is too little open space for the population housed.*

PLATE XIV

Gross Annual Value as an index of production.

Gross Annual Value may also be said to represent an index of prosperity in production, providing its figures are read for a period of years. The long period is necessary since the capacity for production depends upon the heritable parts and the limit they impose. These heritable limits cannot necessarily reflect comparatively insignificant changes in production prosperity but the moment they were changed one way or another a reassessment would take place with a certain time lag, but that does not matter for planning purposes. This contention has been borne out by the investigation into the actual production of certain bakery firms in the city where production is shown quantitatively in their returns by the sale of sacks of flour. These had increased after additions had been made to a mill involving an increase in gross annual value. There is therefore a direct correlation between the two measures. Normally, however, the relation between gross annual value and actual production is indirect. Production measured for a more immediate change can only be shown by the employment level or the actual consumption of material or by the actual output as measured in tons, etc. None of these methods of measurement are commonly used and cannot, therefore, offer a common basis

for the calculation of heritable space requirements : but rental does, as it changes as the heritable space and equipment changes.

Dock facilities, quarrying and coal mining and railway installations, however, are assessed on the tonnage handled each year and interpreted as revenue so that here gross annual value in such cases reflects from year to year on the basis of revenue rather than upon the changes of heritable property.

CONCLUSION.

What are the trends in industrial installations in the city ? These are shown for the seventeen year research period of 1929 to 1946 and tabulated in Appendix 3. The Food, Drink and Tobacco group may be said to be the most important group with paper and printing second. Others have been investigated and reviewed in the Appendix. This review indicates that demands may be anticipated for the Food, Drink and Tobacco industries, supplies and services (especially motor vehicle repair and body building, Distributive and Extractive industries (i.e. concrete and artificial stone). In most other industries existing installations would appear to be adequate to allow for some increase in output though there is a general need for modernisation.

5.—RECREATION SPACES

At first sight Edinburgh would appear to be very well off indeed for open spaces even in the centre of the city but in point of fact she is just as badly off, if not worse in some cases, than other cities for much needed public recreation fields. By comparison with two blitzed cities, Hull and Plymouth, it will be found that when public parks and recreation fields are considered together Edinburgh has a standard of 4·5 acres per 1,000 as compared with 1·18 per 1,000 for Kingston-upon-Hull and 3·6 for Plymouth. However, further analysis shows that the playing fields standard which should be read in terms of modern standard of 4 acres per 1,000 is merely one quarter, namely 1 acre, so far as Edinburgh is concerned. This cannot be corrected merely by converting existing amenity parks into playing fields. Authority playing fields also are well below the minimum standard called for under the Scottish Education Act of 2·0 acres per 1,000 population. For instance, Edinburgh has an existing standard of 0·31 acres of authority school playing fields per 1,000 population, Hull 0·92 and Plymouth 0·62. Though this involves the provision of a substantial balance to bring these facilities into line with the Act it is nevertheless essential as the city is quite inadequately served. Even then the aim is lower than that prescribed for England where the standard under the act is 3 acres per 1,000 population.

Existing Public Playing Fields Facilities.

By way of illustration a survey of football facilities shows quite clearly this marked deficiency in the playing field standard in terms of acres per 1,000 population. For instance, the diagram illustrated on plate no. XIII shows that not only is there maldistribution of playing field facilities but there is also an acute shortage in relation to the known demand in individual areas. The table connected with this diagram indicated that the Pilton area shows such a demand in excess of existing facilities as to restrict a football team to one game in three weeks. Similarly Liberton and Leith Links areas restrict home playing to once in 5 weeks and once in 10 weeks respectively. Even if all of the existing facilities were pooled together the demand is such that no one team could play more than once in two or three weeks. Maldistribution is evident when it is seen that such parts as Inverleith Park have to serve teams as far away as Portobello on the other side of the city for their home matches. The diagram also shows the routes which would normally be followed when the public transport services are used to travel to and from the home district and the home football recreation fields.

Survey for Open Spaces.

This Open Space Survey Map (Folding Map No. 9) shows the existing distribution of the various kinds of open space uses from the public park to the childrens play ground. It also shows the extensive amount of land at present devoted to agricultural use, more than 62% of all the open space is used for one form of agriculture or another. The table shows also that, as yet, only half the total acreage of the city is at present built up—some 16,000 acres out of a total of 32,000 acres. Edinburgh is no exception in providing adequate facilities for one of the most popular Scottish pastimes —the golf course. Next to agriculture the golf courses in the city occupy quite the largest proportion of the total open space. As may well be expected the next largest form of open space is public open space which include such areas as Kings Park, Braid and Blackford Hills, Corstorphine Hill, etc. but what is not expected is the very much smaller proportion of public recreation fields and education recreation fields each of which occupy some 2 or 3 per cent of the total open space acreage.

TABLE III

A. Type of Open Space	Area in Acres	Percentage of Total Open Space	Percentage of Total Area of City
Public Open Space	1,603·41*	9·50	4·93
Private Open Space	895·00*	5·34	2·74
Cemeteries	207·90	1·24	·64
Agriculture	10,531·36	62·85	32·45
Unused Land	628·8	3·76	1·93
Golf Courses	1,986·73*	11·86	6·09
Public Recreation	464·84*	2·78	1·47
Educational Recreation	436·77*	2·67	1·21
	16,754·81	100·0	51·46

TOTAL AREA OF CITY—32,526 Acres

★—N.B.—Taking these into account a standard of 11·7 acres per 1,000 population is obtained on the basis of the 1946 total population of 459,400. For comparative purposes the table below picks out the principal open space uses for the three cities.

TABLE III— B.	Public Parks and Recreation Grounds	Standard per 1,000 Pop.	School Playing Fields (Authority)	Standard per 1,000 Pop.	Private Open Space	Standard per 1,000 Pop.	Cemeteries	Standard per 1,000 Pop
Edinburgh	2,068·25	4·5	145·0	0·31	895·0	1·95	207·90	0·43
Kingston-upon-Hull	379·12	1·18	384·70	0·92	398·44	1·24	219·04	0·68
Plymouth	755·6	3·6	53·8	0·26	152·3	0·74	119·00	0·58

6.—SCHOOLS DISTRIBUTION

The existing schools distribution is shown on this survey of Educational Facilities (Folding Map No. 10) and two typical schools, each representing authority and non-authority types. The schools have been illustrated to show the distribution of the pupils and where they live in relation to their particular school. Table IV gives the figures of this distribution of pupils. It clearly shows that the authority school serves pupils mainly in its immediate district while the non-authority school does in fact serve pupils who come from far and wide. This fact is of value in order that the importance of the geographical disposition of schools in the plan may be fully appreciated. It shows, for example, that Local

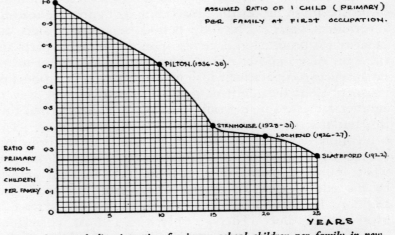

Graph showing decline in ratio of primary school children per family in new Corporation Housing Areas during the inter-war period of 1918—1939.

TABLE IV. SCHOOL.	Number of Pupils.	Number of Pupils Living within 1 Mile of School.	Number of Pupils Living within 2 Miles of School.	Number of Pupils Living within 3 Miles of School.	Number of Pupils Living more than 3 Miles from School	Average Distance to and from School. (Miles.)
George Heriot's School (Senior)	915	162	296	298	159	4·08
George Heriot's School (Junior)	562	89	214	174	85	4·00
Broughton (Secondary)	1,021	549	400	72	—	2·10
Broughton (Primary)	613	605	8	—	—	1·02

Authority Schools serve districts or neighbourhoods while private schools draw their pupils from all parts of the city and from outside. The extent of sharing by several authority schools of one single recreation field is well shown by the example of Broughton School which shares with other schools only 3 football pitches.

Authority Pupil Population.

An estimate of the total pupil population was obtained from the Corporation Education Department for the years 1945-1946 and 1946-1947 in order to estimate the total number of schools required in the Plan. This is as follows and includes all nine age groups from 5-14 plus 16% of the total for the 15 and 16 age groups now to be included for compulsory education :—

	Primary pupils	41,116
1945-1946	Secondary pupils	13,975
	Total	55,091 pupils
	Primary pupils	40,878
1946-1947	Secondary pupils	13,707
	Total	54,585 pupils

This represents approximately 12·0% of the total population which compares with 12% for the County of London. The total non-authority pupils known to be attending private schools in Edinburgh is 10,000 or roughly 2% of the total population of which 1,800 come from outside the city.

Another fact to be allowed for in the Plan is the extraordinary difference in the number of school children of all school ages between a new housing area of a few years old and one of 15-20 years old. The graph below is drawn to show this difference as may be seen between the Pilton Social Survey district No. 39 containing new housing built between the years 1936-38 with 0·71 primary school children per family and Stenhouse Social Survey District No. 54 containing housing built in 1930 with 0·39 primary school children per family living in the district. Two others are also included, Lochend District No. 44 and Slateford District

No. 53 which contain similar housing built earlier still and show a further decline in the number of authority school children of primary school age. All of these ratios are below the average of one primary school child per family for recent housing areas experienced by the Corporation Education Department. All these housing schemes referred to are those carried out by the Corporation or other grant aided schemes but there is reason to suppose that the same conditions prevail in non-grant aided new housing areas.

Condition of Existing Schools.

Most of the existing authority schools in Edinburgh are in an overcrowded state having many with nearly double their normal quota of pupils. The new Education Act will require a very large increase in the number of schools to eliminate this condition. It requires, amongst other things, fewer numbers of pupils per class, that is, 30 per class instead of the pre-war 40 and 50; more commodious conditions and up to date equipment; playing fields of minimum area adjacent to, if not as an extension of, the building site area. Hardly any authority schools in Edinburgh conform to this latter condition while the following facts give a picture of the obsolescence of the present buildings :—

[1] New schools or buildings of a fairly high standard 30%
[2] Schools out of date but capable of modernisation 22%
[3] Schools still more out of date and less adaptable 27%
[4] Schools which should be discontinued as Day Schools 21%

These percentages are only approximate but serve to give an idea of the urgency of the problem of providing for new school sites in the Plan.

Non-Local Authority Education.

Evidence from the University authorities indicate an urgent demand for a large precinct which would bring together the present scattered faculties into one centre somewhere in the vicinity of George Square. The extent of the area required is 48 acres. After circularising all the known private schools in the city from the kindergarten to the big public schools information returned indicated no problem comparable with that facing the Corporation in this respect. With the exception of one public school requiring an entirely new site giving ample playing field space all the other indications either had no change contemplated or minor ones of a kind that could be dealt with more appropriately in the detailed planning stage after the major features of the proposals have been decided.

There is, therefore, no intention to do more than suggest the alternative site for the public school in the plan.

EDUCATION
DISTRIBUTION OF SCHOOL PLAYING FIELDS

WARRISTON PARK — Ⓕ
DIAGRAM SHOWING EXISTING FOOTBALL AND HOCKEY FACILITIES SHARED BY 3 SECONDARY AND 10 PRIMARY SCHOOLS.

FOOTBALL PITCHES
HOCKEY PITCH
TENNIS
BOWLS

PITCH	NUMBER OF MATCHES PLAYED ON EACH PITCH						WEEKLY TOTALS
	MON.	TUE.	WED.	THU.	FRI.	SAT.	
A	2	2	2	2	–	3	11
B	2	2	2	2	–	3	11
C	2	2	2	2	–	3	11
D	–	1	1	1	–	2	5
TOTAL	6	7	7	7	–	11	38

SCALE OF YARDS
220 0 440 880 1320 1760 1 MILE

LEGEND

▨ PLAYING FIELD	■ SECONDARY SCH	□ PRIMARY SCH

KEY TO PLAYING FIELDS

Ⓐ SLATEFORD	Ⓗ JOCKS LODGE
Ⓑ PILTON	Ⓘ NORTHFIELD
Ⓒ FERRY ROAD	Ⓙ PORTOBELLO
Ⓓ WARDIE	Ⓚ CRAIGMILLAR
Ⓔ BANGHOLM	Ⓛ LIBERTON
Ⓕ WARRISTON	Ⓜ HOLYROOD
Ⓖ HAWKHILL	

→ SCHOOL TO RELEVANT PLAYING-FIELD
▼ SCHOOL USING PUBLIC PARK
● NOTE— WHERE NO POINTER IS SHOWN SCHOOL HAS NO ALLOCATION OF PLAYING FIELD EXCEPT ON SATURDAY

KEY TO SCHOOLS

A	1 A	SAUGHTON	(Secondary)	
	2 A	TYNECASTLE	do.	
	3 A	DARROCH	do.	
	4 A	BOROUGHMUIR	do.	
	5 A	GILLESPIE'S (GIRLS')	do.	
	6 A	ST. CUTHBERT'S	(Primary)	
	7 A	GORGIE	do.	
	8 A	DALRY	(Primary)	
	9 A	CRAIGLOCKHART	do.	
	10 A	BRUNTSFIELD	do.	
	11 A	GILLESPIE'S (BOYS')	do.	
	12 A	ST. PETER'S	do.	
	13 A	SOUTH MORNINGSIDE	do.	
B	1 B	DAVID KILPATRICK	(Secondary)	
	2 B	PENNYWELL	(Primary)	
	3 B	ROYSTON	do.	
	4 B	ST. DAVID'S	(Primary)	
	5 B	BROUGHTON	(Secondary)	
C	1 C	HOLY CROSS	(Secondary)	
	2 C	FLORA STEVENSON	(Primary)	
	3 C	VICTORIA	do.	
	4 C	FORT	(Primary)	
	5 C	COUPER STREET	do.	
	6 C	HOLY CROSS	do.	
D	1 D	BELLEVUE	(Secondary)	
	2 D	WARDIE	(Primary)	
E	1 E	TRINITY	(Secondary)	
	2 E	TRINITY	(Primary)	
F	1 F	FLORA STEVENSON	(Secondary)	
	2 F	BELLEVUE	do.	
	3 F	JAMES CLARK'S	do.	
	4 F	BROUGHTON	(Primary)	
	5 F	LEITH WALK	do.	
	6 F	ABBEYHILL	do.	
	7 F	LONDON STREET	do.	
	8 F	CANONMILLS	(Primary)	
	9 F	ST. MARY'S	do.	
	10 F	MILTON HOUSE	do.	
	11 F	ST. PATRICK'S	do.	
	12 F	ST. IGNATIUS	do.	
	13 F	STOCKBRIDGE	do.	
G	1 G	NORTON PARK	(Secondary)	
	2 G	LEITH ACADEMY	do.	
	3 G	ST. ANTHONY'S	do.	
	4 G	LORNE STREET	(Primary)	
	5 G	BONNINGTON	do.	
	6 G	DR. BELL'S	do.	
	7 G	LOCHEND ROAD	(Primary)	
	8 G	HERMITAGE PARK	do.	
	9 G	LEITH ACADEMY	do.	
	10 G	ST. MARY'S (LEITH)	do.	
	11 G	LINKS	do.	
H	1 H	ROYAL HIGH	(Secondary)	
	2 H	ROYAL HIGH	(Primary)	
I	1 I	PARSONS GREEN	(Primary)	
	2 I	ST. NINIAN'S	do.	
	3 I	CRAIGENTINNY	(Primary)	
J	1 J	PORTOBELLO	(Secondary)	
	2 J	TOWER BANK	(Primary)	
	3 J	ST. JOHN'S	(Sec. and Primary)	
	4 J	PORTOBELLO	(Primary)	
K	1 K	NIDDRIE MARISCHAL	(Secondary)	
	2 K	ST. FRANCIS	(Primary)	
L	1 L	JAMES CLARK'S	(Secondary)	
	2 L	LIBERTON	(Primary)	
M	1 M	ROYAL HIGH	(Secondary)	
	2 M	ROYAL HIGH	(Primary)	

USING PUBLIC PARK

1 ▼	JUNIPER GREEN	(Primary)
2 ▼	COLINTON	do.
3 ▼	MURRAYBURN	do.
4 ▼	LONGSTONE	do.
5 ▼	STENHOUSE	do.
6 ▼	CORSTORPHINE	do.
7 ▼	DAVIDSON'S MAINS	do.
8 ▼	GRANTON	do.
9 ▼	NEWCRAIGHALL	(Primary)
10 ▼	NIDDRIE	do.
11 ▼	PEFFERMILL	do.
12 ▼	PRESTONFIELD	do.
13 ▼	SCIENNES ROAD	do.
14 ▼	NORMAL PRACTISING EPIS'C'AL	
15 ▼	ROSEBURN	do.
16 ▼	BALGREEN	do.

NO PLAYING FIELD

1 ●	BLACKHALL	(Primary)
2 ●	CRAMOND	do.
3 ●	ST. BERNARD'S	do.
4 ●	ST. MARGARET'S	do.
5 ●	DUDDINGSTON	do.
6 ●	CRAIGMILLAR	do.
7 ●	PRESTON STREET	do.
8 ●	ST. THOMAS OF AQUINS	(Secondary)
9 ●	ALL SAINTS	(Primary)
10 ●	TOLLCROSS	do.
11 ●	NORTH MERCHISTON	do.
12 ●	CASTLEHILL	do.
13 ●	SOUTH BRIDGE	do.
14 ●	ST. ANN'S	do.
15 ●	DEAN (Temporary Field)	do.

This diagram confirms the extreme shortage of playing field space for the Authority Schools not only by the extraordinary amount of sharing of existing school grounds for those fortunate enough to have one allocated but by the extent of the claims upon the Public Parks which are already overloaded as shown on the diagram on Plate XIII. There are also fifteen schools with only a Saturday allocation of a playing field. To appreciate this present lack of facilities attention is drawn to the extent of sharing at Warriston where three secondary and ten primary schools between them provide a minimum demand for 38 matches in one week which means an average of two matches daily. No pitch can stand more than two or three matches per week if the grass is to be reasonably well maintained. By contrast the Scottish Education Department recommends a minimum standard of 2 acres per 1,000 of the total population as compared with the present standard of 0·31 acres per 1,000, excluding public requirements. For the 1946 total population of 478,769 a minimum of 957 acres is required for Authority School facilities as compared with the present 145 acres of school playing fields. The Plan aims at a slightly higher total population resulting in a larger acreage still.

PLATE XV

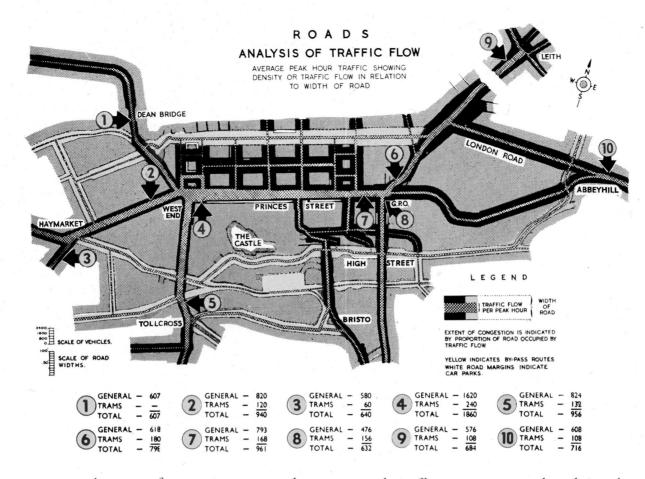

ROADS
ANALYSIS OF TRAFFIC FLOW
AVERAGE PEAK HOUR TRAFFIC SHOWING
DENSITY OR TRAFFIC FLOW IN RELATION
TO WIDTH OF ROAD

LEGEND

TRAFFIC FLOW PER PEAK HOUR | WIDTH OF ROAD

EXTENT OF CONGESTION IS INDICATED BY PROPORTION OF ROAD OCCUPIED BY TRAFFIC FLOW

YELLOW INDICATES BY-PASS ROUTES
WHITE ROAD MARGINS INDICATE CAR PARKS.

1 GENERAL — 607	TRAMS — —	TOTAL — 607	**2** GENERAL — 820	TRAMS — 120	TOTAL — 940	**3** GENERAL — 580	TRAMS — 60	TOTAL — 640	**4** GENERAL — 1620	TRAMS — 240	TOTAL — 1860	**5** GENERAL — 824	TRAMS — 132	TOTAL — 956
6 GENERAL — 618	TRAMS — 180	TOTAL — 798	**7** GENERAL — 793	TRAMS — 168	TOTAL — 961	**8** GENERAL — 476	TRAMS — 156	TOTAL — 632	**9** GENERAL — 576	TRAMS — 108	TOTAL — 684	**10** GENERAL — 608	TRAMS — 108	TOTAL — 716

From the census figures a test was made to ascertain the traffic congestion points by relating the traffic flow to the width of the streets used. Though a street may carry half the hourly traffic flow of a wider street, it can still be more congested owing to its narrowness. Earl Grey Street, known to be too narrow for its traffic, forms the basic unit of density (traffic flow to width of street) from which all other streets are measured for density. [Fig. 1]

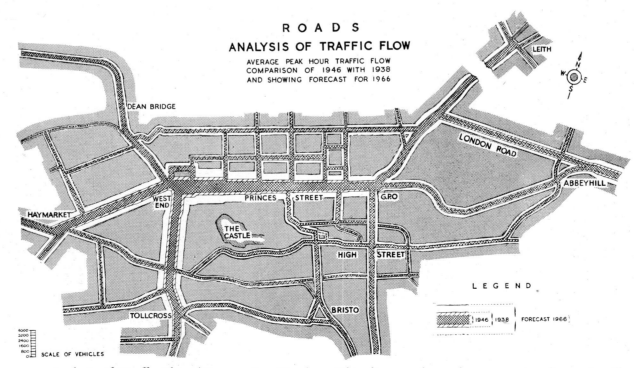

ROADS
ANALYSIS OF TRAFFIC FLOW
AVERAGE PEAK HOUR TRAFFIC FLOW
COMPARISON OF 1946 WITH 1938
AND SHOWING FORECAST FOR 1966

LEGEND

1946 | 1938 | FORECAST 1966

Analysis of Traffic Flow (Comparative Years). This diagram shows the comparative flows of traffic for the three years, 1938, 1946 and for the future year of 1966. The results show how the 1946 traffic is substantially the same as the peak pre-war year. The anticipated traffic in 1966 shows the extent that future traffic may be expected to increase creating a corresponding worsening of congestion. [Fig. 2]

PLATE XVI

East End Traffic [p. 22]

East End of Princes Street Flow. Though the traffic peak hour flow in 1946 was half that for the West End of Princes Street (961 per hour) congestion is nearly as great owing to the more complicated lay-out of the tramway system. There is no doubt that the abolition of the trams in favour of trolley buses would not only greatly ease congestion with present flows of traffic but would make the construction of a traffic roundabout feasible at least for the West End.

East End Traffic [p. 23]

Another view of the East End Traffic. Owing to the lack of adequate car parking facilities only a small number can be parked on the North Bridge (seen in the background) and in St. James' Square. The Theatre Royal area scheme would solve the car parking problem.

West End Traffic [p. 24]

West End of Princes Street Traffic. The present layout of the road intersections have lead to confusion and congestion. It consists partly of a one-way system combined with a two-way traffic use of roads. With the flow of traffic in 1946 (one year before this photo was taken) at the peak rate of 1,860 vehicles per hour, and very nearly the 1938 peak hour flow, this congestion will obviously get out of hand when it doubles itself some ten years or less hence.

PLATE XVII

Waverley Station Entrance [p. 25]

An interesting internal view of the road traffic access to Waverley Station and its departure platforms. There is far too little space for road traffic manœuvring yet the present railway space is also inadequate and requires to squeeze more space from the already too little space for road traffic on account of the narrowness of the valley. This congestion and conflict would be solved if long distance traffic was diverted from here as recommended in the Plan.

Aerial View of Waverley [p. 26]

This photograph taken recently shows Waverley Station of to-day and its extent. There is no doubt that it occupies a substantial area of this magnificent valley unique in character but these roofs do not contribute to its beauty—they mar it.

Aerial View of Waverley [p. 27]

A striking view of Waverley Station roofs from the air.

Aerial View of Waverley [p. 28]

Another aerial view of Waverley Station showing how it dominates the surroundings with its extensive serried rows of glazed and pitched roofs. Yet if only the regional suburban traffic used the station electrification would be possible leading to the possibility of garden roofs with lawns. This is illustrated on Plate XXXV.

PLATE XVIII

7.—COMMUNICATIONS: ROAD AND RAILWAY

ROADS.

Introduction.

The Survey of Traffic taken during August, 1946, on the days when the traffic was known to be at its heaviest, clearly shows by comparison with similar periods during the peak years before the war that traffic generally was approaching the large proportions of pre-war. Such a trend when there were all the prevailing restrictions of the immediate post war period indicates a significant rise in traffic flows over the pre-war year. All the results of the survey clearly show that the heaviest traffic parts of the city are those routes passing through central areas. The Origin and Destination Survey though it was only including traffic which originated from somewhere beyond the city boundaries emphasised that the main bulk of the traffic was making for the central areas. The Traffic Flow Diagram further illustrates this fact by the thickness of the black line in the central parts and rapidly tapering off within half a mile radius of Princes Street. The Accident Map shows that, though the traffic in 1946 was still less by approximately one-third than it was in one of the peak years before the war, accidents were actually on the increase and had already exceeded those for the pre-war year of 1937. Perhaps one of the most important facts revealed by this Survey shows that the greater quantity of traffic is to be found at the West End rather than at any other part of Princes Street. The greater congestion at the East End would suggest that there is more traffic passing that point than at the West End when in fact the survey shows otherwise. The congestion is mainly due to the inadequate design of the road junctions and the presence of the trams. The sharp tapering line of traffic flow on all these main radial routes from the centre shows that the greatest traffic problem is to be found within this half mile radius of Princes Street. It should be noted that this Survey does not give the proportions of the total traffic on any of the routes which may be said to be through traffic. This can only be satisfactorily obtained from an Origin and Destination Survey of the kind already undertaken for the traffic originating beyond the city. This could and should be done with the help of the Police Department. Perhaps one of the most convenient ways of carrying out such a survey with the least delay and inconvenience to motorists would be the preparation of a simple diagram covering the city section by section and issuing them to the drivers of vehicles to be returned with the points of their start and destination filled in. That would then enable the delay caused from the stopping of vehicles to be reduced and the hold up to be confined to points on the fringe of the central area.

Analysis of Traffic Flows.

An analysis of the flow of traffic for three different years—1938, 1946 and an anticipated year is illustrated on plate XVI. This clearly shows the extent to which 1946 traffic flows has nearly caught up with the peak flows of pre-war despite the prevailing post war restrictions. The anticipated flows for 1966 have been plotted, based upon the recognised estimate which doubles pre-war traffic in 20 years time or less. Below this diagram is shown the extent of congestion arising from the 1946 flows, so that any increase in traffic flow will obviously worsen congestion to the point of stagnation if the 1966 flows are reached. Congestion on this diagram is at its worst in Earl Grey Street where the thickness of the black line is least. Therefore, any other road or part of a road in this central area showing an equally thin black line has equal

amount of congestion. The congestion is measured as a density of traffic flow per unit width of street between pavements. At the West End congestion is comparable to Earl Grey Street and is apparently due to the official car park space which reduces the width of Princes Street at this end. Passing from consideration of this density flow diagram to the one showing comparative flows for the three years, 1938, 1946 and the anticipated one for 1966, will give some idea of the scale of increase of congestion anticipated when restrictions are lifted and traffic increases.

Origin and Destination Survey.

Folding map No. 12 shows the destination of all vehicles originating from outside the city in a 4 hour period from 9 a.m. to 1 p.m. The results define the most important parts that attract vehicular traffic. These assessments included only the traffic entering the city and not leaving it. The total amounted to some 3,165 vehicles which passed each of the 11 census points on the outskirts of the city during this 4 hour period. The primary reason for this survey was to test the present need for an outer ring road bye-passing the city itself. The result showed that 326 vehicles or 10 per cent of the total 3,165 vehicles recorded at all origin points had destinations beyond the city, and therefore, could be considered as likely to use such an outer ring road if constructed. Even then they would only give a peak flow of something like 82 vehicles per hour. This would not justify the construction of such a road. The Planning Scheme which follows this survey, however, draws attention to some other important future developments which would change these present conditions and call for such a road to meet the needs of future years. Other conclusions which can be drawn from this survey is the obvious need for an inner ring road to ease circulation about the centre of the town before it seeks its local link road to its destination. 1,304 vehicles, or, 41 per cent of the total vehicles recorded, have destinations in and around the centre of the city that cannot be provided for in any other way than by a ring road, owing to the existing topography. Another factor that emerges is, that at present there is no big demand for an intermediate ring road through the Newington areas. From the detailed nature of the information available a correlation between the Origin and Destination Map and the Traffic Peak Hour Flow Map gives an approximate indication of the amount of through traffic in the total flow of traffic on the main radial routes. For example, 360 vehicles in this 4 hour period made for the city from post 9 at Mayfield or an average of 90 per hour. Since, therefore, at Haymarket the one way traffic for Corstorphine Road is 396 per peak hour about 25 per cent of this traffic consists of long distance vehicles. Similarly, the traffic flow map indicates a two way traffic flow of 716 or 358 one way traffic for the London Road of which some 70 vehicles or one fifth of the total consists of long distance vehicles.

Survey of Accidents.

Though the traffic at the West End in 1946 was two-thirds of the traffic before the war the number of accidents had already risen from 13 in 1937 to 21 in 1946 and there are several similar instances of an increase on other important traffic routes. One of the more interesting conclusions to draw is from the coincidence of the accidents with the location of the shopping streets. Wherever there are shops there seems inevitably to be a conflict between pedestrian and motorist.

This factor has been borne out in most, if not all, other cities in the Kingdom as, for example, on the accident diagram for the city of Kingston-upon-Hull. This clearly adds weight to the proposals in the planning scheme for the segregation of pedestrians from motorists in the shopping streets wherever possible. The shopping precinct is one of the best ways of reducing, if not eliminating, accidents on the roads and in all future development it should, for this reason alone, be adopted as one of the essential principles.

RAILWAYS.

A general indication of the extent of the use of land by the two railway companies, the L.N.E. and the L.M.S. before nationalisation is shown below. There is an uneconomic cutting up of the land and duplication of routes resulting from the extensions of small competing companies of the earlier days of railway development. The uneconomic cutting up of the land is very much in evidence in the Gorgie,

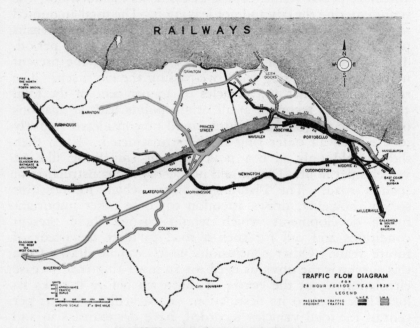

SURVEY OF RAILWAY TRAFFIC.

To assess the relative importance of the routes in the railway system quantitative figures for traffic flows over a 24 hour period were obtained from the L.N.E.R. and L.M.S.R. Companies. It was important to distinguish between the freight and passenger lines so that any improvements contemplated might be considered in the light of present day needs together with information concerning future trends.

Slateford and Haymarket areas where there is much interchange and overlapping of routes used by these two companies. It also became an intrusion instead of an asset where Playfair's development scheme of the 19th century in the vicinity of Calton Hill was interrupted. It is this early lack of appreciation of the importance of the inter relationship between parts in a city's development that creates such problems of bad development which have been left unsolved for half a century or more. Any schemes, therefore, which would eliminate this criss-crossing of routes, in the Dalry area would not only improve accessibility by road and on foot within this area but would also offer better shaped plots of land for building. It is hoped, also, that the railway improvement scheme in the plan will simplify and lessen the amount of railway lines required for good service.

The duplication of routings serving the three most important nodal points for industrial or freight traffic coming in and out of Edinburgh, that is Granton Breakwater Junction, North Leith, and South Leith, result from early competition. Tracing some of these routes it is found for example :—

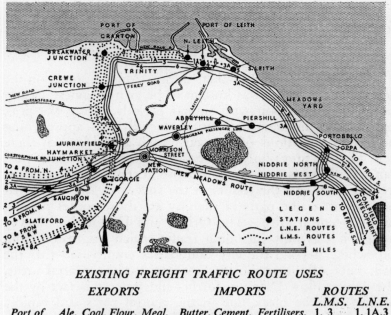

EXISTING FREIGHT TRAFFIC ROUTE USES

	EXPORTS	IMPORTS	ROUTES	
			L.M.S.	L.N.E.
Port of Leith	Ale, Coal, Flour, Meal, Iron and Steel, Paper	Butter, Cement, Fertilisers, Fruit and Vegetables, Grain, Timber, Iron and Steel	1, 3	1, 1A, 3
				3A, 4, 5
Port of Granton	Coal	Esparto Grass, Timber, Wood Pulp	2, 3A, 4	2, 6

(1) The L.M.S. traffic to and from the north where they have the right of way by agreement with the L.N.E., the awkward route is followed from Saughton Junction, via Haymarket West, Morrison Street, where the freight trains then have to be shunted to come back on part of their tracks up a steep gradient to Murrayfield, Crewe Junction and Granton Road and so on to North Leith. The L.N.E. on the other hand, coming in over exactly the same line, does not require to do this in order to reach the same destination. It follows the simpler route through the valley of Princes Street Gardens via Bonnington Junction to North Leith. In order to avoid this the plan shows that a connection could be made between this route from Saughton Junction through to Haymarket West with a short new length of railway line to link up with the route at Crewe Junction.

(2) The L.M.S. route to and from the south and west proceeds via Slateford Junction, Crewe Junction to the Granton Breakwater. The L.N.E. also from the north and west proceeds through Saughton Junction, Gorgie, Morningside and Newington suburban lines, Niddrie, Portobello, Piershill, Trinity and so to the Granton Breakwater. This latter is an incredibly long and devious route for the same destination.

(3) The L.M.S. route from the south and west through Slateford Junction, Crewe Junction, Powderhall and Bath Street Junction to South Leith. This is a duplicate service to the same place by the L.N.E. from the same direction but following another route through Morningside and Newington Suburban lines Niddrie West and North Portobello to South Leith. This L.M.S. Bonnington Line in this latter example is very largely redundant to-day. Central Leith Station has also lost much of its significance from earlier days and it is believed that it could quite easily be acquired without the Railway losing an important asset. There is also the L.M.S. Goods Yard at Morrison Street which is not fully used and might well be acquired for the alternative use the plan suggests.

The gradients on the various routes differ considerably. For example, the route through Morningside and Newington is very unsatisfactory from the point of view of running costs as the gradients which vary from 1 in 70 to 1 in 100 are excessively steep and no freight train of consequence could use this line without the assistance of an extra locomotive.

Marshalling yards as they extend to-day are considered to be inadequate to meet even present day demands. Yet it is a well known fact that the coal field development of the Lothians will create an impossible strain upon the accommodation which they will have to provide.

The Traffic Flow Diagram shows the system that each railway used before nationalisation in the routes primarily intended for freight traffic or passenger traffic. Their relative importance may be assessed from the thickness of the lines showing the density of flow of traffic using them.

Princes Street Gardens.

The L.N.E. line through the Gardens here has for some considerable time been the source of much exasperation to the admirer of natural beauty. There is a very definite popular demand for something to be done to eliminate the ugliness of the station and the noise and smoke caused by the passing and stopping trains. A solution which will enable the covering in of this railway line and the Waverley Station has been put forward in the Plan.

8.—SHOP DISTRIBUTION SURVEY

Retail shopping facilities represent one of the most important of the social requirements of a neighbourhood. Shops are a centre of daily intercourse among friends as well as for the purchase of the family's daily needs. It is common knowledge that if a shopping centre is adequate in size, having a fair number and diversity of shops, the search for the right commodity becomes increasingly satisfying and even fascinating. It is not, however, intended here to argue the merits of the shopping centre, whether large or small as opposed to the scattering of individual shops, but rather to acknowledge the necessity for the grouping of shops and assess the dual requirements for shop space on the one hand and the demand by the public for shop facilities on the other. This is essential, for the Plan must include these requirements with those other social needs already enumerated and explained in the preceding parts of this chapter.

Estimated requirements of a neighbourhood of 10,000 persons.

It is impossible to give a precise answer as to how many shops and stores would be required though it is possible to make a shrewd guess based upon the geographical position of the neighbourhood relative to the city centre where the main shopping centre exists and upon the character of the population to be served and its number. For example, a neighbourhood adjacent to the city centre requires only a very moderate number of shops as compared with one situated two miles or more from the city centre. But such a central neighbourhood requires shops of a local character even if they duplicate those in the main street as, for example, the food provision shop where those in the main street often become known for specialities for occasional indulgence or the shoe and repair shop, as distinct from the fashion shop in the main street.

The number and types of shops given below are, therefore, for general application requiring modification according to the circumstances prevailing of the kind mentioned above. The figure of 10,000 population is taken as a working basis because a reasonable variety of types of shops are then capable of being supported economically. Any smaller population progressively eliminates the scope for choice as between patronising the chain or Co-operative store, for example, or the private retailer, or tends to eliminate an economic demand for the high grade clothing shop or chemist, etc.

This fact adds weight to the need to consider one's planning boundaries so that they contain sufficiently large population units. The economical and administratively convenient size unit has already been established as between 5,000 and 10,000 persons to support a range of local authority schools so that it is important to know of this common factor in estimating for two important social facilities.

TABLE V

NUMBER, SIZE AND TYPE OF SHOPS TO SERVE APPROXIMATELY 10,000 POPULATION

	No. of Shops	Size Frontage in Feet	Depth in Feet	Area	Total Frontage	Total Area
Butcher	8	16	45	720	128	5,760
Baker	7	10	30	300	70	2,100
Grocer	20	20	35	700	400	14,000
Fruit and Fish	4	20	30	600	80	2,400
Green Grocer	6	20	50	1,000	120	6,000
Dairy	2	20	50	1,000	40	2,000
Cafe	2	20	60	1,200	40	2,400
Chemist and Photographer	3	20	30	600	60	1,800
Fried Fish	3	20	30	600	60	1,800
Wines and Spirits	2	15	30	450	30	900
Total Food Shops	**57**	**181**		**7,170**	**1,028**	**39,160**
Drapery	5	20	30	600	100	3,000
Mens Outfitting	4	20	30	600	80	2,400
Footwear	2	30	30	900	60	1,800
Boot Repairs	8	10	20	200	80	1,600
Dyeing and Cleaning	2	10	20	200	20	400
Hardware (Ironmonger)	4	20	30	600	80	2,400
Furniture	2	35	50	1,750	70	3,500
Tobacconist	15	15	30	450	225	6,750
Hairdressing	2	20	30	600	40	1,200
Radio and Electrical	4	15	30	450	60	1,800
Total Miscellaneous	**48**	**195**		**6,350**	**865**	**24,850**
Grand Total	**105**	**376**		**13,520**	**1,843**	**64,010**

The figures quoted indicate the number and size of shops capable of earning a reasonable turnover from a population of 10,000 persons. The information that resulted in these figures was obtained from an enquiry made of the various trade federations or associations and of shops selected by them as being representative. In many instances turnover figures obtained clearly showed the normal extent of the " overheads " separate from the profit and from this an estimate of the number of purchasers or total population required to cover both overheads and profit was assessed.

The influence of the co-operative, multiple or chain store need not, it is thought, alter the calculation providing that the number and size of the departments contained in each store is deducted from the total number and sizes of shops capable of being supported by 10,000 persons. The precise proportion in the number of co-operative stores to private traders is impossible to assess since it must depend upon, inter alia, the sociological distribution of the income groups. Once that distribution is determined for any part of the city the proportions might well be assessed with reasonable accuracy. Meanwhile it is sufficient in the first instance to have the total area for shop sites required for any neighbourhood of a given population total.

CONCLUSION

This civic survey has for its object the uncovering of the salient features for which the plan must make recommendations. They are features which bring to light numerous facts both quantitive and qualitative concerning the living and working conditions of the population. These features whether they be population densities or recreation space provision conjure up a picture in one's mind that may be visualised on the map collectively and geographically or appreciated individually by visits to specific parts of the city. Once the facts are assembled both in tabular and map form close examination can be made because enlightenment is not adequate from perusal of each single proposal but from comparison and correlation between each aspect also. For example, the Registrar General's emigration and immigration figures for the inter-war period require to be correlated and compared with four other facets of the survey—inter-war development map, Dean of Guild Court records, the Social Survey population figures, the Corporation slum and over-crowding records,—before a conclusion could be formed concerning what was possible in development and redevelopment over a period of years. A simpler example of correlated information is, of course, the extraction of net housing areas from the land use survey together with the population figures from the Social Survey.

No attempt has been made to describe in detail what has been discovered for individual districts or for block areas of property because the maps and tables themselves are self explanatory to that extent. They have only to be compared with the proposals to appreciate the extent of development and redevelopment considered necessary. Salient facts are described more as a guide for individual searching than anything else though these also lead in logical sequence to, and give the raison d'être for, the proposals in the Plan.

The aim in the first place, therefore, is to give an overall picture of the living and working conditions, means of entertainment and outdoor recreation and of the public services that make these facets of daily life possible, rather than detailed eccentricities of local significance such as the congested street or the slum tenement or the over used foot-ball pitch. These local facts are important and a solution must be found for them but they cannot be solved independently of the rest of the city since their solution inevitably has repercussions beyond their locality. The sum total of these eccentricities (which is a mild way of describing some of them) gives the total extent of the problems to be solved and paints the overall picture for objective planning.

It is of general public interest also to appreciate what can be achieved from normal expenditure over a period of years and the figure of £25 million spent on all forms of house construction over a 22 year period is of particular significance. If that expenditure could have been guided by a Plan as we understand it, there need never have been the lack of co-ordination between individual developments that add to the head-aches caused by earlier non co-ordination. That this total expenditure in effect involved a distribution of some 140,000 persons is important because it could have included all those living in slums to-day in addition to a good many of those living in other sub-standard circumstances.

For comparison the Civic Survey should be described as a whole and not broken up and distributed among the various sections or chapters of the proposals because the Plan in its initial conception is a global or city wide consideration of the problems from which a broad outline framework is evolved within which the details may be inserted. Detailed comparison in the appropriate context is made possible by the arrangement of the unfolding of the maps clear of the chapter.

Summing up the principal findings of the survey one may enumerate them as follows :—

1. Overcrowding and slum dwelling exists in all its acute forms the worst of which—the " unfit " amount to some 7,000 dwellings or 5·7% of the total 123,265 dwellings in the city representing some 24,926 persons. In varying degrees of unhealthy living conditions a minimum total of 147,408 persons should be rehoused. To provide a good home environment for all at least 262,778 persons require to be rehoused. A new housing policy is needed to relate new house construction with redevelopment.

2. Congestion in the limited amount of recreation spaces available and general need for correcting existing rural distribution.

3. Lack of adequate community facilities in a reasonably spacious environment, i.e., more shops in the suburban areas in properly located centres giving plenty of choice of selection of retailer ; community clubs and health clinic etc.; more and up-to-date local authority schools are required.

4. Congestion of road traffic and dangerous intersections at such points as East and West Ends of Princes Street, Earl Grey Street and Nicolson Street. Evidence of traffic volume being doubled in ten years time.

5. Industry and commerce is scattered amongst residential property to the detriment of both. Evidence of Lothian coal-fields development and dock extensions encouraging influx of industry on a big scale : the sanctity of the city as a capital and cultural city is, therefore, at stake.

6. The traditions of Edinburgh expressed in its heritage of architecture are recorded for preservation wherever possible.

7. Need for central area redevelopment caused by the regrouping requirements of the University faculties into one large central precinct : provision of two festival centres, bus stations and other improvements arising out of the other problems referred to above.

8. From the economic resources measured in pounds, shillings, and pence, building development or population distribution are found considerable when assessed for a 22 year period. This should give food for thought to the habitual sceptics of planning in their cry " it will never happen in my time."

Central Floor Space Survey.

This is an essential requirement for the detailed application of the Plan and has not been undertaken owing to the lack of time. A survey should, however, be carried out in connection with the rebuilding of Princes Street and Leith in particular, and for guidance during redevelopment of commercial areas and for future trends in their four main uses—central office, shopping, hotel and restaurant accommodation.

This would be of particular value in the rebuilding of Princes Street (described in chapter 7), the planning of the central commercial and shopping precincts, the permanent festival centres, and of the government administrative centre.

Finally the survey, it should be remembered, presents a factual record of conditions at a given time, i.e., during the preparation of the Plan. It should be kept up-to-date by means of supplementary surveys from time to time. These will in fact form records of progress and will, therefore, show how far the Plan is being implemented in order to put a stop to unsatisfactory conditions.

More detailed surveys, such as that mentioned above of central floor space areas, should also be put in hand before detailed proposals of certain types are carried out.

The survey in fact, like Planning is a continuing process of investigation and diagnosis, leading to prescription and maintained state of well being.

CHAPTER THREE

POPULATION REDISTRIBUTION

INTRODUCTION. The population of most cities built on rocky prominences, which have in the past been subject to attack, has lived in huddled circumstances in order to obtain the protection afforded by cliff and wall. Such living led to high densities of distribution and overcrowding. There is little doubt that, but for the reasons of safety and defence, Edinburghers would not have been forced to find room for growth by building their tenement flats high in the air, in contrast for instance, to the two storey house and garden of the later suburban development. Though the habit, born of early necessity, still lingers, evidence of a change is not far to seek : Edinburgh built self-contained dwellings with gardens when the first departure from the confines of the old town occurred in the 18th and 19th century developments of George Square and the New Town : again, between the two recent wars the bungalow development presented unusually low density by comparison.

Distribution for Dwelling Types. Despite the fact that high land and property values (and not now reasons of defence as of old and sometimes the " feu " *) still forces up the tenements in huddled profusion in the central areas, this change from the old town tenement life to the house and garden has been a continuing popular trend over the past 200 years, reaching the proportion of 61% of all dwellings erected in the inter-war years. Obviously tenement development in the suburban areas has little to commend it where it is reasonable and feasible to build the two storey dwelling with garden. On the other hand a continuance of excessively low densities of bungalow development over large areas would cause excessive outward development of the city. The Plan shows that within reasonable urban limits of development, the amenities of the house and garden, where most necessary (i.e. for families with children), could be constructed together with suitable flats for childless families provided the whole area conforms to the average density suggested for the zone. In this respect it is well to remember that facilities for the child to play in the open under the mother's watch and care cannot be provided when the house is remotely situated from the ground in a multi-storey block of flats.

Ancillary Land Uses. Population distribution forms the basis for estimating the extent of zoning requirements. So much of population needs for other space uses than for the house and garden has in the past been left to chance or entirely forgotten that there are practically no sites left for shops, community clubs, recreation spaces, schools etc., in the majority of the inter-war development areas. In the older parts previous conversion to provide these needs has resulted in cramped awkward conditions with one ' use ' often in conflict with another. Wherever there is population these ancillary needs are bound to arise and it is the planners task to anticipate and to guide development of all kinds to obtain a reasonable balanced distribution of population together with these ancillary needs.

Limits of Urban Development. Before estimating this distribution, however, an assumption has to be made as a working

★—Derived from the Feudal System.

basis for the ultimate extent of urban growth and a limit defined prescribing its appropriate planning boundaries. Such a limit should in any case be prescribed to prevent the city becoming too large for a number of social, economic and amenity reasons : physically too large a city tends to cause social disintegration or estrangement between the populated parts. (The great " wen " of London is the extreme example of this though there are several other large cities nearly as defective). This danger is considerably increased in Edinburgh by its hilly topography which, together with increased distances, lessens the sense of partnership between neighbourhoods or individual parts of the city. Economically also a large city becomes a burden upon public services and the administration required to perform them. To the farmer such a city is a menace not only because of the lengthening distances from the home market but because of the increasing demand for freedom of access in the fringe areas for week-end exercise of the townsman—a fact acknowledged in the Scott Report on Land Utilisation in Rural Areas. To the townsman his access to fresh market garden produce becomes remote and he has to travel much further to obtain his week-end exercise.

There is also the dread danger of "Black country" development of Midland infamy to guard against in the south eastern portion owing to the development of the Lothian coalfields. A prescribed limit for future urban development to avoid these unfortunate effects is, therefore, of paramount importance.

Regional and National Relationship. Next, a reasonable population total within these confines has to be determined. In this respect two factors must be taken into account : the relationship of the city to the region and to Scotland is one factor and to the needs of the present city population is the other. Consultations with Sir Frank Mears, consultant for the region, and with the Planning Department of the Scottish Office, have indicated that the plan would not conflict with regional development providing the population total does not greatly exceed its pre-war level of 471,000. It would appear to be in the national interest not to exceed this figure and cause further depopulation of the rural areas. The best safeguard would be perhaps the creation of counter attractions in the rural areas by increasing the living and working amenities there.

However, any material increase in population above the 1946 total of 478,769 would not be in Edinburgh's interest either. The present mal-distribution presents too urgent a problem to permit its continuance as the Social Survey clearly shows. For healthy and attractive living conditions this redistributed population will depend upon the amount of possible redevelopment of the outmoded built up areas and from undeveloped land within the city. As the plan indicates it is possible for about four fifths of the present population to live in houses with gardens and still leave a small margin for immigration. The total population ought, therefore, to be limited to 495,600 giving a corresponding total resident population of some 453,000 for whom house accommodation would be required. Immigration created by the potential industrial development in Fifeshire and the Lothians would be amply accommodated outside Edinburgh in the New Towns set aside for them. With redistribution as the most important problem it is proposed that the densities for net housing areas should consist of four zones of 100, 75, 50 and 30 persons per acre. This would give a total estimated resident population including those not permanently resident in Edinburgh of 453,000 persons.

Density Control. The density zones allow also for the important provision of adequate numbers of dwellings within the central area for those who desire and need to live within reasonable distance of their work—at least so far as the principle member of the family is concerned. That is essential for sound economic reasons.

To ensure a redistribution on these lines there must be an adherence to a net residential density control which is reasonably flexible to provide for the greatest variety of development. There is ample ground in Edinburgh that is ripe for development or redevelopment to achieve this and thereby eliminate overcrowding.

This objective to eliminate bad housing and mal-distribution of the population is in grave danger of being defeated by non-controlled occupancy of the land and property. The present form of control limiting private building to 25% of all local authority housing might achieve this though it may not necessarily be the best way. If this danger materialises the city will be faced in the near future with an overspill problem beyond the city boundary with a consequent loss of industry. The absence of such a problem at the moment is Edinburgh's good fortune shared unhappily by all too few cities these days.

Development and Redevelopment. Though there is no whole-sale redevelopment proposed as map number 14 shows and though the Plan looks ahead about 50 years or more, the poorer industrial class housing of the last century has not been excluded.

There is a total proposed residential area of 9,475 acres, excluding shopping areas, in the proposed neighbourhood unit areas of which 4,330 acres consists of property that is either new and of sound construction and lay-out or is of historical, or architectural merit or property that is not too outmoded. This good property, referred to as 'static' areas in the Plan, has been retained even though the net density is frequently much below or much above what it should be for its geographical position. This retention of the existing density lowers the overall average in some neighbourhoods and raises it in others.

Another proportion of the total consists of 2,188 acres of existing built up property requiring redevelopment, either to conform to the zoning proposals, and/or, because the property is ripe for redevelopment anyway. The balance of 2,957 acres scheduled for net residential development consists of property that is at present unbuilt upon land. For the average net densities considered desirable for each particular neighbourhood excluding the 'static' property a total population of 134,061 could be accommodated on the existing unbuilt on land and 147,181 on the existing built up parts scheduled for redevelopment. These and other facts may be read from table XX.

For the whole city a total of 2,310 acres consists of property ripe for redevelopment as it is sanitarily unfit property and/or, is overcrowded on the land. 1,397 acres of this lies within neighbourhood units and 913 acres in the proposed non-residential zones, that is industrial and commerical. 558 acres of this latter area lies in the industrial zone as stated in the chapter on industry. This kind of property is recommended for redevelopment in the Plan.

These net residential areas should be treated as a series of combined operations commencing with the undeveloped parts and ear-marking for the evacuees from redevelopment areas. For example, development at West Pilton should form part of the scheme for the redevelopment of Leith Industrial Zone and of the adjacent neighbourhood units. To take another example there will be found a need for triple operations, involving undeveloped land on the outskirts of the city with redevelopment in existing low density areas in neighbourhoods adjacent to the Dalry and Gorgie industrial zone, and again within the industrial zone itself—all three operational areas to be carried out as one scheme. The total extent of such combined operational areas are shown by the diagram on page 83 but obviously only sections of this total programme can be done at a time and that is where " the phasing " described in the chapter on Realisation comes in.

Planning Standards. Other planning standards included in the gross development required for this 453,000 resident population are 10 acres per 1,000 population for open spaces, an average of one primary school to 5,000 and one secondary to 10,000 population, together with shop and other community building facilities sufficient to meet the needs of the estimated population groups in the neighbourhoods. In application these standards are varied considerably according to geographical, physical and sociological circumstances in each locality or neighbourhood of the city.

CONCLUSION. Map no. 15 shows these zoning areas and their average net densities indicating the population that can reasonably be accommodated within the outer limits of the city together with the appropriate other land use requirements. These outer limits are considered a desirable termination for city building, that is the inner limits of the proposed green belt and wedges.

With 252,778 persons (see Appendix I) out of the total 437,568 resident in the city and living in unsatisfactory conditions for the reasons already stated there can be no doubt where the priority of house construction should lie. A lack of adequate development control during those fateful 22 years of the inter-war period retarded the solution of these problems. For instance, of the 116,298 persons, who came from the older parts of the city, out of the total 139,107 known to have been accommodated in the 43,471 new dwellings erected in this period, only about 16% or 18,320 persons were housed in Corporation housing schemes specifically intended to relieve overcrowding or to effect slum clearance.

This 18,320 population really represented a comparatively small fraction of the total population that would have been considered overcrowded if the second and equally important form of overcrowding had been included, i.e., excessive density of housing or persons per acre and if the standards for measuring overcrowding of rooms were more nearly those considered reasonable today. The pre-war survey by the Medical Officer of Health and Chief Sanitary Inspector under the 1935 Housing Act indicated 22,244 families were deemed to live in overcrowded rooms but under the Housing Act standards children under 10 were only to be counted as half a person while a one year old child was discounted altogether : also a sitting room was expected to be used as a bedroom. Though, for present day regulations, these Housing Act standards still apply it is believed that they will be revised in the near future and the plan anticipates that every human being will be counted as a single person and sitting rooms will not be considered for use as bedrooms. Had the standards been those now anticipated, the estimated total of persons deemed to be living in too small a dwelling would have been doubled. Though the 43,000 dwellings erected in this period would not have completely solved both forms of overcrowding they would have satisfied a great part of it. Also, the more suitable sites absorbed now which are not part of a redevelopment scheme containing bad housing the worse will be the prospects for achieving redistribution without an overspill beyond the city: and any such overspill will cause serious complications.

There is no reason to suppose that this redistribution proposed would not preclude mixing income groups living in the same locality. Mixing as a social advantage is generally admitted and it may be achieved by this redistribution of all income groups living in the outmoded areas recommended for redevelopment in the plan. The large areas of "static" property interspersed among the redevelopment parts also provide the opportunity to correct existing maldistribution.

The following are the main aspects affecting the re-distributing of the population and lead to the proposals put forward in the Plan on folding map no. 14 :—

1. Limit of Urban Development.
2. Planning Standards for Redistribution.
   [a] General Description.
   [b] Density.
   [c] Open Spaces.
   [d] Land for Other Purposes.
       (i) Shop Centres.
       (ii) Other Public Buildings.
       (iii) Car Parking.
       (iv) Schools.
3. Application of Planning Standards.
4. Size and Location of the Communities.

1. LIMITS OF URBAN DEVELOPMENT AFFECTING REDISTRIBUTION OF THE POPULATION.

In Edinburgh there are physical features which predetermine the outer limits : coal working for example has so undermined the land in the south east that building development must essentially be limited by it. In the south the "Pentland Foot" referred to in chapter XI places the physical limit. The safeguard is the Green Belt reservation with its inner limits at Newcraighall and Craigmillar. The Plan shows that existing development has very nearly extended as far as one may dare permit and in parts is seen to coincide with these outer urban limits.

To the south, the outer limits are prescribed well short of the Pentland foot to allow the outer ring road referred to in chapter 4 on roads to have a parkland treatment. The line of urban development may then extend just south of Fairmilehead to round off the existing building development there. In no circumstances should development extend further south than that indicated on the Plan. Such restriction will safeguard the rural environment of Swanston village and provide an adequate foreground of recreational or farmland space to the Pentlands.

In the west and south west lies a vista of comparatively undulating ground between the Corstorphine and Craiglockhart hills where development has already engulfed the villages of Corstorphine and Colinton. Here the presence of railways and the Union Canal influence the population distribution but it is Turnhouse Aerodrome and the need for a "public health" zone centred on Gogar that broadly prescribed the limits of further absorption of the rich agricultural land. The line of the outer ring road finally prescribes the outer limit.

The north western limit is defined by the need to preserve the beautiful woodland belt between Queensferry Road and Barnton railway and of the Almond River, Cramond Foreshore and at Lauriston Castle for public recreation.

The "wedges" of open space referred to in the Recreation Space chapter would effectively prevent existing building development from coalescing into one mass. In this respect topography plays an important role in creating the kind of "spur" development more or less following the valleys.

2. PLANNING STANDARDS OF REDISTRIBUTION : DENSITY, OPEN SPACES. LAND FOR OTHER PURPOSES.

(a) General Description. The space requirements for recreation and public buildings form an important corollary to population distribution. The table below indicates the estimated ancillary requirements for populations of 10,000 according to geographical location. Naturally enough

TABLE VI	10,000 POPULATION REQUIREMENTS Authority Schools			
LOCATION	Total standard in acres/ 1,000	N.S.	P	Secondary
Inner Area	2·4	(4) 6	(2) 9	(1) 9
Suburban Area	2·4	(4) 6	(2) 9	(1) 9
Outer Area	2·4	(4) 6	(2) 9	(1) 9

	Other Community Uses					
LOCATION	Total standard in acres/ 1,000	Shops and Offices	Clubs and Churches	Service Industry	Car Parking	Halls etc.
Inner Area	2·0	6	4	4	4	2
Suburban Area	3·0	8	6	6	6	4
Outer Area	3·5	9	7	7	7	5

The above table gives the average normal building area requirements of a 10,000 population for Authority Schools though considerable variation will occur in application according to the anticipated sociological grouping of the population. Shops and other public building area requirements will probably not vary.

any population total of considerable size requires a shopping centre, library, community club with its hall, craft and lecture rooms, a clinic, cinema, dance hall and swimming baths reasonably near at hand. The housewife does not wish to travel daily a ten mile return journey to buy day to day

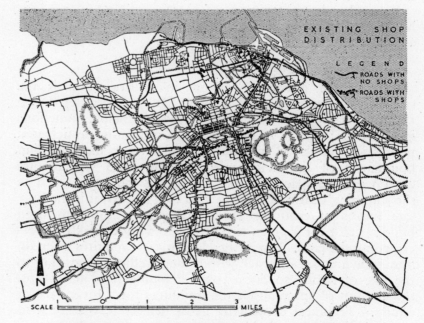

This plan shows the existing distribution of shops which are seen for the most part ribboning the existing main road system. It also shows how little shop provision there is in the somewhat scattered suburban areas by comparison with the older central areas.

necessities in Princes Street, nor does the family want to travel similar remote distances for a place to meet friends.

Yet this has of necessity become a habit with comparatively few exceptions owing to this forgotten factor in housing schemes.

A glance at the shop distribution diagram shows the sparse allowance of shops in the outer areas of the city. In some instances it will be necessary to convert some of the inter-war period development into shops and other community building uses owing to the excessive amount of house building.

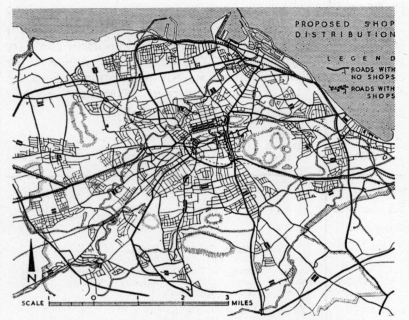

This plan shows the proposals for the provision of shopping facilities in the neighbourhood unit areas. This will correct not only the existing mal-distribution but make up the deficiency in those areas where they are required. It should be noted also that each neighbourhood is provided with a compact sub-shopping centre off the main motor road system.

It is, therefore, of paramount importance to ensure a sufficiency of ground for these purposes and a careful study and research has been made. The Greater London report gave an outline of such requirements as a general guide to local authorities in its region. A similar investigation has been made for Edinburgh and is found in the Civic Survey.

From the above standards of space requirements a population total has been determined for each neighbourhood unit area of the city.

(b) Density Zoning.

One of the governing factors in redistribution is the standard of net residential density. It is a form of Town Planning control which serves two principle functions in the Plan : (a) it is the basis for estimating anticipated population totals of persons living within the planning boundaries of the neighbourhood unit who will require certain ground space uses other than for the home, such as the shopping centre or playing field etc., and (b) it is the only safe means of ensuring a reasonable and minimum sized building plot for a given size of house without risk of over-crowding the land. Just as the Housing Act requires a certain minimum amount of space within the dwellings according to the size of family so does Town Planning need to control the amount of space about the buildings for a given size of family. Technical control by gross density leaves much to be desired as the nimble-witted merely seeks the nearest large open space for his excuse to reduce his building plots in size.

There are four density zones recommended as the controlling medium in all future development and redevelopment of the neighbourhood unit. They are 100, 75, 50 and 30 persons

per *net residential acre and are geographically situated with the highest about the centre of the city and the others circumscribing the 100 density in rings with the lowest forming roughly the peripheral ring of the city. This is known technically as pyramidical zoning.

There is nothing rigid to be interpreted from this form of control as each zone represents an average proposed density within it and reasonable variations either way should be permitted. As regards the maximum density no individual plot should exceed the 100 maximum. Variations, however, can only be achieved in a comprehensive development covering large areas at a time with perhaps 10 acres as the minimum. Smaller areas should conform to zone density as a maximum unless another maximum can reasonably be selected to comply with the general estimates for the zone or neighbourhood. Within such broad density variations local differences of net densities should be permitted according to the size of house or houses to be erected. Clearly a four or five apartment house designed to accommodate a 6 person family should be built upon a larger plot of ground than say a two or three apartment house. This local application of the density principle should not, however, be looked upon as a " rule of thumb " method of allotting building plot sizes but as a general guide. Though for the higher density zones in the centre such an application may require to be more firmly adhered to for the sake of equity, for the outer areas of lower density, it may become merely a general guide with considerable flexibility of application.

These neighbourhood units or population groups, it is estimated, can accommodate the present total population of 437,568 persons with an addition of 15,500 persons in accordance with those standards of density and ancillary requirements. The object at all times must be to keep approximately to the sum total population indicated for these unit areas in order that these ancillary requirements may continue to be sufficient both in quantity and in geographical distribution. For example, if the interpretation of the average density for the zone was exceeded for a number of small unit areas of net housing without any compensating reductions in adjoining areas then not only would the healthy environment of the house be imperilled but the whole balance or distribution of the services such as schools, shops, etc., would be upset.

(c) Recreation Space Standards.

The standard of open space allowances are based generally upon the minimum overall requirements of 15 acres per 1,000 population. This includes 4 acres per 1,000 for public parks, 4 acres per 1,000 for public recreational fields, 2 acres per 1,000 for authority school recreational space 3 acres per 1,000 for golf courses, 1 acre per 1,000 for cemeteries and 1 acre per 1,000 for allotments. Private recreation spaces already exist in sufficient quantity. These standards can only, however, be obtained as an integral part of the general development in a population neighbourhood unit area on the outskirts of the city where the standard of net density is moderate and the amount of built upon land much less. In those areas where the standard of net density is to be higher for reasons previously stated in this chapter the standard of adjacent recreation space must necessarily be lowered in order to avoid too great a dispersal of the population in the central areas of the city where greater compactness is desirable. In these central areas it is suggested

---

★—Net Residential Density means the number of persons that might be expected to occupy a house built within the curtilage of its building plot the area of which is measured from the centre line of the road to the end of the back garden. For flats and tenements the same applies.

that the minimum standard should, therefore, be 4 acres per 1,000 suitably ear-marked to satisfy as much of each of those four categories, public parks, public playing fields, authority school recreation fields and allotments—as can be reasonably obtained. In the outer areas a progressively higher standard is obtained until the point is reached where each neighbourhood unit could be self-contained for almost all of these total requirements.

The balance between the amount that is obtained in the central area and its total requirements of 10 acres is then found in the wedges of open space and the green belt area on the periphery of the town. A detailed account of the open spaces is found in chapter XI on Recreation Spaces.

(d) Land for Other Uses.

Under this group of requirements is included all the school buildings and their hard surface play grounds, shops, offices, social and public buildings, churches, service industry and work shops, car parks, etc. Not included are the areas required for the recreational playing fields for the schools.

(i) Shops and Service Industries.

A special commercial survey carried out in Edinburgh and Glasgow and quoted in the Chapter on the Civic Survey has provided a guide to the amount of ground space required for a given population. There remains to suggest the policy for shop grouping.

In the past the principle of many but small groups containing one each of the different kinds of retailer has been followed but this is not a satisfactory or even convenient form of distribution. A shopping centre should be large enough to offer several shops of each kind covering a comprehensive field of retail trade from the Butcher and Baker to the small tobacconist or cycle or shoe repair shop. Such a centre should be a two-sided shopping street, compact and intimate " to provide a friendly and lively shopping atmosphere " as the Retailers Advisory Committee on Town Planning envisage. For convenience this is also the better form as the smaller shop group either restricts the freedom of choice of retailer, or, causes the extra journey to satisfy that choice in the next small group.

The total needs of a given population depend upon the geographical position of the neighbourhood relative to the main shopping centre of the city. The principle followed here is to reduce the size of this sub-shopping centre in areas nearer the city centre and increase it in areas on the outskirts. The new size of shopping centre requires about 6 acres of ground in the central parts supported by 10,000 population rising to about 10 acres on the outskirts where there may be some 40 to 50 shops of varying size, character and number of types.

The shop centre should be situated away from main traffic arterial routes but adjacent to the principal link road of the neighbourhood unit where it should be centrally placed for convenience of access. This affords freedom from conflict with main traffic, so often the cause of fatal and injurious accidents. The accident survey map gives a good illustration of this conflict.

The service industry may form part of the back premises of the shop, or, it may be apart from it altogether, as in the case of the jobbing builder. A garage repair service and filling station of small dimensions would also require to be apart from the shopping street, though near it.

(ii) Public Buildings and places of Entertainment.

These will vary in number according to the local character and geographical position of the neighbourhood. The community club, clinic, library and art gallery, swimming bath and ice rink, concert hall and cinema should all form a group adjacent to the shopping centre. The bank, post office and Pub. should also be adjacent, but, not necessarily part of the shopping street where an unbroken shop façade is an advantage indicated by the Retailers Advisory Committee.

(iii) Car Parking.

Facilities for this should be on an ample scale as shopping by car before the war was increasing considerably, and, though these neighbourhood centres are within 15 minutes walking distance for the majority of any neighbourhood population group there are still those who use the car as a " shopping basket ", and may wish to increase the variety of choice offered by more than one centre.

The above description of policy for the grouping of all these " other land uses " for the community services aims at establishing single principal centres of community life about the centre of each population group. For Edinburgh these would vary from 7,000 to 20,000 persons.

Such centres could become lively, friendly and, in every way attractive foci of neighbourhoods that would tend to diminish travelling long distances for evening entertainment, social intercourse and cultural pursuits, or, for daily shopping expeditions. These centres do not, however, preclude the " round the corner " shop in different hilly parts, or, where the centre cannot be placed in a central position, but this type of development should be supplementary and not an alternative.

(iv) School Requirements of the Population.

School distribution is yet another corollary to population distribution. The demand for local authority school accommodation is the main concern here though enquiries made of private establishments has permitted suggestions for their requirements also to be illustrated in the Plan. For example, Mary Erskine school, at present situated in Queen Street, requires modern premises, and it is suggested that these might well be situated in one of the green belt areas. This will permit the playing field facilities to be provided side by side with the school.

Contrary to non-authority schools, authority school provision is of distinctly local significance as the proportion of authority to non-authority school children is sufficiently high to create large local demands for accommodation.

Local Authority Schools. The survey gave the existing distribution of those children of all school ages and the estimates for school provision are based upon them. These estimates, however, will need to be adjusted to allow for the redistribution envisaged in the Plan. This raises the complex problem of assessing the sociological regrouping of the population to relieve overcrowding and to obtain close juxtaposition between place of work and home, where desired. Clearly then, any redevelopment in the neighbourhoods adjoining the industrial zones of Leith and Gorgie, for instance, should have a predominance of authority school children. Conversely, those neighbourhoods more remotely placed geographically from industry may be expected to require fewer authority schools.

Next the estimates of totals of authority pupils must be related to the age of the neighbourhood. New development areas, as the survey illustrated, clearly have the high average proportion of one child of " primary " school age to every family of a predominantly lower income group neighbourhood; and after about ten years this proportion drops to about 0.7 per family and to 0.3 after 20 years.

This calls for a long and short term programme of school building with the largest number in the short term period. We recommend that, in every development or redevelopment scheme in a predominantly "authority" area, schools should be provided on the basis of one primary school child per family within the neighbourhood planning boundary. Then at some future period, when the neighbourhood reaches the matured state of an aging population similar to other localities, any surplus schools may be disposed of for other uses.

The minimum standards of site space for building and playing fields set aside in the plan is examined in chapter 10, and covers the range of school requirements from the Nursery to the Secondary School and those for further education.

3. APPLICATION OF STANDARDS.

From the various determinants for a suitable optimum size for the city both in area and in population compiled with regard to the density of distribution of the population the outer limits have been drawn and described. Beyond these limits will lie the green belt and the Pentland Hills as seen in the diagram below. With the population total assessed, re-distribution, together with the necessary ancillary land uses, must now be related to existing physical conditions such as topography and to the distribution of those buildings considered desirable for preservation. The population distribution is, therefore, already predetermined to some extent by such preservation. No neighbourhood unit group of population can be expected to be the same either, in total numbers, or, necessarily of precisely the same character. Such variations between neighbourhood groups will inevitably vary the demand for ancillary land uses and thus create differing results as between one locality and another. There will, for example, be a need for a larger shopping centre in one neighbourhood unit "Area" than in another, more authority schools in one locality than another. The population total recommended for each neighbourhood are those which it is considered the physical nature of the locality will reasonably permit and having regard to the amount of land suitable for building development and of built-up property considered desirable to

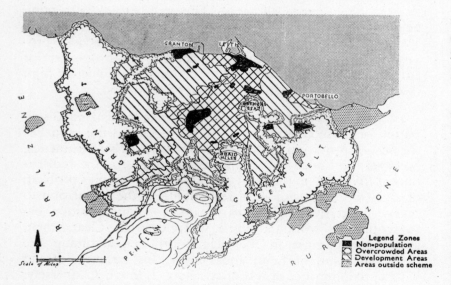

The Plan illustrates diagrammatically the broad conception of the city and its environment where the outer limits of urban development are defined together with the Green Belt reserve and Pentland Foot. These limits, which are more closely defined on folding map No. 14, provide sufficient space for the redistribution of the overcrowded population with a margin for a small additional population.

redevelop. As regards the population character, an assumption has, however, to be made, anticipating the appropriate localities as reception areas for the overcrowded population and for those, not necessarily overcrowded, but living in outmoded property or in some other unsatisfactory circumstances. While at all times the mixing of all income groups

as a sociological necessity may be attained, the results will naturally be influenced by the concerted demands for redevelopment in different areas at one time, together with the development of unbuilt on land in other areas.

Redevelopment Areas. These are determined according to the kind of development considered necessary for a locality to assume its due function in the Plan. It may, of course, be necessary to redevelop to eliminate overcrowding and slum conditions, or, it may be a locality that is best cleared entirely of residential property in favour of a commercial use as in the case of the St. James Square area, or, the proposed industrial zone for Leith or for the University precinct about George Square. The existing conditions of the property is not the determining factor for future land use, but rather for the time when such redevelopment is likely to occur.

Certain areas may well be required for redevelopment to correct mal-distribution of the population caused by an exceedingly low density of development for its geographical position and to provide homes near the place of work. In this respect redevelopment is concerned with the necessary adjustment of siting of the work-place as well as the home.

There will also be the need for redevelopment for the provision of recreation spaces, schools, shops, community clubs, health centres, halls, churches, cinemas, etc., involving a change of existing use to make good local deficiencies. All of these changes occurred from time to time before the war and are occurring to-day as building licences will permit, but they should now be co-ordinated to conform to the land use zoning of the Plan.

The total changes involved in the redevelopment proposals under use zoning and density zoning together are arrived at by an extremely laborious process that includes an examination in detail of every area in the city. The statistical information required for such an examination cannot, therefore, be anything less than a detailed one covering the whole city.

The Survey of the city indicated the geographical position of property which was worthy of preservation, either for its condition or for its convenience of location, or, for its value from the architectural or historical point of view. All such property has, in the main, been preserved in the scheme.

Housing. From the Social Survey it has been possible to assess the total numbers and sizes of houses that would normally be required for the various population groups in the neighbourhood planning areas. The table in appendix I indicates the estimates for house sizes that would be required in any development or redevelopment scheme within these neighbourhoods. These estimates are not intended to be considered as anything else than as a general guide to ensure a reasonable distribution of house types. It is certainly not intended to be considered as a rigid formula, but one to be applied with considerable flexibility. It shows the approximate standard of accommodation which is considered reasonable for a given size or sizes of families and represents a great improvement upon that allowed for in the Housing Act of 1935. It is not one which has any statutory force but it is one which is based upon normal living standards where poverty does not dictate otherwise. There are two departures from the Housing act of 1935, (a) every human being is counted as a single person and (b) only bed rooms are counted as sleeping rooms. The static areas referred to below have been tested for possible overcrowding upon this standard of accommodation. Before allowing for any population going into the neighbourhood area from elsewhere, any overspill from these static areas has been included in the total estimates for land use as well as that for any new population.

4. THE SIZE AND LOCATION OF THE COMMUNITY.

Size.

The size of a community is determined from a number of broad facts such as relationship of the home to the place of work in distance and accessibility: the economic and convenient size and number of a complete range of schools which the population total is required to support: the convenient and attractive size of sub-shopping centre to give as much variety of choice which, also, the population total is required to support. Such factors, considered together, require a 60,000 population total to support a complete range of schools from the nursery school to the secondary school, though the shopping facilities can be supported by smaller groups of population of from five to ten thousand persons. These smaller groups may be considered as sub-divisions to the structure of the community. With these population group sizes as the ideal the advisory Plan, involving as it does the redistribution of the population for the various reasons already enumerated, conceives a regrouping of this population into communities which may vary somewhat either way from the ideal total as local physical or other conditions dictate. It may not be inappropriate at this stage to point out that this essential reshuffling of the population into socially self-supporting communities with their smaller sub-divisions of neighbourhoods might themselves, in the more distant future, become the future ward boundaries for local government administration.

The Population Distribution Table no. XX facing page 90 contains a summary of the results of the application of these ideals. It lists independently the name, the population total and character of each ward in the city to-day, and correlates these with the planned redistribution set forth in the Advisory Plan.

Location of the proposed Communities.

The detailed results are explained briefly in the following community groups which are seven in number, each of which contains approximately six neighbourhood units bounded generally by some physical features such as a railway, road, river or large open space.

Community A. This community occupies geographically an area on the north side of the city with Cramond and Barnton in the northwest corner, North Gyle as its western boundary, Broomhouse and Carrick Knowe to the south and Roseburn to Pilton on its eastern boundary, the total population of which would amount to approximately 91,143 when development is completed. Out of this total population 6.1% are already housed in static lands, the remainder being new population on undeveloped property amounting to 1,200 acres.

The standard of space use requirements for purposes other than housing and recreation spaces varies from 3 to 4 acres per thousand as the neighbourhood units get further from the town centre. This is only to be expected as the further the population group lives from the town centre the more it becomes dependent upon its local facilities for shopping etc.

The recreation space standard also varies from 4 to 9 or 10 acres per thousand population depending upon the proximity to the central areas where the density development must needs be higher in order to allow adequate housing space for those requiring to live near their place of work.

Community B. This community consists of four neighbourhood units with an optimum population total estimated at 49,819 persons. The net density standard for housing development in this neighbourhood ranges from 50 to 100 persons per acre with a standard of approximately 3 acres per thousand for land for other purposes and 4 acres for recreation space.

The area occupied by the four neighbourhood units comprising this community stretches from Pilton in the north to the " New Town " in the south, Blackhall in the west and Inverleith in the east. Most of the built up areas are again static property with comparatively small areas scheduled for redevelopment as, for example, at Stockbridge and Comely Bank and at Blackhall itself.

Community C. This comprises three neighbourhood units with a total population of 50,773 all of which come within the proposed 75 net density zone. Three of the neighbourhoods require a considerable amount of redevelopment, partly to relieve overcrowding, and, partly to clear industry from close proximity to the houses. Redevelopment in any of these neighbourhoods should be considered as part of a triple-scheme involving redevelopment in the Leith Industrial zone and development at West Pilton in neighbourhood unit area A7. The standard of land for other purposes has been taken at 3 acres per thousand and for open space at the minimum of 4 acres per thousand, the balance of open space being found either in the wedges or green belt areas.

Community D. This consists of four neighbourhood units with an optimum population total of 55,501 persons. The standard of density ranges from 50 to 75 persons per acre according to the part of the density zone in which these neighbourhoods lie. The community stretches from Portobello in the east to Lochend in the north west, Duddingston to the south and Craigentinny to the north. The land for other purposes standard, ranges between 3 and 5 acres per thousand according again to the geographical location of the neighbourhood unit group of population. The standard of open space ranges from 4 to 7 acres per thousand.

Community E. This community stretches over an area from St. Leonards in the north to Gilmerton in the south with Craigmillar in the east and Liberton in the west and comprises five neighbourhood groups of population totalling 61,815 persons. The net density of housing development in each of these neighbourhoods varies from 30 to 75 persons per acre. Again there is a good deal of static property in this community mainly centred in neighbourhoods 1 and 2, that is, Newington and Craigmillar, where a good deal of inter-war development took place. There is, however, a substantial area of undeveloped land in neighbourhoods 3, 4 and 5 (Liberton, Gilmerton and Southouse). The standard of land for other purposes in this community again ranges from 3 to 5 acres per thousand while the standard of recreation spaces from 4 to 10 acres per thousand according to the geographical situation of the population groups.

Community F. This community comprises four neighbourhood groups of population totalling 65,471 persons and covers an area from the Meadows in the north to Fairmilehead in the south, Newington in the east and Craiglockhart in the west. This community also covers an area zoned for an average density of from 50 to 75 persons per acre. The standard of land for other purposes varies from 3 to 4 acres per thousand. The recreation space standard varies from 4 to 10 acres per thousand according to the location.

The existing low density areas of the Grange and Merchiston lie in neighbourhoods 1 and 2 of this community group of population. It is suggested that the existing property in these neighbourhoods should be redeveloped to the higher density of 75 in order to avoid the mal-distribution of population caused by excessively low density over large areas persisting so near the centre of the city. Furthermore, if the Dalry and Gorgie industrial zone is to be depopulated in accordance with the zoning principles of industry and home separation, the Merchiston area at least will require to be redeveloped to house a proportion of the workers in this industrial zone. Redevelopment had already shown signs of taking place before the war near Merchiston Castle, on the corner of Colinton Road and Merchiston Avenue, and is a sure sign that there is a demand for increased housing use of land in this locality.

This also applies to the Grange area, except that it might well become a reception area for the people from Merchiston who might wish to settle in this area when redevelopment takes place. The Grange area should also be redeveloped to this 75 density, and it might well be desirable to do so with a development of flats in predominance, in order to preserve as many of the trees which form such an important integral part of the amenities of the locality, as possible.

Community G. This community extends from Gorgie in the north to Juniper Green in the south, Sighthill in the west and Craiglockhart in the east, and contains five neighbourhood groups of population totalling 58,074 persons. This is a mixed area consisting of undeveloped land, property ripe for redevelopment and static property. The two neighbourhoods 2 and 3 contain a total of 53.2 acres of undeveloped land

and a total of 173.6 acres of land ripe for redevelopment or of property for reconstruction to provide community facilities where they are at present inadequate. For example, redevelopment will be necessary on a comparatively small amount of new property in the Chesser Avenue area in neighbourhood 2. There is also some industry which will have to go to make way either for housing development, recreation space or community buildings. One industrial firm has recently conformed to the Plan in moving from here to the Sighthill industrial zone. It is in these two neighbourhoods also that housing development or redevelopment should be ear-marked mainly for the decentralised population from the Dalry and Gorgie industrial zone in addition to neighbourhood unit F.1. The requirements of neighbourhood unit G.1. in this community have been given particular attention to reconcile the many conflicting interests to the development of this locality. The principle of scattering tiny groups of shops of little more than 10 or 12 in number, and often less, appears to have been followed in the recent past. This is in direct contradiction of the accepted principle of shop concentration in large enough centres to provide adequate choice for the housewife. The distribution of other community buildings was also becoming scattered about the neighbourhood without the advantage of cohesion that the properly planned neighbourhood centre can provide. The recreation space distribution appeared to be largely centred upon the huge field of nearly 100 acres between the Sighthill Industrial Estate and the housing development to the east of the Broomhouse Road.

PROPOSED POPULATION AND ANTICIPATED FAMILY STRUCTURE
BASED UPON EXISTING PROPORTIONS.

TABLE VII

No. of Persons in Family	Percentage of Total of Private Families %	Total Private Families	Percentage of Population in Private Families %	Population in Private Families
1	11·48	16,237	3·58	16,237
2	27·01	38,202	16·87	76,403
3	25·60	36,206	23·98	108,618
4	18·00	24,459	22·48	101,836
5	9·36	13,234	14·61	66,169
6	4·43	6,259	8·29	37,556
7	2·10	2,974	4·60	20,821
8	1·04	1,476	2·61	11,811
9	0·53	755	1·50	6,791
10	0·27	378	0·83	3,778
11	0·098	137	0·33	1,513
12	0·036	51	0·13	607
13	0·022	31	0·09	403
14	0·013	18	0·05	245
15	0·005	7	0·02	109
16 and over	0·006	8	0·03	131
Total Private Families		141,432	Population in Private Families	453,028

ALLOCATION FOR COMMUNITY LAND USES

TABLE VIII.

N.U.		Population	Standard per 1,000	Total Allocation	Primary Schools	Secondary Schools	Nursery Schools	Shops and Offices	Community Club and Churches	Public Buildings, Clinics, etc.	Service Industry	Car Parking Roads, etc.	Total not in Housing areas (net)	Total in Net Housing areas	Remarks
			acres	acres											
	1	6,168	3·4/1,000	21·1	nil	nil	(1) 1·6	5·0	4·0	3·0	4·0	3·5	16·0	3·5	Small school allocation reduces overall standard
	2	7,246	4·5/1,000	32·6	(1) 5·6	nil	(1) 2·0	7·0	5·0	4·0	5·0	4·0	20·0	5·0	
	3	14,141	3·5/1,000	49·6	(1) 5·3	nil	(2) 3·6	13·5	7·0	5·0	8·0	7·2	30·0	10·7	Do.
A	4	15,181	4·0/1,000	61·2	(2) 10·0	(1) 8·6	(4) 7·2	12·0	7·5	5·5	5·5	4·9	28·2	7·2	
	5	13,613	3·0/1,000	40·8	(1) 3·6	nil	(2) 2·6	11·5	8·0	5·0	6·0	4·1	20·9	13·7	Do.
	6	16,990	4·2/1,000	71·6	(1) 5·4	(1) 10·0	(2) 3·8	18·0	9·0	7·4	9·0	9·0	30·4	22·0	
	7	17,804	3·9/1,000	69·2	(4) 16·8	nil	(8) 13·6	14·0	6·8	6·0	7·0	5·0	26·8	12·0	
		91,143		346·1	(10) 46·7	(2) 18·6	(20) 34·4			246·4			172·3	74·1	
	1	17,112	3·4/1,000	57·6	(3) 12·8	I technical 8·8 / I Secondary 8·2	(6) 10·8			17·0*			—	17·0	*—As existing
B	2	7,982	3·5/1,000	28·6	(1) 4·4	nil	(3) 4·0	5·0	3·0	2·0	3·2	3·0	16·2	nil	
	3	21,134	2·8/1,000	58·9	(3) 13·1	nil	(6) 10·2	18·0	5·0	4·0	6·0	2·6	27·4	8·2	
	4	3,591	1·3/1,000	4·6	nil	I special 1·6	nil			3·0*			—	3·0	*—As existing
		49,819		149·7	(7) 30·3	(3) 18·6	(15) 25·0			71·8			43·6	28·2	
	1	16,354	3·9/1,000	63·1	(4) 18·4	I Secondary 6·8 / I Special 1·4	(8) 11·4	10·0	5·0	3·0	4·0	3·1	20·8	4·3	
C	2	15,539	4·8/1,000	73·7	(3) 15·0	I Technical 9·6	(8) 12·5	13·5	8·0	4·0	8·0	3·1	19·6	17·0	
	3	18,880	3·3/1,000	62·5	(3) 15·3	nil	(6) 9·2	12·0	9·0	5·0	8·0	4·0	16·0	22·0	
		50,773		199·3	(10) 48·7	(3) 17·8	(22) 33·1			99·7			56·4	43·3	
	1	17,864	4·2/1,000	74·6	(4) 22·0	(2) 18·8	(8) 11·4	9·0	5·0	2·0	4·0	2·4	14·4	8·0	
D	2	16,681	3·4/1,000	56·3	(2) 7·8	(1) 7·0	(2) 3·8	11·5	7·0	5·7	7·0	6·5	23·2	14·5	
	3	7,810	4·0/1,000	31·4	(2) 10·2	nil	(2) 3·4	6·0	4·0	3·0	3·0	3·0	13·8	5·2	
	4	13,146	5·1/1,000	67·0	(3) 13·4	(1) 7·2	(6) 9·4	10·0	7·0	5·0	7·0	80	29·5	7·5	
		55,501		229·3	(11) 53·4	(4) 33·0	(18) 28·0			116·1			80·9	35·2	
	1	14,323	2·8/1,000	40·5	(1) 3·2	(1) 9·6	(2) 2·2	8·0	6·0	4·0	4·5	3·0	14·4	11·1	
	2	12,868	4·5/1,000	57·8	(3) 15·2	(1) 7·6	(6) 8·7	10·0	6·0	4·0	5·3	5·0	22·3	8·0	
E	3	14,579	4·4/1,000	64·5	(3) 16·0	nil	(6) 8·6	12·0	9·0	6·0	8·0	4·9	25·9	14·0	
	4	9,853	6·6/1,000	66·5	(3) 14·2	I special 4·0	(5) 7·6	9·0	9·0	6·5	9·2	7·0	19·8	20·9	
	5	10,192	4·0/1,000	40·9	(1) 5·1	nil	(2) 3·8	8·0	7·0	5·0	7·0	5·0	19·0	13·0	
		61,815		270·2	(11) 53·7	(3) 21·2	(21) 30·9			168·4			101·4	67·0	
	1	12515,	4·6/1,000	57·5	(2) 10·0	(1) 9·6	(4) 5·8	7·0	8·0	4·0	7·1	6·0	18·8	13·3	
F	2	23,854	3·3/1,000	79·7	(3) 14·0	I junior coll 7·8 / I technical 9·0 / I secondary 11·0	(7) 12·0	10·0	7·0	3·0	4·0	1·9	25·9	—	
	3	13,126	2·6/1,000	34·8	(1) 3·2	nil	(2) 3·6			22·0*			22·0	6·0	*—As existing
	4	15,976	3·7/1,000	59·0	(2) 10·3	nil	(4) 7·8	13·0	9·0	6·0	6·0	6·9	23·4	17·5	
		65,471		231·0	(8) 37·5	(4) 37·4	(17) 29·2			120·9			90·1	36·8	
	1	12,772	5·3/1,000	67·9	(4) 16·6	I special 8·4	(8) 13·6	10·0	8·0	6·0	7·0	6·7	32·9	4·8	
	2	20,462	4·8/1,000	98·0	(3) 14·0	I secondary 4·0	(7) 10·4	16·0	13·0	8·0	12·2	12·0	33·2	28·0	
G	3	10,942	5·0/1,000	55·3	(3) 14·2	nil	(6) 11·4	8·0	6·5	4·0	6·5	4·7	22·0	7·7	
	4	6,760	4·7/1,000	32·0	nil	nil	(2) 4·2	8·0	5·5	4·0	5·5	4·8	22·0	5·8	
	5	7,138	4·7/1,000	29·0	(1) 4·0	nil	(2) 2·8	6·5	4·5	3·5	4·2	3·5	14·8	7·4	
		58,074		282·2	(11) 48·8	(2) 12·4	(25) 42·4			178·6			124·9	53·7	
X		9,505	3·1/1,000	29·2	(2) 8·2	I special 1·5	(2) 2·6	2·0	4·0	3·9	4·0	3·0	16·9	—	
Y		841	—	nil	nil	nil	nil	—	—	—	—	—	—	—	An existing residential group incorporated in the plan
Z		5,173	2·2/1,000	11·2	(1) 5·2	nil	(1) 2·4	—	—	—	3·6	—	3·6	—	A special residential unit serving the central area
		15,519		40·4	(3) 13·4	(1) 1·5	(3) 5·0			20·5			20·5	—	
Green Belt		2,685													
Non Pop. Areas		2,228													
Total		453,028		1748·2	(71) 332·5	(22) 160·5	(141) 228·0			583·3			690·1	338·3	

PRINCIPAL FUTURE DEVELOPMENTS FOR EDINBURGH & REGION

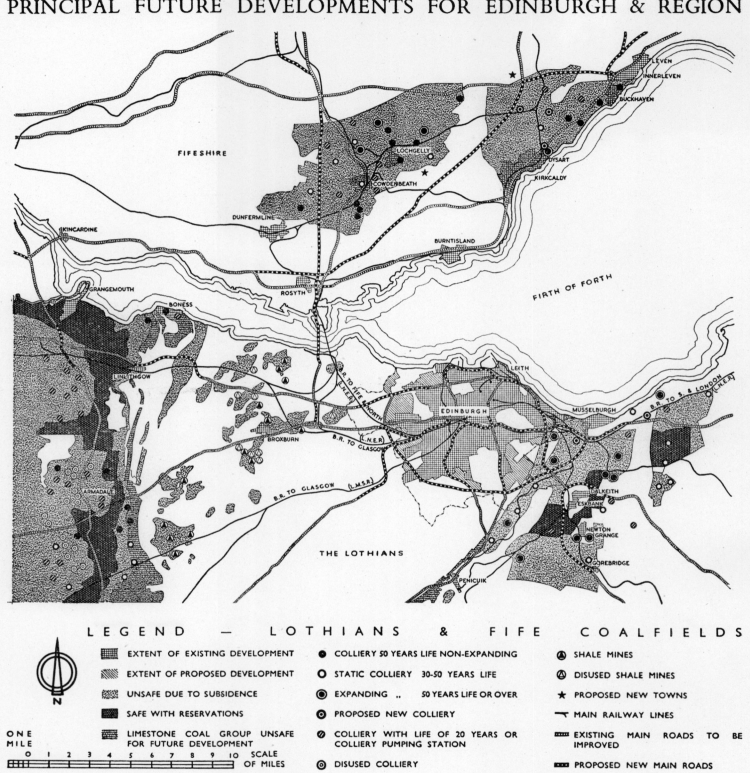

LEGEND — LOTHIANS & FIFE COALFIELDS

EXTENT OF EXISTING DEVELOPMENT	COLLIERY 50 YEARS LIFE NON-EXPANDING	SHALE MINES
EXTENT OF PROPOSED DEVELOPMENT	STATIC COLLIERY 30-50 YEARS LIFE	DISUSED SHALE MINES
UNSAFE DUE TO SUBSIDENCE	EXPANDING „ 50 YEARS LIFE OR OVER	PROPOSED NEW TOWNS
SAFE WITH RESERVATIONS	PROPOSED NEW COLLIERY	MAIN RAILWAY LINES
LIMESTONE COAL GROUP UNSAFE FOR FUTURE DEVELOPMENT	COLLIERY WITH LIFE OF 20 YEARS OR COLLIERY PUMPING STATION	EXISTING MAIN ROADS TO BE IMPROVED
	DISUSED COLLIERY	PROPOSED NEW MAIN ROADS

ONE MILE

0 1 2 3 4 5 6 7 8 9 10 SCALE OF MILES

This diagramatic map shows Edinburgh's geographical and economic position in the region of the Forth Basin not only as it exists but as it will be when the coal field developments reach maturity. Both the Fifeshire and Lothian coalfield developments will cast an increased demand upon the capital city for social, educational, professional and commercial services but on no account should the city encourage a big industrial expansion within its own administrative area. It is more than ever necessary to limit the size of the city both in population and in area. Physical limits to expansion in area are prescribed by subsidence from coal workings and by the topography of the surrounding country.

PROPOSALS
FOR
COMMUNICATIONS

ROADS

LEGEND

EXISTING	PROPOSED	
••••	••••	ARTERIAL ROADS
——	——	SUB-ARTERIAL ROADS
—	- - -	LINK ROADS
••••		ARTERIAL ROADS TO BE WIDENED
═══		SUB-ARTERIAL ROADS TO BE WIDENED
- - -	- - -	ROADS IN TUNNEL
——		RAILWAYS
- - -	- - -	RAILWAYS TUNNELLED
▬	▬	DEVELOPMENT AREAS
～	～	WATERWAYS
		MAJOR OPEN SPACES
		RURAL ZONE

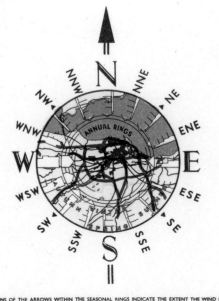

THE PORTIONS OF THE ARROWS WITHIN THE SEASONAL RINGS INDICATE THE EXTENT THE WIND BLOWS AS A
PROPORTION OF THE PREVAILING WEST WIND IN SUMMER.
THE LENGTH OF THE ARROWHEADS WITHIN THE ANNUAL RINGS INDICATES THE EXTENT AS AN ANNUAL TOTAL.

MAP 16

ROADS (Proposals Map)

This Map illustrates geographically the proposed network of roads necessary to promote an efficient transport system. This network has been evolved after intensive survey and analysis of existing traffic conditions and indications for future needs. The Princes Street by-pass, for which several suggestions have been put forward in the past, is clearly necessary and requires to be very closely related to the present route if it is to be wholly effective. Extreme diversions immediately become necessary when a new route is sought clear of the Gardens and Castle, owing to the natural topography of this central area and because of the desire to avoid wholesale demolition of valuable building property by extensive road widenings. To relieve Princes Street effectively there can be no better and more direct route for through traffic than one constructed beneath this street where direct ventilation and daylight is possible without artificial means being found to provide it. A slight infringement upon the Gardens is probably necessary but the suggested colonnade skilfully carried out could make a fine contribution to the architecture of the Gardens and offer yet another enchanting view to the visiting motorist. The basic conception of the scheme embodies the accepted principles of the internal sub-arterial dual carriageway highway with the minimum number of interruptions to the flow of traffic except for essential points of access. To construct the sub-arterials proposed very little if any building demolition is required until the centre of the City is reached, where much requires to be rebuilt anyway. This is rather remarkable in a built-up City almost free from War damage.

1946

PROPOSALS
FOR
COMMUNICATIONS

RAILWAYS

LEGEND

EXISTING   PROPOSED

		RAILWAYS
		ABANDONED RAILWAYS
●	●	STATIONS
○		ABANDONED STATIONS
– – –	- - - -	RAILWAYS IN TUNNEL
▲	▲	SIDINGS
△		ABANDONED SIDINGS
		MAIN ROADS
		DEVELOPMENT AREAS
		WATERWAYS
		MAJOR OPEN SPACES
		RURAL ZONE

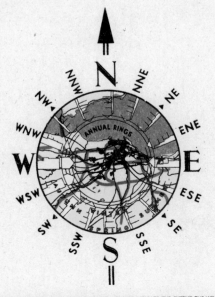

THE PORTIONS OF THE ARROWS WITHIN THE SEASONAL RINGS INDICATE THE EXTENT THE WIND BLOWS AS A
PROPORTION OF THE PREVAILING WEST WIND IN SUMMER.
THE LENGTH OF THE ARROWHEADS WITHIN THE ANNUAL RINGS INDICATES THE EXTENT AS AN ANNUAL TOTAL.

MAP 17

PROPOSALS for COMMUNICATIONS—RAILWAYS

The general plan for the City embraces the railways as an essential part of the transport system, and due emphasis is given to suggestions for any radical or minor changes as may be necessary.

The Survey showed where, as a result of keen competition in the early days of railway enterprise, there is duplication of routes, or where any uneconomic residue of land exists between a network of lines and prevents good development for other purposes, or where there is need for re-planning to meet the needs of the industrial estate or zone as opposed to the present uneconomic scattering or ribboning of factories and workshops. Consultations brought out facts concerning the British Railway needs for expansion in the coalfields. The facts obtained, together with the recognized needs to modernize Waverley Station, eliminate smoke, dust, noise and ugliness from Princes Street Gardens —the heart and pride of Scotland—have called for careful and exhaustive study and deliberation with railway experts. The Waverley Station site is too cramped to deal with both long distance and suburban traffic and still give adequate access for vehicle and pedestrian and elbow-room for the fruit market which is steadily being squeezed out of the valley ; nor can electrification as a preliminary to covering in the railway be so easily and economically achieved unless long-distance traffic can be diverted from the Gardens. The Waverley Station site is retained only as a covered-in regional suburban station in the proposals, with a combined long-distance station on two levels at Morrison Street— the upper to be a terminal for (L.M.S.) traffic and the lower for through (L.N.E.) traffic. Any possible disadvantage arising from a less central position is countered by the distinct advantages to passengers being able in the combined station to transfer from one section to another, while day-to-day regional suburban passengers may still use the modified Waverley Station.

Existing conditions offer a welcome opportunity to provide a combined station on two levels without uprooting the main routes or by creating too huge a station spread out on one level.

The new tunnel proposed beneath the Meadows would connect with the London line via Duddingston at Niddrie for both passenger and freight traffic. It would supersede the badly graded suburban line through Morningside and offers the economic attraction of a 1 in 500 gradient to cope with the expanding coal traffic from the Lothians.

CHAPTER FOUR

COMMUNICATIONS: ROADS AND RAILWAYS

A. ROADS.

INTRODUCTION. Before the question of road planning could be dealt with it was essential to determine where the overcrowded population was to be redistributed, where the main centres of entertainment, commerce, industrial zones, academic areas, etc., were to be situated. In this way a guide to the destination of all traffic and the routes that such traffic would find most convenient was obtained. From this, a system containing the existing or proposed roads shown on map no. 16 was devised. When considering the new system relative to the various destination points, it should be remembered that the existing activities creating present day destinations may not continue to exist under the plan, and may have been altered in accordance with the zoning proposals. Generally, however, though these are local changes, the central area of the city as a whole will still contain the same number of destination centres. The principle changes that affect the existing internal road plan are described later in this chapter. This system was planned so that the destination might be reached as directly as possible without breaking into the precincts to be created out of these various centres of city life. This is a particularly important consideration and is one with which we find ourselves in agreement with the Clyde Report which says, " The main traffic routes " from the south should be kept away from the academic areas " and so far as possible should be located so as to run along " side and not through self-contained communities into which " the city would be divided."

The proposals put forward contain an entirely new system of major arterial roads embodying, wherever possible, the existing radial system and bye-passing to avoid expensive demolition which would otherwise be necessary in order to obtain a good design of traffic road of the dual carriageway type, even in the heart of the city itself. There is no doubt that a system of suitably designed dual carriageway roads is necessary and will become more so in the future as petrol and other restrictions are removed. As an indication of the extent to which traffic was increasing immediately after the war, in 1946 the Traffic Census showed the peak hour flow of some 64% of that in the pre-war year of 1938. The same kind of congestion, well known to many Edinburghers before the war, also began to re-assert itself at the east and west ends of Princes Street and on the other main thoroughfares. Furthermore, the Accident Survey for the year 1946 indicates that, despite the fact that the peak flow of traffic had only reached 64% there was an increase in the number of accidents amounting to 61% above the pre-war figure. Then again, most experts will agree that the pre-war traffic flow will most likely be doubled in the not very distant future. Furthermore, there is the uneconomic burden upon the operating costs of commercial traffic by these typical conditions of the " all purpose " road. With all these factors to be considered nothing short of a complete overhaul of the existing road system would have to be contemplated. Once such an overhaul is agreed upon, the policy can be laid down for its gradual achievement over a period of years.

Achievement of these proposals calls for a bold approach which requires something more than road widening here and there and a short length dual carriageway road that merely discharges traffic on to narrow thoroughfares. There will be a need for new bridges here and tunnels there but none of these suggestions represents new methods untried before, because Edinburgh is noted for its bridge and tunnel construction in the past. For example, North Bridge and South Bridge constructed during the latter part of the 18th century; George IV Bridge, extending southwards, and the approach westwards, was formed in the years 1825-1836 under the authority of a special Act of Parliament at a cost at that time of about £400,000: the important scheme of 1867, in the old part of the town, was authorised by Parliament at an estimated cost of £300,000 for the mere acquisition of old property and the laying out of new streets. All of these together may be said to be comparable to the proposals embodied in the new road system in the plan.

This network consists of a combination of a radial and ringroad system which has been adopted throughout the country in various planning schemes.

Explanation of Main Road System. Though the internal system of the radials and ring roads was determined from the location of the proposed principal destination areas, such as population centres, industrial zones, new railway stations, centres of entertainment, etc., it was necessary to link these up with the road system being planned for the region. Consultations were, therefore, held with the Mid Lothian County Council representatives together with those of the Ministry of Transport and the planners of the Central and South East Scotland Regional Scheme. In general, it may be said that these various interested parties are satisfield with the road plan. As regards the Ministry of Transport representatives, though they have not, as indeed they could not, at the time, give their official approval to the scheme, it may be fairly stated that they are not antagonistic to it. The Police Department held a Superintendant's Conference to discuss the various tentative solutions which were put before them indicating how good traffic circulation could be obtained. Those which have been embodied in the plan generally met with the approval of the Police Department and adjustments have been made to meet criticisms raised.

The principal changes made in the Zoning Proposals which have a bearing upon the re-routing of this main road system, include the new combined terminal station at Morrison Street, which entirely supersedes the Caledonian Station at the West End and the Waverley Station only so far as its long distance rail traffic is concerned; the creation of two Festival centres, one at St. James Square at the eastern end of Princes Street and the other at the Usher Hall at the western end of Princes Street; the new University precinct in the vicinity of George Square which replaces a variety of small industrial and commercial premises as well as residential property; the removal of industry and commerce from the Canongate to make way for houses. These principle changes in the main will only affect internal circulation within the central area, and generally emphasise the need for direct access from the outskirts of the city to the east and west ends of Princes Street with good ring road circulation around the core of this central area. This also applies to Leith and Granton, which still remain as industrial centres though the zoning makes the distribution of industry more compact, which is an advantage rather than otherwise from the point of view of the road system. Apart from these internal re-adjustments of zoning account has also been taken of the new housing development schemes on the outskirts of the city.

DETAILED DESCRIPTION OF ROAD PROPOSALS

1. South Side of City.
   (a) Bridges by-pass.
   (b) Milton Road by-pass.
   (c) Lothian and Morningside Roads by-pass.
   (d) Seafield Road Sub-arterial for Leith.
   (e) Corstorphine & Calder Roads by-pass.
2. North Side of City.
   (a) Ferry Road as sub-arterial.
   (b) Queensferry Street by-pass.
   (c) Northern continuation of the 'Bridges' by-pass.
3. Princes Street by-pass.
   (a) Congestion at East & West ends of Princes Street.
   (b) Possible alternative routes investigated.
      (1) Queen Street alternative.
      (2) By-pass in Princes Street Gardens alternative.
      (3) Cowgate alternative.
      (4) Selected by-pass for Princes Street.
4. A 1. by-pass scheme alternatives.
   (a) Route north of Old Dalkeith Road
   (b) Use of existing Old Dalkeith Road.
5. Bus Stations.
6. Outer Ring Road.

Owing to the topographical nature of the city it is convenient to consider the different features of the road scheme by taking the north side and the south side of the Princes Street area as two separate halves of the city.

DETAILED DESCRIPTION OF ROAD SYSTEM

1. SOUTH SIDE OF THE CITY.

(a) *Bridges By-pass.* The present main road from the East End of Princes Street to Straiton and beyond is by-passed by a parallel route which begins at the top of Leith Walk. Passing under the Calton Hill it crosses the valley containing the railway and then proceeds under the High Street, over the Cowgate and through the Pleasance area (but between the Pleasance and Nicholson Street) where a separate route then forks due southward along the route of the present Causewayside which would be widened. It then continues parallel to Alnwick Hill Road on its western side, and on immediately to the west of Burdie House and so on to Straiton. This new route will carry a large volume of traffic at present using Newington Road and the Bridges, through Liberton etc. It should also be designed as a dual carriageway road in accordance with the modern principle of sub-arterial road design, with sufficient width of carriageway to anticipate the increased traffic in the future.

(b). *Milton Road by-pass.* From this same by-pass there is the proposal to introduce an entirely new road running east wards from St. Leonards Junction beneath Arthur's Seat. It would then run parallel to the old Innocent Railway, past Duddingston to connect up eventually with the Ministry of Transport and Regional road scheme to the east of Musselburgh. This new road would supersede London Road and Portobello Road and its original by-pass of Milton Road which were, of course, a continuance of the original A.1. route to London.

(c). *Lothian and Morningside Roads by-pass.* From the West End, the new by-pass of the present Lothian Road and congested Earl Grey Street is provided on a line immediately west of Gardners Crescent, where it forks eastwards along Melville Drive and southwestwards along the line of the existing Union Canal. The Melville Drive route forms the southern leg of the inner ring road and joins up with the previously described north to south by-pass of Nicholson Street and the Bridges. The southwestern route, which follows along the line of the Union Canal for part of its way, proceeds along the slopes of Craiglockhart Hill to the Colinton Road, where it then branches southwards between Redford Barracks and Colinton Mains and swings more eastwards to connect with the Biggar Road just south of Fairmilehead. After close investigation, it was found that this was the only suitable by-pass which could be constructed for most of its length without disturbing existing property. Providing that the junction with the Biggar Road is suitably designed, there should be every encouragement for motorists coming into the centre of the city to use this entirely new by-pass route in preference to the old congested Morningside Road.

(d) *Seafield Road sub-arterial for Leith.* On the other side of the city Leith is served by a proposed road which runs along the Seafield Road in an easterly direction from Leith until it reaches the Junction with the Portobello Road, where it then branches along an improved Baileyfield Road, east of the existing Duddingston Park Road, to join up with the Niddrie Road, and so southwards to link up with the old Dalkeith Road. At Duddingston, connection is made with the new by-pass for the A.1. road to London.

(e) *Corstorphine and Calder Road by-pass.* In the west, there is the proposal to by-pass the Corstorphine and Calder Roads by introducing an entirely new highway from Roseburn. Running parallel with the British Railway to the Firth of Forth and Glasgow until it reaches Old Saughton, it forks north-westwards to link up with the Glasgow Road just west of Maybury, where traffic would be encouraged by the design of the junction, to use this route in place of the Corstorphine Road, which is now far too built up on either side. The continuation from this junction at Old Saughton due westwards, skirting Sighthill on its northern limits, swings southwards in the direction of Currie and Balerno. This latter route is intended to link up with the Ministry of Transport proposals for the south-western part of the region and is intended also to carry through traffic at present using the Calder Road.

2. NORTH SIDE OF THE CITY.

(a). *Ferry Road as a sub-arterial.* Leith and Granton are really the two main centres on this side of the city that create particular attraction for traffic. Ferry Road has already been considerably widened through most of its length and could well be developed as a dual carriageway road in accordance with the modern principle of sub-arterial design. If this is carried out, there is no reason why it should not form the principal artery connecting Leith with the western limits of the city and the approach route to the new Forth Bridge by means of the proposed abandoned local suburban railway to Barnton, or some route parallel to it, and proceeding on the northern side of Cramond Brig Golf Course to Kirkliston.

This sketch shows the fine south prospect of the southern parts of Edinburgh dominated by the rock of Samson's Ribs for the main approach to the city from the south. There would be no dingy suburbs to traverse. There would be a varied scene of woodland and open field reaching right into St. Leonard's without the need to demolish building property to achieve this Milton Road by-pass.

This pen and ink sketch shows the same scene indicating how this Milton Road by-pass would merge comfortably into the environment.

PLATE XIX

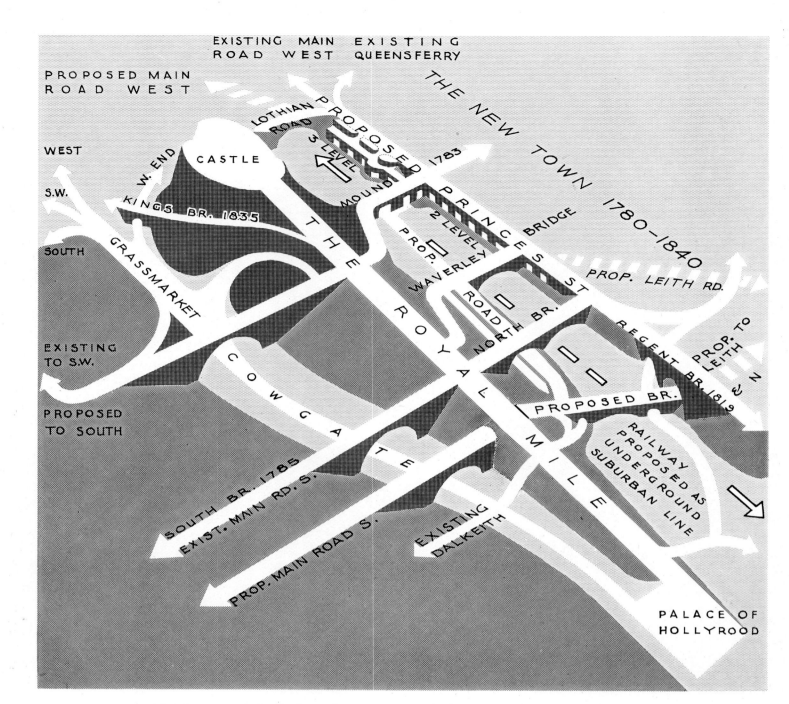

This diagrammatic sketch shows the existing network of principal roads with their date of construction and the proposed new roads designed to meet contemporary and future demands of road transport.

Aerial view from south

[*p. 85*]

Aerial view of central Edinburgh from above Calton Hill

[*p. 86*]

PLATE XX

(b). *Queensferry Street by-pass.* Two main connecting links with the inner ring road to the central areas of the city are considered necessary. In order to give adequate connection to the Ferry Road and the Granton Harbour, one of these connections should begin from the new combined station at Morrison Street and run northwards along Palmerston Place, over the valley of the Water of Leith skirting the Dean Cemetery between it and Daniel Stewart's College, traversing Queensferry Road, crossing Comley Bank at its junction with Orchard Brae Road, and proceeding on to link up with the Ferry Road, Crewe Toll and so on to Granton parallel to the Railway. From Granton it would continue along the sea front to link up Granton Harbour with Leith Port.

(c). *Northern Continuation of 'Bridges' by-pass.* The other main link consists of a continuation of the north to south by-pass of the Bridges from the top of Leith Walk, using the improved Bellevue Road, Inverleith Road, and then connect with the Ferry Road.

3. PRINCES STREET BY-PASS.

The principal and most interesting feature in the road proposals is probably the suggestion for the by-pass of Princes Street. It is not intended to give a detailed description of its possibilities, as that appears in Chapter 7 on Central Planning, but to give here an explanation of the reason for its selection.

(a). *Congestions at East and West ends of Princes Street.* The Traffic Census pointed to the East and West Ends as badly congested traffic intersections—as congested almost as Earl Grey Street. The volume of traffic having reached the proportions of some 1,800 vehicles per hour in 1946, at a time of considerable restriction, is already high, even for a modern dual carriageway arterial, and Princes Street was never intended to carry such quantities of traffic. It would be wrong, therefore, to create an arterial road for rapid and uninterrupted traffic out of Princes Street without some relief. Even supposing such an alteration to Princes Street

were made, there would need to be an enormous roundabout embracing the whole of the block containing Binns' shop, from Charlotte Square to Princes Street to cope with both through traffic and local traffic converging at this point. At the East End, a similar reconstruction would be called for, because not only is the present intersection incapable of dealing properly with present day traffic, but it would require to deal with double that amount in ten or fifteen years time.

The two sketches shown below present the details of the proposals in figure (1) while in figure (2) the existing layout of the roads converging upon the West End together with the temporary arrangements for improved circulation. These temporary arrangements indicate the urgency for a solution and point to the need for a simple junction of Lothian Road and Princes Street which confirms the conclusion reached in the Plan. This conclusion assumes the provision of a by-pass for Princes Street. In figure (1), however, left hand traffic passing from Lothian Road to Shandwick Place can do so without being diverted through Rutland Square as at present and in figure (2) providing the traffic lanes are wider and the roundabout large enough. The roundabout would also eliminate the big diversion imposed in figure (2) such as the one from Lothian Road to Queensferry Street via Rutland Square and Melville Street. Where property space is lost in creating the roundabout (and it would need to be much greater if there was no relief from through traffic) it is made up by the junction design for Lothian Road.

(b). *Possible alternative routes investigated.* Several alternatives were investigated, including the use of Queen Street, a superimposed road upon the railway in the gardens, and the use of the Cowgate.

(1) *The Queen Street alternative.* This is one which has been mooted on many occasions by different investigators in the past, but in considering this as a possible alternative, it was found that no adequate by-pass scheme could be constructed without the demolition of many buildings both at its eastern end and western end. To pull down any of the buildings which form the crescents of the new town extension, would

WEST END TRAFFIC IMPROVEMENT SCHEME.

TEMPORARY ARRANGEMENT FOR EXISTING LAYOUT OF ROADS.

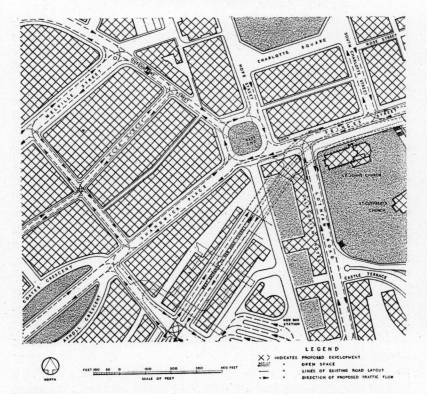

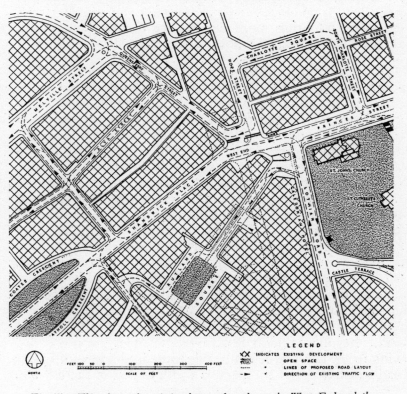

Fig. (1). This is a detail extracted from the City Centre Plan appearing on Plate No. XXIII showing the improvements recommended for the West End.

Fig. (2). This shows the existing layout of roads at the West End and the temporary arrangement for improved traffic circulation.

be to destroy the amenities and architectural composition of the lay out of this fine example of new town development by Gillespie Graham. The loss of any of these new town buildings would mean destroying buildings of considerable architectural beauty and historical consequence while the existing precinctal amenities of the remaining residential property would be destroyed. Without such demolition, it is impossible to obtain a connection for the by-pass with Queensferry Street. Considering this alternative further, it should be remembered that the by-pass of Princes Street should form part of the inner ring road system, which is required to allow for the considerable traffic flowing in other directions than that provided by Princes Street. Therefore, it would be necessary to carry all this improved Queen Street route through to the other new town extension of the Melville Street area in order to link up with the by-pass of Lothian Road and Earl Grey Street. This latter would be essential in order to by-pass the West End. Clearly then, an enormous amount of building demolition would become imperative before this project could materialise, and such demolition would undoubtedly destroy some of the finest examples of the Renaissance architecture of the new town development of 120 years ago. At this western approach, despite the widening of Picardy Place and York Place, further widening would be required involving property demolition. For these reasons, the idea of suggesting Queen Street as the appropriate Princes Street by-pass was discarded. Any other route lying further to the north, not only becomes too difficult to achieve owing to the presence of the Water of Leith valley, but would lie too far away from Princes Street as to have any attraction at all as a by-pass.

(2). *By-pass in Princes Street Gardens alternative.* The suggestion of superimposing the by-pass upon the railway running through the gardens also creates considerable demolition and constructional problems at the eastern and western approaches. Apart from these there is perhaps a more important objection that would be raised that is that the amenities of Princes Street Gardens would definitely be adversely affected. If there is to be any covering in of the railway to improve the amenities of these famous gardens, such a proposition would merely be replacing one nuisance by another. It would sever the gardens in two more effectively than ever and bring more disturbance to the peace of the gardens than the railway does at the moment.

(3). *The Cowgate alternative.* The use of the Cowgate appears at first sight to be an attractive alternative, but again, substantial demolition for road widening would be required throughout its length from Fountainbridge to Holyrood Palace and beyond, in order to obtain a properly designed dual carriageway highway. Such road widening would encounter considerable if not insuperable difficulties at George IV and other Bridges. Even supposing these difficulties could be surmounted, it would be extremely unfortunate if various old centres of Edinburgh, such as the Grassmarket, which lay upon its route, became transformed by the presence of a highway scheme. Furthermore the comparative precinctal quietude in the vicinity of Holyrood Palace would be shattered. Such a scheme could not become effective, without considerable destruction of property and excavation of soil at the south eastern part of Calton Hill in order to provide a good route of highway design and connect up with London Road. Beyond London Road one's troubles are not ended owing to the fact that it brings this route into line with Easter Road which is not of comparable width to that of Leith Walk.

(4). *The selected By-pass for Princes Street.* Having examined these other alternatives, it became clear that the best selection of all would be the route coinciding with Princes Street itself. This would satisfy one of the first essentials of a by-pass, that is, to be effective, it should run parallel and close to the road it is by-passing. Obviously no route could be closer than the one which runs beneath Princes Street. Such a proposition would involve no disturbance whatever to property throughout the greater part of its length as the subsoil consists mainly of grey sandstone which is considered to be ideal from this point of view. It is in no sense a tunnel, owing to the configuration of the land, and direct day lighting can be obtained by means of clear-storey day lighting from above and day lighting on the gardens side. There would, therefore, be no need for artificial lighting nor for artificial ventilation. Financial outlay would be confined to constructional work only, without any additional compensation costs. Compensation is only likely at the two entrances to this lower route, and then it would be in no way comparable with that involved in any of the other alternatives. Property that would be effected at these two entrances are those ripe for redevelopment any way, as for example, the St. James Square area and the slum property behind Lothian Road. Underground services such as the main sewers would not be affected by this scheme, except at the east and west ends. For the most part the existing sewers lie clear of the proposed scheme. The only problem likely to arise would concern the outlets from these sewers which are connected to the main trunk sewer running through the gardens.

The construction is a straightforward engineering job in the opinion of the Ministry of Transport engineers who were consulted in the early stages of its inception. The grey sandstone subsoil raises no insuperable difficulties, in fact its presence is rather an advantage. Natural ventilation and lighting, it was appreciated could be obtained, and that the roundabout beneath the Scottish Academy was feasible and useful as a connection for north and south bound traffic. The cost of construction would be no more than the alternatives already described, and in fact may well be less. Whereas in all the other alternatives, except the Princes Street Gardens alternative, considerable demolition for road widening of good property is involved, including buildings of historical and architectural value, this scheme requires none. Nor is there any violation of any precincts existing in the areas—residential or commercial—along its route, except perhaps in Rutland Square.

4. A1 BY-PASS SCHEME ALTERNATIVES.

(a). *Route North of Old Dalkeith Road.* Considerable importance is attached to the provision of an improved highway development to this south-eastern approach to the city. Two other alternatives have been considered consisting of the use of the Old Dalkeith Road and of an entirely new highway lying approximately mid-way between A68 (Old Dalkeith Road) and A6106 (Dalkeith to Leith Road). This latter route, it is understood, was proposed in order to serve a possible new housing development scheme for a population of approximately 40,000 persons. Owing to the fact that the area in this south-eastern part of the city is liable to subsidence, due to coal workings, such a development would have to be condemned at the outset and the proposed road from that point of view disappears. Even had the housing development scheme been possible, a by-pass running through its middle would contravene the important planning principle of the precinct. It would also break up community development for the Craigmillar area, as recommended in the plan, and would eliminate any possibility of any other adequate selection for community development in this locality. From the communications point of view, this route could not be considered to become a by-pass for the Milton Road, as the proposal in the plan could, owing to the fact that it comes too far southwards to link up with the regional proposals for A1.

(b). *Use of Existing Old Dalkeith Road.* The Old Dalkeith Road is too far south as a by-pass for the Milton Road. Furthermore, it would not be necessary if the Causewayside route was adopted as suggested in the plan. The difficulties of obtaining an adequately designed dual carriageway highway for the Old Dalkeith Road immediately becomes manifest from Cameron Toll onwards into the centre of the city, whereas the route suggested parallel to the old Innocent Railway runs into no great difficulties until the St. Leonards Area has been reached.

5. BUS STATIONS.

Two principal bus stations are recommended in the Plan. One in the Clyde Street area, to replace the S.M.T. use of St. Andrew's Square and Queen Street, and the second at the west end of Princes Street behind the Caledonian Hotel on the site of the present Caledonian Station, which is to be replaced by the combined railway station at Morrison Street. The Clyde Street site is considered the more important one from the point of view of urgency so that St. Andrew's Square may be relieved at the earliest possible date. The S.M.T. have this in mind, and indeed have already acquired property in Clyde Street for a bus station, but it is not recom-

mended that they should have continued direct access for their buses into St. Andrew's Square : nor would it be necessary if the road proposals for this eastern area of the city are carried out, as the most direct access to the new highway system would not be through St. Andrew's Square, but through Picardy Place. Furthermore, the extent of the property acquired by the S.M.T. is by no means adequate if the use of St. Andrew's Square and Queen Street is to be entirely eliminated. The plan, therefore, allows for a much larger bus station than so far envisaged by the S.M.T. involving the acquisition of property to as far as York Place.

The western bus station is a more long term proposal as its construction depends upon the redevelopment scheme for the railway system which, though urgent, is unlikely to materialise for a number of years.

6. OUTER RING ROAD.

The Origin and Destination Survey carried out in 1946 indicates that there was no present need for the construction of an outer ring road owing to the small amount of traffic with destinations beyond the city. There are, however, other considerations, such as the development of the coal fields in the Lothians, which will, no doubt, together with the development of the ring town scheme based upon Dalkeith, create sufficient traffic to make the construction of this outer ring road desirable. The plan, therefore, recommends this outer ring road, but more as a long term policy than otherwise.

B.—RAILWAYS.

INTRODUCTION. Unified railway organisation together with joint control of railway and road transport under nationalisation, brings to the fore questions of over-lapping interests, such as the best form of transport for certain kinds of services, that could not be considered before. Results of competition between Railway companies, arising from a non-unified system of control, are described in the Civic Survey (Chapter XI). The plan assumes that reconciliation between these conflicting interests and those of road transport may materialise in the near future, if for no other reason than of sound economics on the broadest possible basis. Decisions concerning the best form of transport—road or rail—that can best serve public interest for city suburban traffic compared with regional suburban traffic for instance, is one question. To what extent could duplication of railway routes resulting from early railway competition be remedied is another matter for broad policy. Consultations with the railway companies, before nationalisation, over the question of a combined main line station to replace the Waverley and Caledonian Stations indicated critical views of such a proposition. Administrative difficulties were considered by them to be too great if three main stations such as the Waverley, Caledonian and Haymarket were combined all in one. A compromise has since been adopted as a recommendation involving only the concentration of long distance traffic in the proposed new combined station at Morrison Street, and even then, separated on two different levels. This suggestion has still to be considered by the railway executive. Then there is the important question of the marshalling yards, which are admittedly inadequate, even to meet present day traffic demands, and will be still less adequate as the mounting output in the Mid and East Lothian coal fields develops. In view of this it is understood that the railway authorities require a huge yard some three miles long and one mile wide into which they could concentrate the majority of their railway marshalling yard services. Joint consultations with both the Central and

South-east Regional Planning Committee representatives and the railway companies established the fact that such a huge marshalling yard could not possibly be found within the city limits or even near to those limits. As the existing marshalling yard facilities and their reorganisation depend upon the site of this huge marshalling yard, the matter remains somewhat unresolved.

Another factor arising out of the coal field development is an urgent need to provide improved communications between the Lothians and the main line system in the west, as it is anticipated that there will be a considerable increase in freight traffic between the east and the heavy industries in the west part of Scotland. With the export drive for coal there will probably be in addition, considerable increase of freight traffic between the Lothians and Leith Docks.

The improvement by electrification of the unsightliness created by the railways in the Princes Street gardens has been coupled with the problem of solving the problem of congestion at Waverley Station. There does not appear to be enough elbow room in the valley to maintain a combined suburban and long distance passenger station and still give adequate parking facilities and other means for road and foot access to the public. Since, therefore, it seems unlikely that any satisfactory electrification scheme can be evolved for the long distance passenger traffic, sufficient to justify the covering in of the station and the railway, separation of the two systems would seem desirable. Since the regional suburban traffic could be more easily electrified and, therefore, facilitate covering in of the suburban line, and since there is a strong case for such a centrally placed station as the Waverley for the daily suburban travellers, the suggestion of confining the valley to regional suburban traffic only has been made.

PROPOSED NEW SYSTEM.

Having regard to the various problems just alluded to, it has been decided to recommend that serious consideration be given to the proposal of separating the main line passenger traffic from the suburban passenger traffic which at present uses the Princes Street Gardens route. In that way a modified Waverley Station becomes possible with adequate space without even using the whole width of the valley, while long distance passenger traffic may be combined on a two level railway station at Morrison Street. Facilities for stopping suburban traffic at this combined station should also be possible so that a link may be obtained between it and the new modified railway station.

To meet the requirements of the increased freight traffic, which at present has to use the badly graded Newington—Morningside suburban line, a new by-pass route is suggested running parallel to the old Innocent railway where it would enter a new tunnel at St. Leonards and proceed beneath the Meadows and emerge at the other side of the combined passenger station to link up with the main line to the west. If this were done, an easy gradient of 1 in 500 or less would be possible as compared with existing gradients of 1 in 70 and 1 in 100 on the suburban line. Not only are the gradients bad on the suburban line but it is inadequate in width to cope with any considerable increase in freight traffic. Any widening of this suburban line would meet with considerable difficulties owing to the need to widen the cuttings which would involve riparian buildings.

Leith Dock Requirements.

With the extension of the Leith Dock facilities, comes the urgent need for marshalling yards and goods station facilities. Coupled with these requirements is the general need, for a railway scheme improvement in this part of the city for a continuation of the line from South Leith over to North Leith, and so on to Granton, together with the reconstruction of Leith and the readjustment of the siting of industries over a period of years. It is felt that these suggestions will provide the best means of access to both docks and industry. Consultations with the Leith Dock Commission indicate that they welcome the suggestion of the proposed link up between South Leith and North Leith on the lines suggested in the Plan. This obviously would provide better communications between North and South Leith than the tortuous route which meanders through the Docks, or alternatively, via Piershill and Bonnington. The plan indicates a marshalling yard to the south of Commercial Street which conforms to the Leith Dock railway plan.

SUMMARY OF NEW RAIL SYSTEM.

Goods Yards. The plan provides for two principle goods yards, one in Leith near to the Docks and one at the east end of the city at Meadowbank. These two would replace the existing Leith Walk goods yard. The other goods yard is a large one situated south of West Coates where there exists a number of single storey domestic properties which are considerably out of date. This goods yard would replace the Lothian Road and Morrison Street goods yards. The South Leith L.M.S. goods yard could be retained in addition if required. The "standage" yard at Craigentinny for coal might well be replaced if the new marshalling yard on ground reclaimed from the sea were constructed at South Leith. Such a replacement would make the Marine Gardens a much more attractive feature as a recreation space than at present.

Proposed rearrangements of existing routes. The main railway system allows, as already stated, for the joining up of South and North Leith with Trinity. This link would then replace the Piershill and Trinity L.N.E. line to North Leith and Granton. It would also make redundant the L.M.S. line from Crewe Junction via Newhaven Junction to Seafield.

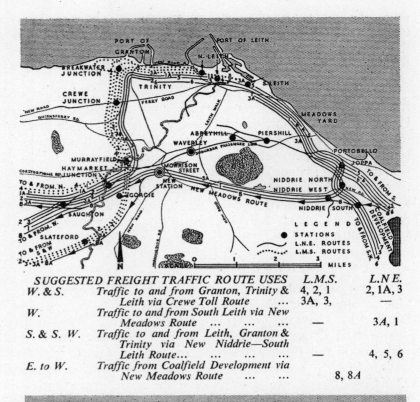

SUGGESTED FREIGHT TRAFFIC ROUTE USES

		L.M.S.	L.N.E.
W. & S.	Traffic to and from Granton, Trinity & Leith via Crewe Toll Route	4, 2, 1 3A, 3,	2, 1A, 3 —
W.	Traffic to and from South Leith via New Meadows Route	—	3A, 1
S. & S. W.	Traffic to and from Leith, Granton & Trinity via New Niddrie—South Leith Route		
E. to W.	Traffic from Coalfield Development via New Meadows Route	4, 5, 6 8, 8A	

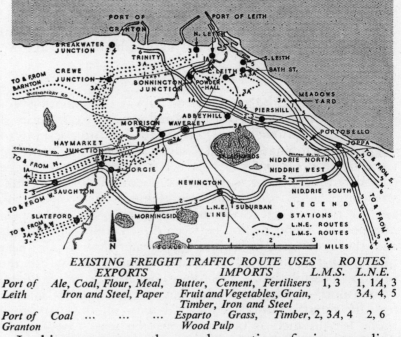

EXISTING FREIGHT TRAFFIC ROUTE USES

			ROUTES
	EXPORTS	IMPORTS	L.M.S. L.N.E.
Port of Leith	Ale, Coal, Flour, Meal, Iron and Steel, Paper	Butter, Cement, Fertilisers Fruit and Vegetables, Grain, Timber, Iron and Steel	1, 3 1, 1A, 3 3A, 4, 5
Port of Granton	Coal	Esparto Grass, Timber, Wood Pulp	2, 3A, 4 2, 6

In this western area the conglomeration of criss cross lines at Gorgie could be greatly simplified in the following manner. The L.M.S. Gorgie to Murrayfield would be replaced by the regraded route via Gorgie Junction, and by means of a viaduct over Haymarket, to Murrayfield. By the same new link in a different grade, a connection could be made with Haymarket itself and the new goods yard.

It was mentioned in the Civic Survey that the L.M.S. use of the L.N.E. route into Morrison Street goods yard and doubling back to Murrayfield, Granton and North Leith would be replaced by the new link joining Murrayfield with the main L.N.E. line west of Haymarket West Junction at a reasonable grade of 1 in 200.

The present freight line using the Morningside—Newington suburban line would be replaced by a new link from Duddingston beneath the Meadows to Haymarket West Junction.

The proposals if carried out would result in a saving of some 13 miles of surface tracks or 25 per cent of existing total mileage. Such saving would release ground amounting to some 160 acres as well as offer the opportunity for a more up-to-date system of economic gradients, suitably disposed service yards and passenger stations.

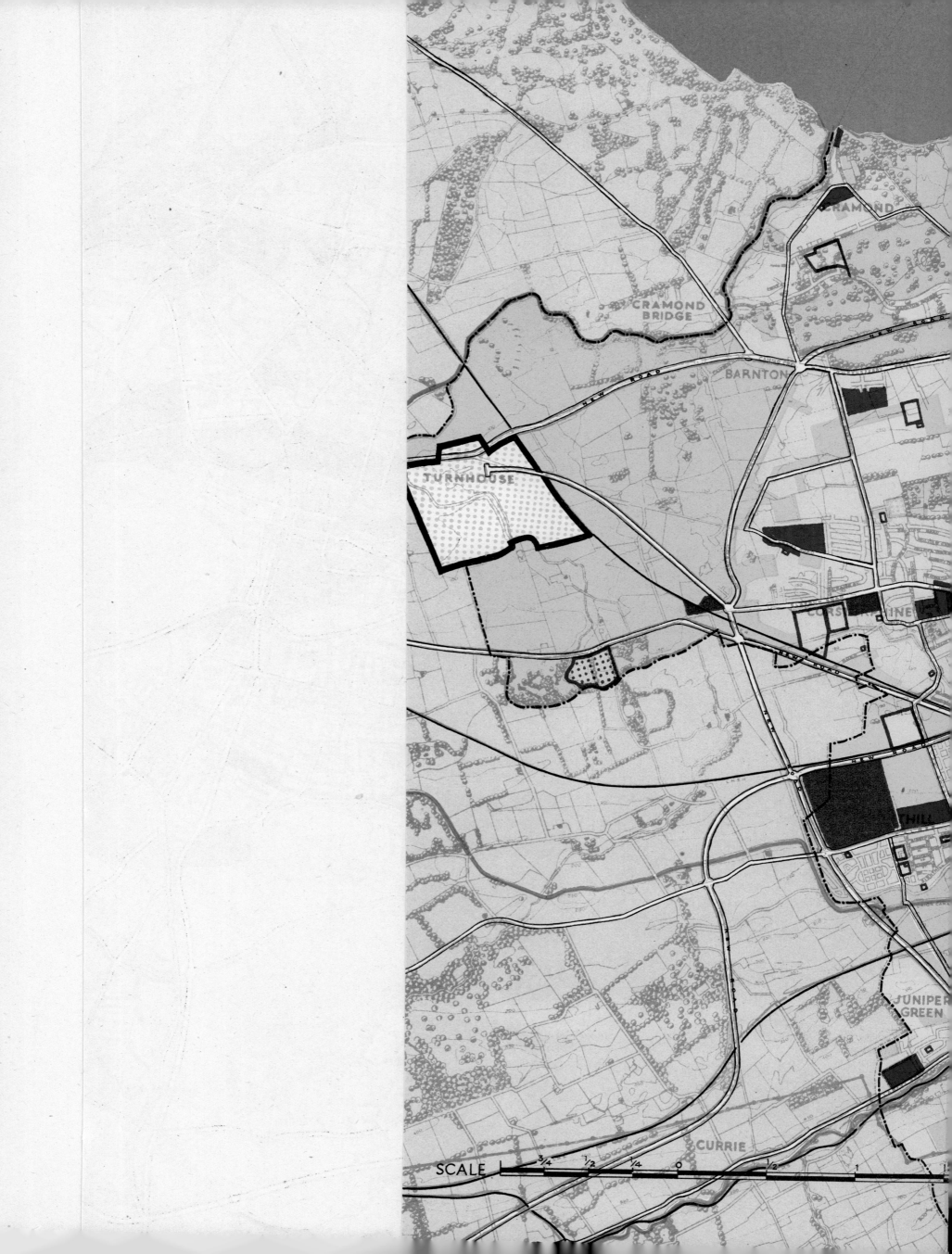

CRAMOND

CRAMOND
BRIDGE

BARNTON

TURNHOUSE

CORSTORPHINE

JUNIPER
GREEN

CURRIE

SCALE   ¾   ½   ¼   0   ½   1

MAP 18

GENERAL DEVELOPMENT

The general Development Map shows the broad classification of land use recommended in greater detail on the other maps. It shows the net residential areas, open spaces generally, industrial zones, and land generally for other purposes. In this way the broad summation of needs for the City as a whole are illustrated. The communication system is also shown to complete the general picture of requirements, but for detailed study each aspect is dealt with separately or in combination with other aspects on individual maps. This general framework appears with the building development areas interlaced with open spaces whose principal features consist of such magnificent existing parks as that surrounding Arthur's Seat. Though this is one of Edinburgh's most remarkable features, materially casting its influence upon the proposals, the topography elsewhere is no less interesting and important. The Castle and Royal Mile between it and the Palace of Holyroodhouse is situated on a sloping ridge that determines the route and may be traced from many vantage points in the City. The influence of the topography upon the general pattern of development is paramount and is the direct cause of many of its characteristics, such as the concentration of the main radial routes upon a bi-focal centre—the radials themselves are mostly determined by the hills and valleys.

CHAPTER FIVE

ZONING : COMMUNITY PLANNING : PRECINCTS

IF Communication is the dynamic aspect of planning, zoning might be described as the static; it is concerned with the use of land, both the nature of that use and its intensity. But generally, in this chapter, the nature or character of the use will be implied by the term zoning while its intensity of use is described in chapter three. Communication and zoning are, therefore, the two fundamentals of physical planning, and it is impossible to say which is the more important; the engineer may put Transport first : the Surveyor Land Use : the planner sees these as twin poles whose dialectical resolution produces the Plan.

All land, except that directly used for routes of transport, must be zoned for a specific use : afterwards, it is necessary to expatiate upon the special requirements and motive forces within the different zones, Residential (in which the question of intensity of use is of first rate importance) Industrial (in which the needs of different types of industry are analysed) Open Spaces (in which the components of a park system are allotted) Commercial (in which estimates of floor space must be made) Educational, etc.

Closely allied to zoning, but distinct, is the principle of Community Planning : this is chiefly applied to residential areas which, in addition to housing zones, contain open spaces, focal centres (commercial, small service industrial and other zones) combined into a neighbourhood unit. Several of these are further grouped together to form a Community.

There is also related to general Zoning and grouped Community planning the Precinct Principle. This aims at safeguarding individual zones or parts of them or whole communities, from outside influence, either by alien uses or by traffic invasion, which has no business with its occupants. A precinct may possibly coincide with a special ad-hoc zone, e.g. a University precinct whose predominant zoning use only occurs in that one area.

There is not any increased freedom from claims for compensation which has always been unclaimable in respect of restriction imposed on the development of land, whether these restrictions prevented an owner from disposing of his property for the most immediately lucrative use, or for putting the maximum number of buildings upon it which the land could carry (building bye-laws being of course a fixed statutory safeguard of certain standards). But the definition of the term "development" prevented the Minister from exempting from compensation a total prohibition of building on undeveloped land. This is now completely changed, with the important result that the *amount* of land zoned for development (in contrast to that left open in the neighbourhood of the town) can now be limited in accord with a more precise estimate of population and industrial needs.

The object of a Plan, such as this, in relation to zoning, is to give a broad picture of the general development needs of the city, the location of the different characters of development, their suitable intensity (especially with regard to housing density); and, as a consequence the amount of land so required, in other words the extent which it is desirable the city should cover, whether continuously or according to some other pattern. A margin of extra land to allow a certain freedom of choice must be left : the trouble under the former acts was that this margin was too great, being

determined by the wish of many landowners to get their land zoned for the utmost possible development. Landowners who for various reasons refused to sell for development, and who were formerly held to blame as impeding unlimited expansion, are now found in many cases to have helped in the creation of the Green Belt.

In determining the extent of land required for these various zoning uses, including the Green Belt, the Plan for Edinburgh has been co-ordinated with the development taking place in certain parts of the immediate region. Edinburgh in this respect bears a certain resemblance to Cardiff, where with the exception of the S.E., the mining operations stop a long way short of the boundary of the city : but whereas Cardiff sprang into importance as the metropolis of a mine field, Edinburgh's secular capital existence finds itself confronted with this new growth on and beyond its periphery. Both towns, however, are fortunately quite differently situated to Coventry whose mining, hitherto on its outer edge, now threatens to undermine the centre of the city itself.

In addition to these broader issues there are the more detailed advantages to the internal arrangement of the city, both existing and extended, of a general zoning plan based upon a careful factual survey and an equally considered prognostic of population and industry. There is much sorting out of mixed uses dating from the middle years of the last century to be done. The revision of transport, especially rationalisation of railways will tend to a more logical industrial grouping. The decentralisation of a certain proportion of the population, in some cases not to change use-zoning but to reduce density zoning ; in other cases, caused by a change of residential use to an industrial use; or again the opposite effect of the removal of industry from cramped quarters; or in other cases, to create open space where was formerly building : all these and other changes in the existing town will point to well-defined needs on new land, and will give much greater precision to the allocation of land than has hitherto obtained.

In this general sorting out, there will be an opportunity of avoiding conflicting use, which is so frequent in an ancient city, where we see a palace hemmed in by breweries, houses overshadowed by factories or railway shunting yards, industrial buildings prevented from expansion by housing, commercial shopping centres thronged with through traffic, open spaces shrouded in smoke, river valleys blocked with industrial waste and effluent, and many other discordancies.

There is nothing unusual in the types of zone that are required to meet Edinburgh's needs. There will be :—

(a) *Residential zones*, distinguished by density, but leaving a good deal of discretion as to whether houses or flats are built, provided the overall average density is maintained. The usual special buildings will be allowed in by consent. As it is the modern policy to group together shops and other commercial buildings, it will probably be found better to provide a zone for these within the Neighbourhood or Community, as part of the Centre rather than to allow them in the residential zone by consent. The same applies to the smaller industrial buildings which may be permitted within a residential neighbourhood centre.

(b) *Industrial Zones*, distinguished according to type of work carried on. The usual segregations of types of industry shown for each of the zones. Special industrial zones for factories emitting fumes, the general industrial zones with heavy machinery but not emitting fumes, the light industrial zones not containing factories of the first two kinds, Dockside industrial zones for industries requiring dockside facilities but not of the first two kinds, neighbourhood service industrial zones for small industries of a very local character. Though a full description of the location of these sub-divisions of industrial land use and their purpose is given in Chapter 6, it is well to emphasise here the importance of disposing them geographically so that no nuisance is imposed either by one upon workers in another, or by the whole zone upon adjacent residential zones.

(c) *Commercial and business*. In the centre of an old city there must always be a considerable number of "combined" uses and it will have to be decided whether it is possible to separate these into small zones in which a predominant use may be fostered or to allow a large number of permissive uses. The smaller the subdivision into definite zones, the easier it will be to administer; but it will take longer to determine the predominant use—some combinations are not very convenient to either use, e.g., offices and shops; on the other hand shops and hotels may well be associated (as in the case of Princes Street).

(d) *Control of Building heights and bulk in architectural design*. In order to keep a reasonable scale of rebuilding in the inner part of the New Town (George Street, etc.) as compared with the possibility of great average height increase in Princes Street (where the vast open space in front will allow this), the prescription of Floor Space indices as recommended in the Mannual for Central areas issued by the English Ministry of Town and Country planning, will doubtless be helpful. But this method of height and bulk restriction, which has been found so necessary for the limited area of the City of London, is not perhaps so essential in Edinburgh. Its relation to the aesthetic requirements of architectural harmony must also be taken into consideration. A balance between the practical requirements of the buildings themselves, the needs of the neighbours' for light and ventilation and the dominating claims of the Capital City of Edinburgh must be struck. Bye-law control, however drastically applied by means of angles of vision or obstruction and floor space indices, is not enough.

(e) *Recreation Zones*. These can perhaps be more fully described under Open spaces, as forming the "Park System." Those which are designated for permanent open use, whether of a public or private character, do not come under the machinery for regulating development. At the same time there may be within the Green Belt, areas primarily zoned for agricultural use, but in which a limited amount of other building may be allowed, e.g., industry connected with farming and public institutions. Such areas may be described as Rural Zones in which great care will have to be taken so that much building is not allowed that the rural character is lost. Village growth is closely allied to this aspect of Open Space zoning.

(f) *Cultural Zones*. It is doubtful whether it is wise to prescribe an actual zone for Cultural use. Sir Frank Mears has described a "University Mile", grouping, in a loosely knit whole, many interrelated buildings, serving however varied uses, such as a Hospital, Art School, Museum, University, etc. Probably the less legally defined, but even more widely protected "Precinct" may be the better method. This may fall within a larger zone of more general application. It may also be necessary to protect a precinct not only from intrusive discordant building, but from through traffic.

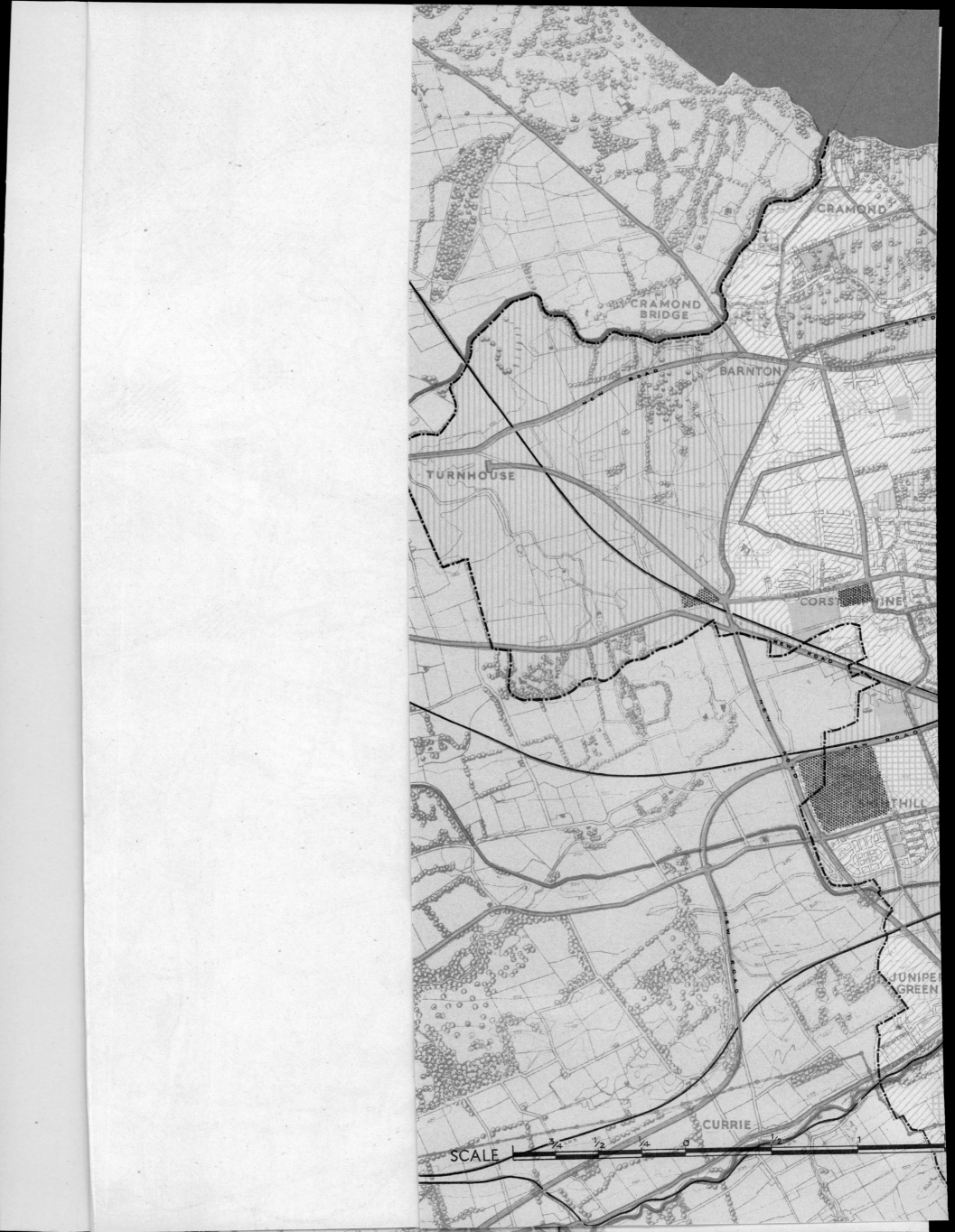

CRAMOND

CRAMOND
BRIDGE

BARNTON

TURNHOUSE

CORST[ ]INE

[ ]THILL

JUNIPE[ ]
GREEN

CURRIE

SCALE   ¾   ½   ¼   O   ½   1

MAP 19

INDUSTRIAL DEVELOPMENT and ZONING

The Industrial Zones are proposed to meet the requirements of expansion and modernization and to effect the separation of factories and large workshops from residential property.

Correction of the present scatter shown by the Survey of existing Distribution of Industry should be undertaken in accordance with these proposals : this would, of course, be spread over a period of years. Existing residential property in the Industrial Zones should be pulled down and alternative up-to-date accommodation be made available in the residential communities for the displaced families. Realization of the increased area for Industry will be achieved as land is set free by these demolitions.

The Table in the Appendix shows how the existing groups could be modified or, in some cases, eliminated to fulfil these requirements.

The Industrial Zones are mostly formed out of existing groups. Each zone is classified broadly by the cross hatching to indicate the nature of industry considered suitable for the locality.

These classifications are :—

SPECIAL INDUSTRIAL ZONES to accommodate noxious industries and industries that are liable to cause any nuisance when in proximity to residential areas.

GENERAL INDUSTRIAL ZONES to accommodate the heavier type of factory and warehouse, and those which require easy access to railways, docks, etc.

LIGHT INDUSTRIAL ZONES to accommodate the lighter types of factories and warehouses and establishments which may be a combination of industrial and commercial use.

SERVICE INDUSTRIAL ZONES to accommodate city service establishments such as Public Transport Garages, milk and food distribution centres, etc., together with the smaller workshops and stores ancillary to the purely commercial areas.

NEIGHBOURHOOD SERVICE INDUSTRIAL ZONES to accommodate the local workshops, stores, garages, etc., serving the several neighbourhoods within communities. (These Zones are not plotted on the Industrial Zoning Map, but have been calculated on the basis of 10% of the allotment of " land for other purposes " in each neighbourhood.)

The precise acreages allotted to each Zone will be found in Chapter 6 and Appendix.

CHAPTER SIX

INDUSTRY.

INTRODUCTION. The mix up of industry with housing contravenes one of the chief principles of good town planning—use zoning. There is no academic theory in this principle as its specific aim is to maintain the integrity of the city's character and the prevention of economic deterioration of house property and of the well being of those who live in the houses. John Buchan, in his book called "Memory Holds the Door," describes vividly how the home of his childhood was not only hemmed in by industry, but, at all times was smelling of wax cloth while one of two streams became foul with the discards of the bleaching works. With zoning control in its negative use there need be no fear of an industrial invasion of the city and its residential areas. Its positive use should be a corrective one involving redistribution to eliminate present mal-distribution of existing industry. Such control makes possible the creation of the trading estate—an acknowledged advantage. Land use zoning, therefore, represents one of the best safeguards for industry and home alike. This chapter, therefore, sets out to explain in what manner this principle has been applied.

Relationship of home to work place. Linked, of course, with this important question of zoning, is the relationship of the industrial zone to the housing zone. For example, the neighbourhood units adjacent to these industrial zones must be capable of accommodating at least the greater part of the workers of all income groups, for, as the Clyde Report correctly says, "it is unwise to build houses if there are no industries near-by for the inhabitants," and vice versa. In this respect it may quite well be necessary, as in the Merchiston area, to increase the existing density of development in order to make room for the depopulated persons from the proposed industrial zones of Gorgie and Dalry. This is essential in order to prevent mistakes of the past to which the overcrowding in the morning and evening of the transport facilities is largely due.

Decentralisation of Industry. The Industrial Survey appearing in Chapter 2 and Appendix 3 describes the types of industries that exist in Edinburgh. Those that may reasonably be considered 'mobile' and 'non-mobile' are described subsequently in this chapter. The mobility of industries is important as it gives an indication of where to look for the industries that might be decentralised along with the overcrowded population. There is nothing new in the movement of industries away from old congested centres to the outskirts of the city. This has been going on over the past 200 years. Unfortunately, however, nothing has been done to co-ordinate this movement with a policy for the elimination of congestion or with adequate safeguards to ensure accommodation for the workers in the new areas selected by these industries. Omissions of this kind have certainly been made even in recent years. It is important, therefore, that decentralisation of industries be correlated with that of the overcrowded population. This fact is also appreciated by the Clyde Report where it states " . . . . . the exodus from the con-" gested housing areas of considerable numbers of the popu-" lation will require the corresponding removal of several of " the industries from these areas."

Limit to Industrialisation. We confirm the anticipation in this report that the redevelopment of the congested areas should not primarily be done to encourage new industries, but rather, for the rehabilitation of existing industries in the city. Some new industries should be encouraged to set up in Edinburgh if only to preserve and rejuvenate industrial life. But this should not in any way be carried to excess, if the other important question of preserving the city's present character as the administrative capital of Scotland is to be achieved.

As a guide, it is suggested that the yard stick for determining the extent of industrialisation might be based upon the proportion of the city's insured persons engaged in industry relative to the proportion of the country's insured persons also engaged in industry. The extent of pre-war industrialisation is indicated in this manner in the analysis of the trends for the period 1929-1939 in Appendix 3. A limit in area of the industrial zones ensures an optimum limit for industrialisation.

Regional influences to industrialisation. The danger of over-industrialisation is particularly prevalent now that the Coal Board's policy is known to include a great expansion of coal extraction from the Lothians, coupled with the steady closing down of the coal pits in the Lanarkshire area. In this respect the report of the Scottish Coal Field Committee (December, 1944) considers that there should be a balancing programme of expansion on a large and dramatic scale in the Forth basin to offset the decline in the coal fields of west and central Scotland. Though it is not anticipated that such heavy industries as the Clydeside steel industries will move from their present region to this eastern part of Scotland, it is probable that there will be considerable industrial expansion in the neighbourhood of Edinburgh. It is in the Fifeshire and Lothian region rather than in Edinburgh itself that industrial developments should in the main be confined. In any case there are relatively few areas on the outskirts of the city that are suitable for industrial trading estates of the kind envisaged in the Clyde Report. In fact, it may be said that no large scale industrial development could take place in Edinburgh until such areas as Leith, Gorgie and Dalry industrial zones are redeveloped.

Future of industrial development. The Civic Survey, illustrates on maps the distribution of existing industry and clearly indicates the predominating areas of industry. Apart from the well defined concentrations in Leith and Gorgie there has been a general spread of minor concentrations between these two main ones which has resulted in almost continuous industrialisation from Leith to Slateford.

There are two large industrial zones proposed, and several smaller ones shown on folding map no. 19, each of which has been determined having regard to convenience of location to meet the needs of industry and the needs of the community generally. The larger zones such as Leith and Gorgie have zone sub-divisions for special industries emitting fumes: for general industries with heavy machinery plants where noise, smoke and dust is likely to be unavoidable, but do not emit fumes from processing: for light industries, not of these first two categories: for Dock industries not being special industries but requiring dock-side facilities.

These zone sub-divisions are suggested so that no nuisance may be imposed either by one type of factory upon the workers of another, or by the whole zone upon adjacent residential zones. Care, has therefore, been taken where other factors such as means of access, etc., permit, to set aside the "special" zones to the lee of residential areas and to create cut-off open spaces where this cannot be achieved. Also the fringe of the industrial zone as a whole, where it is nearest the residential zones, is set aside for the light industry category. About the core of these larger zones should be created a commercial zone for offices. In Leith industrial zone will be found all four categories, Special, General, Dockside and Light industrial zones, and in addition, a commerical zone for offices. In the Gorgie zone the same number of categories are also considered necessary except the dockside industries.

(i) *The Craigmillar zone*, where breweries are already established, is set aside for "special" industries with King's Park as the "cut-off" open space between it and the residential zones on the leeward side.

(ii) *The Niddrie zone*, which embraces the existing coalfield ancillary activities and marshalling yards, will probably remain for such uses for a long time to come. It cannot be made larger owing to the underground workings for coalmining. Its use class will, therefore, be for "special" industries.

(iii) *The Kings Road zone* embraces the existing Portobello electric power station and ancillary buildings. The boundaries of this zone are drawn to include also the local industries of Portobello, such as the Glass bottle manufacturing industry, and to allow of enough room for the completion of the Power Station building programme. Otherwise the zone should be strictly limited to permit the 'town' to achieve an attractive redevelopment as a sea-side resort. The use class is for general industries.

(iv) *Meadowbank* includes a number of substantial industries such as steel foundry, brewery maltings, etc., but sufficient area has been prescribed to permit redevelopment for one at least of the principal breweries in the Canongate. There should not be a very large zone created here, as the intention is to free the immediate environs of King's Park from an excessive industrial use and maintain a predominating residential character. The use classes of industry will, therefore, be "general" and "special" industries.

(v) *Annandale Street* already contains large service industries, such as motor body repair and construction works, and it is suggested this group might form the nucleus for such establishments to a limited extent. The boundaries of the zone are, therefore, drawn to allow only for a limited expansion. The use class would correspond to the statutory interpretation of "general" industry of the large service type.

(vi) *St. Leonards* contains amongst other "general" industries a brewery and distillery. With King's Park to the lee of this group, so far as the prevailing west wind is concerned, there would be no danger of affecting a residential area with fumes and smoke. "General" industry is the principal use class, though "special" industries, such as the brewery, will create an additional use class for the zone. This latter class should not be greatly extended.

(vii) *Sighthill* is a new area being developed upon virgin ground, and provides an additional work place for the new housing areas in this western part of the city. Its industry use class should be confined to the light industry kind which does not cause nuisance from smoke, fumes, dust, etc., to the adjoining residential areas. The "cut off" recreation space on the leeward side is an additional safeguard for this.

(viii) *Port of Leith*. The industrial port of Leith is Edinburgh's outlet for the export and import of goods for industries with external trade. It also serves the regional industries, of which coal is the most important. Its prosperity may be measured by the tentative programme of development at present in its first stage. The ground space so gained within the Dock area is about 50% giving of additional building space of approximately 34 acres.

The measure in water area provided by this programme would amount to over 100% increase.

(ix) *Newhaven*. This fishing port is no longer adequate to contain anything but the smaller drifter type of trawler. Though the Dock expansion does not absorb the port, it will obviously be necessary eventually in order to round off their foreseeable requirements. In any case the new road system cannot avoid disturbing the village layout on account of the topography of the area.

(x) *Granton*. This port is retained in the scheme as a secondary one to Leith, where it is understood the Leith Dock Commission have given up their interest in the Fishing industry in favour of Granton. This harbour can take over the Newhaven fishing industry and give the modern trawler adequate facilities.

The Plan aims at creating a number of industrial zones in which there will be no housing permitted in accordance with the principle of segregation already alluded to. Owing to the obvious predominance of industry in Leith and Gorgie indicating an economic necessity for industries in these areas, two main zones proposed are based upon these two localities. Others may be seen on folding map no. 19. The demarcation line for each of these zones has been carefully assessed mainly to permit of more commodious sites for existing industry in the zones, and for those that will require to be moved into them from the proposed housing areas, or zones, and for a certain amount of new industry. As regards new industry a total of 34 acres will be available as the Dock Extension programme at Leith progresses. Other factors taken into account in assessing the boundaries of these zones are partly to create compact ones containing areas of an existing predominance of industry, and, partly, by the physical barrier of a major arterial road. The physical factor is often the determining one, as it gives a convenient and defined break between housing areas and those of the industrial sites.

Other smaller zones are indicated on map 19 and require no further description. The following headings contain further details of the main aspects considered in the plan for industrial development :—

1. Principal Existing Industries.
   Mobility of industries and their extent.
2. Extent of Industrialisation and Areas required in zones.
3. Geographical Relationship between homes and Work Place.
4. Leith Redevelopment Area.
5. Gorgie—Dalry Redevelopment Area.
6. Conclusion.

1. PRINCIPAL INDUSTRIES.

In the appendix 3 of this Report will be found a number of analyses indicating the relative importance of the various kinds of industries that exist in Edinburgh. Of these the food, drink and tobacco groups, paper and printing, transport undertakings, miscellaneous constructional undertakings are,

EXISTING DISTRIBUTION OF LEITH INDUSTRIES

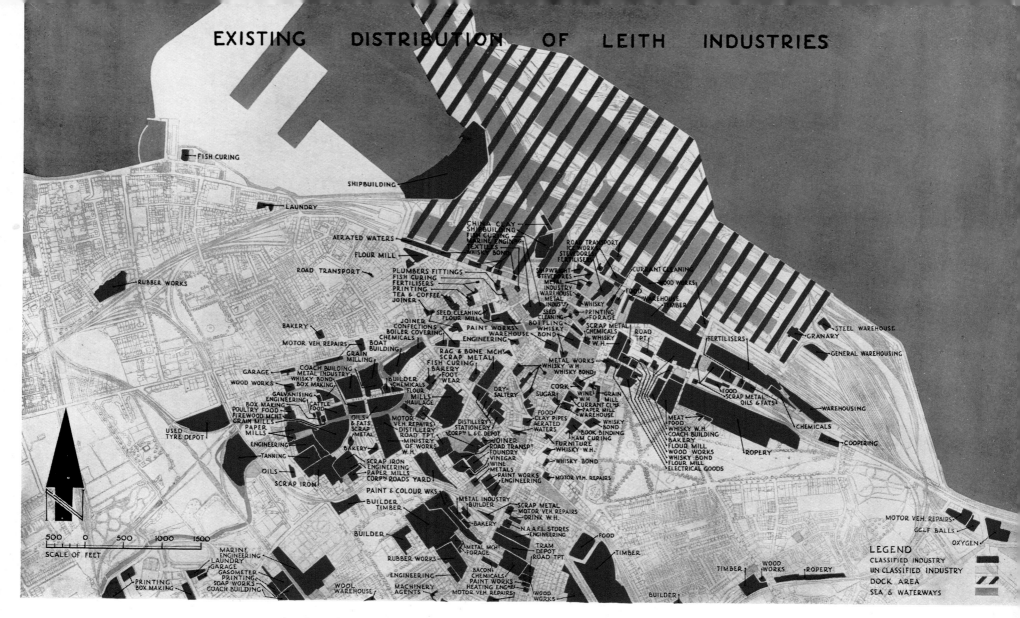

The above drawing shows the existing distribution of Leith industries (shown in red) and the type of manufacture or other industrial use carried on in these individual installations. A comparison with the proposal contained on Plate XLI will show how the proposed zone includes the area of Leith which is predominantly industrial. Though the zoning proposals involve a loss in housing acreage there is a corresponding gain to housing outside the zone.

Aerial view of Leith from the south-east [p. 83]

Aerial view of Leith Docks from the north-east [p. 84]

PLATE XXI

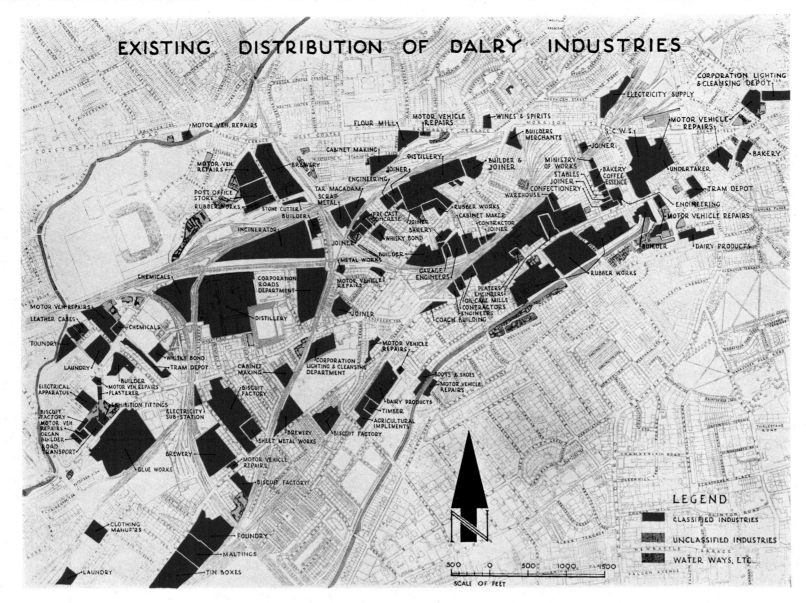

EXISTING DISTRIBUTION OF DALRY INDUSTRIES

The above drawing shows the existing distribution of industry in the Dalry locality. The site area occupied by these diverse industries are shown in red and the names give the type of manufacture or activity carried on. It is proposed to make the industrial zone for this locality sufficiently large to embrace most of these industries and to take in the intervening areas at present occupied by housing or other property for industrial expansion and for incoming industries from the areas zoned for residential use.

[p. 97]

Aerial view of Dalry area in the foreground showing the rubber works fronting on to the Union Canal. The proposed industrial zone embraces these and stretches further to the west.

[p. 98]

Aerial view of Gorgie and Slateford in the foreground with the Firth of Forth in the background and to the north. The proposed industrial zone is contained west of the railway lines.

PLATE XXII

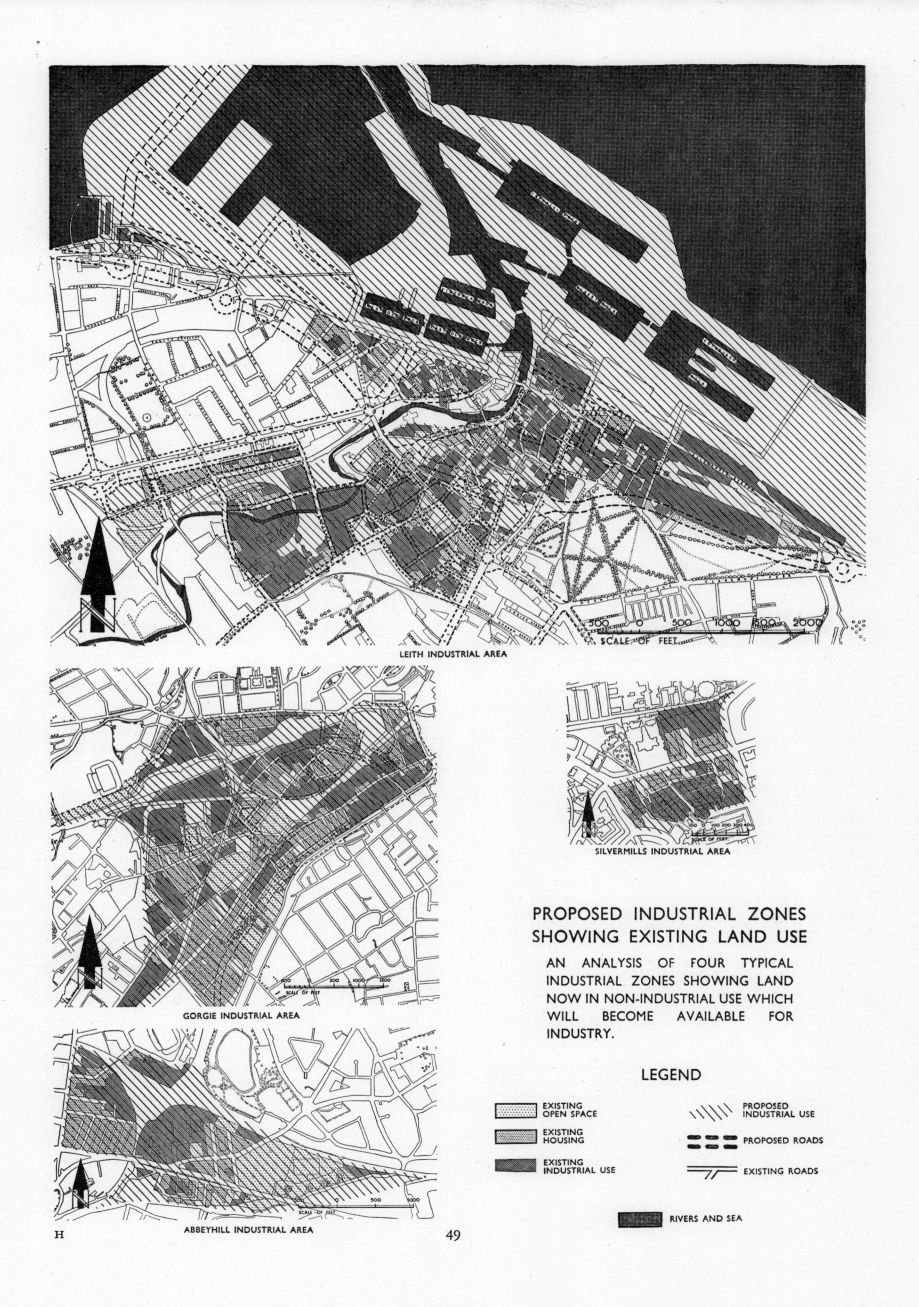

LEITH INDUSTRIAL AREA

500   0   500   1000   1500   2000
SCALE OF FEET

SILVERMILLS INDUSTRIAL AREA

GORGIE INDUSTRIAL AREA

ABBEYHILL INDUSTRIAL AREA

PROPOSED INDUSTRIAL ZONES
SHOWING EXISTING LAND USE

AN ANALYSIS OF FOUR TYPICAL
INDUSTRIAL ZONES SHOWING LAND
NOW IN NON-INDUSTRIAL USE WHICH
WILL BECOME AVAILABLE FOR
INDUSTRY.

LEGEND

EXISTING
OPEN SPACE

EXISTING
HOUSING

EXISTING
INDUSTRIAL USE

PROPOSED
INDUSTRIAL USE

PROPOSED ROADS

EXISTING ROADS

RIVERS AND SEA

H

49

the most important ones. With the exception of the paper and printing trade, they are shown to have, in the Trends Survey, a continuous tendency for expansion. Considering that the printing industry of Edinburgh was, in the past, one of the most important in the country, it is significant to find that it has shown in recent times a tendency to remain either more or less static, or to decline. This is believed to be on account of the lack of modernisation of equipment, and a corresponding deterioration in the quality of the aesthetic in its craftsmanship.

'Mobile' and 'Non-mobile' Industries. In the Civic Survey, the distribution of mobile and non-mobile industries was indicated and their geographic distribution is seen on Plate no. XI. It will be seen that in Leith social survey district, excluding the Dock Commission area, there is a total of approximately 18 industries containing mobile installations, and 23 containing non-mobile installations out of a total of 41 industries. The mobile installations occupy approximately 116 acres, and the non-mobile 135 acres. In the Gorgie—Dalry locality there are approximately 8 industries containing non-mobile installations, occupying some 80 acres, and 26 containing mobile installations occupying some 144 acres. The non-mobile were determined upon the basis of industries which were regarded as particularly difficult and costly to move, such as power stations and iron foundries or chemical works, where their installations are integral with their buildings.

In this latter respect, the extent of mobility or otherwise of an industry is often determined, not so much from the nature of the building installations, but from the economic relationship to its raw materials, its water supply, its access to rail and, or, dock facilities, or to its association with other installations or ancillary trades. A typical example of an industry tied to its present location by its requirements for rail and dock facilities is, of course, the shipbuilding and repair industry.

The converse of these types, namely, those described as mobile industries, may be said to consist of industries whose equipment may easily be dismantled and re-assembled, or those that require scrapping or substantial modernisation and those that are of the small compact type of industries that could more conveniently and economically be accommodated in what are known as "flatted" factories. Examples of these mobile industries are the saw milling industries and some of the general engineering industries such as the machine tool, and agricultural manufacture.

The important conclusion to draw from these facts is, that, apart from the general inconvenience and cost of moving factories to new sites in a decentralisation scheme, there should in many cases be no fundamental economic reasons to prevent their removal. In fact, given a good conveniently shaped site with satisfactory transport access and general services, there is every reason to suppose that such removal would be an advantage to the industries concerned than otherwise. Continuing congested circumstances, on the other hand, are not.

2. EXTENT OF INDUSTRIALISATION AND AREA REQUIRED IN ZONES.

Conclusions from the Survey of Trends in Industry indicate that, before the war, Edinburgh was not tending to become an industrial city. That is to say, though there was industrial development, by comparison, it was less than the average for the country as a whole. This pre-war development, however, increased during the war-time period to quite a considerable extent. In order that this more recent trend could be fully

allowed for, it was first of all necessary to obtain an approximate estimate of the proportion of the total industrial population resulting from this development. From this proportion and from the relative industrial worker density ratios arrived at from the Civic Survey, a guide was obtained to assist in finding the proper demarcation line for each of the industrial zones, the total area of which would be sufficient to allow for this recent trend, and for a reasonable number of new industries to come into the city. The present proportion of Edinburgh's total population engaged in industry is 90,000 or 19·7% of its total population in 1946, as compared with Great Britain's proportion engaged in industry which is 9,614,000 or 20·3%. The Table below gives the present situation for insured workers with Glasgow and Manchester added as two well known industrial cities.

TABLE IX
COMPARATIVE INDUSTRIAL POPULATION (1946)
(Thousands).

	Total Pop.	Ind. Pop.	% of Total
Edinburgh	459·4	90·1	19·7%
Manchester	668·7	222·6	33·3%
Glasgow	1050·0	300·0	28·6%
Great Britain	*47300·0	9614·0	20·3%

*Estimated

It is recommended that this relationship should remain roughly the same in order to preserve the existing character of the city and prevent over industrialisation. For comparative purposes, the total area at present occupied by all industries for which information has been analysed is 1,100 acres and that which is allowed for in the zones is 1,508 acres.

The analysis of some of the zones in diagram form on page 49 show how the industrial land use is obtained and what kind of properties are affected. Tabulated data may also be seen on Table XXVIII in Appendix 3.

This 1,100 acres of ground space occupied by existing industries includes both those which, by modern standards, are congested and those which use ground space uneconomically in the planning sense. Allowing for these prevailing conditions the amount of additional space represented by the above difference is a conservative one.

3. GEOGRAPHICAL RELATIONSHIP BETWEEN HOMES AND WORK PLACE.

A study analysing the existing relationship of Place of Work and Place of Residence of the present population has been given in the Civic Survey, Chapter 2. The extent of travelling to and from the existing concentrations of industry and the homes is fairly considerable in some instances, as for example in the centre of Edinburgh, where the principal wage earners live as far away as Pilton, Sighthill and Duddington. In others, such as Granton and Leith, there exists a curious interchange, consisting of people who live in the industrial area of Leith and work in the industrial area of Granton and vice versa. One of the objects of the Plan is to make it possible to eliminate unnecessary travelling. In the redistribution of the population, resulting partly from the proposal to depopulate the proposed industrial zones, and, partly, from the redevelopment of the proposed residential zones to eliminate overcrowding, a reshuffling over a period of years enables a solution to be found to this problem. Such a solution will require a determined attempt to correlate the redevelopment of the overcrowded housing areas with the redevelopment of the industrial areas. It will call for an increase in density of housing development in some areas, particularly those adjacent to the Gorgie—Dalry industrial zone, and even a change in some instances of the existing predominating character of the neighbourhood. It is impossible to pre-determine where everyone should live in order to satisfy these economic and social considerations, and there is no suggestion made for any dictatorial policy to that end. The contention is, however, that when redevelopment takes place in an area involving house construction, prior consideration should be given to the opportunity that this reconstruction offers, for those who may need to live in that locality to be near their place of work.

4. LEITH REDEVELOPMENT AREA.

The area of this zone lies between Leith Docks to the south-east and Bonnington to the south-west and is bounded by Leith Links to the east and Trinity on the west. There is a large amount of existing industrial property much of which is ripe for redevelopment. It is not proposed to give a full description of the detailed proposals for this zone, as this appears in the chapter on Leith and Portobello (Chapter 9). A brief description, therefore, of the kind of industries that might be encouraged to set up in this zone, or that of the Leith Docks will suffice. The industry which occupies the greatest area is saw-milling. It occupies over 10% of the total industrial space of this locality. This is interesting as saw-milling represents one of the mobile industries reasonably capable of being moved. Other industries consist of shipbuilding, milling, ropemaking, coopery, baking, etc. many of which are non-mobile types.

Industries particularly suitable for the neighbourhood of the port, and which are less well represented in the locality are the wood-box making and cardboard manufacturing industries. These are particularly suitable to the port area owing to their dependence upon sea communications. Both are well represented in greater Edinburgh but not in Leith itself. There would, therefore, appear to be a case for encouraging these units to move from their sites in other parts of the city to the port when disturbed by redevelopment or modernisation schemes.

The Leith industrial area has been redesigned to provide zones for different types of industries and for the business interests of the port. These are based upon the predominance of existing types. Leith has, however, been redesigned and though, as many as possible of the existing roads, are retained, considerable re-orientation of the general layout has been necessary to eliminate a bad layout of roads. This, is described in Chapter 9.

GORGIE—DALRY.

The largest type of 'user' of industrial space in this locality, which lies to the south of the Haymarket, consists of the 'drink' group of industries which occupies over 10% of all the existing industrial space. Others consist of general food manufacturers and distribution, rubber, general engineering, baking, and so on. The curtailment of the western spread of the industrial area will involve the redistribution of certain of the mobile industries as, for example, those in the general food distribution group, coopery and laundering and some of those in the general engineering group. There will, however, be ample room for these in this south-west industrial zone of the city when slum clearance begins.

CONCLUSION.

It may be said that the principal requirement in the plan for industry is the regrouping of existing industries into zones, to avoid congestion of site planning for industries on the one hand, and for the proper environment of the home of the worker on the other hand. Coupled with that is the other equally important aspect which requires that industrial development for Edinburgh as a whole should not be permitted to become so predominant a feature of the city's activities as to change the character of the city. The fact that there are a large number of mobile industries in the two principal industrial zones of Leith and Gorgie amounting to some 44 industries out of a total of 75, indicates that there must be some prospect at least of reshuffling to achieve this essential segregation from the home. This prospect is enhanced by the fact that the mobile industries in these two districts occupy some 240 acres, in addition to a considerable acreage of out of date housing property lying intermingled with these industries. Furthermore, the areas in which these mobile industries are located, are, for the most part, areas of bad layout of the kind referred to in the Town and Country Planning Act of 1947.

An indication of the extent to which it is thought that Edinburgh's industry might be permitted to expand is illustrated in folding map no. 19. An important guide for the total land area assessment is the estimated total industrial population that might be expected (assuming full employment) from the industrial development occupying this total area. This total industrial population, taken as a proportion of the total city population anticipated in the plan, is then correlated with the same proportion for the country as a whole, which may be said to represent a reasonable datum. The table in the appendix furnishes in greater detail a comparison with Great Britain and the two principal industrial cities of the United Kingdom, namely Glasgow and Manchester. It is felt that so long as this index relationship remains the same, there is no need for any fear of over-industrialisation, or of the city changing its character.

CHAPTER SEVEN

CENTRAL PLANNING

INTRODUCTION. Central Planning covers all the aspects of development which, for clearness, must ordinarily be considered separately under their respective headings; the synthesis being accomplished under the Master Plan. Here, at the centre, it is impossible to disentangle the interlocking, though some obvious attempt must be made to take one aspect at a time: the whole, however, builds up into a close piece of counterpoint. Thus, in this one section of the report, road traffic, railway stations, detailed statutory zoning or precincts varying from civic and government centres to groups of tenements in the Canongate, civic design on its most extended scale, open spaces, preservation of historic buildings, and monuments and many utilitarian functions such as markets, car-parks etc. must all be considered simultaneously on plan and as conjointly as the written word will allow.

In the planning of central Edinburgh, topographic and historic considerations are of paramount importance. It might be thought that the violent natural features which dominate the central scene would give the planner his chief difficulties: and indeed, if symmetry and regularity on a scale of Roman extravagance were attempted, the site would prove almost intractable, to this artificial approach. Even the New Town based upon Renaissance conceptions of formality found the easier site north of the loch sufficiently difficult, after the first fairly level piece had been used by James Craig. On the southern side of the ridge great bridging streets have been carried across the valley, so that a casual visitor entering from the south, unless he is quick to note the Cowgate, enters High Street on the level. But in spite of the great mass of human effort "we have some possessions", as Stevenson says, "that not even the infuriate zeal of the builders can utterly "abolish and destroy. Nothing can abolish the hills, unless "it be a cataclysm of nature which shall subvert Edinburgh "Castle itself and lay all her florid structures in the dust. And, "as long as we have the hills and the Firth, we have a famous "heritage to leave our children."

Of the human handiworks which have overlaid these natural features, there are many that have acquired an historic interest and possess an architectural value. These are ranked of equal and in some cases of more ardent importance than the natural features. Nothing is so likely to arouse controversy and opposition as change or destruction of any of the ancient human landmarks of this city. This cherishing of the heritage of the past is laudable but it makes the work of the planner more perilous.

Paradoxically, it is the former consideration, highly varied topography, which helps rather than hinders the preservation of the historic and architectural appearance of the city, while permitting proposals of sufficient boldness to cope adequately with modern problems. There is fortunately, no war-time destruction in central Edinburgh, but the sudden changes in level, the high ridges and deep valleys, allow a whole system of road improvements to underlie the existing features of the city, tunnelling here, bridging there, in order to effect the highly complex traffic solution which present traffic congestion and interference require and future increase will render absolutely imperative. Thus it may be said that these conditions have led to the very boldness of many of these

proposals, the diversion of Leith traffic from Princes Street for instance, or the three decker road under North Bridge, or the three decker to Princes Street, or the passage under the Canongate and the diversion of the main line (L.N.E.R.) under the Meadows. The solutions themselves, are also the means of rendering them almost invisible, e.g., the duplication of Nicholson Street, the combination of the Railway Terminals and others. There are no disastrous widenings of existing roads proposed, nor new roads cutting gashes through precious areas, no precincts invaded, no favourite or valued pieces of architecture demolished, by these very necessary utilitarian proposals. There will be, it is true, a slight alteration to the Castle valley gardens, where the lower road will be seen through arcades as it lies at a lower level. There will also be the immense gain in amenity through the elimination of all but an electric route through the valley, a greatly reduced Waverley Station, and the recovery of the valley below the Calton Hill.

The following are the headings under which these central improvements will be described in some detail: but in every case a reference to map on Plate No. XXIII will show interrelationship of them all:—

[1] Roads system in the central area: brief description: Bye-focal Plan: the carry-off of through traffic.
   (i) The effect on Princes Street, the Gardens, the Mound and North Bridge.
   (ii) The effect upon the High Street and Pleasance.
   (iii) Melville Drive.
   (iv) The junction of Leith Walk and Princes Street.

[2] Central Railway alterations: brief description.
   (i) New combined station.
   (ii) The St. Leonards and Meadows route.
   (iii) New Waverley Station from the valley.

[3] Recovery of the Castle Gardens Valley.

[4] General improvement of the Royal Mile.
   (i) Surrounding Holyrood: breweries and Gasworks
   (ii) Precincts: administrative and residential.
   (iii) Pleasance and St. Leonards residential neighbourhood.
   (iv) West Port and Morrison Street residential neighbourhood.

[5] Central commercial and shopping precinct: Princes Street, Melville Street, etc.
   (i) The gradual transformation of the new town: shops: industry.
   (ii) Industry in Central Area at back of Princes Street.

[6] Two festival and entertainment centres: Usher Hall and St. James Square.
   (i) Usher Hall.
   (ii) St. James Square.

[7] Enlargement of Government Administrative centre.

[8] University precinct: removal of Bristo Street.
   (i) Traffic problem.
   (ii) George Square.

[9] Grassmarket and Heriot's School.

[10] Water of Leith Walk in Central Area: Dean Village.

[11] Central Markets.

DETAILED IMPROVEMENTS DESCRIBED.

1. *Road System in Central Area.*

The City, as already explained in chapter 4, is greatly influenced by the sharp contrasting topography and its road system, perhaps more than any other aspect of planning, is affected by it. The interruption, by the Castle and ridge of the Royal Mile, to the two valleys through which the Dalkeith and Lanark radial roads pass, has created a bi-focal centre situated at the east and west ends of Princes Street. Princes Street, therefore, becomes a link of great importance between these two foci in the central area, so that any by-pass scheme to relieve its traffic congestion must of necessity run parallel and as close as possible to it. For this, and other reasons already stated in the Roads chapter, the route for this by-pass has been selected to run beneath Princes Street itself, where it forms the northern leg of the inner ring road of this central area. It creates an interesting and important contribution to the amenities of this magnificent valley—the heart and pride of Scotland.

PRINCES STREET BYE-PASS SCHEME

The scheme is a three decker one, the uppermost deck being existing Princes Street which would become primarily a service link road with all through traffic diverted from it. The middle one, some ten feet below but beside it, would be for car parking and promenade; the lowest, lit and ventilated naturally by the colonnade and 'clear storey' windows would be the by-pass for all through traffic. Both Princes Street and its by-pass would carry bus traffic, but with local stopping buses on Princes Street and long distance buses on the by-pass. There would be no need for ventilating towers in this valley as the 'clear storey' gives ample daylight and ventilation to the carriageway furthest from the open side. The open side would be architecturally designed as a continuous colonnade, intercepted only at intervals where ramps or steps are provided for pedestrian access to the Gardens, as at present. Above, Princes Street is narrowed to the same width existing in front of the Scottish Academy building, i.e. 40ft., to allow a broad strip of tree planted green. Some 10ft. lower, yet still above the by-pass, is the 40ft. wide car parking terrace running more or less the length of Princes Street. This terrace could accommodate some 200 to 300 cars at one time as well as offer an additional promenade to pedestrians. The visiting tourist may then drive on either one of three levels and admire this magnificent panorama with a southern aspect.

At the Mound, the by-pass has a traffic underground roundabout where vehicles may flow freely and uninterrupted, either up on to Princes Street, or away out across the valley beneath the North Bridge to the new North to South by-pass of the ' Bridges.' Its sides would continue the open colonnade treatment.

Waverley Bridge and Cockburn Street form an intersection with this southerly outlet to pick up the Waverley Station taxi and other traffic making for the southern suburbs.

(i) *The Effect on Princes Street, the Gardens, the Mound, and North Bridge.* This project offers a wonderful opportunity for a feat of engineering and of architectural achievement. There would be little disturbance to existing services, sewers and the like, though it is believed that these sewers are becoming overloaded already and may need relaying anyway. There would be no compensation to pay the existing frontagers of Princes Street as the sub-soil is sandstone and money expended would be confined mainly to constructional costs except at the two points of entry where property is less expensive than at the West End and East End. This scheme reduces the need for an expensive reconstruction scheme at the West End, although reconstruction there should take place even for local traffic. Traffic up the Mound would still continue, though its destination should be much more local being confined to the High Street, University and Lauriston Place.

At the North Bridge an interesting three level road scheme emerges from the road system with Market Street retained as a local road; the east to west link between Waverley Bridge and the new North to South by-pass of the " North Bridge " running parallel to Market Street and passing beneath the arches of the North Bridge. It consists of the North Bridge retained primarily as a link road with all through traffic taken off it, and seen spanning the two at right angles. At the junction of Chalmers Close and Jeffrey Street, the actual intersection with the new North to South by-pass is made by means of a roundabout half built into the hillside of the ridge of the Royal Mile. The other half spanning Market Street with daylight admitted through to the street below. The new North to South by-pass of the North Bridge would be seen emerging from the black rock of Calton Hill and thrusting its arched concrete structure of mellow colour across the valley retrieved from the ugliness of the railway goods yard.

(ii) *The effect upon High Street and the Pleasance.* From its intersection with its Waverley Bridge and Princes Street link, it carves a way through the ridge flanked by the tall High Street buildings of mediaeval origin, and without disturbing any buildings of consequence, passes beneath the High Street. It then continues southwards to pass over the Cowgate, as does the present " south " Bridge, before striking ground level near Drummond Street and between the Pleasance and Nicholson Street. This by-pass forms the eastern leg of the inner ring road system.

(iii) *Melville Drive.* At St. Leonards the southern leg of this ring road passes westwards to follow the tree planted avenue of Melville Drive, and thus introducing, by contrast to the other parts of the system, a boulevard flanked by the sweeping Meadows separating the University from the residential suburbs. (These Meadows will offer a similar outlook to the new University precinct as Christ Church meadows do for Oxford University.) The new two level main railway station is reached at Morrison Street having passed immediately west of Gardner's Crescent. Though Rutland Square would be transformed owing to the need to enter the low level Princes Street, its east and west flanking buildings could be retained though their reconstruction as office buildings would be more appropriate.

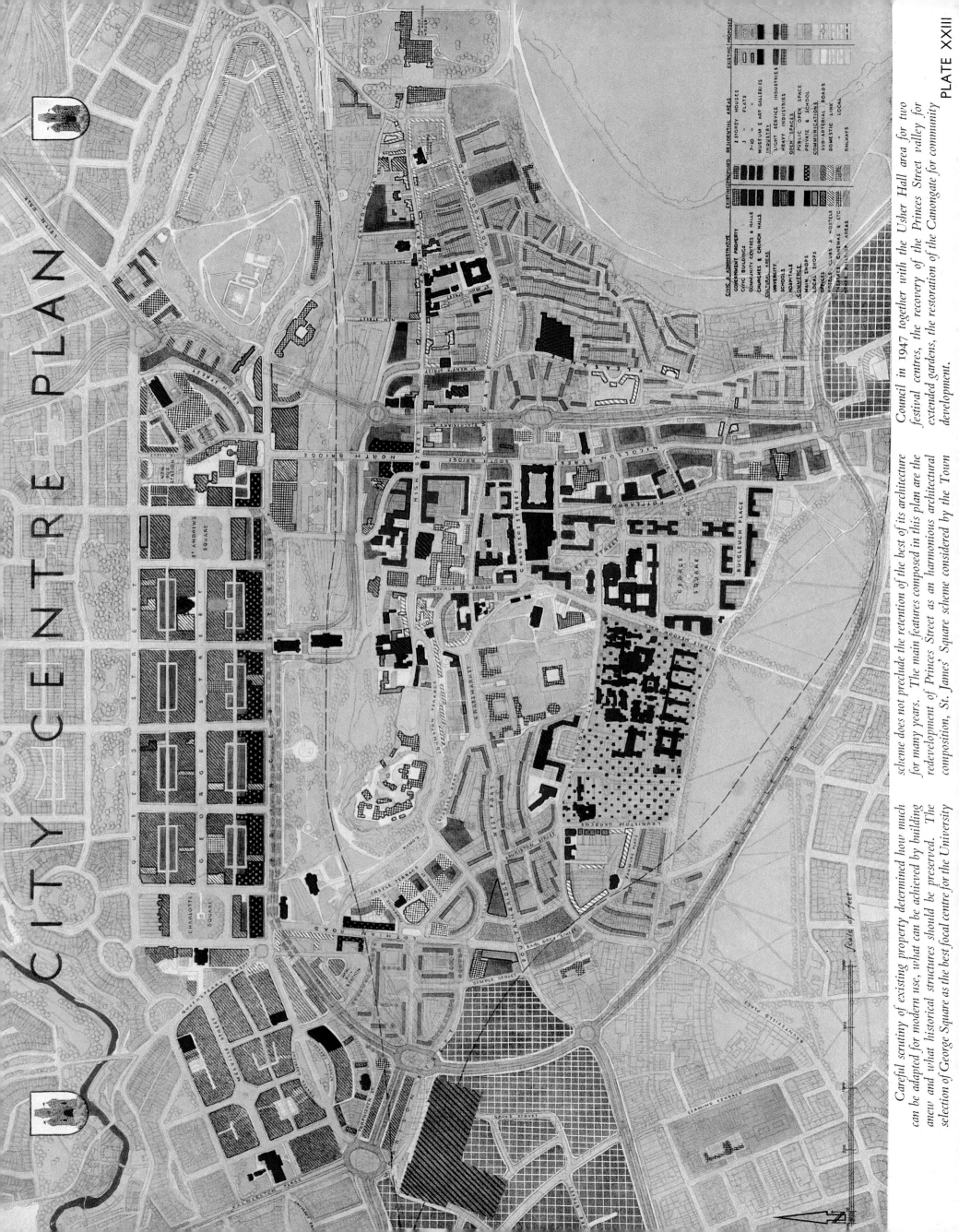

CITY CENTRE PLAN

Scale of feet

PLATE XXIII

Careful scrutiny of existing property determined how much can be adapted for modern use, what can be achieved by building anew and what historical structures should be preserved. The selection of George Square as the best focal centre for the University scheme does not preclude the retention of the best of its architecture for many years. The main features composed in this plan are the redevelopment of Princes Street as an harmonious architectural composition, St. James' Square scheme considered by the Town Council in 1947 together with the Usher Hall area for two festival centres, the recovery of the Princes Street valley for extended gardens, the restoration of the Canongate for community development.

EXISTING | PROPOSED

CIVIC & ADMINISTRATIVE
GOVERNMENT PROPERTY
CIVIC BUILDINGS
COMMUNITY CENTRES & HALLS
CHURCHES & CHURCH HALLS

CULTURAL AREAS
MUSEUM & ART GALLERIES
UNIVERSITY
SCHOOLS
HOSPITALS
COMMERCE
MAIN SHOPS
LOCAL SHOPS
OFFICES
HOTELS CLUBS & HOSTELS
THEATRES CINEMAS & ETC.

RESIDENTIAL AREAS
2 STOREY HOUSES
FLATS
3   "   "
7-10   "   "

INDUSTRY
LIGHT SERVICE INDUSTRIES
HEAVY INDUSTRIES

OPEN SPACES
PUBLIC OPEN SPACE
PRIVATE & SCHOOL

COMMUNICATIONS
SUB-ARTERIAL ROADS
DOMESTIC LINK
LOCAL
RAILWAYS
PRE-BUILT AREAS

This is an aerial view of the south side of the city with Nicolson Street cutting down the centre of the photograph. The property to the left of this road south of Chambers Street would be mostly required for the proposed University precinct scheme. George Square may be seen at the bottom left-hand corner.

Aerial view of University Precinct   [p. 39]

Aerial view of St. Andrew Square   [p. 40]

[p. 41]

[P. 41]. An aerial view of Waverley Station showing the High Street and St. Giles Cathedral in the foreground.

Great King Street   [p. 81]

[P. 81]. An example of the New Town architecture is seen in this view of part of Great King Street which is situated on the north side beyond Princes Street and Queen Street.

PLATE XXIV

(iv) *The junction of Leith Walk and Princes Street.* The significance of Leith Street as the only important link existing between Leith Walk and Princes Street would diminish considerably with the construction of the " Bridges " by-pass and Princes Street by-pass, especially as direct access is obtainable between Princes Street and its by-pass at Frederick Street. The Princes Street by-pass is, therefore, also a means of access to the Mound as well as a by-pass of it. The turning of Leith Street into Picardy Place via Broughton Street (widened) and the closing of its junction with Leith Walk is deliberate to " precinctalise " this important shopping street.

2. *The Central Railway Alterations.*

So many Edinburgher's and their friends at home and overseas have uttered piteous outbursts at the spoiling of Princes Street Gardens that no improvements for railway needs could be investigated without this factor at the back of one's mind. Many also have expressed the opinion that no inconvenience would be caused to long distance travellers by rail arriving at a station situated even well away from the centre; but none have thought of the daily suburban traveller not benefiting from a centrally placed station. There lies the crux of the geographical problem for passenger traffic, though the economic problem explained in chapter 4 is connected with it. The alterations in this central area include a new two level combined station at Morrison Street for all long distance traffic but with suburban connections. Also, the retention of a modified Waverley Station is suggested to meet only the daily suburban and regional passenger traffic which might well be electrified with the help of the Scottish hydro electric schemes. If the London traffic had still to be admitted through the Gardens, then that traffic too would have to be electrified before complete covering-in of the railway and station would be feasible. Diverted, as it could be, in tunnels beneath the Meadows, an all electric railway in Princes Street gardens then becomes possible together with the restoration of the valley to a verdant one.

(i) *The Combined Station.* This is situated at Morrison Street and would occupy the site of the present marshalling yard. The area required would be relatively less than at Waverley, as there is no suggestion of moving suburban and regional passenger traffic. Furthermore the two main stations of Waverley and the Caledonian would operate one above the other as the levels of the present railway system demands. The lower station, being a through one, connects with the east coast route while the upper station is a terminal like the present Caledonian. These two stations together, would become an important focal point on the new road system where the main western radial road meets the inner ring road at the Haymarket.

(ii) *The St. Leonards and Meadows Route.* This forms the main link between the main London line at Niddrie with the main northern line and Glasgow line at the Haymarket. One section of this new route follows the existing route of railway enterprise of the last century—the old Innocent railway. With improved gradients the new route will pass by means of twin tunnels beneath the Meadows and Earl Grey Street. Offering a 1 in 560 gradient it would be an attractive alternative to the present Newington—Morningside suburban line for freight traffic from the expanding coalfields.

(iii) *The New Waverley Station from the Valley.* If the long distance services are withdrawn from this route through the Princes Street gardens, Waverley Station would no longer require to be so big (or cramped) as it is now. Never was a more complicated set of exits and entries presented to the traveller for such an important station. They not only affect the economic administration and maintenance of an awkward structure, but the convenience of the travelling public. The scheme now proposed eliminates these eccentricities and presents a boldly conceived eletrification scheme including the entire covering in of the station beneath a roof of lawns and terraced gardens.

3. *The Recovery of the Castle Gardens Valley.*

The railway development blotted Edinburgh's copy book badly in bringing the railway uncovered through this magnificent gift of nature. It is strange how little respect for nature appears to have been given even by the new Town builders, when they heartlessly used this valley as a dumping ground for the excavated material from their workings. The Mound, so created, and now covered by the blackened National Art Gallery and Royal Scottish Academy, has introduced aesthetically an unfortunate horizontal element that only a sentimentalist can fail to appreciate. Bridges there must be, but their open spans of arch construction do not interrupt the continuity of elongation of the natural valley formation: the solidity of the Mound with its superstructure of buildings most definitely does.

With the covering in of the railway and station the Valley Gardens may be greatly improved and extended to restore the original shape of the valley. Additional space for out door physical recreation as a centre for olympic or national games becomes a possibility. The present Waverley market, which was the subject of an architectural competition before the war to transform it into an indoor centre for amusement and physical recreation, would be capable of greater possibilities than so far conceived in the winning design. The successful architects in this competition have already reported favourably in this wise.

When considering the implications of the railway scheme the value of such improvements to Waverley Market, the valley generally and Princes Street, the potential building development for central area housing west of Lothian Road, must be weighed in the balance.

4. *The General Improvement of the Royal Mile.*

An idea is given in chapter 8 on Canongate and Royal Mile proposals, its architecture and zoning. It remains, therefore, to fill in the gaps to complete the picture of the overall scheme.

Of the Royal Mile consisting of three unit areas, two of which (the Lawnmarket and High Street) are for administrative, commercial and central community buildings and the third (the Canongate) is zoned for residential development. The latter presents difficult problems of zoning. In the past, attempts have been made to reconcile the desire to preserve the old residential character of the buildings and continue a large scale industrial use of buildings. This leads to a travesty of architectural design. A continuance of the present mixed use of houses and industry, with freedom of architectural expression, might satisfy the architectural aspect of the problem, but there will be no lasting satisfaction from the town planning aspect: there will be no healthy or convenient living or working conditions. A thinning out of residential buildings to ameliorate living conditions, or to allow for the present industrial expansion, offers no lasting solution, with the prospect of future industrial expansion in the locality, of which there has been ample evidence recently.

(i) *Surroundings of Holyrood: Breweries and Gasworks.* With the presence of Holyrood Palace, this problem assumes national significance. A royal Palace enshrouded in a black pall of smoke from time to time and the air permeated with factory processing, is no fit place for a Sovereign to dwell, any more than a commoner in the surrounding houses.

There can only be two possible solutions :—

(a) A gradual decentralisation of industry to other more suitable and industrially convenient sites, allowing for expansion of the residential use of buildings to recover the original residential character.

or

(b) A retention and eventual expansion of the existing predominance of commercial and industrial use of property and a total elimination of residential buidings. In that event the Palace would be untenable.

From the historical and sentimental aspect, industry should go. From the point of view of the general requirements of good city development, industry should go, because better communications and more elbow room for expansion is available in the industrial zones on the one hand while on the other, adequate space for living is required in the centre to avoid over decentralisation of the existing population from the central areas.

The gasoholders are retained, as they represent an essential part of a principal distribution centre of radiating gas mains for the whole of east and south-east Edinburgh, and to put them out of sight, total submergence below the ground would be cheaper than readjusting many miles of gas mains. There is also little, if any smell, from gasoholders as distinct from gas works.

The Plan, therefore, proposes decentralisation of industry to the zones recommended for them, and, as a first step, the property immediately opposite the Palace should be cleared as far back as Queensberry House. This would permit the Brewery to continue operating on the remainder of its site west of Queensberry House and garden for, say, another ten or fifteen years, while the ground so released would be redeveloped to house some 200 persons at 100 persons per acre net density. The reconstruction programme already contemplated by the Company concerned, of which this disturbed brewery section forms a part, might well take place, not in the Canongate, but at their Meadowbank site, where railway access is available together with its Maltings. This brewery section could then form the first stage of such a programme. Such a progressive reconstruction at Meadowbank would, therefore, not only contribute materially to the proper redevelopment of the Canongate but would bring together all its scattered units as one harmonious whole.

(ii) *Precincts: Administrative and Residential.* The main administrative centre of the city still lies about the old High Street, though there have been many offshoots both of local government as well as of central government departments to other parts of the city, notably George Street, Melville Street and St. James Square. The suggestions for redevelopment in the High Street, part of Mr. MacRae's Royal Mile Report have been adhered to, as the location could not be better. It is hoped to reinstate all the Corporation departments in a considerably augmented building adjacent to the City Chambers, while the Police department building on the opposite side of the High Street would be reconstructed and extended. The National and Corporation Central Libraries could take place as indicated on either side of George IV Bridge. Other administrative centres are allowed for including the Government administrative centre at Calton Hill.

(iii) *Pleasance and St. Leonards Residential Precinct.* There are two residential precincts suggested for this central area as may be seen on the City Centre Plan, Plate No. XXIII One embraces St. Leonards and the Canongate, and one is situated in the vicinity of West Port and Morrison Street. The estimated population total for the St. Leonards unit amounts to 8,702 persons, based upon the density zoning proposals of 100 persons per net residential acre. The layout plan suggests a mixed development of two storey housing and 7 to 10 storey blocks of flats on the assumption that lifts will be installed in the latter. It is possible to obtain, as already mentioned in the Population Distribution chapter, 50% two storey dwellings with private gardens and 50% as dwellings in flats, with communal gardens, in a 100 net density zone. Two primary schools with their playing field allocation, have been allowed for in the layout together with community and other public or important city cultural buildings which are already existing. The standard of public open space allowed for within the confines of this unit is scheduled at 1·3 acres per thousand owing to the fact that Arthur's Seat adjoins the area and would bring up the balance to 4 acres per thousand allowed for in this central area. The great mass of Arthur's Seat itself, of course, is not included in the standard as that is considered to be one of the major open spaces used by citizens all over the city, while the flat parts that lie close to this unit may reasonably be considered of prior importance to the population in the immediate locality. It will be seen from the Plan that the major part of the flats allocated under the density zoning scheme lie about the proposed north to south by-pass road of the 'Bridges' route where tall buildings would be an advantage architecturally and where the necessary greater space between the blocks of buildings can be readily obtained. The two storey dwellings on the other hand should be sited in terraces on the steep slope approximately west of the line of the existing Dumbiedykes Road. It is important that the buildings should be kept low in height in this area in order to make the most of the magnificent views of Arthur Seat that would then be obtainable: and, as the population distribution proposals permit of such a density, there is no reason why these two storey buildings should not be carried out in order to safeguard this important amenity aspect. The new road layout would, of course, entail an almost total abolition of the existing domestic road system, of which Brown Street, Arthur Street and Salisbury Street are typical examples that require to be eliminated anyway, as they run steeply against the existing contours.

(iv) *West Port and Morrison Street.* The total population that can be housed in this area amounts to 7,276 persons at the proposed density of 100 persons per net residential acre. Additional land has been obtained in the Plan from the proposed abolition of the old railway goods depot adjacent to Lothian Road. On the other hand, land consisting of very mixed and derelict property has been redeveloped in the vicinity of West Tollcross, Lochrin, for essential primary school buildings and playing fields to meet the requirements of this population. Again flat development is recommended for the property areas adjacent to the ring road that passes to the south and west limits of this locality. Though West Port and Fountainbridge are also areas scheduled for tall blocks of flats, two storey dwellings may be seen located immediately west of Lauriston Street and Panmure Place. In that way, the desired mixed development of two storey houses with gardens, and flats is again obtained, which together provide accommodation for the above mentioned total population allowed for in the population distribution proposals for the whole city.

The above perspective sketch shows the manner in which the present Lothian Road Goods Yard can be redeveloped as part of a housing community when this part of the railway proposals are carried out. The aim at the same time is to provide a suitable setting for the Usher Hall which forms the nucleus of one of the two festival centres.

Usher Hall from Railway Goods Yard   [p. 58]

This photograph shows the present ugliness which forms the foreground to the Usher Hall where some of the principal parts of the Festival programme are enjoyed. This goods yard becomes redundant under the railway scheme and offers an opportunity that may be seen in the perspective above.

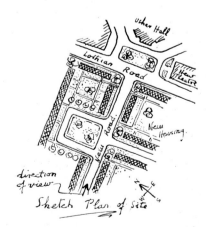

This sketch plan shows the arrangement of the buildings which would be constructed on this goods yard and the arrow shows the direction of the view pictured by the perspective above.

PLATE XXV

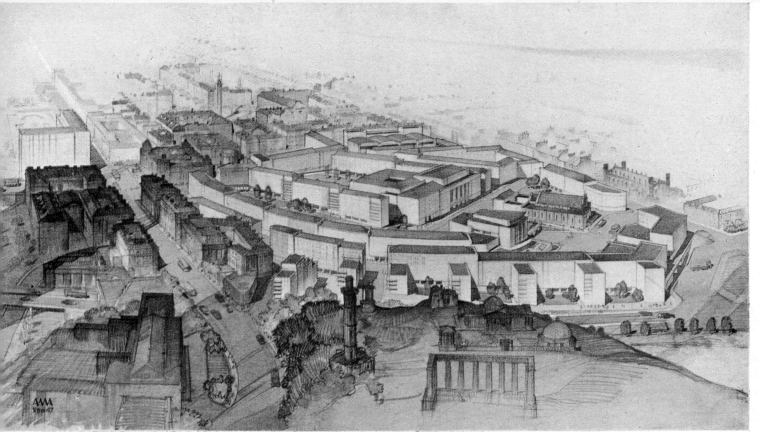

This perspective represents the first esquisse study for St. James' Square/ Leith Street scheme. The amended scheme may be seen on Plate XXVII, p. 82.

This photograph shows in the foreground part of the St. James' Square/Leith Street area as it exists to-day. The bottom left-hand corner shows the roofless building of the Theatre Royal and the awkwardly shaped piece of built-up property separating Leith Walk from Picardy Place. Rising steeply in the background is the Calton Hill which would give a fine setting to this festival centre.

[p. 70]

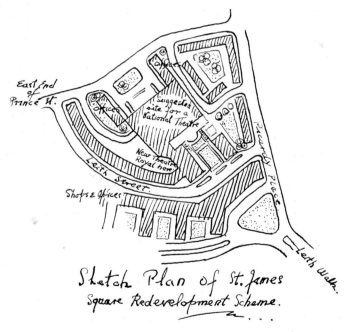

Sketch Plan of St. James Square Redevelopment Scheme.

This is another view of this locality for the festival centre showing the intensely built-up habitations. See p. 79 and p. 78 on Plate XXVII for typical close up views of the kind of property to be found here.

[p. 69]

PLATE XXVI

5. *Central Commercial and Shopping Precincts* : *Princes Street, Melville Street, etc.*

These central commercial and shopping precincts are based upon Princes Street, Melville Street and Shandwick Place and Leith Street. The locations of these proposed land uses are manifestly necessary, as they form the hub of city commercial life. The total extent, however, is one which calls for searching investigation, in order to ensure that no more residential property is absorbed than is absolutely necessary for this purpose. A glance at the Land Utilisation Map of the existing use of property for this area shows beyond doubt that the area zoned for this commercial use of land, corresponds very closely to an existing predominant use. In total ground area there is not a very great increase contemplated, but the total floor area can be very considerably increased as and when the demand arises. This demand is considered likely to arise from the future Lothians and Fifeshire industrial developments, which will increase the commercial importance of Edinburgh as the capital city. To meet this, additional floor space area is provided in the Princes Street architectural scheme, involving the increased height of many of the existing buildings, and, in the St. James' Square and Leith Street redevelopment scheme, where the upper storeys should be for commercial use rather than the existing residential use. It should be borne in mind also that there is every reason to avoid fragmentary groups of housing in this commercial zone not only because of the desire to avoid the inevitable conflict between the domestic use of buildings and a commercial one but in order to conform to the principle of community planning where a minimum total population of 5 to 10 thousand persons is required to support minimum community services. For this reason a convenient line has been drawn based upon the road widening scheme for Palmerston Place with Drumsheugh Gardens and Chester Street, Queen Street and York Place forming the northern limits as may be seen upon the City Centre Plan.

(i) *The Gradual Transformation of the New Town from Residential to Office, Shop and Industrial Use.* Early maps of the 'New Town' of Edinburgh clearly showed that this area which lies about a central axis between St. Andrew's Square and Charlotte Square and Melville Street, was designed for residential buildings. George Street was the principal street with Princes Street and Queen Street definitely taking second place. Rose Street and Hill Street, which run parallel and immediately behind George Street formed the 'mews' of this residential development. This former " grid iron " form of planning is fortunate and lends itself admirably to the modern requirements of a commercial centre. If the transformation could have been controlled architecturally, there is no doubt that there could not have been a better form of design for present day needs. Rose Street lends itself admirably for a service road for delivery vehicles to the shops, but the increased height of the buildings fronting this street should, of course, have been much more limited. Light and air have been denied to many of the habitable rooms and much of it now has become slum property. The Plan suggests that in the architectural reconstruction scheme, these back areas of Princes Street and George Street should be replaced with a much lower construction of buildings with the ground floor dedicated in the main for loading bays and car parking. This is a method which has been adopted before as a means of overcoming the difficulties of vehicular access to central built up areas. Some examples of this are to be found in New York City and elsewhere.

(ii) *Industry in Central area at back of Princes Street.* The local types of industry found in the survey in George Street, Princes Street etc., are of a small local workshop type whose trade lies about this centre of commerce. For this reason it would be appropriate for these small workshop industries to be located in the reconstructed Rose Street and Hill Street as indicated on the Plan and illustrated in its three dimensions on the large scale model for this central area.

6. *Festival and Entertainment Centres* : *Usher Hall and St. James Square.*

These two centres, one at the Usher Hall behind the towering mediaeval castle, and one at St. James Square, should satisfy the needs of a bi-focal communication centre. This is yet another instance of the influence that topography in Edinburgh has in the distribution of land use. The Castle ridge and valley together with the Calton Hill, so divide the centre from the eastern and western parts of the city that it would be wrong to concentrate the needs of the Festival and other cultural functions in one centre. In both, it would be necessary to provide concert halls, theatres, cinemas and, in particular, the music practice rooms and studios for the creation of a centre for educational purposes. One of the principle purposes of the Festival is to increase the understanding of music and drama and, as much as possible, develop local talent. To achieve this, it is felt essential that adequate accommodation suitably grouped and designed to attain almost a collegiate atmosphere, must be provided in these centres.

(i) *Usher Hall.* As regards location, there is already the nucleus of such a centre in the Usher Hall, Lyceum Theatre and Synod Hall, situated between Lothian Road and Castle Terrace. With its important front to Princes Street Gardens and the Castle, the slopes down to Kingstables Road can be made into attractive terraced gardens as part of the general composition, while the redevelopment of the built up portion of the area could include little forecourts or patios as local centres for social contact.

(ii) *St. James Square.* The St. James Square area was selected because it offers a natural compact area close to the eastern communication centre, with magnificent views from its steep slopes to Leith Walk, of the Firth of Forth and the Fifeshire mountains. Here it is suggested that Edinburgh might find the most appropriate site for a Civic Theatre and Concert Hall with music practice rooms and lecture rooms in the upper storeys. The basement floors would provide additional garage accommodation. The huge building containing this theatre and concert hall would be approached from St. James Square, but the principal front should be the one overlooking the terraces which offer a magnificent view of the Firth of Forth.

These terraces, the principal one of which would be situated on the roof of the proposed underground garage to be constructed mainly upon the site of the present Theatre Royal, would be on the north eastern side. The Theatre Royal, which was gutted by fire in 1946, was the subject of consideration by the Town Council in July 1947, when application was made by the proprietors for consent to reinstate their burnt out building. The whole of this Festival Centre Scheme was prepared in advance of this report at the request of the Town Council so that it might guide them in considering this application. Consideration resulted in refusal of consent to the application and encouragement was, therefore, derived to go forward with this scheme and include it as one of the principal features of the recommendations in this report. The Secretary of State for Scotland subsequently turned down the appeal made by the applicants against this decision.

Evidence was given that the whole of the area could not be redeveloped adequately without the removal of the Theatre Royal from its present site. Further, from the architectural stand-point both the Roman Catholic Cathedral which abuts on the present Theatre Royal site and the Theatre Royal could then be given a suitable architectural setting. Moreover, a more appropriate place could not be found for the essential garaging facilities urgently required to relieve congestion at the East End of Princes Street, in Leith Street and York Place than the site of the Theatre Royal. The magnificent view of the Firth of Forth already referred to could not be satisfactorily obtained without the removal of this Theatre.

Apart from these aspects, the whole scheme from Greenside and Calton Hill to York Place on the Northern limit of the area was ripe for redevelopment within the meaning of the Town and Country Planning Act: that is to say, the area consists of a bad lay-out of roads and derelict or slum housing. The Social Survey indicates, for example, that the new site proposed for the Theatre Royal contained only six reasonably fit dwellings out of a total of 283, while another back area of property immediately behind, contained only one fit dwelling out of 255.

About this Festival Centre, there are the Leith Street shopping centre buildings, those fronting York Place and Greenside which should be reconstructed for other commercial purposes, the existing population of 3,763 persons to be decentralised and redistributed in the alternative residential areas suggested in the Report.

TABLE X.

St. JAMES' SQUARE AREA.

Block	Fit Dwellings	Fit Pop.	S-S Dwellings	S-S Pop.	Unfit Dwellings	Unfit Pop.	Totals Dwellings	Totals Pop.
14	7	23	23	77	16	53	46	153
15	17	54	22	69	62	195	101	318
16	13	38	1	3	—	—	14	41
17	1	3	62	184	192	568	255	755
18	—	—	9	24	1	3	10	27
19	8	32	22	86	3	12	33	130
20				No Housing				
21	7	22	76	236	201	623	284	881
22	—	—	13	64	—	—	13	64
23	—	—	3	15	1	5	4	20
24	6	24	31	125	21	85	58	234
25	2	8	39	154	248	978	289	1,140
Totals ...	61	204	301	1,037	745	2,522	1,107	3,763

Figures in heavy type other than totals refer to property affected by the new Theatre Royal scheme.

7. *Enlargement of the Government Administrative Centres.*

St. Andrew's House, built just before the war, set up a new government administrative centre on the slopes of Calton Hill. Since then Government services have expanded enormously to an extent that the present building is totally inadequate to house all the departments now required. At the same time it is known that the Royal High School lying on the opposite side of the road, but further to the east of St. Andrew's House, is scheduled for removal in the school provisions for the future which have been allowed for in the school planning section of this report. It is proposed, therefore, that this building should be if re-modelling is not feasible to provide the additional accommodation required in this new government administrative centre. The architectural merits of the existing building are known and appreciated but it is felt that there is an overriding claim for reconstruction in this case, as it has outlasted its useful life. It is, therefore, proposed that this building site should be developed as an extension of St. Andrew's House.

The buildings flanking Royal Terrace and Regent Terrace were originally designed as magnificent dwellings in the 'grand manner' of the renaissance period. These buildings have steadily been converted into offices and hotels on account of their extreme difficulty of up-keep as dwellings. The hotel use of these houses is known to be unsatisfactory owing to the 'rigid' nature of their original design making them impossible of reasonable conversion. To add these to the list of buildings for preservation would burden Edinburgh and its ratepayers unduly and deprive the city of accommodation which is far too valuable to be lost. The Plan, therefore, suggests a complete re-modelling of these dwellings as hotels. The geographical position is close enough to the centre of the City and the festival centre of St. James Square to make it a most desirable place for hotel accommodation.

8. *University Precinct : Removal of Bristo Street Traffic.*

The University Centre put forward as a scheme by the University authorities on the advice of their consultant Dr. Holden, forms the major part of a huge cultural centre stretching from the Grassmarket and Cowgate in the north to the Meadows in the south, Lauriston Gardens in the west and Potterrow in the east—an area of some 112 acres in extent. This cultural centre would contain not only the University precinct, both existing and proposed, but such buildings as museum, art display centres, etc. Indeed, the Scottish National Gallery might well be transferred to this centre where it would be better placed and room for expansion could be provided.

The siting of this cultural precinct is determined partly by the fact that many of the buildings required are already situated there such as the Old University building itself, the M'Ewan Hall and medical departments and the adjoining hospital of the Royal Infirmary which holds close liaison with the medical school of the University.

(i) *Traffic Problem.* Bristo Street would of necessity be closed in order to obtain the precinctal qualities desired for this cultural centre. It is a road used by both local traffic and long distance through traffic, though the local traffic is predominant. Bristo Street forms an integral part of the route to the southern part of the city via George IV Bridge and the Mound. It is anticipated that this traffic would normally use the north to south by-pass of Nicholson Street and the 'Bridges' with which connection is obtained by the new road running parallel to Market Street and beneath the North Bridge. In this respect, the Police department which has examined the problem in relation to this proposal is satisfied. It is known also that the Lauriston Place traffic, that normally uses Teviot Place and Marshall Street, could quite conveniently be brought on to the north to south by-pass via Forrest Road and Chambers Street. It should also be borne in mind that the commercial vehicles at present using Bristo Street and Potterrow would no longer do so once the University buildings have replaced the commercial premises that attract them.

The city transport services affected by the scheme would be adequately met, in the opinion of the Transport Department,

Model showing Central Area Proposals from north-east

This photograph shows the amended scheme worked out on a 1/500 scale model for the St. James' Square Festival Centre. Details of the scheme for the proposed theatre and concert halls together with the garden terraces built upon the site of the present Theatre Royal appear in Appendix V. Advantage has been taken of the topography to obtain a series of terraces built upon excavated ground to form one or more floor levels for garaging facilities. Beneath these terraces would run the tunnel entrance to the Princes Street three-tier road scheme. This tunnel entrance should be constructed at the same time as the new Theatre Royal and new concert halls are constructed together with their garaging facilities.

[p. 82]

Property lying between St. James' Square and Leith Street   [p. 79]

[P. 79]. This shows more property lying between St. James' Square and Leith Street. Where there was once back gardens or yards these have now been completely built over by multifarious industrial workshops which have both restricted the limited light to the habitations and destroyed their amenities.

Backs of tenements behind St. James' Square   [p. 78]

[P. 78]. This shows a typical view of the backs of the existing tenements behind St. James' Square which now consist of an indescribable collection of derelict buildings. These buildings have been very little altered since they were constructed in the late 18th century.

[p. 80]

This is a typical communal staircase to the tenements in St. James' Square which is traversed daily by the many families occupying this multi-storey tenement. Obviously such property should be demolished at the earliest opportunity. It is upon such property that the new Festival Centre would arise and from which many families would be transferred to new housing schemes to be provided for them.

PLATE XXVII

[P. 67]. *This is a birds eye view of the property facing Morrison Street most of which will be rebuilt in the scheme for the new combined station. The site of the station is upon the goods yard seen at the extreme right-hand corner of the photograph.*

[p. 64]

[p. 68]

Usher Hall area from Castle   [p. 65]

Arthur's Seat and North Bridge   [p. 59]

St. Cuthbert's Church from Castle   [p. 66]

[P. 64]. *A view of the Usher Hall area from the Castle showing the terraced gardens in the foreground.*

[P. 65]. *Another view of the Usher Hall Festival Centre area as seen from the Castle.*

[P. 66]. *The two churches, St. Cuthbert's and St. John's, at the West End as seen from the Castle. Corstorphine Hill may be seen rising from the wooded slopes in the background.*

[P. 68]. *This is a general view of the west central part of Edinburgh with the Castle dominating the scene. The Grassmarket is seen in the middle-left flanked by tall tenement buildings.*

[P. 59]. *Edinburgh vies with many famous continental cities in presenting this fine view from Princes Street of Arthur's Seat and Salisbury Craggs. The old cast iron North Bridge appears in the foreground.*

PLATE XXVIII

This is an aerial view showing the Usher Hall at the bottom right-hand corner dominated by the Castle which provides a magnificent setting for the projected Festival Centre. The serried roofs of the Caledonian Station seen in the foreground will be replaced by a modern hotel, the station itself being replaced by the combined station at Morrison Street in the railway scheme. Convenience of access to this Festival Centre may be appreciated from the close proximity of Princes Street which is seen on the extreme left-hand side of the photograph.

[p. 36]

[p. 38]

[p. 110]

[p. 37]

[P. 110]. This shows a view of the New Town area extending northwards beyond Queens Gardens. It shows Great King Street joining Royal Circus with Drummond Place and forms the core of this part of the New Town extension. Development further northwards rapidly deteriorates as it reaches the Silvermills area seen to the middle-left of the picture.

[P. 38]. An aerial view of the High Street with St. Giles Cathedral in the middle foreground.

[P. 37]. A view of St. Andrew's Square which forms the terminal feature of George Street.

PLATE XXIX

A fine view of the eastern central part of Edinburgh showing Arthur's Seat in the foreground with North Bridge and Waverley Bridge crossing the valley and the railway which passes through it. It is a great pity that this station and railway have been allowed to dominate this famous valley. By diverting the main line railway by means of the tunnel proposed under the Meadows it would be possible to cover in this railway and station and retrieve the valley for terraced gardens. St. Andrew's Square is seen in the bottom left-hand corner of the photograph and the Scott Monument looming up in the centre.

[p. 74]

General View *[p. 75]*

An aerial view of Eglinton Crescent and Grosvenor Crescent and of St. Mary's Cathedral which forms part of the new town western extension. It is doubtful whether the existing buildings will for ever provide a convenient and economic form of habitation, but the road layout may be retained should rebuilding in the future prove necessary.

General View *[p. 73]*

This is an aerial view of the new town showing Charlotte Square in the foreground and St. Andrew's Square in the background linked by George Street. Princes Street is seen parallel to the gardens on the right-hand side dominated by the Castle while Queen Street and its gardens are seen defining the northern limit of the New Town on the left-hand side of the photograph. Calton Hill is seen in the background and the West End of Princes Street together with the Caledonian Hotel and Station in the bottom foreground.

PLATE XXX

by this same system of roads, while No. 9 bus service with its terminus at Greenbank could quite well proceed via Lothian Road and the local by-pass of Earl Grey Street suggested in the City Centre Plan. From the traffic point of view this cultural precinct does not present any insuperable problems and Middle Meadow Walk which was at one time considered as a relief road required by the closing of Bristo Street would be preserved as an essential feature maintaining access between the Royal Infirmary and the University proper.

(ii) *George Square.* Some of the existing buildings around George Square are relics of the first developments that took place outside the Old Town and were the one time habitations of some famous Scotsmen including Sir Walter Scott. The Square has a domestic character of some considerable charm though the buildings present a strange sense of the incongruous between the comparative coarseness of this early masonry of Naysmith's and the delicacy of the doorway architecture. Recent alterations have however entirely altered the north side and parts of the other sides also and have destroyed much of this original charm. Though the old buildings are not without historical and architectural interest, the Square, as a whole, should not be rated as high as some in the 'New Town' such as Moray Place and Anne Street, where there are no incursions. The case for preservation should not only take the architectural and historical value into account but also the possibilities of what can be achieved by building anew. The use of the Square in the University proposals hinges largely on the fact that it is the only large open space about which the larger University buildings could find a suitable setting. In this respect there must be no repetition of the mistake made in the past of allowing other development to 'crowd' the scheme as was permitted in the case of the Old University buildings whose position and scale cannot be appreciated without clearing the buildings on the opposite side of Nicholson Street. If, however, George Square could not be reconstructed for these larger buildings in the University Scheme, another open space would have to be created of comparable scale in the locality. There is, therefore, economy in the use of existing features in these proposals of the University authorities. Another factor that has been considered is the presence of a large number of University buildings already in George Square. It is suggested therefore, that the University might be permitted to proceed with the rebuilding of the north side in such a way that the new buildings would be neighbourly and in harmony with the existing buildings on the other three sides of the Square where the majority of the old buildings are still existing. Though it is hoped that it might be possible to make use for many years of the existing buildings on these other three sides they should not stand in the way of a good architectural development scheme with the total transference of the square to University use. Care should at the same time be taken to ensure that the existing public accesses are not in any way curtailed.

9. *Grassmarket and Heriot's School.*

Adherence to the suggestions of the Royal Mile Report by Mr. MacRae for the extension of Heriot's School by two wings fronting on to the Grassmarket is made as seen in the Plan. This extension represents important requirements of the Heriot School Authorities and would appear to hold a prior claim for the redevelopment on the south side of the Grassmarket.

10. *Water of Leith Walk in the Central Area: Dean Village.*

This walk represents one of the most attractive parts of the whole of the Water of Leith Valley as it is to-day. It is partly accessible to the general public though the majority of its gardens are semi-private of the kind which is frequently found in Edinburgh to-day. Access to these parts may only be obtained as a member contributing to the up-keep of the gardens. It is suggested that these gardens should now be acquired for complete freedom of access to the public in order to make the whole of the valley scheme a public promenade from one end to the other, as described in the chapter on recreation spaces. The suggestion is put forward for a considerable thinning out of some of the trees in the present gorge-like part of the valley, as it is felt that the number of trees excludes too much sunlight and obscures the attractive course of the Water of Leith itself. An interesting old print of this part of the valley shows a very sparse allowance of trees and shrubs with the result that the lawns on the slopes of either side of the river are much more attractive than to-day. A reproduction of this old print appears on Plate No. XLVIII. The Dean Village which lies on the westward side of the Dean Bridge, which spans the Water of Leith Valley, contains some very interesting old buildings and warehouses which, it is felt, could be restored for modern use. Much of the additions to the village in the earlier part of this century might well be demolished and rebuilt to harmonise more satisfactorily with the old character of this village.

11. *Central Markets.*

The principal market in the central area is, of course, the fruit market, at present using Market Street adjacent to Waverley Station. There is a meat market also at Fountainbridge, though the slaughtering now takes place at Slateford. The fruit market was at one time in the Waverley Market building though an early plan shows a much larger place for it lying opposite and on either side of the North Bridge. It also occupied a greater width of the valley, since given up for use by the railway. The squeezing out, by railway development, of this market, has thrown Market Street into a chronic state of congestion where S.M.T. buses and other vehicles have considerable difficulty in making their way through the conglomeration of market vehicles and baskets of vegetables. Since the development of road transport, the importance of this area as a market centre, originally dependent upon railway transport no longer exists. In view of this and the possibilities brought out in the Plan for the recovery of the valley for recreation, it is proposed that a new fruit market centre should be set up at Morrison Street which now becomes in the Plan a very important focal centre of the communication system. It would also be close by the new railway termini should any future advantage be found in such proximity.

The meat market at Fountainbridge could also be located in the same area and its present site used for building a new school.

Fig 1.

Fig 2.

Fig 3.

Fig 4.

Fig 5.

Fig. 1—The above shows the proposals in the plan for redeveloping the Theatre Royal area. Architecturally the problem is one of providing a proper setting for three important public buildings— a civic theatre and concert halls, new Theatre Royal and the principal Catholic Church. The composition requires a terraced garden space in front and beside these buildings so that their shape, scale and proportion may be satisfactorily appreciated. The terraced garden could be used for sitting-out space and refreshment and with garage space beneath.

Fig. 2—The two important public buildings shown are the old Theatre Royal and Roman Catholic Cathedral seen crammed together each vieing with the other for domination giving an unsatisfactory architectural front to Broughton Street. A less satisfactory arrangement could not be conceived: the theatre shuts out daylight from one side of the cathedral and the latter prevents the essential provision of emergency exits along one side of the theatre.

Fig. 3—This shows the proposed rebuilding at the top of Leith Walk.

Fig. 4—This indicates an idea of the nature of the rebuilding proposed at the rear of the new Roman Catholic Church.

Fig. 5—This is a suggestion for the treatment for reconstruction of the lower part of Leith Street.

PLATE XXXI

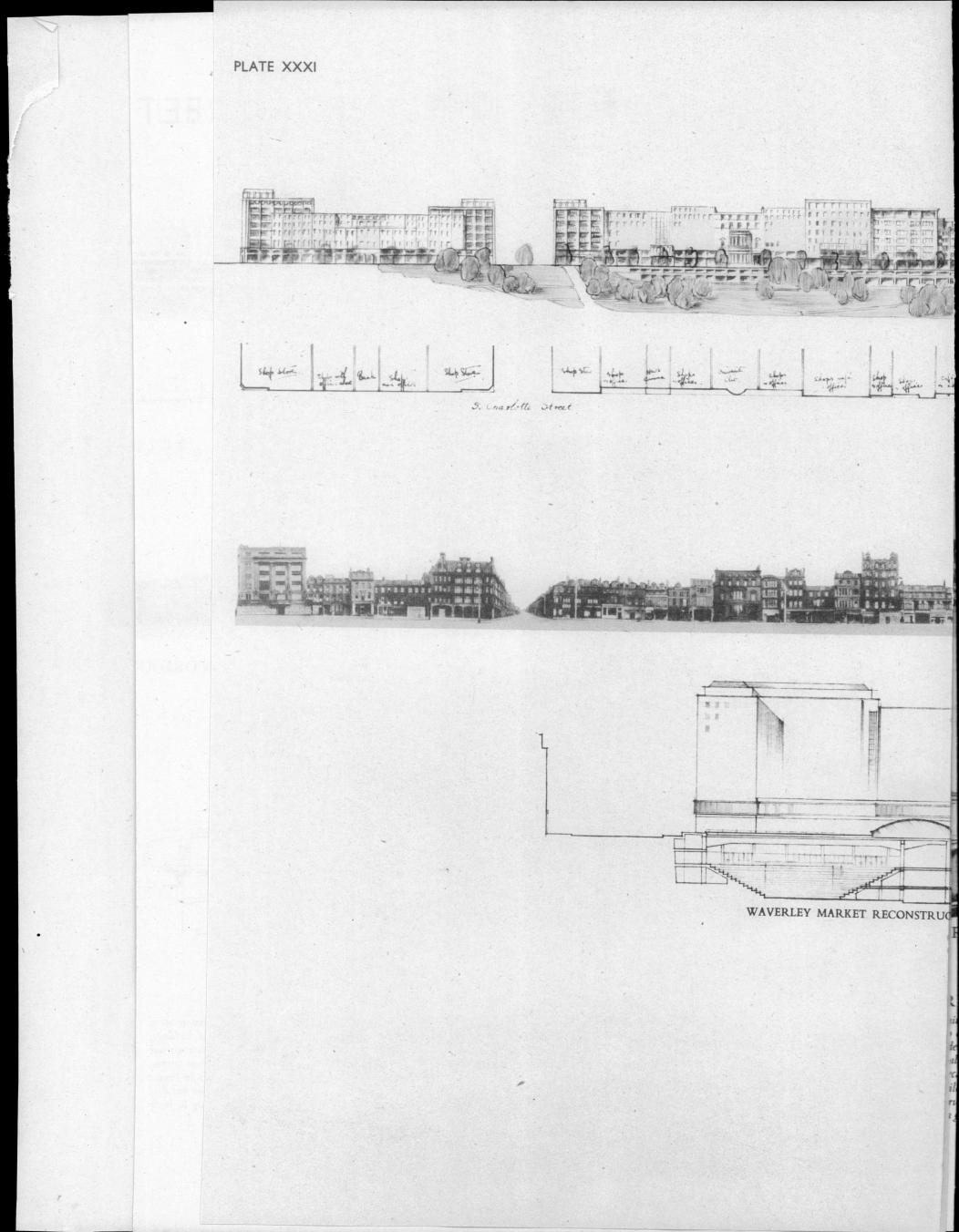

S. Charlotte Street

WAVERLEY MARKET RECONSTRUC

Waverley Bridge

North Bridge

Hotel   shop
         store   shop + office   shop
                                   store

S. S.t David Street

water
frees   hotel   shop
                  offices book.

S. S.t Andrew Street.

Register House

Derek Phurstan

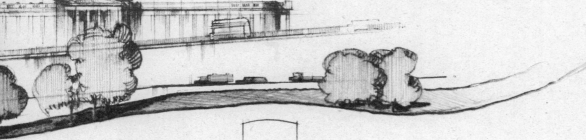

RDENS SHOWING THE

EET

CHAPTER EIGHT

URBAN ARCHITECTURE: MEDIAEVAL AND RENAISSANCE

THE MODERN PROBLEM

INTRODUCTION. No city could show more clean-cut examples, each excellent in themselves, in close juxtaposition and yet distinct, of the two great historic types of planning and architecture, the picturesque and formal, the mediaeval and classical, than Edinburgh. In spite of a considerable amount of rebuilding and an almost wholesale change of use, the High Street and Canongate on one side of the valley, and the New Town on the other declare their completely different aesthetic and social philosophies to the most casual observer. Everything is present to heighten the contrast: the old Town, starting from a rugged castle rock, descending along the crest of a ridge and ending in a Palace backed by an extinct volcano of savage barrenness: the New Town sitting pretty on a gentle slope, the terminal features of its main regular street a church and bank facing across the prim grass and trees of a town square. Architectural treatment is no less antithetical: although High Street and Canongate contain fewer mediaeval buildings than is often supposed, the general effect of the individualistic treatment of the 17th century buildings is mediaeval; and there are numerous incidents, St. Giles Church, the Tron, the Tolbooth, gateways, varying widths, deflection from the straight, different height and above all the descending level, to produce a picturesque (in the literal sense) scene. In the new Town, with the exception of the front of Princes Street, which is indeed irregular without being picturesque (in any sense) and which will be studied in detail later, the sober level character of what is popularly known as Georgian architecture is maintained, in spite of a few recent exceptions.

Finally, by way of contrast, may be opposed the northern front of the Old Town—to the valley, to the southern facade of the New Town—the already mentioned Princes Street. It is interesting to observe that whereas both these town fronts (and it is rare in a British town to find a town front at all) are largely composed of modern buildings, the Old Town has fared better than the New: Playfair's Gothic towers may not be very real gothic, certain banks and newspaper buildings may be in overblown neo-georgian and Patrick Geddes Hostels may be a little fussy and flimsy, but the general effect topped by Pugin's splendid spire is undeniably satisfying to the amateur of the sharawaggi, even if one discounts the real, the genuine, the utilitarian picturesque of the sublime castle and rock which sheds its lustre over the whole scene. And yet, such is the benificence of atmosphere and perspective, and distance-lending enchantment, there are views from above the Mound, such as our artist has caught, where the New Town, characteristically dominated by its green-domed church, shows up, in spite of the Princes Street anarchy, surprisingly well. Of course, it must be remembered that in Edinburgh, the topography, the very anatomy of the landscape, is eternally noble.

It is fortunate that Edinburgh possesses a full survey of old and new towns produced by Mr. MacRae to show not only what exists but what is worthy of preservation. How such preservation can be carried out consistently with the living needs of a community has two aspects: the application of protective regulations and the principles governing changing conditions. It is of the greatest value to have available an authoritative opinion upon what must at all costs remain intact as compared with that which, though worthy of retaining, may have to give way to more insistant demands.

There will be many cases of individual rebuilding required within these areas of architectural importance which will call for sympathetic treatment (whether administered under legal control or under enlightened architectural practice) but it must be remembered that sympathy must be shown not only towards the work of the past but to the needs of the future.

But two problems must be faced in any plan for the city, both owing to the importance of the situations and to the imminent redevelopment on a large scale: these are the High Street and Canongate, and Princes Street. Their different characters (already mentioned) call for the exercise of different approaches: High Street and Canongate are largely a question of enlightened continuance of an existing tradition: Princes Street needs the creation of something new to take the place of what is there now.

It need hardly be necessary to state that these two problems are not merely a matter of finding a suitable aesthetic solution to each. There are the equally important factors of use and bulk (or floor space) zoning which must be decided upon before any rebuilding scheme is contemplated. The original use for which these old parts of Edinburgh were built may be found to have been departed from, e.g., in the New Town the original residential user has been largely changed to commercial, which is in conformity with planning requirements. This changed use naturally affects the building and to attempt to cloak it with a semblance of the original use is a false piece of development. This applies equally where, as in the lower Canongate it is decided to continue an existing use; here a non-conforming industrial building may be prepared to hide itself behind a domestic mask: this skin-deep conformity leads not only to insincere building but to anomalies in zoning of deep-seated mal-adjustment. Again, the change in bulk or floor space will alter the height of the building and introduce a new factor into its external appearance which must be boldly faced.

There is, therefore, the closest inter-relationship between the use and volume (or floorspace) of the property and its external appearance, calling for utilitarian and aesthetic co-operation. There is perhaps a modern tendency★ to suggest that if practical requirements are met, a satisfactory architectural appearance is inevitable. This is not the place to discuss so complex a problem: but even if it were demonstrable that this result is possible in a single buidling, it is much more remote for the groups of buildings that form a town, a neighbourhood or a street. Some more detailed remarks upon the narrower subject of stylistic harmony or contrast will be found in the section upon rebuilding Princes Street.

There is also the further question of the degree or absence of administrative control, also affecting this vital question of

★—In English Mem. on Rebuilding.

third dimensional appearance, during a period of rebuilding.

A detailed account of the proposals affecting these two distinct localities of the city is given below.

1. The Old Town.
   (a) High Street and Canongate.
   (b) Zoning Proposals: three distinct zones: Castle Hill and Lawnmarket, High Street, Canongate.
   (c) Mr. MacRae's Royal Mile Report.
       Analysis of proposed changes.
   (d) The Breweries.
2. The New Town.
   (a) A conscious effort at Planning.
   (b) Princes Street Architectural Scheme.
       (i) Use and Height Zoning.
       (ii) Architectural Composition.

1. THE OLD TOWN.

(a) *High Street and Canongate.*

This masterpiece of nature, the ridge from the Castle to Holyrood, stands clear above the centre part of Edinburgh. As seen from Blackford Hill Sir Walter Scott describes it as follows :—

> " Where the huge castle holds it state,
> and all the steep slope down,
> Whose ridgy back heaves to the sky,
> Piled deep and massy, close and high,
> Mine own romantic town ! "

There lies the historic centre of the city seen from miles around, with the Castle as its dominating feature and the Royal Palace terminating at the lower end of this " ridgy back." It was the smoke haze seen hanging round and above it by people on ships in the Firth of Forth and by people at work in the quiet country fields that gave it the name of " Auld Reekie." A close observation confirms expectations of smoke begrimed walls that present a gloomy contrast to the modern building in this age of electricity. The dinginess of these flanking buildings is strange and surprising to those who expect something better of such a Royal centre. Holyrood Palace " stands great and silent in a workmen's quarter " and many breweries and gas works " says R. L. Stevenson. Can the Palace be retrieved from such squalor or must it for ever be condemned to these alien surroundings ?

The great pile of buildings mounting high on this ridge presents a multi-storey aspect of sky-scraper character to the stroller along Princes Street, though in the High Street itself there is no such abnormality to be appreciated. It is quite bewildering to the untravelled Englishman who enters a building from the High Street, descends several storeys apparently into the bowels of the earth, only to discover himself one or two landings still above ground. It is characteristic of these dwellings or " lands " as they are locally termed. To the European this is no new experience. It is typical of walled cities built in precarious positions where defence against marauders forced compactness of structure necessitating buildings of considerable height and density.

The architecture, influenced by the lofty nature of the structures, follows a vertical vernacular of mediaeval character with corbelled corners and turret windows. The turnpike stair is much in evidence with its tall rounded projection rising to the full height of the building and often simply roofed by a continuation of the main roof over it. There is nothing of an Elizabethen character of the half timber type except Huntly House with its oversailing second storey.

Property use has, since the earliest times, been mixed. Trades started in the homes of the craftsmen may be considered a mixed use of little nuisance to one's neighbours. In fact it is an asset and convenience to all, but such mixing is poles apart from the comparative industrial giants of to-day which have now grown up among the dwellings. They grew as deterioration spread among the property after the well-to-do left for the New Town and George Square developments. In fact, industry not only swallowed up many of the houses built in the 16th and 17th centuries upon the original garden spaces, but have also built higher and more intensely than ever. The latter ' permitted-development ' is undoubtedly the cause of great deterioration of housing property and loss of revenue in the Royal Mile as we know it to-day. The City Architect in 1945 reported that only 65% of the total of both frontages of the Royal Mile now consists of dwellings and, only 7% of these were up to modern standards. The Social Survey in 1946, carried out in connection with this report, indicated 50% of the dwellings in this district as unfit for human habitation. They form a very thin veneer to the non-residential users on the erstwhile garden space behind : slumdom is the inevitable result of such permitted encroachment. Not one of the "lands" or "hotels" can be described as providing normal standards of decent living in this Royal Mile stretch from Castle to Palace. Let the sentimentalist reflect, for it is indeed easy to be a conservator of others' discomforts. When the rich lived there, they were able to maintain an aggregation of comfort not known to-day. Now, however, there is nothing but an aggregation of discomfort, for the populace have not the means to provide otherwise.

To-day, as of old, a single house (in the English meaning of the word), may be occupied by 40 or 50 families living sometimes separately, sometimes sharing apartments—mainly in mean and hideous conditions of discomfort. (The Social Survey of 1946 showed 55 families sharing apartments in the Canongate district). Is this habit of living, born of troublous times for reasons of safety and defence, to be perpetuated as an ancient tradition worthy of preservation ? Or is the house and garden protagonist of the inter-war years a trend of enlightened times ? Defoe said of the old town " . . . . for though many cities have more people living " in them yet I believe that in no city of the world so many " live in so little room."

What then is the answer ? To pull down and rebuild in a modern idiom or to reconstruct in the traditional manner ? Either is possible, though the latter may mean sacrificing in some small measure the conveniences of a house planned and designed as a truly modern residence. As the old buildings have a generous distribution of windows the prospects for modern internal planning are good. Before that can be agreed upon, however, an important town planning decision of zoning for the most appropriate land use must be made. It is no solution to rebuild houses there if the factories are allowed to remain and to permeate the air, even to the innermost room, with the smells of processing and with smoke and grime. The unequal fight that such conditions impose upon the family will soon reduce the new buildings to slumdom once again. It is no solution if the continually expanding factories of these past 200 years are allowed to continue. It is important, therefore, to define what we mean when we say : ' let us restore the character of the Royal Mile.' Is it the character of to-day or the character of 200 years ago ? They are, in reality, two entirely different conceptions. The Royal Mile has changed its character over the past 200 years immeasurably, and will continue to do so in direct conflict with a rehousing programme so long as factories are permitted to stay. It is a medical fact that no family can exist healthily in close proximity to factory processing. Mr. MacRae in his Royal Mile Report estimated, after close consultation with the

Grassmarket at Night   *[p. 43]*

This floodlit scene of the Castle dominating the tall tenements
in the West Bow provides a striking and characteristic view of mediaeval
Edinburgh.   Restoration to retain the architectural character of the old
city is recommended.

PLATE XXXII

Castle Esplanade [p. 44]

[P. 44]. This is a view of the Castle Esplanade approached by the narrow entrance of Castle Hill seen in the background with the draw-bridge and arch in the foreground. Pugin's Gothic Spire of Tolbooth Church rises in the background. Sir Patrick Geddes' castellated Outlook Tower is also in the background with the Camera Obscura housed in the roof.

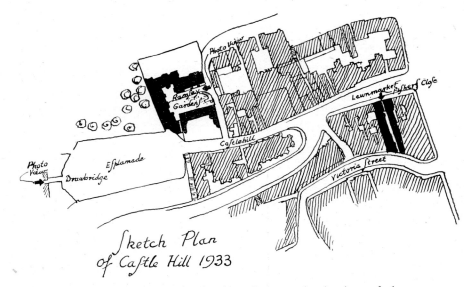

Sketch Plan
of Castle Hill 1933

This is a sketch plan showing the locality of the Castle Esplanade in relation to the High Street as it appears in present-day Edinburgh.

[P. 45]. This is a view of Fisher's Close and retains one of the few mediaeval streets that run down the side of the ridge which contained the old mediaeval town of Edinburgh. Careful detailed planning and considerable restoration work for these buildings is urgently required. The Plan recommends that industry should be cleared from the locality in order to provide good healthy surroundings to the new homes that can be created.

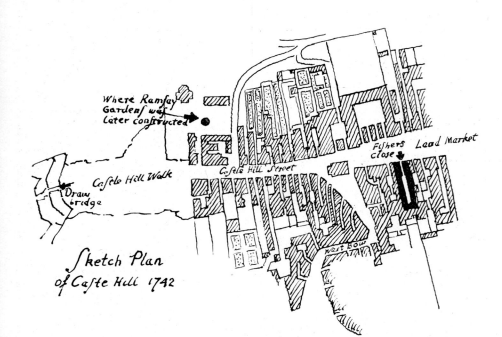

Sketch Plan
of Castle Hill 1742

This sketch is an extract from Edgar's Map of Mediaeval Edinburgh of 1742 showing how much the locality has changed in plan.

Fisher's Close [p. 45]

PLATE XXXIII

Ramsay Gardens [*p. 46*]

[P. 46]. Behind Castle Hill on the northern slopes lies the delightful residential part of Ramsay Gardens. They represent a recent development of this century. They have been retained in the Plan.

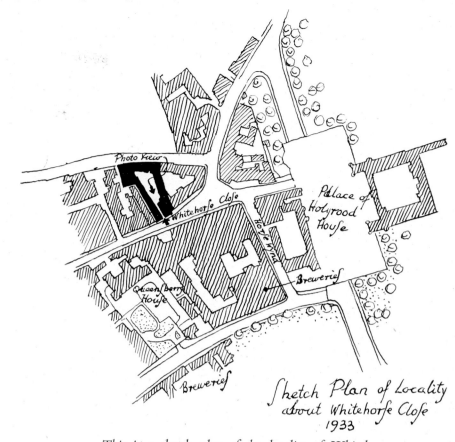

Sketch Plan of Locality about Whitehorse Close 1933

This is a sketch plan of the locality of Whitehorse Close as it appears on Ordnance Plans to-day. A comparison with the extract of Edgar's Plan shows the change that has taken place since 1742.

[P. 47]. At the foot of the Canongate and behind it lies Whitehorse Close which is recommended for restoration for residential use. It will be necessary to retain as garden space the property already demolished to the west of the close in order to give adequate internal light and air to the restored dwellings. Until a firm decision is made to remove the breweries none of this property should be used as homes.

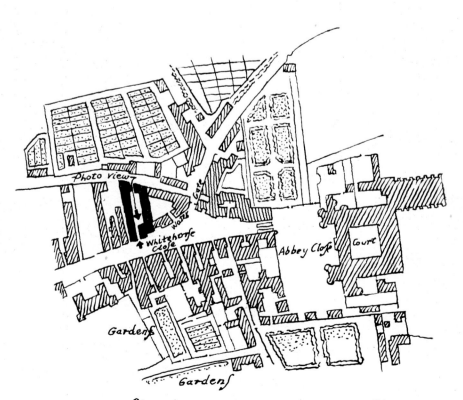

Sketch Plan showing Whitehorse Close in 1742

Whitehorse Close [*p. 47*]

PLATE XXXIV

This is a photograph of the 1/500 scale model showing the Princes Street scheme and the extent of change possible by covering in the railway and station to form garden terraces. The new road proposals which include the by-pass of North Bridge, the colonnading required to give light and air to the bye-pass of Princes Street seen beneath it, the new link between the North Bridge by-pass and the Princes Street by-pass at the Mound give an exciting result to the many improvements suggested for this central part of Edinburgh. Tremendous improvements are possible in the reconstruction scheme for the Waverley Market and in the delightful prospect for new garden architecture. Details of the new architecture for both the Princes Street scheme and the High Street can only be finally determined in co-operation with individual developers. Only the appropriate massing and proportion of building structures are shown.

PLATE XXXV

Medical Officer for Health, that, if this mixing of dwellings and factories was to continue as indicated in his plan, the present population of some 10,000 persons would have to be reduced drastically to less than one third. There would be no community life for this remaining population if scattered in small groups of 100 here and 50 there, over one third of a square mile. We cannot therefore, adhere to a scheme which retains a domestic use under such a serious handicap, until it is agreed to remove industry from the Canongate and St. Leonards areas as a basic essential and continuing policy over a period of years.

In the general analysis of the character and conditions of the Old Town it is necessary now to refer to existing particular aspects so that a comparison may be made with the proposals.

Zoning : Survey and Proposals.

Survey : The Royal Mile falls naturally into three parts, Castlehill and Lawnmarket, High Street and Canongate.

Castlehill and Lawnmarket is almost equally residential and non-residential in the use of property. The High Street on the other hand containing most of the principal administrative buildings of the capital has comparatively very little housing left. The Canongate, to the visitor, would seem distinctly residential but, if time permitted, a peep behind this street facade would show a great deal of non-residential use of property built over what might at one time have been the gardens. In fact the non-residential use definitely predominates as may be seen from the survey plan in the pocket at the end of this report. It is not proposed to enumerate all the buildings considered worthy of preservation as this is done quite adequately in Mr. MacRae's Royal Mile Report. A sufficient idea can be obtained from the Land Utilisation Survey showing some 60 buildings in the Old Town as worthy of preservation.

Proposals : Three distinct zones, Castlehill and Lawnmarket, High Street, Canongate.

Castlehill and Lawnmarket. On the north side, the existing buildings about Ramsay Gardens are retained for residential use. The buildings between the Church Assembly Hall and Bank Street should be reconstructed as dwellings to a height of not more than three storeys, unless lifts can be installed, when they could be reconstructed to their present height. Milne's Court Gladstone's Land and 435 Lawnmarket are to be retained at their original heights and lifts should be installed. Milne's Court should be for residential use while Gladstone's Land should be continued as offices and 435 Lawnmarket converted into offices.

On the other side, Riddle's Court is recommended as a Community Club and the buildings behind it and Johnstone Terrace are to be reconstructed as three storey flats or higher if lifts can be installed. The other side of Castlehill is recommended for commercial offices or educational use.

High Street. This is clearly an administrative centre of long standing and tradition and as there is ample evidence of increased demand for accommodation by the various Corporation Departments—(indeed there was never more clamant need for reconstruction of antiquated premises as the authors have good cause to appreciate !)—this locality is recommended for exclusive use of the present predominating one. Such development would entail the removal of some hundreds of families in dire need of fairer homes. This has been allowed for in the population redistribution proposals.

The heights of the new buildings would have to be carefully regulated to fit in with the general character of the area and in relation to the width of the street, in order to ensure adequate layout in accordance with the recent memorandum published by the Ministry of Town and Country Planning on floor space indices.

Canongate. Generally, it is proposed that the new buildings should be constructed to conform to the residential zoning proposals of the area, with heights of buildings reduced to approximately three storeys above High Street level. Variations from this might well be necessary in order to fit in with the existing historical buildings retained in the scheme. As the Canongate forms part of the central area zone of 100 persons per acre density, the flat development would permit a fair proportion of two storey dwellings with gardens to be constructed in the redeveloped portion behind the Canongate. Here it is suggested that the closes might well be retained as a means of access to these two storey dwellings which would then be constructed in terraces to maintain the character of closes.

MacRae Royal Mile Report.

The buildings listed for preservation in the Royal Mile Report for the Canongate has been adopted in the Plan. Change of use, however, has been prescribed for the following buildings as a departure from the Royal Mile Report. These changes become possible only if the clearing of the area of industrial premises as a progressive policy over a number of years is adopted :—

All buildings on the north side of the Canongate frontage are scheduled for the same use as in the Royal Mile Report, i.e., residential and public uses such as churches, educational, cultural and social. Changes of use for property lying between the Canongate and Calton Road shows the S.M.T. Bus Depot at New Street being replaced by residential development. The suggested removal of this bus depot adheres to the principle of use zoning and is made in the knowledge that a new site for the depot can be found at the Annandale Street Industrial site. It would be more easily accessible to the new proposed S.M.T. Bus Station behind St. Andrew's Square. The present traffic routes to and from this depot are completely inadequate to meet the demands created by its presence. Another change indicated is at Abbeyhill where the area should be cleared for redevelopment for residential use instead of a museum as indicated in the Royal Mile Report. The properties requiring reconstruction on either side of Gilchrist House and Huntly House would become residential in place of industrial and public use. On the other side of the Canongate changes include Chessels Court recommended for residential use and the House of Nisbet of Direlton, described as one of the most interesting buildings in the Canongate. This change from public or educational use would only be made possible if the industrial properties lying close to them are removed.

Street improvements recommended for the Royal Mile include the proposal for the new North to South by-pass of the Bridges route, where it runs on a line immediately adjacent and to the east of Blackfriars Street and where it would not involve the demolition of any building of architectural or historical consequence but would require the demolition of much derelict property of little consequence. It is important that this road should not only run parallel to the Bridges but come as close as reasonably possible to the route it is by-passing in order to avoid as little interference as possible with the layout of the High Street. It is suggested that this road should run immediately beneath the High Street with the latter forming a bridge over it. The topography is sufficiently varied to permit this road to pass beneath the

High Street and still have 'head room' to pass over the Cowgate.

Holyrood Road and the Cowgate will not require any material widening in the scheme as indeed it is virtually impossible to obtain continuously owing to the bottle-necks at the arches of the South Bridge and George IV Bridge.

Use of materials for the special restoration and reconstruction of the Canongate area so far as the buildings that flank the street are concerned should be of local stone, but it is suggested that the two storey dwellings behind might well be built of a more modern material.

(d) *The Breweries.*

While the Royal Mile Report recommends the removal of the brewery from the north precincts of the Palace in order to improve the immediate environment in that part, difficulty appeared to arise in carrying out a consistent policy so far as the brewery west of the Horse Wynd is concerned. If it is important for the one to go, it is just as important for the one in the Canongate also to be moved as there never was a case where greater conflict between property use existed. Royal Palaces and breweries cannot be said by any stretch of the imagination to make good neighbours. Furthermore the Horse Wynd itself requires to be rerouted sufficiently far west to enable a good local traffic intersection point to be created at its junction with the Canongate and with Holyrood Road, and, at the same time to provide a reasonably generous grass strip between it and the Palace buildings. Situated upon the site to the west of the Wynd and of the present brewery, dwellings could be erected at a density of 100 persons per net acre to accommodate approximately 200 persons between Horse Wynd and Queensberry House. It is suggested in Chapter 7 that if the brewery, which at present functions as two separate units, were moved to the Abbeyhill or Meadowbank site in two stages there should be little disturbance of business.

The removal of two other breweries is also necessary if the complete redevelopment of the Canongate is to be suitable and adequate for residential use. The ground released by such further removals would amount to 32 acres for the construction of some 1,000 dwellings, quite apart from additional property in the immediate neighbourhood affected by these industries that would also be released for redevelopment for housing.

The architectural development could then assume a domestic character with materials and style in keeping with the traditions of the locality. The redevelopment about the precincts of the Palace might well consist of more expensive flats to contribute substantially to the cost of the redevelopment.

Queensberry house, it is suggested, should be retained for institutional or cultural uses with some modification to the present building to restore it to its original size and character. The garden space on the south side should also be retained.

2. THE NEW TOWN.

(a) *A Conscious Effort at Planning.*

The Edinburgh New Town was a deliberate piece of municipal extension, in which the Town Council took the initiative. It was carried out in units which have a certain though not quite complete coherence. Four such neighbourhood units may be easily discussed. The first was designed by James Craig, 1766, with its central feature of George Street lying between the two famous squares: it was intended to house between 3,000 and 4,000 people. Separated by the well marked cut off of Queen Street Gardens is the second unit, planned by Robert Reid, 1802, with a similar central feature, Great King Street lying between Royal Circus and Drummond Place, neither of which is closed, as are St. Andrew and Charlotte Squares: this unit is about the same size as the first and was jointly promoted by the City, the Heriot Hospital Governors and another owner. The third was a piece of proprietary planning for the Earl of Moray by James Gillespie; it is smaller and has not the neighbourhood quality of the other two (but richer architectural treatment). Fourthly the fragment of the ambitious plan prepared for the City by William Henry Playfair in 1819: this great scheme, starting with even grander features than the others, was, after 1830, overwhelmed by the intrusion of the railway and the general disintegration of nineteenth century industrialisation.

There is no need to add anything to the admirable survey which Mr. MacRae has made which includes many smaller areas of this renaissance planning and building of which George Square, south of the Old Town has become recently famous. Mr. MacRae also explains the technical methods, in addition to feuing control, which were used to obtain continuity of frontages. Of course, by far the strongest control was exercised voluntarily and almost instinctively by " a galaxy of architects enthusiastic in the practice of the classic revival ": in addition there was the common use of a number of similar building stones " supreme in quality " and worked according to the highest standard of craftmanship; and a public prepared to support and appreciate the work and to forego, as householders, the advertisement of highly individualised frontages.

The New Town has not always been held in equal estimation. After its first enthusiastic reception by the polite period, there followed the neglect of anything fine by the industrial age, coupled with the romantic attachment to antiquity encouraged by Sir Walter Scott, whose creation of Abbotsford shows his hankering after the Old Town's glamour. When Stevenson published his " Picturesque Notes on Edinburgh " in 1879, he could write " It is as much a matter of course to " decry the 'New Town' as to exalt the Old; and the most " celebrated authorities have picked out this quarter as the " emblem of what is condemnable in architecture." But R.L.S. himself considers that " to the unsophisticated, who call anything pleasing if it only pleases them, the 'New Town' of Edinburgh seems in itself, not only gay and airy, but highly picturesque." This, and what follows, is perhaps an unusual angle of admiration, but it marks the beginning of the rise of Georgian art in public favour, as something not severe or dull but humanistic and urbane. Thence praised, the 'New Town' becomes one of the foremost examples of the art of townplanning in its domestic vein: it is used in the text books with Bath and Bloomsbury. Simultaneously societies both in England and Scotland are found to study, popularise and protect Georgian Architecture, and Edinburgh becomes one of the most devoted centres of this cult.

But in spite of this canonisation of the 'New Town', criticism is heard from time to time and often, it must be confessed, unwarranted. R.L.S. for example, accuses the architect of being " essentially a town bird, and he laid out the modern city with a view to street scenery and to street scenery alone. The country did not enter into his plan . . . . . " Barry Parker, twenty years later, fresh from planning Letchworth, where the country certainly invades the garden city, makes a similar complaint. The view over the Forth should have been open to every house on a series of terraces, and incidentially the piercing north east winds. The architect's avoidance was intentional: more serious is the criticism of the Moray, Ainslie and Randolph Places and Crescent turning their backs upon the lovely glen of the Water of Leith: on the other hand the beautifully landscaped park on Calton Hill on to which the back gardens of the Royal and Regent terraces give,

St. George's Church  [p. 42]

    This floodlit view of St. George's Church designed by Playfair retains much of the features of Robert Adam who originally conceived the layout for Charlotte Square in which this church stands as the dominant feature. There is no doubt that Playfair appreciated the importance of lifting this building above the domestic scale that Adam conceived in order to provide a strong enough terminal feature to the vista of George Street. In this respect Playfair's lofty dome is probably more successful than the one originally designed by Robert Adam.

PLATE XXXVI

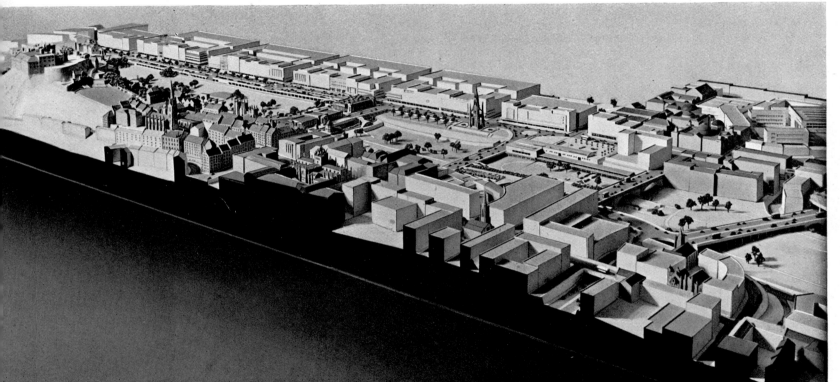

This first esquisse study for Princes Street seen from this frequented part shows how an overall composition can be appreciated and how the ugly confusion of styles and silhouettes of to-day can be avoided.

Here the architectural study is more satisfying and from less rigidity in height and bulk to an orderly rhythm of silhouette a wide variety of expression is possible. Echoing the natural emphasis of the Castle Rock opposite an assymetrical composition focuses attention upon the principal intersection at the Mound. The Academy should not be overwhelmed by an unrestricted height and bulk of new buildings opposite and repeat the mistake in London of the Cumberland Hotel overshadowing the Marble Arch.

[p. 93]

[p. 63]

[p. 62]

[P. 63 and P. 62]. These two photographic views taken together give a fairly comparable view of the existing architecture which it is proposed to correct in the manner shown in the view of the model above.

PLATE XXXVII

is a real contribution to urban domestic planning and is much superior to the London Squares, as private open space accessible without crossing a road.

Another unjustifiable criticism is that the authors of the plans did not provide for through traffic. On the contrary they wisely wished to exclude it from a residential area, which is all that they were at the time concerned with.

Finally a recent and more searching criticism has been levelled at the architecture itself, not so much by modernists (some few of whom can see no merit in the past) but by discerning amateurs who point to the mellower materials of Bath or Dublin or the greater abundance of fine detail in Bloomsbury. Charlotte Square is generally exempted from this accusation of grimness and austerity, not mitigated by a certain heavy monumentality found in Moray Place. The very fineness of the masonry, its large stoned ashlar, its resistance to decay but its acceptance of grime, are set against Stevenson's gaiety: was there perhaps less smoke in his day?

Some space has been devoted to an analysis of the virtues and possible defects of the New Town, as due regard to the value of its claims must be paid during the change of use from domestic to commercial which has taken place almost entirely in the original unit designed by James Craig. The buildings, few of which, according to Mr. MacRae are the original ones (but which have replaced them in a congruous style), have stood up to the changed use without entirely disintegrating the prevailing architectural character: and the new buildings, even in George Street, are so far, with one or two exceptions reasonably harmonious. The problem of continued rebuildings is somewhat similar here, mutatis mutandis, as in High Street or Canongate, i.e. there is a background against which each new proposal can be assessed.

(b). *Princes Street Architectural Scheme.*

The rebuilding of Princes Street which is inevitable during the next 50 years, or less, presents perhaps the biggest, certainly the most spectacular problem of civic design in Great Britain, surpassing in interest, because of its history and individualism, the south bank of the Thames. The whole subject of architectural treatment, uniformity, controlled sanity and anarchy— can here be explored.

Originally this was a street front of uniform houses of little architectural interest: though Craig could not exactly be accused of turning his back upon the valley, loch and castle, he certainly lavished his fine efforts upon George Street and Adam gave the final touch of distinction in Charlotte Square. A considerable number of these small Princes Street frontage houses still remain more or less altered. Two things can be said at once: these original buildings are of no value as a guide (in contradiction to many of the " lands " in the Old Town) and further, the original principle of uniformity cannot for one instant be maintained. A Scottish version of the Rue De Rivoli might be imposing but it could never be imposed. The attempts made in Leeds and Hull are not encouraging.

The next point to decide is whether there are any of the later buildings which should be retained. This is a much more debatable question. The advocate of the clean sweep is taking the easier course: the timid preserver of many fronts in good condition would compromise a fine result. In the scheme illustrated three or four buildings alone are retained.

(i) *Use and Height Zoning.* The problem of use zoning is not a serious difficulty here: with the exception of three clubs, several small banks and two large insurance offices, the use is a fairly uniform dual one of shops with hotels (and occasional offices) over. This combined form of zoning★ is a satisfactory one, particularly for this actual site which faces south and has splendid views of the Old Town seen across the valley. The one sided shopping street may be against the rules, but is here successful owing not only to its attractive southern aspect but to its importance as a promenade between the east and west ends of the city centre.

The bulk or floor area required is, however, debatable: if uniformity of skyline is to be aimed at, are maximum and minimum heights to be prescribed, entailing variable floor space indices? And not only variation in floorspace, but in heights of rooms? (e.g. the floor above a shop may be a low storage mezzanine or a lofty café).

(ii) *Architectural Composition.* We are now arrived at the crucial point as to whether a strict composition or rhythmic sequence or individual freedom is to be aimed at. A composition which proposed anything like a balanced or symmetrical design, based upon the four long centre blocks, the two shorter " square " (Charlotte and St. Andrew) blocks and the appendage next the Register House, would be almost as difficult as the rigidity of a uniform front. One must not forget the unusual opportunity afforded by the topographical nature of the locality in appreciating an end to end composition. It would be possible and reasonable for a symetrical emphasis and an overall composition at the Mound. In the other extreme is complete freedom, conditioned only by floor space indices. This freedom from control of height, design or material would appear to be recommended by a recent writer† who relies upon the general higher level of modern architecture to produce a finer result than that which Princes Street presents to-day. Unfortunately for this belief, it cannot be said that practising architects represent a new " galaxy " of consistent design such as obtained in the mediaeval or renaissance periods.

The first stage in control is that which was exercised under the 1932 Act, in which each building was examined separately and passed as an individual design, with an occasional reference to " good neighbourliness." The English Memorandum carries this a step further and suggests that " it is desirable in general that, subject to Floor Space Index and day-lighting controls, developers should have considerable freedom concerning the block form and height of their building. On the other hand, it is highly desirable that the composition and general effect of a street should possess both balance and a reasonable measure of continuity and cohesion."

Is there a half-way house between the rigid uniformity of design such as Adam imposed (under the power of a single superior owner) in the rebuilding of Charlotte Square, and a complete anarchy of presumed high artistic quality? An attempt at a rhythmic sequence is the answer, prepared strictly as a sketch design and subject to continual modification as individual proposals are submitted for rebuilding: a kind of partnership set up between the developer's architect and the planning officer resulting in a contribution within this overall framework, with the rhythmic sequence offering the greatest elasticity and variety.

This is what is proposed in the modest attempt shown on Plate no. XXXI. In preparing this, certain broad principles and guiding ideas have been observed and it is hoped that too much attention will not be given to individual details which must inevitably reflect personal approaches to design. A certain baldness or " packing-case " effect may perhaps be attributed to a desire to avoid any appearance of imposing stylistic

★—Not mentioned in the English Memorandum.

†—Hon. Lionel Brett, Spectator 20/2/48. " Aesthetic Major Generals."

details. The following points may be noted: (a) generally speaking the ownership frontages have been respected, though certain combinations of narrow plots have been suggested. (b) It is assumed that redevelopment will take place, on the basis of private enterprise, piecemeal; and therefore, it will be a considerable time before any grouping becomes manifest. (c) While it is not thought feasible or necessary to attempt any regular composition in the individual blocks, the street openings, three of which include rising vistas emphasised by statues, should be symmetrical, as an echo of the original design: (this, however, need not occur at South St. Andrew Street). (d) As a maximum height to be allowed, the comparatively new building of Messrs. Binns at the extreme west-end has been taken. Where for aesthetic reasons lower vertical fronts are needed, the principle of set back (if greater floor space is required) for upper storeys used in the City of London Plan should be adopted. (e) Considerable use for variety of effect is made of the play of frontage between the original building line and the forecourt line. (In many of the older buildings this has produced a bay window treatment, e.g. in the three Clubs.) (f) A uniform shop front treatment has been tentatively suggested: this means a frame including the mezzanine and leaving absolute freedom for the actual shop front. (g) The change of level along the street has been adjusted to each block: this means that floor lines do not run through from one end to the other. The changes between blocks are slight and would be quite imperceptible.

It is contended that, with some such framework, without imposing harsh or genius-cramping restrictions, it may be possible to bring about some general harmony of redevelopment, coupled with a higher standard of architectural design than is shown for the most part in the existing buildings in Princes Street.

It should be unnecessary to add that the present sketch should be taken as only a first tentative effort. A detailed survey (on the lines recommended in the Memorandum) must be undertaken and the use and floor space needs of each owner of a building ascertained, analysed and agreed, within the scope of planning requirements.

Finally the traffic improvements proposed, entailing a three decker Princes Street and an open arcade upon the gardens will add another factor, and one capable of most imposing treatment to the general appearance—so vitally important, from the Gardens and the Old Town.

Preservation of the old city and Castle by means of remodelling and restoration is proposed but Princes Street requires rebuilding upon modern lines in contrast to the old. This aerial view of part of the large scale model shows how these contemporary ideas for redesigning Princes Street can provide harmony by contrast especially with the intervening garden valley to give the desired setting to old and new. The terracing and colonnading proposed for the Princes Street by-pass and car parking terraces give the architectural link required between garden and building.

[p. 91]

Bakehouse Close

[p. 17]

"Bakehouse Close"—a piece of Royal Mile building restoration in the old town.

[p. 90]

This part of the 1/500 scale model shows the Usher Hall and the new buildings for one of the two Festival Centres strikingly situated beneath the Castle Rock. No more inspiring setting could be found than this.

[p. 92]

This part of the 1/2500 scale model of the town centre gives an interesting plan view of the proposals. George Street is seen in mid-foreground flanked by the rectangular building blocks and terminated at each end by Charlotte Square at the right end and St. Andrew's Square to the left.

PLATE XXXVIII

This aerial view shows part of the 1/2500 scale model for Leith development. Leith Walk is seen traversing the middle left of the photograph and linking central Edinburgh with Central Leith at the Kirkgate before joining the main east to west road at the second roundabout. Ferry Road joins this east to west road at a roundabout near the Water of Leith. The Dock Extension Scheme is seen in its completed form on the right-hand side of the photograph.

[p. 89]

Aerial View of Leith Docks [p. 87]

Lamb's House, Leith [p. 48]

[P. 87]. This is an aerial view of Leith and Docks from the west.

[P. 48]. This is Andrew Lamb's house (a prosperous merchant who received Mary Queen of Scots on arrival from France), which is preserved in the scheme as a fine example of Scottish mediaeval architecture. It is also situated in the mediaeval part of Leith, the street network of which is recommended for preservation in the Plan. The house is the oldest in Leith and was recently restored. The suggestion for its use as a maritime museum is a satisfactory one.

[P. 88]. An aerial view of Leith Docks at the estuary of the Water of Leith. The area at the bottom of the photograph and to the left of the Water of Leith is part of the "Citadel" site recently decided by the Town Council to be the subject of an application under the new Act of 1947 for scheduling as an area of comprehensive development.

Aerial View of Leith Docks [p. 88]

PLATE XXXIX

LEITH LINKS

Gt. JUNCTION STREET

COUPER STREET

COMMERCIAL STREET

LAMB'S HOUSE

BERNARD STREET

CONSTITUTION STREET

LEITH REDEVELOPMENT
AERIAL VIEW

PLATE XL

PLATE XLI

PLAN FOR CENTRAL LEITH

LEGEND

HISTORIC BUILDINGS
SPECIAL INDUSTRY
INDUSTRIAL SITES
GENERAL DO
LIGHT SERVICE DO
DOCKS
SHOPS & OFFICES
COMMUNITY & CIVIC BUILDINGS
EXHIBITION HALL
PUBLIC OPEN SPACE
PRIVATE OPEN SPACE & SCHOOL GROUNDS
CEMETERIES
NO STOREY HOUSES
DO
PARK HOUSES
DO
SEVEN STOREY HOUSES
EXISTING HOUSING RETAINED
SCHOOL
HOSPITAL
SUB-ARTERIAL ROADS
OTHER ROADS
BUS STATIONS
RAILWAY

A. M. GRAHAM

This plan shows in outline and in some detail the proposals for the residential and industrial redevelopment of Leith. A separate zone is suggested for industry of all kinds cleared of any existing housing. Likewise the areas surrounding this zone are suggested for residential redevelopment cleared of any existing industry. Such zoning illustrates one of the fundamental principles contained in the report and accords with one of the accepted planning principles. Re-orientation of most of the existing streets is recommended to eliminate the existing bad layout: rerouting of the existing rail system is foreshadowed together with essential goods station services and marshalling yard facilities. These are partly to provide for the impending Leith Dock expansion and partly to supersede the old L.N.E. Leith Walk to Trinity line and the old L.M.S. Newhaven to Bath Street line. Resiting of industry to conform to the zoning proposals will contribute to the redundancy of these old rail routes. Care has been taken to preserve the existing buildings of historic and architectural value and particularly the layout of roads in old Leith centred upon St. Bernard Street.

CHAPTER NINE

LEITH AND PORTOBELLO

LEITH.

INTRODUCTION. Leith lies to the north-east of central Edinburgh and occupies approximately 1,300 acres. Its commercial centre and docks are linked with central Edinburgh by the broad highway of Leith Walk. Over recent decades its character as a populated town has been steadily changing until to-day its use of land has become predominantly industrial or commercial. The land utilisation survey map in the pocket of the report shows the extent of industrialisation though there is still a considerable population in this old town totalling some 57,000 residents. Although there has been decentralisation over the past 30 years of something like 23,000 persons the gradual squeezing out of the residential use of property by an expanding industrial use has created high "net" densities of 600 and 700 persons per acre. This industrial use of property is now 40% of the total area as compared with 25% of the total area in residential use. In attempting to meet this trend a specific area of some 278 acres is zoned solely for industry with a core of commercial offices situated in the oldest part of Leith. As redevelopment in this zone takes place for incoming industry the existing overcrowded and outmoded dwellings will be eliminated. Conversely, as industry vacates the land it occupies outside this zone so ground will become available for redevelopment for new dwellings to accommodate the population decentralised from this zone. This is an example of the kind of "combined operation" referred to in chapter 3 on Population Redistribution.

Redistribution of Leith's Industries. Leith's place in the Plan acknowledges, as of old, its importance as the port of Edinburgh: a position that enhances the value of its industrial hinterland consisting of general engineering, milling, baking, chemical, metal working, etc. It is not suggested that all industry at present occupying land in the survey area for Leith should be accommodated in this zone. If the present overcrowding of the residential parts is to be eliminated and new homes constructed reasonably near the work place there will have to be decentralisation of industry from this district into some of the other zones described in chapter 6 on Industry. This recommendation is made with the knowledge that the neighbourhood unit groups of population nearby this Leith zone can accommodate the whole of its workers at a comfortable density without excluding others from living there who work elsewhere: also there is a substantial proportion of 'mobile' industries in the district sufficient in number to indicate that no uneconomic decentralisation is put forward. For example, industry, both mobile and non-mobile, at present occupies some 158 acres in the proposed zone leaving 120 acres available for redevelopment either for expansion of these existing industries or for some of those occupying land in the district but outside the zone. However, as the whole of the 278 acres of the zone will eventually have to be redeveloped to replace for example, outmoded property, it is suggested that the reshuffling will result mainly in the retention of those industries economically 'tied' to the district. As their acreage is assessed at 133 acres there should be ample margin to be found in the remaining 145 acres either for an expansion of 109% in land occupancy for these 'tied' industries, or for a proportion of the 'non-tied' or

partly for entirely new incoming industries, or for some combination of all three types.

Reorientation of existing street system. The existing lay-out of the streets is by no means satisfactory either for the building sites provided or for the circulation of traffic that requires access from one part to another. Nevertheless the Plan has not made such an entirely clean sweep of the existing road lay-out as might have been expected but has in fact used quite a considerable number of the existing roads. Many aspects have had to be considered: for example, the provision of a remodelled railway system consisting mainly of a link up of north with south Leith, separating the old core of the town about Constitution Street from the southern part, which is intended for the industrial zone. Increased facilities for goods stations and marshalling yards have had to be anticipated if the port and industrial requirements are to be adequately met. There is also the important provision of through road sub-arterials to connect the industrial zone and port with the other parts of the city. In this respect some difficulty has been experienced in providing the through road between north and south Leith without disturbing more than is necessary the amenities of Leith Links on the one hand and the buildings of historical value together with important industrial properties on the other. It has been impossible to avoid entirely such disturbances either to the industrial concerns or the amenities.

Further details of the Plan are described below:

(1) Leith as a Port.
(2) Proposed new layout.

1. *Leith as a Port.*

Within the Firth of Forth area there are seven major ports, four on the south bank and three on the north. All of these provide extensive accommodation for overseas and coasting vessels. They consist of Leith, Granton, Bo'ness and Grangemouth on the south bank and Methil, Kirkcaldy and Burntisland on the north side. Of these, Leith is the largest and is the second largest port in Scotland. Leith is situated some 20 miles from the open sea and is controlled by the Leith Dock Commission which was created in 1838 when dock undertakings were removed from the control of the city of Edinburgh. At present it includes the inner and outer harbours giving a total water area of 105 acres with some 27,300 lineal feet of quayside. Of the imports, grain is the most important though there is a considerable tonnage also of timber, cement, flour, fertilizers, paper making materials and general goods. The principal export is coal from the Lothians while iron and steel also form part of the trade of the Port. When the dock extension programme is completed it will be by far the largest port on the east coast of Scotland. Considerable initiative to this expansion has been given by the commencement of the deep water quays for Messrs. Ranks new grain silo and flour mill.

Leith Industries. Excluding the docks the largest users of industrial space are saw milling, ship and boat building, milling, rope manufacturers, metal working, and general food production followed by chemical, coopery, baking, etc., warehousing, iron founding, general engineering, patent colour, printing, leather and tanning manufacture. Of these industries the following are considered to be most suitable for the port area owing to their reliance upon dock facilities, marine ship building, saw milling, chemicals and coopery, oils and fats, warehousing, iron founding and general engineering.

The industries less well represented in Leith and which are also of the kind requiring port facilities are wood box making and card board manufacture. Both of these are well represented in Greater Edinburgh but not in Leith itself. There would, therefore, be a case for encouraging units of these industries to move from other parts of Edinburgh near to the port. Such movement of industry would considerably facilitate the redevelopment of the proposals in the plan. The kind of new industries that might be considered desirable to stimulate the trade of the port and of industrial Edinburgh generally are the motor and aircraft manufacture industries including ancillary trades, plaster board manufacturers and plastic manufacturers. All of these are hardly represented either in Leith or in greater Edinburgh.

2. Proposed New Layout.

The layout for Leith industrial zone has been designed to provide convenient and economically shaped sites for the different types of industries and in other business concerns of the port and of those already existing which may not necessarily require port facilities. The detailed zoning of the area influences the layout of the roads : it consists of warehousing and general industry adjoining the docks and to the north-western side of the Water of Leith, a zone for special industries on the west side of the dock extension; the south-eastern side consists of the commercial core of the old town bounded by Constitution Street to the south east and the Water of Leith to the north west, the general industries zone and a zone for special industries on either side of Salamander Street; a light industrial zone is suggested for the foot of Leith Walk and Gt. Junction Street area; a general industry zone in the Bonnington Area and light industry again along the frontage of Ferry Road.

The natural focus of commercial activity in Leith is the river crossing nearest the docks. Here it is proposed that a river side park with café and recreational facilities could provide the open space amenities required by both office and industrial workers. There are too few amenities of this kind in the heart of Leith and now that the dock expansion scheme is going forward the importance of providing such amenities is greater than ever.

It is appreciated that when allowing for this dock expansion scheme together with the additional space for industrial development which it entails, Salamander Street and Commercial Street will become much more useful as feeder roads within the commercial area and will, therefore, become quite unsuitable for through traffic. It is for this reason that the whole of this dock side area has been by-passed leaving the old mediaeval centre of the town which already contains a number of offices, banks, etc. to form the heart of the business community. The character of the existing street lay-out with its closes and wynds and particularly the irregular shape of Bernard Street has been retained together with the most important buildings of historical and architectural value. The remaining buildings should be pulled down and reconstructed upon modern lines and the height should be more suitably related to the widths of these old streets having regard to the need for ample light and air to all of the work rooms. For this latter purpose see publication on redevelopment areas referred to in Chapter 8.

The principal feature of major importance is, of course, the new main sub-arterial road that passes on the north side of Leith Links and across the Kirkgate to the north of South Leith Church. It then passes across the north corner of Henderson Gardens to a point just south of the Hospital in Mill Lane where an important traffic intersection is required to pick up Sherrif Brae before crossing the Water of Leith. Passing Leith Town Hall it curves northwest-wards at the foot of Leith Fort to join the new main entrance to the dock extension. From here it follows the foreshore to Granton.

Another main feature is the new rail link between north and south Leith already referred to. The most suitable place for a new goods station, which will probably be required to cope with the general industrial improvement of the zone, would be situated in the area on the north side of this road and the old mediaeval part of the town to the north of Charlotte Street. In addition there is the railway marshalling yard required for the Leith Dock Extension which should be located at the foot of Leith Fort between the Docks and the sub-arterial road in order that it may satisfactorily work in with the rest of the railway proposals for this district. It is essential for these railway facilities to be provided well clear of the docks in order to avoid congestion.

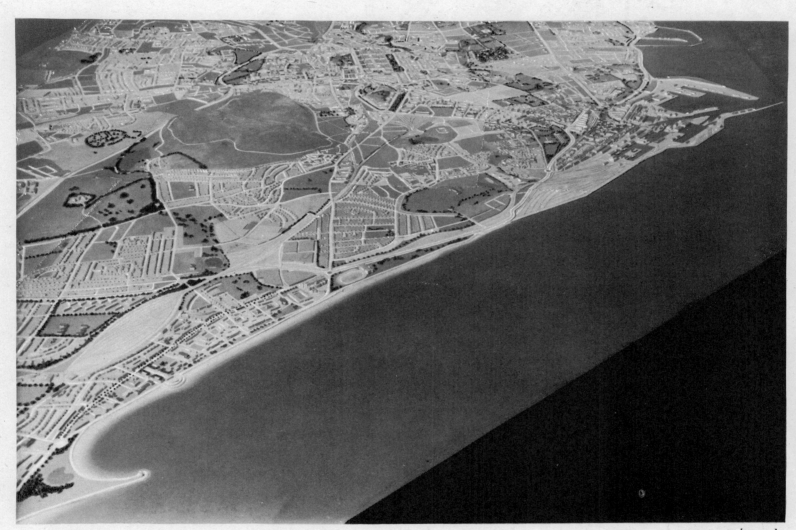

[p. 94]

This shows the Portobello Development Scheme as it appears on the 1/2500 scale model. The reclamation scheme and storm barrier for protecting the Promenade is seen in the bottom left-hand corner and a similar projection into the sea is seen in front of the neighbourhood centre for the area. It is hoped to increase the recreational facilities by these means particularly the Promenade foreshore. Leith is seen in the top right-hand corner of the photograph and Edinburgh at the middle-top.

PLATE XLII

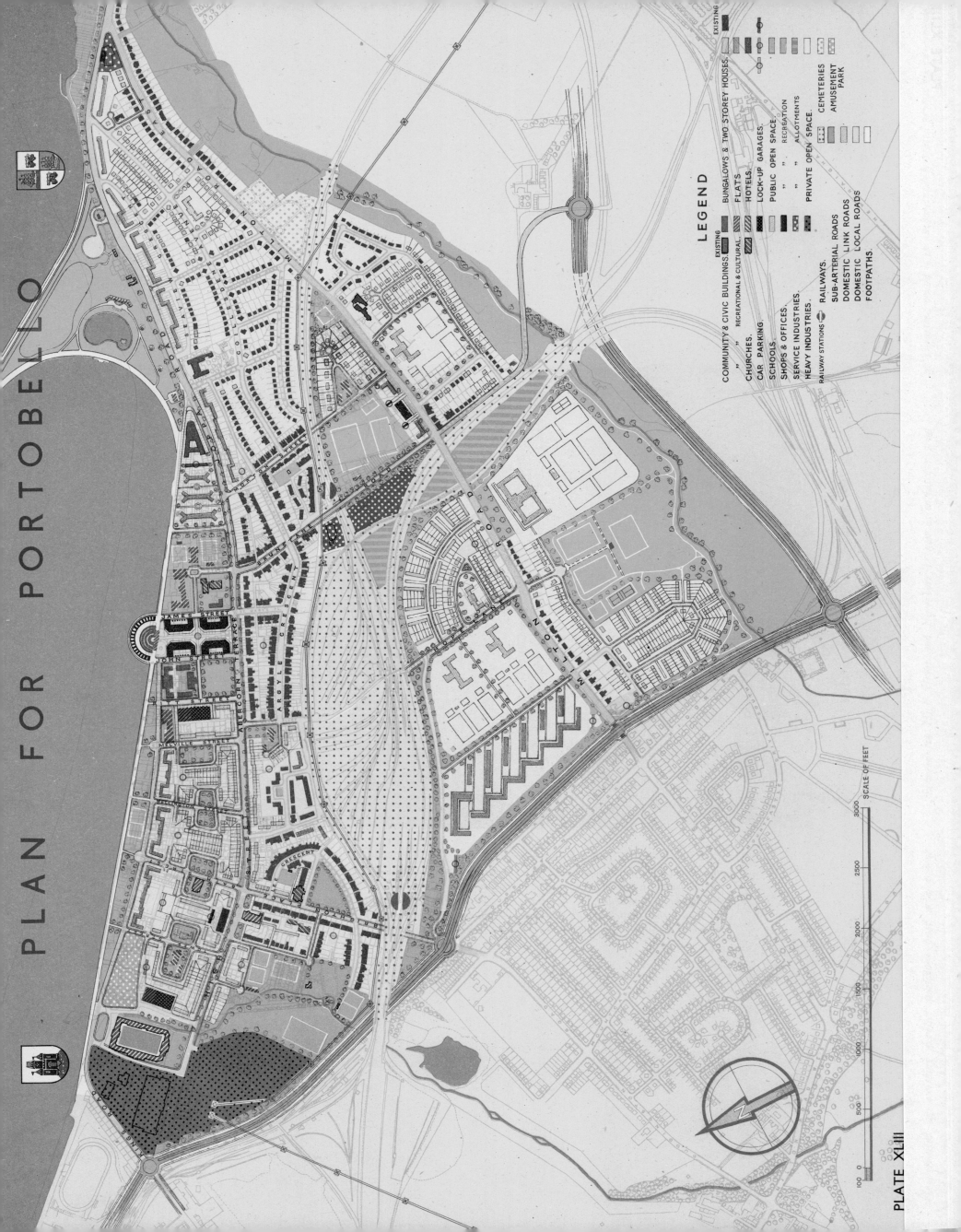

PLAN FOR PORTOBELLO

LEGEND

EXISTING

COMMUNITY & CIVIC BUILDINGS.
"   "   RECREATIONAL & CULTURAL.
CHURCHES.
CAR PARKING.
SCHOOLS.
SHOPS & OFFICES.
SERVICE INDUSTRIES.
HEAVY INDUSTRIES.
RAILWAY STATIONS.

BUNGALOWS & TWO STOREY HOUSES.
FLATS.
HOTELS.
LOCK-UP GARAGES.
PUBLIC OPEN SPACE.
RECREATION.
ALLOTMENTS.
PRIVATE OPEN SPACE.

CEMETERIES
AMUSEMENT
PARK

RAILWAYS.
SUB-ARTERIAL ROADS
DOMESTIC LINK ROADS
DOMESTIC LOCAL ROADS
FOOTPATHS.

SCALE OF FEET

100 0   500   1000   1500   2000   2500   3000

PLATE XLIII

PORTOBELLO.

INTRODUCTION. When considering Portobello one inevitably raises the burning question of redevelopment of built up areas. When can attention be turned to the improvement of built up areas? That is the areas left behind by the pre-war annular outward spread on to undeveloped land that offered less difficulty to develop. For years cities have been spreading outwards on the undeveloped parts within their domain and ignoring the older parts which are allowed to deteriorate at an ever increasing rate. Portobello like Leith has reached the stage of almost complete dereliction over much of its built up area. This is a serious situation that is perhaps not fully realised. This kind of abandonment of the old parts is rather like the movement of farmers in the U.S.A. and elsewhere who have continually moved across the continent in search of unturned pasture and left behind soil-eroded land that has resulted in the present danger of world starvation. The uneconomic burden of the derelict built up areas is another danger resulting from such abandonment. While new areas like Cramond foreshore present new opportunities where similar mistakes of uncontrolled commercialism can be avoided, backs cannot for ever be turned to Portobello where complete clearance from the foreshore to the High Street represents only one of the essential measures that should be taken. The prevention of continued sea erosion and undermining of the promenade is another. The elimination of unsatisfactory living conditions in those parts brought out by the Civic Survey is yet another.

Portobello is a sea-side resort which has become part of Greater Edinburgh. It is not only the resort for Edinburghers but also for the citizens of her sister city, Glasgow. It is situated on the north-west of Edinburgh and covers an area of approximately 246 acres. Adjacent, lies the other town of Joppa which now merges with Portobello, adding a further 387 acres. Both are separated from central Edinburgh by Arthur's Seat and Duddingston Park. Portobello has quite a considerable amount of industrial use of property which represents some 27% of its total area: 41% is occupied by housing giving a total population of 8,568 persons living at an average net residential density of 85 persons per acre. There is a standard of 3·8 acres per 1,000 population of public open space but no school recreation space. Joppa on the other hand has only 1% of its area used by industry while 30% is occupied by housing giving a total population of 3,491 at an average net residential density of 29 persons per acre. Its existing standard of public open space is 0.8 acres per 1,000 population and it again has no school recreation space. It is really the much newer suburb of the two as it consists mainly of interwar housing development while Portobello is almost equally residential, industrial and commercial in character.

The Plan.

The proposals, a detailed illustration of which appears on plate No. XLIII, adopts for its planning boundaries a much larger area intersected in more than one place by the main railway routes and a marshalling yard of the British Railways. As Portobello and Joppa, Neighbourhood Unit D.4., will have a dual function of providing for a permanent resident population and for a holiday making population there may be some advantage in having a separation of the kind imposed by these railway routes.

The total area of the proposed Neighbourhood Unit embracing these two townships amounts to approximately 617 acres of which 316 acres is zoned for net residential development at an average density of 50 persons per net residential acre of the new development and redevelopment areas accommodating a total population of 9,820 persons. In addition there is a total of 120 acres of existing housing development retained in the scheme which it is estimated could accommodate a total population of 3,280 persons. The total potential population after allowing for the relief of overcrowding would be approximately the same population as exists to-day, that is, 13,000 persons. The remaining land would be developed for such ancillary population needs as public buildings, including shops, civic and commercial buildings and recreation space.

The Plan for Portobello, therefore, proposes a redistribution of its existing population at a much more satisfactory density together with the above mentioned land use requirements. It aims at the creation of an entirely new centre situated about John Street which would include the main shopping centre instead of the present scatter further west along the High Street. The whole of the area between the High Street and the foreshore is recommended for redevelopment owing to the derelict nature of existing property. Such complete redevelopment makes possible readjustment of the existing distribution of land uses of which the new shopping centre is an example. The new areas on either side of Milton Road are taken in for housing, schools and open space development to achieve this redistribution of the population.

Road System.

Through road traffic is diverted from its present use of the High Street to link up with the proposed by-pass of Musselburgh which passes at the southern extremity of this Neighbourhood centre at the Figgate Burn. This means that traffic from Leith would continue along the improved Baileyfield Road consisting of a dual carriageway and proceeding southwards on the east side of Park Avenue until it reaches the Musselburgh by-pass. This new road not only by-passes Portobello but represents the most direct route for the new A.1. arterial road by-passing Musselburgh. The existing High Street does not give such a direct connection. Traffic destined for Portobello and coming from the Seafield direction would pass along King's Road and along the new local road provided in the foreshore redevelopment scheme. This new promenade road would afford adequate access to the different parts of Portobello and Joppa.

The High Street and its continuation eastwards to Joppa would then become a tree-lined avenue with green margins, giving access to the sea front at various points along its length and with the Community Centre as its dominant feature. It would have no direct connection for traffic with the main arterial high-way running east or south, and thus create a precinct.

Industry.

The existence of Portobello Power Station at King's Road precludes the possibility of providing the right kind of setting for the bathing pool. As both of these existing structures are new there is no suggestion made to amend this disposition. For existing industry, of which the power station and a bottling works are the largest, an area has been set aside in this northern part of Portobello. A small trading estate situated adjacent to the power station should provide sufficient space for the existing scattered units of industry in other parts of the locality.

Sea Front and Promenade.

One of the most urgent problems for Portobello is a solution to the effects of sea erosion upon the promenade. Expert local knowledge, indicated from a study of approximately 50 years of the nature of the tides along the coasts of the Firth of Forth, that the sand which used to sustain the promenade wall remained there only so long as there was an obstruction such as the old Portobello pier, projected into the sea. The contention is, that, owing to the impact of the strong flood tides against the ebb, any form of obstruction projected into the sea will cause silting up on the westward side. Furthermore the gradual undermining of the Portobello promenade wall dates almost from the removal of the old pier. There is substantial evidence based on past experience that leads to the conclusion that the construction of a new sea wall projecting out into the sea as indicated in the plan would have the desired effect of causing silting up along the whole length of the promenade wall and at the same time creating a valuable and considerable addition to the promenade beach throughout its length. This projection would have the effect also of reclaiming land for additional recreational space from the sea similar to that indicated along the Cramond foreshore.

Also there is the suggestion to widen the esplanade west of the community centre, the building line being kept back to form a continuous sweep of residential flats with broad green strip for rest and recreation along this part of the sea front, and with the amusement park and open-air swimming pool at the west end. The main approach to the open-air swimming pool will be improved by straightening out the esplanade and reclaiming a strip of the foreshore at the estuary of the Figgate Burn.

The Community Centre would comprise recreation and club rooms, cinema and dance hall, gymnasium and baths, theatres (open-air and indoor) in addition to business and civic offices. Provision is also made for grouping the many kiosks and shopping booths which form a feature of any seaside holiday resort. Car parking towers on the mechanised car parking system could be provided at the amusement centre as well as in the vicinity of the Community Centre.

Extending eastwards from the Community Centre are situated other flats and two hotels, and in order to improve this area the whole of the land between the coastal road and the sea front is shown cleared to form a green strip facing the Firth. In order to restore some of the former attraction of the beach by accumulating sand and to protect the esplanade from recurring damage it is suggested that a sea-wall enclosure or storm barrier, indicated in the plan, to encompass a bay would render the beach better and safer for boating and bathing. In the area of land thus reclaimed a quiet retreat with a paddling pool for the recreation of the young could be provided and a short hole golf course or putting green for their elders.

Much of the land to the south and east of the neighbourhood is allocated for public open space because of underground workings, and in consequence the need for the existing public park is lessened. It is, therefore, suggested that this park land should be utilised for two primary schools and residential flats, being land suitable and favourably placed for such a use.

If these suggestions in the Plan are adopted, of which the foreshore scheme is not the least important, the opportunity for restoring Portobello and recreating the kind of sea side amenities for which it has been famous, can be taken. Edinburgh will then be able to offer contrasted sea-side facilities when both the Cramond foreshore and Portobello schemes are substantially complete. Tourist traffic, already encouraged by the setting up of the Festival, will then have this added attraction while the resident population will be living in a considerably improved environment.

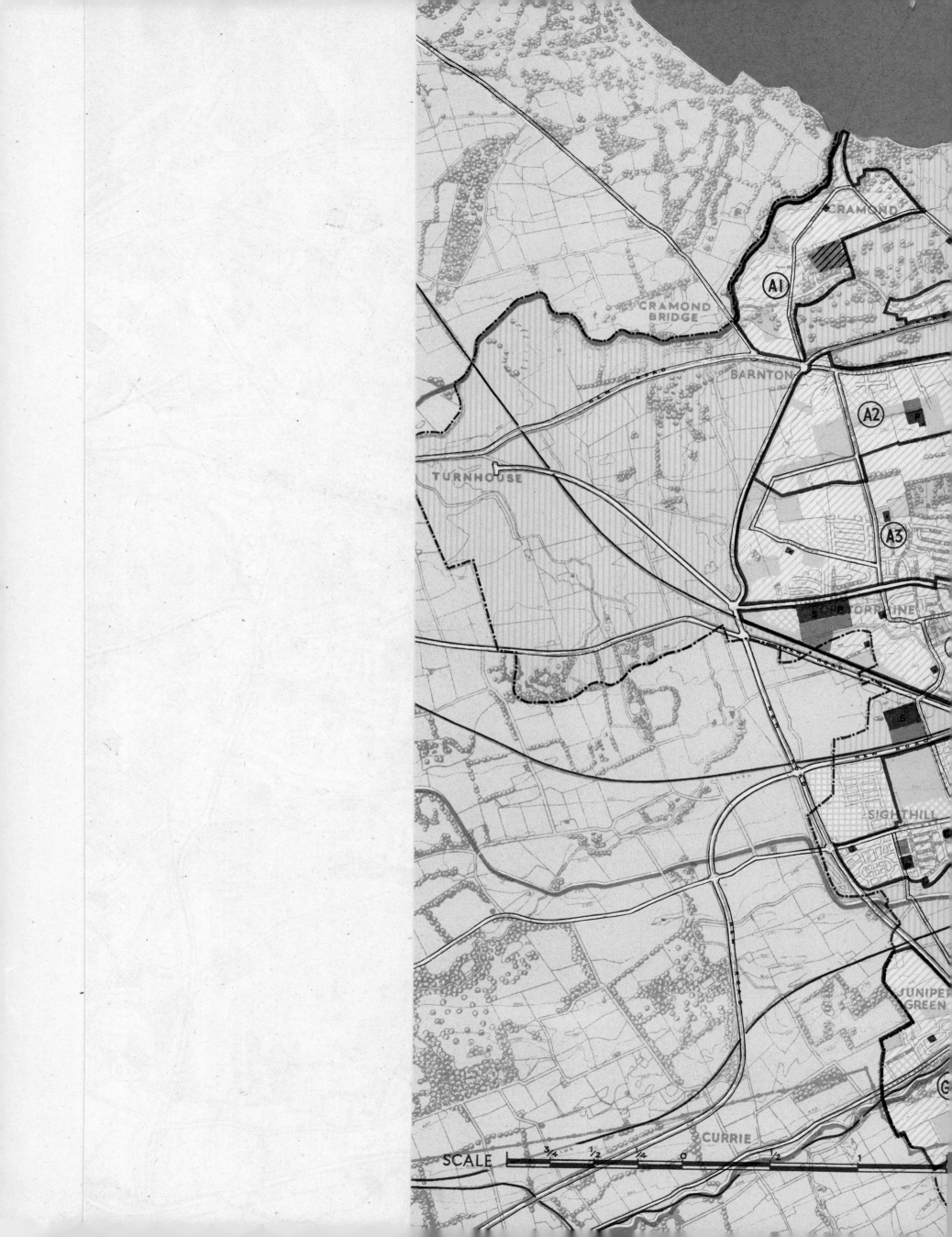

CRAMOND

CRAMOND
BRIDGE

A1

BARNTON

A2

P

TURNHOUSE

A3

CORPLINE

SIGHTHILL

JUNIPER
GREEN

CURRIE

SCALE
¾ ½ ¼ 0 ½ 1

MAP 20

SCHOOLS (Proposals)

These are provided on the basis of the modern standards recommended by the Scottish Education Department and include the nursery, primary and secondary schools and technical colleges including further education for adults and adolescents.

Each neighbourhood unit is provided with nursery and primary schools together with their playing field requirements within its boundaries, but its secondary school and playing fields are for the most part either in the green belt or in some of the existing private open spaces to be built upon. It has been an urgent necessity to make use of one or two small golf courses which lie well within the confines of the city in order to satisfy some of these essential and minimum educational needs. This was not thought unreasonable particularly as the golf courses could be re-opened in the green belt without undue inconvenience to the older generation.

The plan suggests a programme of school development which for the primary schools would have a forty size of class room for the short term period as recommended by the Scottish Education Department. It is anticipated, however, that their recommendation of a thirty size of class room for the long term period would automatically be achieved as the population in the new development areas settle down to a balance of child and adult population normally found in matured communities. In this latter respect the plan conforms to the findings of the Civic Survey.

CHAPTER TEN

EDUCATION

INTRODUCTION. Edinburgh is one of the foremost centres of education in the country, possessing a most comprehensive provision from the nursery school to the University. Broadly, there are three kinds of educational service available—the University, the local authority schools and the independant establishments such as the Merchant Company and George Heriots and numerous smaller ones including some in the embryo stage. No plan can be adequate which ignores the needs of the educational services for site space. Even in cities where educational services are not so prominent a feature as they are in Edinburgh it would be wrong not to study the population requirements in this respect. They are just as much a complement to housing as house construction is in a population distribution scheme. It is because there has been insufficient school provision allowed for in town plans in the past that this essential need has now become so acute.

Another factor to be considered is the effect of the University scheme and the new Education Act upon existing provisions. The act renders most of the local authority schools out of date whilst the University scheme aims at regrouping in one area its various departments. This follows the declared policy of the University, " . . . to regain the sense of unity which is essential to a healthy corporate life there must be a reversal of the policy of dispensing its activities over a wide area of the city." At present the various departments are scattered over a wide area. The proposed integration of the University departments would involve the complete redevelopment of Bristo Street and George Square and the Plan must, therefore, show the extent of the scheme and the best position for the University in relation to kindred organisations and the Plan as a whole.

Consideration has also to be given to the needs of the independent establishments some of which are of world wide reputation.

Perhaps the most important difference from a planning point of view between these three different kinds of establishments is that the local authority schools are intended primarily to serve the district in which the school is situated while the independent establishments and University are not. This requires the siting of the local authority schools close to the community or neighbourhood they should serve. The ' Independents ' on the other hand, may seek their sites over a much wider area, while the University must be centrally situated in order to be near the public buildings provided for advanced cultural pursuits.

The Education Plan, therefore, deals with the requirements of each of these three establishments, the main features of which are described in the following order :—

(1) The University Scheme.

(2) The local authority Schools.

    (a) School distribution in the Plan.

    (b) Standards of accommodation for site space.

1. THE UNIVERSITY SCHEME.

There have been two schemes put forward for an internal scheme—one from the University authorities embracing George Square and one from a group of societies interested in the preservation of the buildings around the Square and who base their scheme upon one prepared by Sir Frank Mears sixteen years earlier. But neither of these schemes can be properly considered without first appreciating the wider issues involved.

What are these wider issues ? First is the question of zoning. The Societies scheme includes the east side of the ' Bridges ' by-pass which is required for residential use and any encroachment there would not leave sufficient area for community development. Furthermore the existing buildings in connection with slum clearance schemes carried out before the war in this locality are too new to be removed and would become isolated residential blocks of buildings if the new University were constructed there.

On the other hand the west side of Nicolson Street should not be residential owing to the predominance of important existing cultural buildings, in addition to the teaching hospital of the Royal Infirmary. This is clearly seen in Sir Frank Mear's earlier plans. If the precinct were placed to the east as the Saltire Society favoured there could be no integration between the precinct and the kindred establishments such as the College of Art and the museum etc., (as the Outlook Tower Association, considered essential) without moving these establishments into the eastern area where there is not even room enough for the University faculties. And what of the old University ? That would have to be moved too if the same precinctal conditions were to be obtained to include this building. No bond can be properly established between this building and a development to the east when it is separated by the existing thoroughfare and its by-pass.

Next is the communications aspect of the Plan. Nicolson Street will always be an important thoroughfare as it is not intended that public service vehicles should be entirely diverted on to its by-pass. Therefore, it would present a physical division between one precinct development and another, i.e., the University (if based upon George Square) and the residential community proposed for St. Leonards. The by-pass is another physical division of more importance. Neither of these roads could be altered in their purpose nor could the by-pass be placed elsewhere if it is to function adequately.

On the other hand traffic now using Bristo Street could be satisfactorily diverted on to one or other of these two roads— Nicolson Street or its by-pass. There would not in our opinion be any need to open up Middle Meadow Walk to take this Bristo Street traffic. This opinion is shared by the Transport Department of the Corporation who are satisfied that the adjustments to the present road system indicated in the Plan would meet their requirements and by the Police Department who agree that most of the traffic using Bristo Street comes from the Princes Street area and would naturally use the by-pass when constructed.

It would, therefore, be impossible to create a self-contained unit for this University development if it were situated to the east of Nicolson Street where precinctal unity between the Old University and the hospital could not be maintained and where the residential development to the east side would be adversely affected.

George Square.

If the west side of Nicolson Street is accepted as offering the most practicable solution, there is the question of detailed land use affecting George Square. Owing to the total area required by the University, George Square could not be left out of the scheme. Whether its old buildings are retained and adapted for such faculties as can effectively use them is a matter for investigation by the Corporation and the University Authorities. These considerations should not be limited to a mere preservation of the buildings on the grounds that they have great architectural merit. The architectural qualities of the buildings in this Square are not to be compared with those in the 'New Town' or some of its adjacent areas, such as Moray Place and Ainsley Place. Furthermore, the architectural unity of the Square has already been destroyed by earlier development on the north side. On the other hand this fact should not necessarily determine the future of the Square. Again wider issues must also be taken into consideration. Not only should practical needs of administration in the disposition of the various departments in this area be considered, but the fact that at least some of the buildings require a large open space in front of them to give them an appropriate setting. If these faculties could not be located in George Square a similar area of open space would have to be found elswhere in this locality. There must be no repetition, for example, of the mistake made in the case of the Old University building where the environment is exceedingly cramped. In addition to zoning it is largely an architectural question and any question of preservation of existing buildings should be considered in the light of what can be achieved by building anew.

2. THE LOCAL AUTHORITY SCHOOLS.

There are two main aspects to be considered in the provision of schools for the various population groupings in the Plan : the first presupposes a given sociological distribution of the income groups—the upper, the middle and working classes; and the second is a certain minimum standard of accommodation to be provided for each type and size of school. As regards the first consideration, the distribution must be related to the zoning proposals for land use where the question of distance of the home from the place of work is involved. As to the second consideration, the minimum standard of accommodation is based upon the recommendation of the Scottish Education Department, the main substance of which is subsequently related. This accommodation, of course, includes not only the number of classrooms and their size but the amount of playing field space that such a school should have. That playing fields ought to be situated adjacent to the school and if possible form part of the same site is manifest from the advantage of improved environment and from the convenience of administration. This matter of the external environment is important as it plays a great part in the psychological influence the school has upon the student and the success or failure of his mental and physical development. The truth of the old Greek belief that human fitness depends upon the concurrent development of an active, healthy body and mind is generally admitted, but the means of attaining this have not always been provided, as schools and their playing fields are often separated by miles of built up property in between. This condition has been aggravated by the sharing of what little playing field space has been provided.

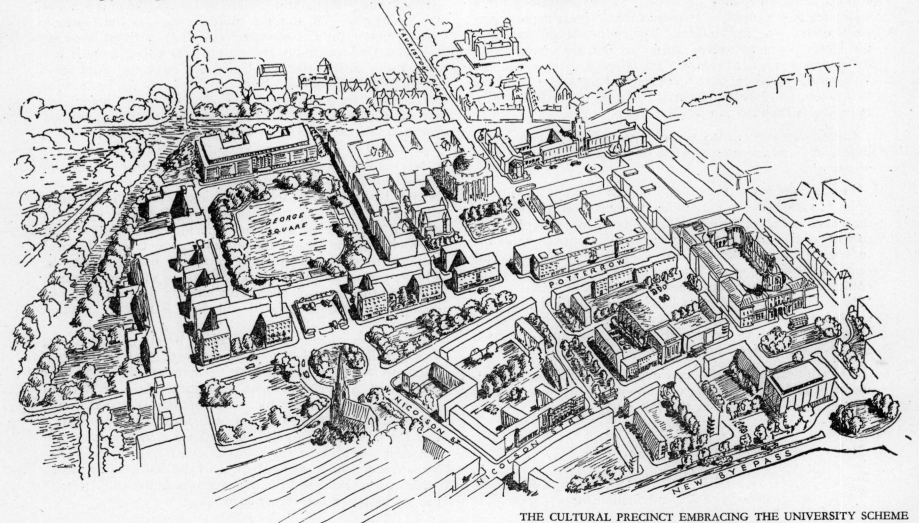

THE CULTURAL PRECINCT EMBRACING THE UNIVERSITY SCHEME

George Square [p. 72]

The architecture of the buildings in George Square of which the above are samples by no means deserve pride of place in Edinburgh's heritage. Why then allow them to stand in the way of a great project?

Queen Street [p. 71]

There is much of this architecture in Edinburgh as seen in the above photograph which many would claim to be of higher architectural value than those of George Square. One cannot, however, expect to preserve everything if improvements are to be made to meet present and future needs.

This sketch shows how inadequate in scale are the existing buildings around George Square for a town square. Larger buildings are required to improve the composition of a garden square with town buildings. This can be done in the University Scheme.

This sketch shows the sort of scale of building required by the University for which the large open gardens of George Square adequately provide the right amount of open space as a setting. If forced to build elsewhere a similar area of open space would have to be created out of built-up property to achieve a comparable setting.

[p. 96]

George Square as seen from the air is half as large again in size than Charlotte Square yet the riparian buildings are similar in scale.

[p. 95]

Charlotte Square as seen from the air was designed by Robert Adam though not completed by him. He shows a better sense of proportion relating size of building to size of open space than was the case for the buildings around George Square.

PLATE XLIV

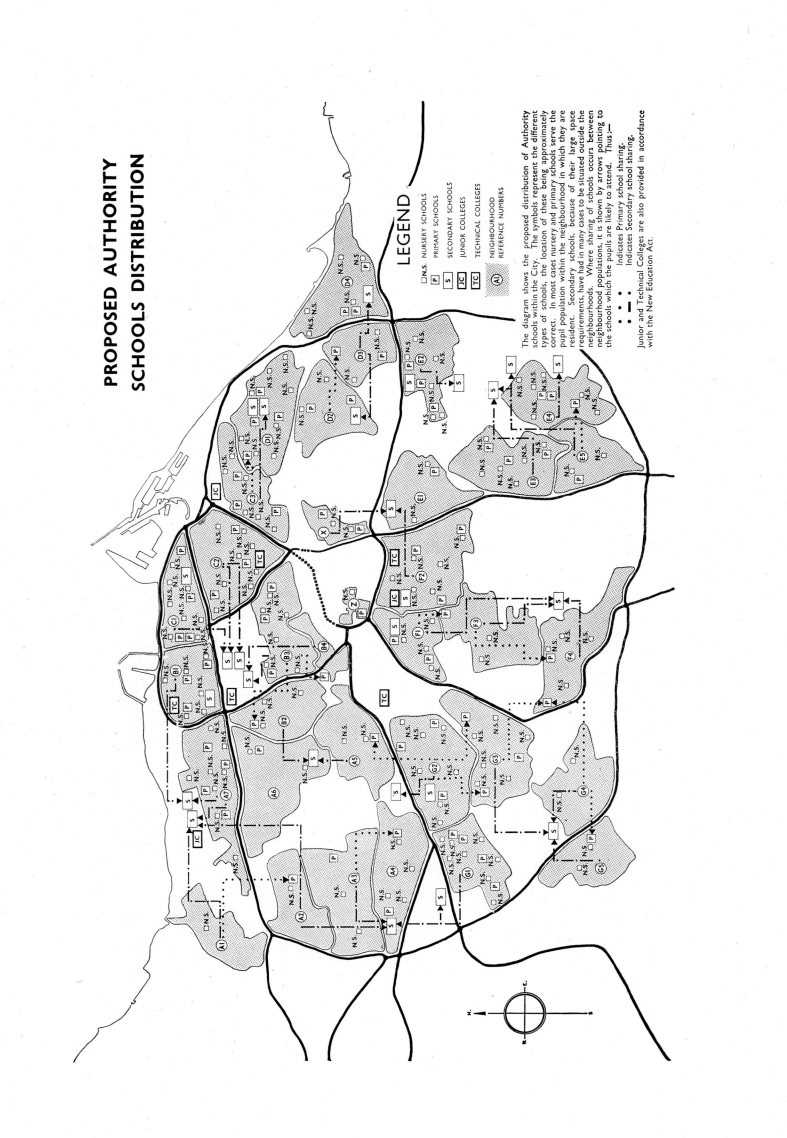

PROPOSED AUTHORITY
SCHOOLS DISTRIBUTION

PLATE XLV

LEGEND

N.S. NURSERY SCHOOLS

P PRIMARY SCHOOLS

S SECONDARY SCHOOLS

JC JUNIOR COLLEGES

TC TECHNICAL COLLEGES

A1 NEIGHBOURHOOD
REFERENCE NUMBERS

The diagram shows the proposed distribution of Authority schools within the City. The symbols represent the different types of schools, the location of these being approximately correct. In most cases nursery and primary schools serve the pupil population within the neighbourhood in which they are resident. Secondary schools, because of their large space requirements, have had in many cases to be situated outside the neighbourhoods. Where sharing of schools occurs between neighbourhood populations, it is shown by arrows pointing to the schools which the pupils are likely to attend. Thus:—

· · · · Indicates Primary school sharing.
·—·—· Indicates Secondary school sharing.

Junior and Technical Colleges are also provided in accordance with the New Education Act.

TABLE XI.

ANTICIPATED DISTRIBUTION OF LOCAL AUTHORITY SCHOOL PUPILS

LOCATION OF HOME

Location of School

Footnotes (right margin):
- + I T.C.
- + I T.C. (P./F. at Inverleith).
- * Includes I Fee Paying School.
- + I J.C. + I C.C. (All P./F's at Braids).
- (P./F. at Carrick Knowe).
- + I J.C.
- I.J.C.
- I.J.C.
- I.J.C.

Summary columns (right of table): Central Shopping Area | Total Pupils | Total Schools | Average Pupils per School

School location	Total Pupils	Total Schools	Average Pupils per School
A	—	1	—
	666	1	666
	541	1	541
	1082 / 1063	2	541 / 1063
	667	1	667
	464 / 702	1 / 1	464 / 702
	2400	4	600
B	1643 / 800	3 / —	548 / 800
	575	—	575
	—	—	—
	2301	4	575
C	—	1	—
	2577 / 806	4	644 / 806
	2552	3	851
D	1914	3	638
	2392 / 2053	4	598 / 1027
	582 / 698	2* / 1	582 / 698
	1112	2	556
E	1960 / 697	3 / —	653 / 697
	439	1	439
	1769 / 552	3 / —	590 / 552
	1975	3	658
	1736	3	579
F	578	1	578
	1200 / 915	2 / —	600 / 915
	1945 / 854	3 / —	648 / 854
	600	1	600
G	2105	4	526
	1834 / 818	3 / —	611 / 818
	1904	3	635
X	—	1	—
Y	600	1	600
Z	1200	2	600
	600	1	600
Total	**43113**	**72**	

Bottom summary rows:

	Central Shopping Area
Total Primary	650
Muirhouse	2146
Inverleith	3367
Prestonfield	1122
Craigmillar	800
Braids	953 / 400
S. Gyle	984 / 200
Carrick Knowe	1053
Kingsknowe	874
Leith Links	875
Crewe Toll	—
Gorgie Industrial	—
Drum (Gilmerton)	—
Little France	950 / 392
Total Secondary	23800 / 992

NOTE.—Primary Schools and Pupils thus: 2577. Secondary Schools and Pupils thus: 818.

Reference to this is made in the Civic Survey, but it is sufficient to quote here the example of Warriston School playing field which contains three football pitches to meet the demands of 33 games per week from 13 schools. In fact there is a total of only 145 acres of playing field space for all the City's schools giving a standard allowance of 0·3 acres per 1,000 population, as compared with the minimum requirement of the Scottish Education Department of 858·5 acres for the estimated total population in the Plan, giving a standard of 1·95 acres per 1,000.

School Distribution in the Plan.

This is shown on map no. 20. The primary schools and secondary schools allowed for in the Plan would serve an estimated total pupil population of children of all ages up to the new school leaving age of 16. This estimate of authority pupil population is based upon the figures obtained from the Education Department of the Corporation for the years 1945-46 and 1946-47 and referred to in the Civic Survey. The geographical disposition of these schools has been related to the decentralisation proposals of the plan and the anticipated sociological grouping of the redistributed population. Though it is hoped that there will be a greater intermingling of all income groups than hitherto, the existing over predominance of the lower income groups in such areas as Craigmillar and West Pilton cannot be ignored nor can it be corrected for a very long time. This is not to suggest that no area should have a predominance of lower income groups as this would be impossible to avoid in certain areas adjacent to the industrial zones, if we are to provide against excessive travelling for those who can least afford it.

The number of pupils has been found to vary considerably in the population of new housing areas according to the length of time the locality has been established. The number of schools will require to be reviewed every five years when a fresh Development Plan has to be submitted to the Central Department as the new 1947 Act demands. The Plan, however, indicates the probable ultimate number to be required : but it should be realised that while such localities as Sighthill and Craigmillar now have approximately 0·7 primary school children per family, in fifteen or twenty years, the ratio may well have fallen to something nearer 0·3. The Civic Survey describes this varying factor in the distribution of the pupil population.

Sharing of Schools between Neighbourhood Units. The aim is to make each neighbourhood unit self sufficient for its education but this could not entirely be expected except for the primary schools. Though the aim is to provide for population groups of approximately 10,000 persons there are often variants of this total. While there is always a large enough population group to support at least one primary school, frequently, there are insufficient pupils to support economically a 600-800 size of secondary school. It is necessary, therefore, to group the secondary schools in an area as reasonably equidistant as possible from the population groups they are intended to serve.

The technical school is another example where sharing between community groups of neighbourhoods is necessary. In a built up city this sharing is a help, as the choice of areas in which to find a suitable site is increased and the opportunity of selecting sites where the playing field can be included with the school building site greater.

In order to explain how the geographical disposition of the schools together with their playing fields shown on map no. 20 is determined the diagram on plate no. XLV illustrates the relationship of these schools to the population groups or neighbourhood units.

Standards of Accommodation for site space.

As a basis the Scottish Education Department have indicated, in advance of their memorandum on school and playing field accommodation, a reasonable standard of site space that should be provided. This is set out below and includes the requirements for the nursery school, primary and secondary schools up to 16 years of age and for the adolescents. While endorsing this recommendation, it is felt that the space allowances for the secondary schools are unnecessarily small, particularly for those that may be situated in the Green belt or Wedge areas of the plan. The allowance for these schools of 800 pupils would be only 16 acres for playing fields as compared with the English standard of 13 acres for 450 pupil size of school.

Nursery Schools. These schools serve the age groups 2-4 inclusive. (Parents are not compelled to send children and the Scottish Education Department take the view that the nursery school movement will have made very satisfactory progress if half the children of the age group are in such schools within 20-25 years). These schools will be mainly of two sizes : one-two play room schools for 40 to 50 children in all and, two-four play room schools for 80 to 100 children. The second type would be built only where housing is so dense that the 100 children coming to school would have to travel a relatively short distance, say quarter of a mile. The site for the two play room school should be 1 acre and for the 4 play room school 1½ acres, the building site should be flat but the rest of the area might with advantage have a variety of contours.

Primary Schools. These schools deal with age groups from 5 to 11 inclusive. The normal primary school will include 14 classes, two per age group of 40 and in addition two backward or tutorial classes of 20 each. The school roll will, therefore, be 600. The site should be 4½ acres for the buiding site and hard surface play ground. Alongside or near by a further site should be provided for play pitches requiring a total site acreage of approximately 4½ acres. Looking to the future, classes will fall below 40 and therefore, there will arise in the foreseeable future a need for more schools. The Plan anticipates a 30 size of class room giving a school roll of 460 pupils.

Secondary Schools. Secondary school education under the Education (Scotland) Act of 1945 envisages the raising of the school leaving age to 16. It is almost certain that within foreseeable time the size of class will be reduced to 30. For these reasons more sites may have to be earmarked for secondary school purposes than are immediately required and these are anticipated in the Plan. The kind of school recommended in the Plan for the accommodation of the junior and senior schools up to the school leaving age of 16 is a school roll of from 800 to 1,000 in order that the school may have a diversified programme with a top class of economic size. Each of these schools should be built on a site of 9 acres allowing for a hard surface play ground space around. In addition playing field space of 12 to 16 acres according to the size of school for the football, hockey, tennis and other games should be provided. The schools should be situated at convenient sites between the city proper and the peripheral points where they may serve the groups of neighbourhoods from which the pupil population will be coming.

Further Education. Junior Technical Colleges to serve part time or full time students mainly of the 16 to 18 age groups would be required for every 50,000 of the population. The requirements regarding the site and playing fields are the same as required for secondary schools.

CRAMOND

CRAMOND
BRIDGE

BARNTON

TURNHOUSE

CORSTORPHINE

SIGHTHILL

JUNIPER
GREEN

CURRIE

SCALE ⌞ 3/4   1/2   1/4   0   1/2   1   1'

MAP 21

OPEN SPACES (Proposals)

A standard of 10 acres per 1,000 population has been adopted for each community representing the planning standard recommended partly by recognised authoritative opinion and partly by statutory legislation. This standard represents a minimum total of the various kinds of open space facilities required by any one community of population. These various forms of facilities may be broadly subdivided as follows :—

4 acres per 1,000 population for public recreation fields.

3 acres per 1,000 population for public parks, boulevards, etc.

2 acres per 1,000 population for authority school playing fields as recommended by the Scottish Education Department.

1 acre per 1,000 population for allotments.

It is not proposed, however, to provide more than 4 acres per 1,000 for those communities in the 100 and 75 density zones nor more than 7 acres for the 50 density zones while there is a chance to provide the balance in the green belt and wedges. With these essential minimum standards within the communities themselves the maximum possible population compatable with good healthy living environment can be maintained. The 9 acres per 1,000 can reasonably be obtained within the 30 density zones since they contain much undeveloped land, but the remaining 1 acre per 1,000 for allotments might well be found in the wedges and green belt.

The over all city open space system includes, of course, the whole of the open space created by this standard together with all those five natural features with which Edinburgh is blessed, such as the mountain of Arthur Seat and the Braid, Blackford, Corstorphine and Craiglockhart and Pentland Hills, together with the Water of Leith and the various burns. The resulting over all standard must, therefore, of necessity be much higher when including these abnormal hilly features. In association with the Regional Planning Committee it is suggested that the Pentland Hills should be preserved as a natural reserve or national park.

CHAPTER ELEVEN

RECREATION SPACES

INTRODUCTION. Edinburgh is one of those capital cities like Paris and London, which, owing to the possession of certain spectacular open spaces of world-wide renown, give a somewhat misleading impression of wealth of park lands. But if the Champs Elysees and Hyde Park are patently visible, how much more arresting are the three rugged hills in the centre of Edinburgh where nature has lent a hand, in place of the landscape architect? And not only are these three rocks in the centre, but three other hills, Braid, Blackford and Corstorphine vary the urban scene somewhat further afield with large areas of rough ground or native woodland. More remarkable still, the actual foot of one of Scotland's National Parks, the northern spur of the Pentlands is thrust across the city's boundary. Then, in contrast to these municipally enclosed crags and mountains, there is the mighty Forth, with, preserved as by a miracle, a fringe of beautiful coastal scenery along its shores; there are views from Lauriston Castle grounds which are almost unbelievable when it is remembered that there is a city of half a million inhabitants within a few minutes reach.

There is no need to enlarge upon the beauty of the Castle Rock or the fantastic group of architectural monuments on the Calton Hill—the view from the North Bridge might be a dream of Piranesi—could any other city be so prodigal of a precipice descending into a railway yard, and yet forming the base to the back of its official National Building (St. Andrews House), here grouped like the monastery of the Grand Lama of Tibet?

The mere convenience of disposal of excavated earth has created another obstruction to a natural feature: the Mound, crowned with two classic national buildings presents the hard horizontal line of a dam across the valley of the loch.

But Arthur's Seat must always carry off the prize: its volcanic origin produces here, in contrast to the luxuriant sophistication of the slopes of Vesuvius, a wild remote savageness. The city is to be congratulated that nothing has been done to tame this: the people, except on rare occasions (when there is skating and tobogganning) do not surge on it in crowds: it has the incalculable value of solitude in the midst of a mighty city: and there are moments and views when there is the illusion of mountainous country stretching illimitably. And what of the view from the garden of Prestonfield House?

An efficient system of recreation spaces to meet the needs of a town must, however, consist of other than these gifts of nature. There must be playing spaces for young and old, for violent exercise and peaceful leisure, distributed at certain intervals throughout the urban mass. There is also the surrounding country which marches up to the edge of the town and defines its limit of spread. Finally there is the dynamic or traffic aspect of recreation spaces: the field paths, parkways and riverside walks.

There may thus be grouped four major aspects of Edinburgh's Park or Recreation Space System:

(a) The natural features: Arthur's Seat, the Castle and valley and Calton Hill in the centre, Corstorphine, Blackford and the Braid Hills in the suburbs and the Pentland Foot on the outskirts. The large areas occupied by these are to be regarded as additional—a gift from nature, to the distributed acreage of open space.

(b) The recreation space based upon a population demand distributed according to a standard and planned in sizes and at intervals as required, so far as this is possible. This section of the park system will also take cognisance of private open space which meets the needs of a certain section of the population.

(c) The surrounding Green Belt and wedge of open country which penetrate into the built up area. The Green Belt, as defined in the Scott report, serves a dual use (agriculture as well as recreation), and contains some areas given wholly up to recreation. It also links through the Pentland "foot" connection with one of the National Parks of Scotland.

(d) The footpaths, parkways and riverside walks, which in some cases are situated within wider open spaces and in others: thread their narrow way through built up areas.

A detailed account is given under headings mentioned below:—

1. Distributed recreation spaces.
2. Green Belt and connection with National Park.
3. Parkways.
   (a) Footpath system.
   (b) Water of Leith.

1. DISTRIBUTED RECREATION SPACE.

Existing Distribution.

As has already been hinted, the Open Space Survey Map of Edinburgh gives a somewhat misleading impression to those who do not know the city; the amount of green of all kinds shown appears to suggest an ampleness of recreational space, which does not, in fact, exist except for those who climb Arthur's Seat or who play golf. The Survey of Open Space shows that of the 32,526 acres of the city's area about one half is built up and the remainder open space. Some 11,000 acres of this open space is agricultural while 5,386 acres consist of golf courses (37%) spectacular open space (e.g. Arthur's Seat) (29%) private open space (16%) public recreation space (8·6%) non-authority schools (5·4%) local authority schools (2·7%). The true position of the recreation space, which should be distributed on a population basis, becomes apparent when it is realised that the city's acreage for 1,000 persons is 1·0 acre for public recreation (as compared with the minimum 4 acres per 1,000 recommended for central areas) and 0·31 (not all of it directly accessible) for local authority schools as compared with 1·95 as required. The standard usually adopted for distributed open space (including for schools), is 10 acres per 1,000 of the population. The 5,386 acres of Edinburgh's total of all kinds represents a standard of 12 acres per 1,000 an impressive figure until it is realised that no less than 82% is either in exclusive private possession or is largely composed of irregular masses of rock and precipice!

The Garden.

In the past, its safety where preservation is needed has been uncertain : its provision in slum clearance schemes almost non existant. The original gardens of the old Town have long since been built upon while high density tenement development at Craigmillar and Pilton have squeezed out all hope of garden provision. Yet there is nothing which contributes to the beauty of our environment so much as does the garden : nor anything which encourages the means for self expression and physical exercise for which all too little room is allowed in these utilitarian days. Those who have lived in the tenements built to the favourite high densities of some inter-war builders and who now live in the standard temporary house must be thankful for the small mercies their tiny gardens represent. Yet the one time stifled urge has been released at last and delightfully prim little plots are to-day emerging to promise well for the future beautiful environment that is a much needed blessing for the temporary house.

When considering the density of distribution of the houses and population it is hoped the garden will not be a thing fenced off, which might be necessary where the provisions of recreation space elsewhere is inadequate. The garden should be seen by all to be most appreciated.

Proposed Distribution.

The distribution proposed in the plan aims at providing as near as possible to the approved standards in all areas of development and redevelopment and within the planning boundaries of the neighbourhood units. It is appreciated that to obtain in the central areas the ideal allowance of all kinds (15 acres for every 1,000 population in all) is not feasible on account of the enormous disturbance that would be caused to property. Furthermore, such a distribution would collectively result in a more widely flung distribution of the population and require a greater area of building development for the city as a whole. As, however, the standard 10 acre is considered to be essential some will have to be found in the green belt and wedges, while the balance, the barest minimum of 4 acres per 1,000 population should be provided within the central and more compactly built up parts of the city. Nothing less than the 4 acres would adequately relieve the congestion at present experienced on the existing public and school recreation spaces. Warriston Road recreation ground, for instance, has had to be relaid with ashes owing to excessive use.

The plan recommends, therefore, a distribution of 4 acres per 1,000 population for all purposes in the central areas, the balance being found in the green belt and wedges. For the intermediate and outer areas the basic allowance recommended varies from 7 to 10 acres per 1,000 population within the neighbourhood units.

The details of distribution embodying these requirements are shown on map no. 21 but it will perhaps be of interest to give a brief description of some of the more important spaces suggested. These consist in the main of existing unbuilt on ground.

Niddrie House Estate. This comes within the Neighbourhood planning unit E2 at the south-east part of the city. A substantial portion of the estate is liable to subsidence due to underground coal workings. The part scheduled for public recreation is east of Niddrie Burn, while the beautifully wooded park and banks of Niddrie Burn are recommended for public parks. The balance next to Niddrie Mains road contributes to the housing development for the locality.

Duddingston Mains Golf Course. This was an existing open space and was used as a golf course before the war but has since been ploughed up for agricultural use. It is suggested in the Plan that this might well provide for new development consisting of two primary school sites totalling 9 acres and two primary school playing fields totalling 9 acres with the remainder for new housing development. To replace this recreation space some ground on either side of the Brunstane Burn and to the south of Milton Road which is liable to subsidence and, therefore, unsuitable for building purposes is recommended for public recreation space and school playing fields.

Sea Coast Reclamation at Portobello. 32 acres could be reclaimed from the sea to provide some of the recreation space requirements for the Portobello neighbourhood unit. It would serve a double purpose because this reclamation would at the same time give the protection required to prevent further sea erosion to the Portobello Promenade wall.

Seafield Golf Course. This is an open space which was taken over during the war for a camp and has since been completely disfigured. It is recommended that the whole of this area be used to help meet the needs for secondary and primary school sites and their playing fields for the community in this part of the city.

Eastern Slopes of Arthur's Seat. These slopes of Arthur's Seat come within Neighbourhood Unit D2 and in order to prevent further encroachment on them by building it is proposed that some of the recreation space requirements for this neighbourhood unit should be found here, thus serving the double purpose of recreation and the preservation of the slopes.

Prestonfield Golf Course. This golf course comes within Neighbourhood Unit E1 and though it still functions as a golf course to-day, it is felt that the community in the locality should have a prior claim to its use for essential football and cricket facilities ; it is, therefore, scheduled for public recreation space to meet these requirements. The golf course could quite well be transferred to one of the green belt areas instead.

The environment of Prestonfield House is to be preserved as a public park while the house itself might eventually be used as a community club.

The north west portion of this Prestonfield area, which is suggested for the new site of the Royal High School and playing fields consists of allotments and two large houses. The present Royal High School at Calton Hill could then be remodelled for the extension of St. Andrew's House.

Burdiehouse Burn, Liberton. This is required for part of the public park for the community and preserves a ' greenway ' separating Neighbourhood Units E3 and E4.

Gracemount Estate. This estate should be acquired mainly for open space providing public recreational facilities while the house might be used as a community club. A stretch of ground to the south west of this proposed recreation space should be allocated for a shopping centre to serve the neighbouring population group.

Carrick Knowe Golf Course. As it has not the hilly topography of many of the golf courses of Edinburgh this one does not lend itself so well for golf course use though it has very attractive surroundings. It is suggested that a more appropriate use would be for public recreational space mainly for secondary school and playing field accommodation.

2. GREEN BELT AND CONNECTION WITH NATIONAL PARK.

The encirclement by a Green Belt is perhaps more necessary in Edinburgh than in most other isolated Towns★. Usually the inner edge, the so-called Urban Fence, can and indeed must be sharply defined, the outer edge shades off imperceptibly into the surrounding country. If the Scott Committee's definition of the Green Belt be accepted, viz : that it represents an area in which the dual use of agriculture (in its widest sense) and recreation (not in the intensive form, but as the townsman's use of the country for relaxation), then it is clear that the further out from the town, the thinner this use becomes, with the ever widening radius; certain well-known places which once were unfortunately misnamed beauty spots are an exception to this principle of the general dispersion of recreational intensity.

In the case of Edinburgh, however, there is, at any rate on the Haddington side, a developing area, the Lothian Coalfield beyond the Green Belt, which is thus caught between expanding Edinburgh and encroaching Lothian : its essential role of an intervening space is therefore of immense importance.

How much of the open land surrounding Edinburgh is still required for growth and decentralisation, is shown in the population chapter 3 and on folding Map 14. It is well that a limit should at length be called to this continuous spread. But how can it if new housing development continues to be mainly devoted to immigrants instead of to the relief of the existing overcrowded areas ?

R.L.S. in his notes on the Edinburgh of his day, deplored the villa extension that was rapidly going forward. It is true that there was great charm in the old compact city, and even in living memory there was the great expanse of level ground open to the Forth, once Fettes and the Queensferry Road were passed. It would indeed have been grand if the Green Belt could have carried along in a width of one mile from Dalmeny Park and Cramond to Leith, with Granton as no more than a coastal episode. But no-one, not even Queen Elizabeth in England† or Mary Queen of Scots in Edinburgh, could confine the old mediaeval city or even the New Town. The growth was inevitable, but it might have followed better lines. The low density spread of recent years, which covers so much ground, was probably a reaction from the densely crowded "Lands" of the Old Town, coupled with the habit of a home on one floor.

The Green Belt must be pushed out beyond these far-flung suburbs, which not only approach the Forth but straggle nearly up to the Pentlands. Consequently it cannot be confined to the city boundary as at present existing owing to its irregular shape, particularly on the west. The outer limit of the Green Belt has been determined in close co-operation with the consultant to the regional plan.

There are several wedges of open land, that start from the Green Belt and penetrate into the built up area.

Green Wedges.

(1) *North Western Wedge.* At the north western parts of the city there are some beautiful woodlands, the foreshore of the Firth of Forth, the wooded estate between Queensferry Road and Barnton railway and Corstorphine Hill. If these natural features were linked together and preserved from building development they would contribute a very fine wedge of park land from the sea shore to Corstorphine.

★—As distinct from Towns like Glasgow which forms part of a Conurbation.

†—See Proclamation to limit the size of London

(2) *The Broomhouse Wedge* consists of rich farmland lying in a triangular shaped area between two railways and the proposed outer ring road. The plan recommends a continuance of the farm land or nursery use but with a secondary school and its playing fields and perhaps a nine hole golf course to be situated on part of the ground on either side of the Broomhouse Road. The whole would make an extended form of open space preserving a kind of public health zone situated about Gogar.

(3) *Kingsknowe and Hailes* offers another wedge of open ground consisting of a golf course and rich farm land with the Union Canal running through its midst. Its existing use and features should be preserved to retain this wedge of open space between the Colinton and Sighthill communities.

(4) *Dreghorn and Redford* is practically all War Department property which is needed by the Department mainly as open training ground. This requirement meets with the desire for a wedge of open space, but care must be taken to preserve public access in safety as it offers some of the best means of approach from the city to the Pentlands. With the City Hospital grounds, this wedge forms a useful extension of the greenbelt.

(5) *The Braid and Blackford Hill* wedge is one of the most extensive and comes closely into the centre of the city most of which is accessible to the public. Some parts about Mortonhall still bar the right of way to the open country and steps should, therefore, be taken on the lines suggested in the section under footpaths.

For fine vistas of woodland and open hill none could be better than the prospects that can be enjoyed from the various vantage points. Certainly housing development should not be permitted here.

Craigmillar and Holyrood Park. As a devious tract of land, this wedge preserves the present country character lying between Niddrie Mains and Liberton. It embraces Arthur Seat in the heart of the city, Craigmillar Castle and the surrounding rich nurseries and other agricultural holdings. The secondary school sites with their playing fields are situated below the Castle and away from its sloping foreground which is such an essential feature of the composition of the landscape. Though it links up with that part of the green belt where the coalfields lie the area is remarkably free from disfigurement.

3. PARKWAYS.

The means of getting about on foot, on horseback, or even on a bicycle, without using a road, on which motor cars assume the prerogative, is one of the provisions of a plan. These Park-ways will sometimes pass through public recreation spaces, sometimes through land under cultivation and sometimes through built up areas. An attempt at a system of communication, comparable to a road system should be made : but it should always be borne in mind the park traffic system attaches more importance to pleasantness of route than to directness, hence the special attraction of the river valley parkway, for all that it meanders. There are three streams in the Edinburgh area, one passing through its midst, the Water of Leith, one on its western boundary, the river Almond, and a little removed toward the east, the North Esk. Although all the valleys of these streams have been used for industry (the Almond least so) they contain features of extreme and even romantic beauty. Without attempting to clear out industry (which, in contrast to the similar Sheffield streams, has not left them), it is proposed to

77

make at any rate the Water of Leith and the Almond continuously accessible to the outer verge of the Green Belt: thus there may be a riverside walk from Bonnington near Leith to Balerno.*

[a] *The Footpath System.*

Within the city there are a number of path-ways which pass through some extremely interesting natural scenery and from which delightful views of Edinburgh's hills and landmarks may be seen to surprise the new-comer. In a number of cases these foot-ways are rather fragmentary, being enclosed by the building development of past years. An attempt, however, has been made to show how it might be possible to link up at least some of these foot-ways to create a useful and interesting greenway system. The Water of Leith Valley is an example of this fragmentary accessibility for the public owing to the fact that it is mainly in private ownership of one sort or another.

The following are suggestions for this footpath system :—

In the western area, starting from inside the city, it would be possible for the citizen to obtain the magnificent promenade walk from Granton along its fore-shore to Cramond from which three alternative routes are open to him. First is the existing one, accessible by means of the ferry at Cramond from which runs the beautiful Dalmeny Park walk to South Queensferry. The second would be along the river valley of the Almond passing through Cramond Brig and Craigiehall to Turnhouse. The third would be from the fore-shore through Silverknowes, Blackhall to Murrayfield and Hillwood by means of Corstorphine Hill and its woodlands.

Other local routes are also suggested as, for example, from Long Green in Dalmeny Park crossing Queensferry Road at Dolphington, through the woods to the railway embankment near the river Almond.

The next important system from the city would, of course, be the Water of Leith Valley which is described in some detail further on.

After that is the Union Canal route which in the Plan could commence right from the centre of the city where it would pass parallel to one of the proposed arterial radials at Slateford. The Canal would then be reached whence an interesting walk of diverse scenery right through East Hermiston to Ratho and beyond could be enjoyed.

As an off-shoot from this main route it is suggested a new access might be provided from Hermiston on the Canal along to the Gogar Burn through Dalmahoy on the north side of Dalmahoy Hill to the Water of Leith at Balerno.

South and East. The most important route in this part of the city is via Braid Burn and it is suggested that there would

*—Its counter-part is to be created in the new 'Thames Walk' at present under consideration by a joint consultative committee of the local authorities concerned.

be little difficulty in creating one of the most interesting routes of all, from Portobello to Colinton Mains. Through Northfield it would pass by way of the Figgate Burn, through Duddingston where a woodland path might be created, through Bridgend and the policies of the Inch, passing Nether Liberton and Liberton Dams, Hermitage of Braid, Braid Burn Valley, Craiglockart and so on to the devious routes that diverge at Colinton Mains into the Pentland Hills.

All these existing and proposed footpaths may be traced upon folding Map no. 22 showing the green belt wedges and footpath system.

[b] *Water of Leith.*

This offers one of the finest riverside walks that any city could wish for, but few, if any of the citizens of Edinburgh know the full extent of the scenery that may be seen and enjoyed by following the course of this river from its mouth in Leith to the city boundary at Juniper Green and beyond. This is hardly surprising since the greater part of its banks lie within property of many ownerships that bar the way to the public. Snatches of the delightful views and world-famous landmarks of the city are known to many, such as the one seen at Powderhall but these merely whet the appetite for more. Many more views are to be had as those shown on plate no. XLVI clearly illustrate.

There is room for considerable improvement in the different parts of the course of the river where there are many uncared for portions of the banks and derelict buildings requiring repair. Even in some of the more beautiful parts of the valley, particularly at the Dean Bridge, the existing landscape has become over-wooded. The Plan, on plate no. XLVI shows a number of architectural suggestions for indoor and outdoor recreation, knit together by careful landscaping of varying character. For example, in the Leith Industrial area a public park would be created out of the derelict areas on both sides of the river for the benefit of visitors and for a lunch hour walk for citizens working there.

At Powderhall a new stadium and racing track is suggested upon much more generous lines than exists at the moment. It should, in fact, be possible to obtain a running track for olympic and other athletic purposes. In other parts of the system where the flanking communities follow its route the natural contours of the locality have predetermined the need for community centres to be located about the banks of the river, for example, Stockbridge which is neighbourhood centre for Neighbourhood Unit B3, also Roseburn for A5, Slateford for G3 and Colinton for G4. The whole scheme in essence should be a public walk by the Water of Leith from Bonnington to Balerno interspersed by varying recreation facilities.

PLATE XLVII

This perhaps presents one of the most charming views of Arthur's Seat and the Salisbury Crags as seen from Bruntsfield Links in the heart of the city. The row of trees in the middle foreground mark the route of Melville Drive which forms the northern link of the proposed inner ring road for the city.

PLATE XLVIII

W L Leitch

Fig. 57 St Bernard's Well

This is a reproduction from a lithograph print by W. L. Leitch of St. Bernard's Well in the valley of the Water of Leith. It is situated in one of the most charming parts in this valley and it is important to appreciate the need for good landscape design. Whether or not it presents a faithful interpretation of the extent of tree and shrub plantation of an earlier century there is no doubt that the valley at this part looks far more attractive with a few groups of well placed trees than the gorge-like profusion of trees that exists at present and which obscures for the most part the natural features of the river side and its banks. The photograph on the opposite page, Plate XLIX, gives a bird's eye view of this part of the valley from the opposite direction.

Randolph Cliff [*p.* 50]

This bird's eye view of the Water of Leith valley shows how excessive is the existing tree plantation. The result produces this gorge-like wilderness which excludes from view too much of the riverside walk. The protection from the sun afforded by this natural growth is more appropriate for tropical parts than in the northern climes where heavy rain-fall together with dense woods tends to produce a dank atmosphere.

PLATE XLIX

An interesting view of the spire of Tolbooth Church in Castle Hill seen against the background of Arthur's Seat. Views of this kind are typical of Edinburgh with its sharply contrasting contours.

Old Tolbooth Spire [p. 18]

Cramond Brig [p. 60]

[P. 60]. *This bridge provides one of the principal points of access to the city from the north. It is situated on the boundary of the city and is called Cramond Brig.*

[P. 54]. *In the heart of Edinburgh lies one of the old village communities of Dean. This view shows the old arched bridge spanning the Water of Leith which meanders through the village itself. Considerable restoration work is called for in the redevelopment scheme for this village.*

Old Dean Bridge [p. 54]

PLATE L

CHAPTER TWELVE

VILLAGES

INTRODUCTION. It was from 1920 onwards that the rural communities of Corstorphine, Cramond, Newhaven, Colinton, etc., were absorbed by expanding suburbia. In the historical chapter their traditional and historical associations are mentioned when they had not yet become mere dormitories of the great city.

The purpose of this chapter is to explain what is left of them—of their buildings and environment—that determined their character and to discover their new role in this expanded growth not only of to-day but of to-morrow as anticipated by the Plan.

Corstorphine.

Entering this part of the city (for it is no longer separated from Edinburgh as of old) one becomes aware of the remains of a community centre of rural scale and character. The church with its curiously squat tower is situated in a green setting and although the tombstones of its yard have begun to extend from behind the church there is still a pleasant green on the south side. The removal of the railings from the low stone wall marking its boundaries provides the delightful impression of a village green. May it remain so. One storey cottages to the west of this green together with an absence of large or tall buildings maintain the scale of a village centre while tall groups of trees enhance the rural scene.

Less fortunate is the town character given to the layout of St. Margarets Park where simplicity should have been the key note, the lack of which is in strange contrast to the village-like one storey pantile roofed cottages near by.

These relics of rural life probably owe their preservation to the fact that commercialism was more attracted to the main Corstorphine Road that lies to the north and that traffic by-passed the area. The whole village now lies on the fringe of the 19th century spread from the city and is surrounded by a motley collection of 20th century bungalow and two storey houses of which some consist of that strange hybrid of the city tenement—the " flatted " two storey dwellings. The choice of materials is perhaps the worst feature of both the 19th and 20th century buildings which offer a monotonous dullness and general lack of cheerful colour.

The Plan recommends a redevelopment of the old village centre to create a neighbourhood centre for a further enlargement of the present population. Care should be taken to maintain the village scale and character. In no circumstances should blocks of shops with high tenements be constructed like those recently built on the Corstorphine Road.

Juniper Green.

This village lies at the extreme south west part of the city and appears now as a mere incident on this part of the main Lanark Road where 19th and 20th century ribboning has contributed to the general featureless character of the development.

It is recommended that a well defined shopping centre, together with adequate public buildings, should now be the aim for the centre while the neighbourhood should become a reception area for some of the decentralised population under the general scheme for redistribution.

Colinton.

Situated on the steep slopes of the Water of Leith in the south-eastern part of the city, Colinton is a definite village centre with a small group of shops. Again it is a community that has not suffered as so many have from being situated on a main road. The village owes much to the fact that the Lanark Road by-passes it to the north-west. Its role as a week-end rendezvous is not in any way lessened on that account but on the contrary is made all the more attractive. The magnificent walks in the Pentland Hills area are by no means the only attraction however, as this part of the Water of Leith provides really superb scenery at the " Dell " and the walks along the river banks. If the Water of Leith Scheme is carried out, Colinton and its riverside park will play an important part. Care should be taken to preserve the interesting and charming group created by the positioning of the Church, Manse and church yard which have for their setting the beautiful wooded slopes of the Water of Leith. A view of the crescent shaped wooded slopes is interrupted by the old house in the Corporation-maintained church yard and something should be done to correct this.

In the Plan the existing nucleus of community life at Woodhall Road is expanded, and the neighbourhood unit centred upon it should become a reception area for decentralised population.

Swanston.

Here at the southern extremity of the city and nestling beneath the shadow of the Pentlands is the " Clachan " village made famous by Stevenson. Charmingly situated on the lower slopes of Caerketton Hill of the Pentlands it is screened from view by high trees offering complete seclusion —a writers paradise. The three sided green of stone cottages set apart from the " clachan " cottages are a more modern addition as, no doubt, is the white-washed walled house with its picturesque garden. They introduce a rather formal note by comparison with the irregular placing of the thatched " clachan " cottages but none the less pleasing for that. The condition of the thatched cottages, however, is poor : they appear to have been neglected and some do not have the healthy living accommodation that is possible by careful restoration.

The village and farm is essentially a place of quiet retreat and is probably not greatly frequented by week-end pleasure seekers as the principal walks in the Pentlands do not pass through here. However, its peace has, according to Stevenson, been disturbed on more than one occasion in Edinburgh's chequered history. For example, the farm opened its doors hospitably to the Covenanters when a night conventicle was held upon the Pentlands. Another event was the descent of some of Prince Charlie's highlanders who raided the farm during a foraging expedition.

Edinburgh Corporation is interested in this locality for another reason. The springs that rise and gather in the place called the dell are a source of important water supply and the sheltered field containing them was purchased by the Corporation a long time ago. But this was not the only interest, according to Stevenson, who refers to the cottage in the dell as a "municipal Pleasure House" where "with jovial magistrates and public funds" a place suitable for "junketing" was found.

As one emerges from this secluded place one is immediately confronted with the fringe development of suburban Edinburgh that is anything but attractive. With the rounding off of this recent development suggested in the Plan a last chance is available to the city to create something more worthy as a front to the proposed National Park for the Pentlands which penetrates into this part of the proposed Green Belt. There should not be any building development here.

Liberton.

This place lies on the rising ground to the south-east of the city. It has no village features since originally it was a hamlet situated at the cross roads of the main Lasswade road and Kirkgate.

Taking this old focus as the new centre for a neighbourhood unit a new focus for shopping and community activity may grow up to serve the new development in the locality.

Gilmerton.

Lying to the south east of the city and south-east of Liberton this place consists of a main street serving a population whose principal occupation is mining. The village contains miners rows (now derelict but still standing) and one or two charming cottages, but otherwise it is featureless.

In the Plan the main street is to be redeveloped as a shopping centre with its group of community dwellings adjacent.

Duddingston.

This place is situated beneath the heights of Arthur's Seat and on the fringe of King's Park. Any development either in the village or in the immediate vicinity should be carefully considered from the point of view of its effect upon this magnificent landscape. Indifferent "suburbia" has already encroached upon the fringes of the village and care is required to preserve the scale and character of this old part. It consists of a single street, dog-leg shaped on plan with one old Inn on the corner—The Sheeps Heid—and the part Norman church. The whole is by-passed by the thoroughfare to the east. It serves as a happy rendezvous for those seeking company, perhaps within sound of the skittle alley, before returning along the green road overlooking Duddingston Loch in its misty evening setting. As it lies on the extremity of the neighbourhood unit, the focus of community life would naturally tend towards Northfield where a new centre is recommended in the Plan. Redevelopment suggested for this old part should be carried out to retain the best of the existing features.

Dean Village.

This village lies on either side of the banks of the Water of Leith beneath the Dean Bridge which provides the link between the new extension and the north western section of the New Town. It is rather a confused conglomeration of buildings which derive a considerable amount of charm in certain instances from such irregularity. In fact anything but an informal layout for development in such a deep ravine as here would be absurd.

There are a number of mills dating from the time of David I of Scotland which were among the conveyances of his Royal Charter to Holyrood Abbey. Some 17th century cottages exist on the south bank. A particularly charming one just restored is situated at the corner of the very old single arched bridge that spans the stream. Indifferent remnants of 19th century buildings join the village with the road leading to the famous Dean cemetery and on to Queensferry Road. On both sides of the stream there is room for considerable improvement and restoration of old buildings following the example so recently carried out at the corner of the old bridge.

The village forms an important feature of the Water of Leith scheme and contributes to the great variety of changing scenery that can be linked up in a continuous parkway system. It is recommended therefore that redevelopment should take the form of restoration of that which is worthy of retention and a general thinning out to reduce congestion of living conditions.

Cramond.

The village is situated at the north west corner of Edinburgh in the charming setting of the wooded Dalmeny Park from which it is separated by the Almond river. It presents an entirely different scene to the weekender or casual visitor. It lies at the junction formed between riverside walk provided along the banks of the river Almond and the new promenade now nearing completion along the coast of the Firth of Forth. The village is well placed to satisfy the needs of promenaders who will no doubt increase considerably in numbers. In addition there are the yachting activities of the local club. The yachts add pleasantly to the scene as they rock lazily at their moorings. Historically the village goes back to Roman times. It occupies the site of an important Roman station with a military way connected with the great English Watling Street. Its name Cramond is Celtic signifying "the fort upon the Almond."

In the Plan Cramond retains its present role and assumes yet another—the centre for the daily activities of the rapidly developing neighbourhood which should become a reception area for the decentralised population in the redistribution scheme described in Chapter 3. It is anticipated that the population moving into the locality in the scheme would not be all of one income group.

Spring Glory [*p. 51*]

*A charming view of the public walk through part of the Dean
Village during spring time.*

PLATE LI

[P. 55]. *This is a view of the Haven at Cramond which provides one of the few opportunities for pleasure yachting activities near the city. A ferry at this point links Dalmeny Estate for public access with the Cramond Foreshore development which terminates at its estuary.*

Haven, Cramond [p. 55]

Cramond Inn [p. 61]

Lauriston Castle [p. 53]

Swanston Village [p. 52]

[P. 53]. *This shows the original portion of old Lauriston Castle situated well within the city confines. It is situated in a charming estate and is recommended for preservation in the Plan. It was presented to the city as a bequest and is preserved as a museum together with its internal furnishings.*

[P. 52]. *These are some of the old clachan cottages at Swanston Village which nestles beneath the shadow of the Pentland Hills. Considerable restoration work is necessary in order to obtain comfortable dwellings comparable with any modern housing. Such restoration work was very successfully carried out in different parts of the country before the war.*

[P. 61]. *A view of the whitewashed Cramond Inn which is situated just above the Haven seen in the adjoining photograph. Cramond Village is a seaside place which adds considerably to the diversity of choice for week-end recreation.*

PLATE LII

PART IV

CHAPTER THIRTEEN

REALISATION

INTRODUCTION. A Development Plan as its name implies is in no sense a contract drawing or series of blue prints, intended as in the case of a Building to be carried out in every detail and at once, as a single operation. It should be regarded much more as a programme of works to be realised at different times : and it is one of the advantages of a programme that while it gives an indication of the whole, there are opportunities of reviewing or improving some of the later items when they fall to be realised.

The time-factor, in a word, enters as an essential feature into the plan. Though the scheme of Development is presented as a whole, it will be separated into periods, which may take in the aggregate 50 years to complete. The whole plan is not only split up into these realisation periods but the separate sections may equally be subject to period planning. Thus the road system proposed contains many obvious and necessary improvements which can and should be put in hand at once : others, which may involve the destruction of existing buildings which still have a certain " life " before them, will inevitably be postponed to a later date. Housing improvement, again, is always being undertaken sectionally; the plan merely gives a more logical programme, fitting it in with other requirements such as location of industry, provision of playgrounds, neighbourhood centres etc. There is also the highly important synchronisation of public services : working to a comprehensive plan of development has here an economic significance of first importance.

The Plan, indeed, stands as a whole : it is not a fortuitous collection of separate items, bound up together in a Report. Nevertheless, paradoxical though it may appear, certain separate features can be abandoned without vitiating the rest : it is not a precarious card-castle—one dislocation and the whole falls to the ground. There are certain main features, to which indeed the authors attach first-rate importance, which could either be transposed into a remoter period category or even abandoned without destroying the other essential features. This particularly applies to interests generated externally such as long distance railway traffic, as compared with essentially internal problems such as the breakdown of overcrowding. The main line diversion of the North British railway under the Meadows is a proposal which we believe to be feasible, advantageous for rail transport and terminal facilities, and also of inestimable value to the general amenity of a capital city at its very centre point of spectacular beauty. But the road plan has so been devised that its main central proposals would still stand if Edinburgh found itself prepared to tolerate the smoke nuisance in the Waverley valley.

While this admission is made with regard to certain major features of the plan it must not be stretched to mean that sections of the plan can be mutilated and excised indiscriminately, until no coherent scheme remains.

There is another aspect of the Development Plan presented as a whole which requires a word, not indeed of apology, but of explanation. To the business man, it is apt to look like an expensive piece of work; so many proposals, so many operations, so much rebuilding, so much city extension :

surely we can never afford it, i.e. the whole scheme. But a little reflection will show that the vast majority of works proposed under the plan are things that must be done anyhow, if the City is to keep pace with the bare essentials of modern existence.

Traffic congestion, which at the moment is being slightly ameliorated by temporary police expedients, must sooner or later be fundamentally solved by permanent planning : the west end of Princes Street cannot be left in its present makeshift condition nor can the industrial traffic from Leith be allowed to continue to find its way along Princes Street to the detriment of the shops. These improvements may well be expensive, but they are unavoidable. Again Parliament has placed a statutory obligation on Local Authorities to eliminate slums, to decongest the overcrowded centres of our cities and to provide new houses to take the place of those condemned for various reasons. The Plan does no more than indicate how and where this should be done and in conformity with other essential features such as schools, community centres, shops, open spaces, etc. In these respects the Plan does not necessarily add one single pound to the cost.

But there are frankly certain features proposed for the sake of general convenience and amenity, proposals not extravagant in view of one of the most beautiful cities in the world. A mean and clipped solution might indeed save a few pounds of present expenditure : but would it pay in the long run ?

Railway improvements in general, and the Waverley Station in particular, might be thought extravagant : but in all those in which the public critic may scent amenity it will be found that convenience and ultimate economy have also been in view.

Finally perhaps the most spectacular proposal of all, the rebuilding of Princes Street may be mentioned. What city, it may be superficially queried, could possibly afford this gigantic architectural conception, three quarters of a mile of continuous new building ? But careful enquiry has shown that with the exception of one or two quite new buildings and three clubs, the whole frontage is ripe for reconstruction; though not of course as a single gigantic operation. But is this rebuilding to proceed in single unrelated units or as part of a considered conception which, while avoiding the monotony of the Rue de Rivoli of Paris, may oppose a great facade of ordered variety to the infinite historic picturesqueness of the old town across the valley ? No extra cost, indeed a simplification of individual designs would result if a scheme somewhat upon the lines of that proposed were adopted.

But still granted all this, the practical man asks, how much is it going to cost : he cannot approve of a scheme without having some figure to seize hold of and to cling to as a refuge from nebulous ideals. In the light of the above remarks about the inevitable building, it is still difficult to give an estimate of the cost of the other works entailed by the Plan, if it is accepted. These works, as has been suggested will probably be spread over at least 50 years and no one can forecast the cost of works at so remote a period. At most it might be possible to give an approximate estimate of the first five-year period works.

In addition to Public Works which must be paid for by public money, there is the realisation by planning control over

Private Enterprise. Much of the detailed working out of the plan comes under this head ; Housing Schemes (other than those of the Corporation), Factories located in industrial Zones or Trading Estates, Shops and many more buildings. Now ambitious plans for control in the past were dogged by the fear of the bogey Compensation. It is true that certain requirements such as reasonable density restrictions were exempted from claims when approved by the Minister : but especially in the improvement of central areas and also in the keeping open of a green belt (where building value was automatically being created by the spread of urban influences) the Planning Authority was paralysed. The recommendation of the Uthwatt Report as embodied (with certain modifications) in the 1947 Act have changed all that : the Planning Authority need no longer prepare blank schemes without a single road proposal, as was the case of the London County Plan under the 1932 Act. A great liability for the cost of schemes is thus disposed of under new legislation.

Finally it may be pointed out that in order to realise the housing proposals of the Edinburgh Plan, it will not be necessary to create a satellite to deal with decentralised populations.

In this respect this Plan differs radically from those prepared for London, Manchester, Glasgow and Hull. Both increased growth of and decentralisation from Edinburgh proper can be accommodated within the immediate periphery of the city, and within the inner line of the green belt. The anticipated growth in the Region is not an Edinburgh growth at all, but an expansion and development of the Lothian coalfield. This is being dealt with by Sir Frank Mears and is self contained so far as local requirements are concerned : the effect upon Edinburgh will be undoubted but will be indirect, affecting her cultural institutions, shopping and amusements : provision for these reactions to the coalfield development has been included in the Plan.

Redistribution of the existing population and industry.

This represents one of the most important aspects of the plan because many of the proposals depend upon this redistribution. For example, there must be adequate provision of houses of the right kind and size, of schools, open spaces and so on.

The diagram (2) page 83 shows the amount of decentralisation required from specific areas either to relieve over-crowding or to separate the home from industry as the zoning proposals indicate. Its aim is to identify certain redevelopment areas as reception localities for workers of all income groups where alternative accommodation may be found when redevelopment commences. The diagram shows that although the total movement of population is vast it is not a mass migration taking place all at once. The Town and Country Planning Act lays down that only as much of those areas that are ripe for redevelopment and can be acquired in 10 years may be designated for redevelopment at one time.

Industry too requires new sites for old and redevelopment cannot be confined to existing housing areas when it is necessary for demolished slum property to be given over to industrial development or vice versa.

The planned redistribution should, therefore, be a combined operation of clearance of overcrowded and substandard houses and congested or outmoded industrial premises. The ball may be set rolling by the acquisition of house property in Leith, demolished to make way for industry which is being cleared from areas in the proposed neighbourhoods of C.1., C.2. etc. Similar operations may be started in the St. James Square area combined with clearance of commercial property in the proposed neighbourhood of St. Leonards.

The Financial Aspect.

The statutory authority for acquisition as already stated is now placed in the Local Planning Authority's hands through the power of "designation." Compensation that laid the cold clammy hand over all well-meaning schemes for central improvements in the past is now restricted to the use value at the time of acquisition and no amount of argument can any longer make it appear to have any greater or lesser value. There is, therefore, no need to look upon central area improvements as necessarily more costly operations than undeveloped land on the outskirts of the city. Slum condemned houses for instance would carry very little value for the buildings. The land they stand upon may be of higher value than land on the outskirts of the city. Furthermore it is impossible to set an immediate value in advance of the negotiations that must arise between property owner and the valuer. Still less is it possible to anticipate precisely what the value of a building or piece of ground will be five years hence or the cost of labour and materials.

As a guide however the answer might well be found in the history of works in the inter-war development period when £38 millions were spent in 22 years on all forms of new building enterprises. An estimated average over a period of years covering booms and slumps is less misleading than estimates for the immediately possible. £25 millions of this total were spent on housing projects alone which involved a redistribution of 140,000 persons of which some 26,000 were immigrants from outside the city. The inter-war map no. 2 shows where they were housed and diagram no. 1 on page 83 shows where the majority came from and in what quantity. There is no great difference between their numbers and that proposed in the Plan but the co-ordination of planned distribution now proposed is quite different from this inter-war movement of population. If the same spending power is available over the next 22 year period free from the disturbance of war there is every hope of a similar number of people being rehoused : there must, this time, however, be control to ensure that the majority of house construction in the city is devoted to the relief of the overcrowded population. To overlook this important fact again is to create worse problems later involving an overspill beyond the city boundary.

The Festival Centres.

These two centres are based upon outmoded property (both housing and commercial) which brings the limit of time for realisation much nearer than would otherwise have been possible if the property had been new. Even though they were conceived before the first international festival was held in 1947, they were believed to represent a probable demand. There was nothing concrete to show when popular demand might cause early achievement but since then two festivals have been held with great success and, stimulated by the Grassmarket suggestion for a new centre with up to date buildings, popular imagination has been fired. Further encouragement has been given by the Government's decision to contribute £1 million towards the National Theatre on the south side of the Thames leading to a similar promise for Scotland should public subscription make a comparable start to that of the National Theatre Funds. Both these new factors were unpredictable and now place the achievement nearer in point of time.

The moral to be drawn is, that, providing the assessment of the population needs is reasonably and accurately made, it is of the utmost importance to include all in the plan and to ensure eventual achievement by gearing present policy to allow for the long term projects. Support (in terms of money) for a project may bring the necessary impetus overnight.

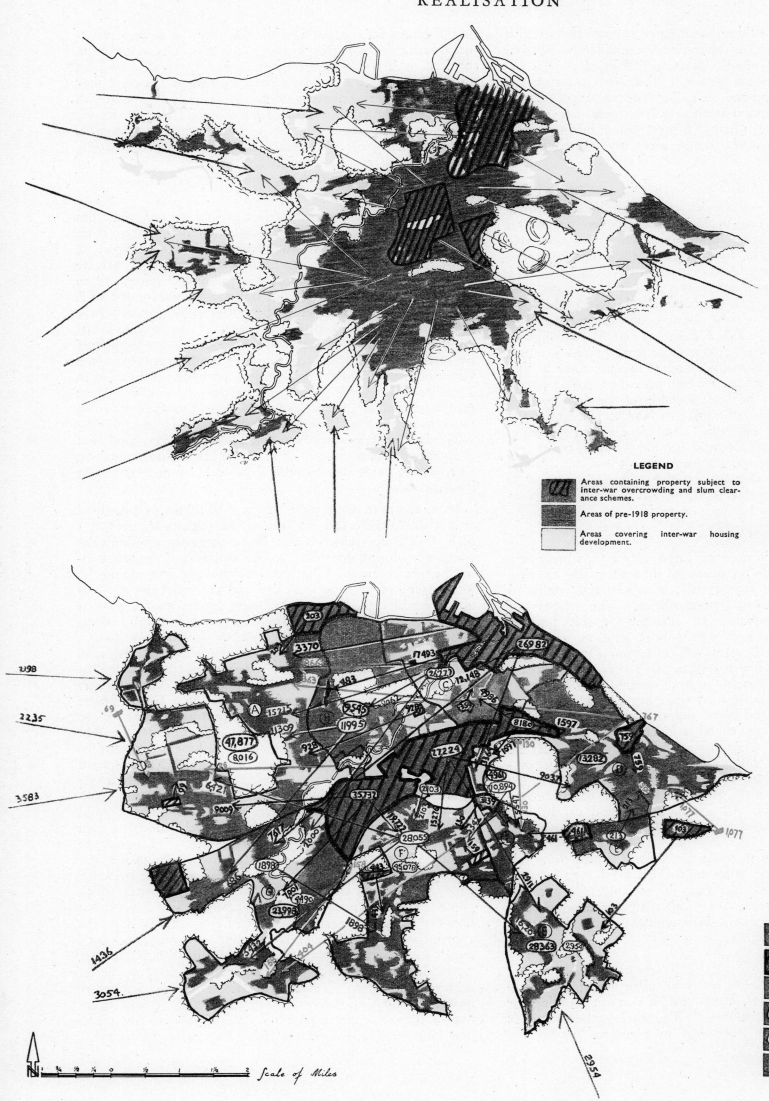

LEGEND

Areas containing property subject to inter-war overcrowding and slum clearance schemes.

Areas of pre-1918 property.

Areas covering inter-war housing development.

DIAGRAM I.

Without a civic survey to record the extent of past activity there can be no appreciation from which to determine an aim for future development. The extent of inter-war building shown in yellow proved that in 22 years some £25 million was spent in constructing some 43,471 dwellings. Into these new homes came 139,107 persons of whom 22,809 were immigrants from outside the city and 116,298 were residents in the pre 1918 dwellings, 16 per cent of whom were moved under the slum clearance schemes. Had this building activity been controlled as part of a co-ordinated policy, overcrowding and slums would largely have been eliminated.

Note.—The arrows show the direction of population movement into the new houses, the brown represents 18,200 persons moved under the Slum Clearance Schemes, the red represents 98,098 persons who moved from comparatively good housing areas and the black represents 22,809 immigrants from outside the City.

DIAGRAM II.

This diagram shows how the four prevailing evils—outmoded or sanitarily unfit dwellings, overcrowded dwellings upon the land, overcrowded families within dwellings and the mixing of homes with industry—can be eliminated by means of the combined operation described in Chapter 3. The arrows indicate the anticipated movement of population likely to result from such redevelopment in its total extent spread over a period of some 50 years. The total population to be rehoused in the city is approximately 286,402 persons resulting in an anticipated movement of 189,897 persons to new districts as compared with 139,407 persons in the 22 year period between the wars. Guidance as part of a national policy for town and country of future house building is essential to achieve the above results without a future overspill of population beyond the city.

LEGEND

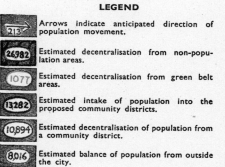

Arrows indicate anticipated direction of population movement.

Estimated decentralisation from non-population areas.

Estimated decentralisation from green belt areas.

Estimated intake of population into the proposed community districts.

Estimated decentralisation of population from a community district.

Estimated balance of population from outside the city.

Scale of Miles

83

but there would be nothing but disappointment and anguish if earlier development had been permitted and now baulked its realisation. Self-styled "practical" folk claim the expediency of the moment as the yardstick to measure the value of a set of proposals. A major redevelopment scheme is impatiently condemned because a few years may be lost to an individual concern before it may reopen business even though greatly improved circumstances are offered on an alternate site.

The Schools, Recreation Spaces and Community Centres.

The provision of community clubs and local authority schools and their playing fields in the plan merely interpret the requirements of the Education Act. The collective requirements, of course, look vast yet they only represent the bare minimum considered by present day standards. The fact that these standards are very different from those that exist only shows the parlous condition in which the local authority schools all over the country have been allowed to fall. The matter is not one for dismay but of challenge to put right what is wrong. Again there is no precise estimate of the cost that can reasonably be made because there is little or no precedent over a long enough period to make even an average assessment for the new standards set. Nor is it possible to assess accurately what the price of land will be under the new Act for 'existing use value.' Sufficient to say, therefore, that there is a statutory demand for these requirements and government grants to assist achievement when the demand in a locality becomes clamant. If these demands are not to be baulked by earlier development, advance knowledge as indicated on the plan becomes essential.

Roads and Railways.

It is often cheaper in the long run to select an entirely new route through unbuilt on property than to widen existing roads when planning for arterial or sub-arterial routes to meet present and future contingencies. The by-pass of Princes Street is probably an example of this because Queen Street or Cowgate would both involve expensive demolitions, whereas the proposal in Chapter 4 involves cost of construction only, for its length of Princes Street. Realisation is also more attainable in long continuous stretches at a time than in the case of road widening which, in fits and starts, presents good and bad conditions for a long period of time. This is not a general condemnation of building demolition for road widening as this alternative must be considered according to the merits of the case. It is important when considering the prospects of achievement to appreciate that many of the proposals for main road improvement do pass through either unbuilt on land or through property ripe for redevelopment within the meaning of the Act.

It has been said that the collective cost of similar proposals for various towns and cities in the United Kingdom runs into hundreds of millions. That is probably true but it is doubtful if the collective cost of all road widening schemes together with their by-pass links would be any cheaper in the long term view either.

Conclusion.

" If you are planning for one year, plant grain; if you are " planning for ten years, plant trees; if you are planning for " a hundred years, plant men." The analogy between this Chinese proverb and realisation in planning lies in the implication of a continuing aim attaching the same sense of importance for integrity between the long and short term project. All the suggested improvements of a town plan cannot be realised in a day, a year or in many years yet they represent the essential needs of men in succeeding generations. Changes in the environment of our homes and factories are continual from one generation to another: they mature in form as each generation makes its own contributions: the ultimate result in its entirety is analogous to the heritage of our great cathedrals which are representative of the work of many generations.

Financially, a scheme can normally only be achieved from the resources of city funds or those granted by statute from national funds. But through the application of present legislation it is possible to harness the efforts of private enterprise as measured in money by guiding development to conform to the plan. It is not unknown however for such resources to be supplemented by public subscription where local enthusiasm for a project is great. For example, initial popular demand for the national theatre in London supported by voluntary contributions caused a supplement from the Government and made this project possible. Likewise, as a symbol of the new Warsaw rising on the ashes of the old, the proposed road beneath the centre of the old town appealed so much to public imagination that half the cost is being met by voluntary subscription: even when housing accommodation is so scarce several blocks of flats that stand undamaged on its route are being demolished in the enthusiasm to complete its construction.

If our aim of to-day is to be kept in view it must be presented as a whole picture and, so long as the various features of a plan, which represent this aim, do no more than indicate the complete solution according to our aspirations, the plan cannot be overcharged. What can be grandiose in showing the total extent of housing development and redevelopment to obtain healthy and convenient living conditions for all that need them even if their construction may take many generations to complete ! The plan would be totally inadequate if it excluded all foreseeable requirements. Official estimates indicate 4 million new houses required for the country, at the present rate of approximately 150,000 per year, planners must look ahead for 25 years for completion. The complete picture is important also to ensure integration between those parts of the plan capable of early achievement—the first designation areas of immediate accomplishment for example —with those of subsequent years. How much less awkward would have been Gillespie Graham's problem for extending the New Town had Craig left more elbow room for the development of the Earl of Moray's estate or if Craig himself could have been permitted to consider more logical boundaries than those limited by the Earl of Moray's estate. The avoidance of such obstructions imposed by land ownership of the past to the proper development of the area is one of the principal aims of the Town and Country Planning Act of 1947 which permits the conception of the development area beyond the limits of immediate realisation: or of land ownership to the appropriate physical boundaries. By assessing the total requirements of the community and recording them on a plan, we anticipate a greater development than is possible of achievement within a single generation: but the legislative powers at our disposal make realisation of these total needs over a period of years possible with whatever adjustments may be necessary to meet the circumstances of the future.

APPENDIX No. 1

POPULATION AND HOUSING.

This Appendix contains details of some of the principal features of the Social Survey carried out in 1946. There is presented a number of tables from which certain statements contained in Chapters 2 and 3 have been made. The following details are presented :—

1. Dean of Guild Record of Property Development of all kinds between the years 1918 and 1939 are shown in Table XII.
2. Table XIII sets out data concerning the residential and industrial use of land in each social survey district of the city.
3. The movement of population in and out of the city is recorded upon Table XIV which has been built up from figures provided by the Registrar General.
4. Statements are set forth in Tables XV and XVI giving for each district the existing distribution of family and house sizes. If these are correlated upon a given standard of accommodation an estimate of balanced distribution of accommodation can be made. Table XVIII applies a test for a suggested standard of accommodation or relationship based upon current social trends for the existing totals of family and house sizes compared with those allowed for in the Plan.
5. The condition of dwellings all over the city is given in Table XVII and in terms of the sanitary facilities and conditions prevailing.
6. Information concerning the Place of Work in relation to the home is illustrated by Table XIX which gives the totals of principal wage earners geographically distributed into their working and residential districts.
7. A statement describing the three forms of unsatisfactory living conditions is given for the redevelopment areas.

RECORD OF DEAN OF GUILD COURT WORK, 1918-1939.

TABLE XII.

| YEAR | Shops | NUMBER OF FLATS IN TENEMENTS | | Apartments | | | | | Tenement, buildings | Houses | Villas | Public or other Buildings | Alterations | APPROXIMATE VALUES | | | | | |
		1	2	3	4	5	6	7						Houses	Villas	Public or other Buildings	Tenements	TOTAL	ALTERATIONS
1918	—	—	—	—	—	—	—	—	—	—	—	3	35	—	—	£15,450	—	£15,450	£24,820
1919	—	—	—	88	10	42	—	—	35	1	—	67	97	£900	—	255,565	£122,264	378,729	196,540
1920	—	—	81	108	178	54	18	—	99	59	—	110	146	72,814	—	437,973	314,541	825,328	275,058
1921	—	—	—	276	138	47	—	—	142	34	42	106	139	45,642	£62,340	245,339	502,352	855,673	205,981
1922	6	—	—	95	19	—	—	—	34	57	29	130	188	68,250	44,680	602,872	126,000	841,802	276,343
1923	—	—	47	320	6	8	—	—	56	383	106	157	243	353,467	178,125	566,837	159,836	1,258,265	376,767
1924	6	—	66	762	2	6	—	—	113	561	48	190	222	503,015	105,750	756,420	398,153	1,763,338	305,741
1925	18	—	172	362	9	6	—	—	83	763	41	265	230	685,355	79,750	469,889	251,406	1,486,400	227,038
1926	33	—	160	788	54	—	—	—	180	1,526	23	320	221	1,063,175	51,750	555,079	424,160	2,094,164	294,748
1927	49	—	156	1,338	18	—	—	—	401	659	9	271	227	595,090	17,150	839,950	574,671	2,026,861	423,585
1928	54	—	37	47	21	—	—	—	19	604	15	586	235	546,020	30,050	748,480	51,981	1,376,531	362,580
1929	42	—	216	176	—	—	—	—	72	769	6	344	248	695,820	9,150	925,985	121,626	1,752,581	476,265
1930	42	—	58	470	17	5	—	—	99	828	4	286	187	703,745	6,350	592,070	175,100	1,477,265	336,650
1931	57	—	324	899	34	—	—	—	215	1,323	4	284	201	1,004,530	10,050	314,350	357,360	1,686,290	314,000
1932	133	—	300	1,591	278	—	4	—	380	2,549	—	401	200	1,634,440	—	474,460	616,900	2,725,800	311,970
1933	112	28	100	652	158	7	—	—	160	2,409	—	457	235	1,691,285	—	288,070	277,025	2,256,380	326,280
1934	97	—	42	736	167	30	3	—	172	3,187	—	370	226	1,943,700	—	430,275	355,125	2,729,100	378,170
1935	147	—	36	833	124	32	21	—	184	3,513	—	471	301	1,782,870	—	839,340	412,280	3,034,490	645,500
1936	58	—	8	1,055	926	59	10	—	368	2,305	—	489	300	1,418,920	—	769,180	821,230	3,009,330	611,650
1937	62	—	2	185	107	3	—	—	43	2,426	—	600	265	1,453,440	—	1,208,041	144,300	2,805,781	527,405
1938	38	—	—	330	653	30	24	—	188	1,126	—	555	278	853,595	—	917,772	483,350	2,254,717	456,260
1939	42	—	3	266	410	—	—	—	119	1,111	—	319	196	743,630	—	616,855	286,900	1,647,385	286,755
TOTALS	996	28	1,808	11,377	3,329	329	80	—	3,162	26,193	327	6,781	4,620	£17,859,703	£595,145	£12,870,252	£6,976,560	£38,301,660	£7,640,106

1 The Table above gives a record of Dean of Guild Court work from 1918 to 1939. It will be seen from this Table that there were 16,951 flats in tenements, 26,193 houses and 327 villas built in this inter-war period giving a total of 43,471 dwellings of all kinds. Since the Social Survey records an average of 3.2 persons per family the estimated total population living in these dwellings would be approximately 139,117 persons. The total approximate cost of these dwellings was estimated at £25,431,408.

2 Existing residential and industrial use of land. The following Table XIII shows the existing nature of each district in the city by the present use of property and the extent of particular use such as industry in proportion to other uses such as residential. From such data an assessment can be made as to the predominant character or use of each district.

3 Inter-war immigration and emigration. Table XIV below shows the population movement in and out of the city between 1918 and 1946 up to the year of the Civic Survey. It shows that in the years immediately following the first world war an emigration trend of movement was followed by an immigration trend from 1924 up to the outbreak of the second world war in 1939. This is important as it occurs at a time of large scale house building from which the conclusions stated in Chapters 2 and 3 are made. From the Birth and Death figures an assessment has been made to determine whether the city population has a large population " natural increase " This " natural increase " averages, for the 29 years tabulated, 1,400 annually but it is difficult to determine to what extent emigration has influenced this annual " increase " Much depends upon future national policy regarding counter attractions in the rural areas before a forecast can reasonably be made for future years.

4 Tables XV and XVI show the distribution of family and house sizes for each Social Survey district in the city. Reference has already been made in the Civic Survey Chapter to the relationship between house and family sizes according to the existing standard under the 1935 Housing Act and one based upon contemporary conceptions for minimum accommodation. These conceptions follow the improved standard in which the bed rooms only are counted as sleeping quarters and children of all ages in the family are taken into account. Table XVIII represents a correlation based upon the improved standard of minimum accommodation for a given family size. The table is in two parts, the first giving the existing population in totals of family sizes correlated with the existing totals of house sizes including existing property to be preserved in the Plan (i.e. static property), assuming subdivisions follow-ing present day social trends. The second half of the table covers the areas scheduled in the Plan for redevelopment and new development but excludes the static property from the application of the standard. The result of the test in the latter half of the table would naturally produce a conservative estimate of the number of house sizes that may be anticipated in future development because it ignores " subdivisions " which might be permitted in parts of the proposed static areas. In the event of " subdivisions " the population total would, therefore, (assuming one family per dwelling) be increased.

This table does not represent a rigid rule of thumb method but a guide to detailed development and used with reasonable flexibility of appli-cation. It is also one which might well replace the rather arbitrary regulations imposed at present by the Department of Health.

TABLE XIII. EXISTING RESIDENTIAL AND INDUSTRIAL USE OF LAND.

Dist. No.		Total Area (Acres)	Total Indust. Area	Indust. Area as % of Total Area	Total Resident. Area (Acres)	Resident. Area as % of Total Area	Total Population	Net. Resident. Density
1	High Street	92	10·1	11	12·49	13·6	4,590	367·5
2	Grassmarket	30	10·6	35	5·21	17·4	2,028	389·3
3	Princes Street	1,674	13·8	1	7·34	0·4	1,663	226·6
4	Canongate	84·5	33·3	39	10·33	12·2	4,369	422·9
5	Pleasance and St. Leonards	106	20·4	19	53·85	50·8	16,263	302·0
6	George Square	106	5·7	5	33·78	31·9	6,270	185·6
7	Lauriston	85	0·5	1	12·84	15·1	1,954	152·2
8	Fountainbridge and Tollcross	126	32·8	26	61·82	49·0	13,074	211·5
9	West End	183	4·1	2	62·82	34·3	4,405	70·1
10	Stockbridge	130	5·5	4	83·71	64·4	12,811	153·0
11	North Side	121	25·6	21	64·69	53·5	8,854	136·9
12	East End	192	24·8	13	50·79	26·4	9,120	179·6
13	Abbeyhill	45	8·7	19	16·27	36·2	3,388	208·2
14	Kings Park	582			1·50	0·26	35	23·3
15	Prestonfield	280	0·5	0·2	90·44	32·3	4,996	55·2
16	Newington	269	7·3	3	183·88	68·4	6,399	34·8
17	Marchmont	174	4·8	3	117·70	67·6	10,741	91·3
18	Grange	330	6·7	2	219·31	66·5	3,579	16·3
19	Bruntsfield	104	0·7	1	67·38	64·8	3,393	50·4
20	Merchiston	178			155·85	87·6	6,723	43·1
21	Dalry	191	60·4	32	58·99	30·9	17,571	297·9
22	Haymarket	143	5·5	4	67·36	47·1	3,635	54·0
23	Belford	124	6·6	5	27·37	22·0	1,088	39·8
24	Craigleith	578	1·8	0·3	206·12	35·7	6,777	32·9
25	Goldenacre	396·5	13·6	3	84·66	21·4	3,212	37·9
26	Broughton	232	44·5	19	64·72	28·0	7,582	117·2
27	Easter Road	123	21·8	18	48·83	39·7	10,262	210·2
28	Meadowbank	118	8·0	7	46·83	39·7	6,978	149·0
29	Piershill and Willowbrae	304	4·1	1	122·18	40·2	6,764	55·4
30	Duddingston	955	3·4	0·4	206·08	21·6	4,288	20·8
31	Craigmillar	824	59·9	7	112·68	13·7	14,391	127·7
32	Blackford	352·5	27·8	8	48·12	13·7	1,878	39·0
33	Morningside	610·5	9·9	2	384·33	63·0	14,236	37·0
34	Gorgie	285	51·9	18	92·11	32·3	15,420	167·4
35	Roseburn	122	25·9	21	15·18	12·4	1,264	83·3
36	Murrayfield	317	0·5	0·2	174·23	55·0	2,238	12·8
37	Ravelston	144			44·77	31·1	540	12·1
38	Blackhall	595	1·4	0·2	241·83	40·6	4,423	18·3
39	Pilton	437	9·6	2	188·87	43·2	14,933	79·1
40	Granton	513	246·6	48	179·92	35·1	12,247	68·1
41	Trinity	285	6·0	2	173·27	60·8	5,623	32·5
42	Newhaven	46	22·5	49	31·10	67·6	3,892	125·1
43	Leith	1,309	526·2	40	327·42	25·0	57,338	175·1
44	Lochend	210	3·7	2	133·95	63·8	10,019	74·7
45	Craigentinny	419	13·1	3	197·49	47·1	8,968	45·4
46	Portobello	246	65·6	27	101·10	41·1	8,568	84·7
47	Joppa and Eastfield	387	3·2	1	116·54	30·1	3,431	29·4
48	Newcraighall	361	67·2	19	19·62	5·4	1,366	69·6
49	Gilmerton	1,309	13·1	1	85·83	6·6	2,227	25·9
50	Liberton	2,450	28·0	1	191·78	7·8	4,048	21·1
51	Braids and Fairmilehead	2,430	28·9	1	186·12	7·6	2,363	12·7
52	Craiglockhart	604	0·5	·08	152·72	25·3	2,559	16·8
53	Slateford	300	59·0	20	105·13	35·0	7,076	67·3
54	Stenhouse	205	3·2	2	119·43	58·2	8,809	73·8
55	Saughtonhall	257	1·8	1	107·90	42·0	4,481	41·6
56	Corstorphine	1,332	12·2	1	492·38	37·0	12,562	25·5
57	Davidson's Mains	741·5	4·8	0·6	153·86	20·7	2,199	14·3
58	Colinton	2,494·5	54·8	2	280·34	11·2	5,544	19·8
59	Kingsknowe	449			68·55	15·3	1,239	18·1
60	Sighthill	1,047	5·9	0·6	145·51	13·9	7,112	48·9
61	Juniper Green	402	1·8	0·4	74·10	18·4	1,663	22·4
62	Turnhouse and Maybury	1,970	26·4	1	27·37	1·38	346	12·6
63	Barnton and Cramond	1,016	·2	0·02	169·08	16·6	1,753	10·4
		32,526·0	1767·2		7187·77		437,568	

5 Table XVII below segregates the total 123,265 dwellings in the city into three categories, " fit ", " substandard ", and " unfit " measured in terms of sanitary facilities provided in the dwellings and by their structural defect such as dampness and others prescribed by the Sanitary Inspector in his Housing Survey.

These facts contained in this table give a general indication of the totals of dwellings which will probably require replacement in the near future. They certainly indicate the total of dwellings which are out-moded so far as internal building is concerned and might well be more expensive to convert into modern dwellings than it would be to rebuild entirely afresh. Comparison with the layout of the roads in the local-ities in which these dwellings are situated, and with the survey showing the density of distribution and of the extent of mixing with industry, should present conclusive evidence for complete redevelopment. These latter factors give the nature of the environment which could only be improved by a general redevelopment scheme while these internal conditions give an indication of the nature of the dwellings them-selves.

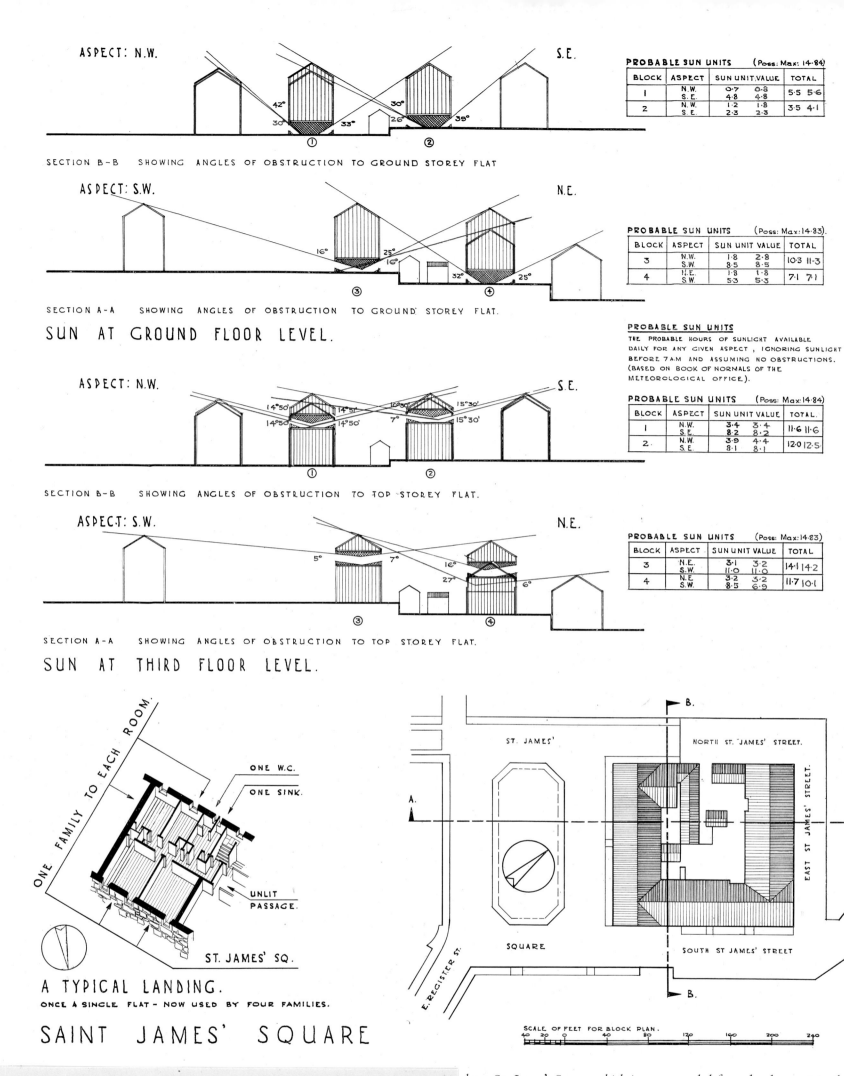

SECTION B–B SHOWING ANGLES OF OBSTRUCTION TO GROUND STOREY FLAT

ASPECT: N.W. — S.E.

PROBABLE SUN UNITS		(Poss: Max: 14·84)	
BLOCK	ASPECT	SUN UNIT VALUE	TOTAL
1	N.W.	0·7 0·8	5·5 5·6
	S.E.	4·8 4·8	
2	N.W.	1·2 1·8	3·5 4·1
	S.E.	2·3 2·3	

SECTION A–A SHOWING ANGLES OF OBSTRUCTION TO GROUND STOREY FLAT.

ASPECT: S.W. — N.E.

PROBABLE SUN UNITS		(Poss: Max: 14·83)	
BLOCK	ASPECT	SUN UNIT VALUE	TOTAL
3	N.W.	1·8 2·8	10·3 11·3
	S.W.	8·5 8·5	
4	N.E.	1·8 1·8	7·1 7·1
	S.W.	5·3 5·3	

SUN AT GROUND FLOOR LEVEL.

PROBABLE SUN UNITS

THE PROBABLE HOURS OF SUNLIGHT AVAILABLE DAILY FOR ANY GIVEN ASPECT, IGNORING SUNLIGHT BEFORE 7 A.M. AND ASSUMING NO OBSTRUCTIONS. (BASED ON BOOK OF NORMALS OF THE METEOROLOGICAL OFFICE).

SECTION B–B SHOWING ANGLES OF OBSTRUCTION TO TOP STOREY FLAT.

ASPECT: N.W. — S.E.

PROBABLE SUN UNITS		(Poss: Max: 14·84)	
BLOCK	ASPECT	SUN UNIT VALUE	TOTAL
1	N.W.	3·4 3·4	11·6 11·6
	S.E.	8·2 8·2	
2	N.W.	3·9 4·4	12·0 12·5
	S.E.	8·1 8·1	

SECTION A–A SHOWING ANGLES OF OBSTRUCTION TO TOP STOREY FLAT.

ASPECT: S.W. — N.E.

PROBABLE SUN UNITS		(Poss: Max: 14·83)	
BLOCK	ASPECT	SUN UNIT VALUE	TOTAL
3	N.E.	3·1 3·2	14·1 14·2
	S.W.	11·0 11·0	
4	N.E.	3·2 3·2	11·7 10·1
	S.W.	8·5 6·9	

SUN AT THIRD FLOOR LEVEL.

ONE FAMILY TO EACH ROOM. — ONE W.C. — ONE SINK. — UNLIT PASSAGE. — ST. JAMES' SQ.

A TYPICAL LANDING.

ONCE A SINGLE FLAT – NOW USED BY FOUR FAMILIES.

SAINT JAMES' SQUARE

ST. JAMES' — NORTH ST. JAMES' STREET. — EAST ST. JAMES' STREET. — SQUARE — SOUTH ST JAMES' STREET — E. REGISTER ST.

SCALE OF FEET FOR BLOCK PLAN.

... about St. James' Square which is recommended for redevelopment in the ... ected vertically in the four sections A–A and B–B above, and the extent ... e angles of light created by building obstruction in front of the dwellings. ... by the sunlight angles in black and the resulting number of sun units in ... urgh lies in its By-laws. For comparison the probable building height ... the corresponding sunlight angles and the resulting number of sun units

... llings for sun light no real improvement is possible without re-orientating ... t conditions. The existing road system will not permit this. Assuming ... N.E. aspect in Block 3 of Section A–A obtains more sunlight if Block 4 ... of dwellings lost in the operation, but those in the lower stories obtain no ... to the full height likely to be permitted under the By-laws.

PLATE LIII

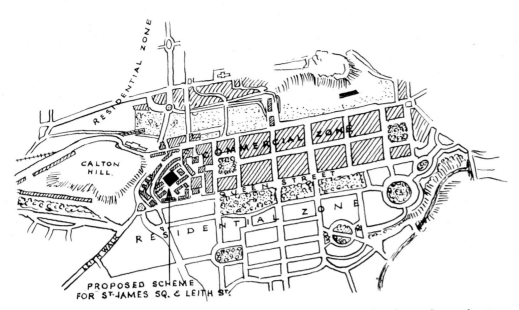

Being closely situated to the East End of Princes Street the above shows the St. James' Square—Leith Street scheme well placed for a Festival Centre to serve the eastern half of the City. The area is too small for residential development but as a natural link with the commercial zone to the west it also affords a chance to meet the increasing demands for up-to-date office accommodation and to eliminate slums.

[p. 105]

[p. 104]

The shadow that these tenements cast upon those on the opposite side of this narrow street, North St. James' Street, illustrates how the majority of the dwellings obtain very little sunlight owing to the lack of sufficient space about the buildings.

This photo shows the steep character of the street layout of this locality, where the gradient of this street, Little King Street, is 1 in 9. This road is eliminated in the redevelopment scheme for the area.

[p. 112]

This aerial view shows the Playhouse Cinema built upon a site which is still largely residential. It is a typical example of how commerce takes advantage of lowering property values when deterioration sets in and quickens the process by the additional loss of amenity it creates.

The St. James' Square—Leith Street Area is shown in the middle-top of this aerial view. The Playhouse Cinema is the white building appearing in the bottom right-hand corner.

[p. 111]

PLATE LIV

6 Table XIX below gives the totals of the principal wage earners who were found during the 1946 Social Survey to be living in one locality and working in another. The geographical relationship between these localities is illustrated in the diagrams on plate VI. To read these facts from the table the vertical columns under the heading of " Working Districts " gives the totals of principal wage earners working there and segregated into totals placed horizontally opposite their residing district. For example, " Working District D " contains a count of 5,979 principal wage earners who live and work in this " Working District " and 3,887 who work in district " D " but reside in district " B." Conversely the totals residing in a district and working in another district can be assessed by reading the table horizontally.

The value of these results lies in the guide they offer in the search for a suitable location for the home relative to the distance from the place of work. These results, for example, have been used in diagram 2 appearing on page 83.

REGISTRAR GENERAL'S POPULATION STATISTICS FOR THE YEARS 1918—1946.

TABLE XIV.

Year		Deaths	Births	Natural Increase (or Decrease)	Population Total incl. Immign. and N.I.	Population + N.I.	Immigration Gain	Emmigration Loss
				Total population excluding influence of Migration and Natural increase or decrease } 443,461				
1918	* Edinburgh	5,090	4,828	262‡	333,883	—	—	—
	Leith	1,333	1,699	366‡	83,828 } 443,534	—	—	—
	Suburban	379	348	31‡	25,823	—	—	—
1919	* Edinburgh	5,583	5,612	29	338,060	333,912	4,148	—
	Leith	1,360	1,900	540	84,281	84,368	—	87
	Surburban	404	435	31	26,080	25,854	226	—
1920	* Edinburgh	4,442	7,773	3,331	312,212	341,391	—	29,179
	Leith	1,218	2,487	1,269	81,476	85,550	—	4,074
	Suburban	288	584	296	27,509	26,376	1,133	—
1921	Edinburgh	6,048	9,028	2,980	425,582	424,177	1,405	—
1922	,,	6,447	8,772	2,325	428,200	427,907	293	—
1923	,,	5,875	8,662	2,787	429,000	430,987	—	1,987
1924	,,	6,312	8,404	2,092	429,800	431,092	—	1,292
1925	,,	6,138	7,843	1,705	432,000	431,505	495	—
1926	,,	5,710	7,926	2,216	433,900	434,216	—	316
1927	,,	6,066	7,621	1,555	435,300	435,455	—	155
1928	,,	5,872	7,420	1,548	436,800	436,848	—	48
1929	,,	6,442	7,304	862	438,000	437,662	338	—
1930	,,	6,038	7,307	1,269	439,800	439,269	531	—
1931	,,	5,726	7,164	1,438	443,042	441,238	1,804	—
1932	,,	6,032	6,960	928	447,800	443,970	3,830	—
1933	,,	5,964	6,835	871	452,773	448,671	4,102	—
1934	,,	5,873	7,188	1,315	457,099	454,088	3,011	—
1935	,,	6,132	7,037	905	460,877	458,004	2,873	—
1936	,,	6,226	7,391	1,165	464,139	462,042	2,097	—
1937	,,	6,544	7,375	831	466,817	464,970	1,847	—
1938	,,	5,974	7,547	1,573	469,448	468,390	1,058	—
1939	,,	6,169	7,300	1,131	471,897	470,579	1,318	—
1940 †	,,	6,802	6,930	128	447,010	472,025	—	25,015 §
1941 †	,,	6,545	6,934	389	462,952	447,399	15,553	—
1942 †	,,	6,152	7,386	1,234	464,910	464,186	724	—
1943 †	,,	6,338	7,605	1,267	468,495	466,177	2,318	—
1944 †	,,	5,979	7,908	1,929	474,281	470,424	3,857	—
1945 †	,,	6,147	7,362	1,215	476,173	475,496	677	—
1946 †	,,	6,485	9,350	2,865	478,769	479,038	—	269
				44,385 Less 293‡				
TOTALS		180,133	224,225	44,092	—	—	53,638	62,422

* During these years Edinburgh did not extend to its present boundaries and to give comparable figures Leith and the Suburbs must be added.

† The figures quoted for the years 1940 to 1946 include, in addition to the civilian population, persons in the Services who are normally resident in Edinburgh.

‡ Indicates Natural Decrease.

§ The large decrease from 1939 to 1940 may be attributed to the number of evacuees still absent from the City in 1940.

REDEVELOPMENT AREAS.

There are three forms of living conditions which can create a state of unsatisfactory living, the combination of which are generally found to create slums. These three conditions, that is, dwellings mixed with industrial property, dwellings having net densities in excess of 100 persons per acre and dwellings that are sanitarily substandard and, or, unfit. Where all three conditions occur in any one area, the property usually presents problems for redevelopment requiring early solutions. The population in these areas for Edinburgh is assessed at 134,081 persons or 30.5 per cent of the total existing population in the city.

These three conditions, where they occur separately, often lead to this combination of all three and it is important, therefore, to extend the areas containing the three conditions to include those where one or more conditions can be the cause for further deterioration.

Taking one of the more serious conditions there is a total of 252,010 persons living in out-moded property containing inadequate, by modern standards, sanitary facilities. Though some part of this population may be living in property capable of modernisation, deterioration cannot be stemmed if the immediate enviroment is also unsatisfactory either because the density of the development is too high or because it is situated among various kinds of industry. Out of this total of 252,010 persons only 36,661 are found to be living in dwellings that do not also include one or more of the other conditions while 74,567 also live at an existing net density of higher than 100 persons per acre and 6,701 live in areas mixed with industry. Evidence of the geographical location of these areas may be seen on the diagram on page 18 and though they are not at present slums, from past experience it is known that they lead to slums even though the structures themselves are strongly built.

Excess net density is caused by too many people living on too small an amount of ground which is formed from an overcrowding of dwellings together in built up areas. It is determined by two criteria :—

(a) From the appropriate density in zones for the whole city, which is assessed from broad planning considerations such as the appropriate optimum population for the city on the one hand and the amount of suitable housing land available on the other.

(b) The maximum density that may be permitted in each of those zones which is compatible with a healthy and convenient living environment. In this respect no one can reasonably claim, for example, that the Corporation's pre-war housing schemes at either Niddrie or Pilton is happy where the ground is over built with too little ground left for the amount of demand for communal use the occupied flats have created. The ground is down trodden and derelict in appearance and incapable,

DISTRIBUTION OF FAMILY SIZES IN DISTRICTS.

TABLE XV.

Dist. No.	1	2	3	4	5	6	7	8	9	10	11	12	13	14	15	16	Totals Families	Total Persons
1	257	335	295	238	139	88	40	17	10	6	1	1	—	1	—	—	1,428	4,590
2	94	139	144	101	73	27	19	8	6	3	—	1	—	—	—	—	615	2,028
3	127	175	153	78	34	19	9	3	1	2	—	—	—	—	1	—	602	1,663
4	222	351	291	210	129	63	44	21	20	3	1	1	—	—	—	—	1,356	4,369
5	743	1,289	1,226	896	507	250	121	53	27	12	1	—	—	—	—	—	5,125	16,263
6	382	557	472	342	174	87	38	26	9	2	1	1	—	—	—	—	2,091	6,270
7	86	143	122	96	62	38	19	9	5	3	—	—	—	1	—	—	584	1,954
8	582	1,191	1,027	708	386	168	93	30	18	12	4	—	1	1	1	—	4,222	13,074
9	270	471	340	209	109	60	27	11	5	4	—	1	1	1	1	1	1,511	4,405
10	673	1,159	1,002	695	372	172	81	32	14	5	6	—	1	—	—	4	4,216	12,811
11	525	900	747	474	225	103	55	16	4	5	2	—	1	—	1	—	3,058	8,854
12	555	863	742	461	228	127	54	31	13	7	1	—	1	1	—	1	3,085	9,120
13	147	338	305	206	89	38	13	3	2	2	—	—	—	—	—	—	1,143	3,388
14	2	—	6	—	3	—	—	—	—	—	—	—	—	—	—	—	11	35
15	138	369	331	277	144	94	49	31	9	5	—	—	1	—	—	—	1,448	4,996
16	211	654	508	394	181	74	29	18	7	1	1	—	—	—	—	—	2,078	6,399
17	515	1,168	898	609	289	117	44	19	9	6	—	1	—	—	—	—	3,675	10,741
18	129	360	292	194	100	45	24	7	6	3	—	—	—	—	—	—	1,160	3,579
19	224	398	309	153	78	35	15	11	1	2	—	1	—	—	—	—	1,227	3,393
20	381	786	578	337	167	71	33	10	7	2	3	—	—	—	—	—	2,375	6,723
21	746	1,586	1,542	1,092	490	199	73	46	14	1	—	—	—	—	—	—	5,789	17,571
22	117	313	271	185	107	63	25	14	8	2	2	1	1	—	—	—	1,109	3,635
23	52	84	100	62	33	15	7	2	—	—	—	—	—	—	—	—	355	1,088
24	210	751	638	462	163	50	15	8	1	1	—	—	—	—	—	—	2,299	6,777
25	112	336	262	205	81	34	17	7	2	2	—	—	—	—	—	—	1,058	3,212
26	254	743	670	464	214	85	27	20	3	2	—	—	—	—	—	—	2,482	7,582
27	473	1,032	957	629	260	97	44	7	8	2	—	—	—	—	—	—	3,509	10,262
28	296	697	675	431	157	60	37	9	7	—	—	—	—	—	—	—	2,369	6,978
29	149	445	515	426	204	92	62	26	13	9	5	—	—	—	—	—	1,946	6,764
30	99	360	361	255	113	51	32	16	9	4	2	—	—	—	—	—	1,302	4,288
31	118	379	513	507	476	394	242	162	100	68	32	10	8	2	2	—	3,013	14,391
32	82	191	182	125	46	17	4	1	—	—	—	—	—	—	—	—	648	1,878
33	767	1,722	1,463	437	437	159	51	24	10	4	—	—	—	5	—	—	5,079	14,236
34	615	1,495	1,420	881	425	163	59	31	14	8	2	2	—	—	1	—	5,116	15,420
35	43	146	134	66	28	9	4	4	1	—	—	—	—	—	—	—	435	1,264
36	39	189	185	129	66	41	9	6	3	2	—	—	—	—	—	1	670	2,238
37	24	59	55	31	13	2	2	1	—	1	—	—	—	—	—	—	188	540
38	143	487	431	305	107	31	9	—	1	—	—	—	—	—	—	—	1,514	4,423
39	74	538	813	676	432	307	240	133	97	50	25	15	4	1	—	—	3,405	14,933
40	132	576	728	654	425	259	155	85	35	23	8	5	2	—	—	—	3,087	12,247
41	165	504	525	360	169	60	21	7	3	—	—	—	—	—	—	—	1,814	5,623
42	134	287	289	242	131	66	28	7	4	1	—	—	—	—	—	—	1,189	3,892
43	2,306	4,906	4,589	3,308	1,728	772	345	159	80	39	4	1	4	2	—	1	18,244	57,338
44	170	535	608	522	324	212	116	66	34	17	11	1	2	—	—	—	2,618	10,019
45	128	574	614	556	317	155	75	33	15	9	3	2	2	1	—	—	2,484	8,968
46	319	719	669	443	253	146	63	33	14	6	—	—	—	—	—	—	2,665	8,568
47	138	327	314	225	97	33	6	3	3	1	1	—	—	—	—	—	1,148	3,431
48	22	79	96	80	54	21	11	7	2	2	1	—	—	—	—	—	375	1,366
49	46	154	166	120	76	38	13	9	9	2	1	1	—	—	—	—	635	2,227
50	131	425	377	252	100	42	10	6	2	4	—	—	—	—	—	—	1,349	4,048
51	65	260	231	146	71	18	3	1	1	—	—	—	—	—	—	—	796	2,363
52	111	240	229	184	74	22	5	1	—	—	—	—	—	—	—	—	866	2,559
53	145	517	574	378	238	121	49	25	16	6	—	—	—	—	—	—	2,069	7,076
54	79	390	490	518	365	165	96	54	29	10	7	2	1	1	—	—	2,207	8,809
55	109	390	421	292	138	47	14	9	1	1	—	—	—	—	—	—	1,422	4,481
56	325	1,190	1,280	874	311	98	24	12	9	1	1	1	—	—	—	—	4,126	12,562
57	55	194	173	139	71	26	9	7	2	—	3	—	—	—	—	—	679	2,199
58	146	425	503	392	169	64	19	9	3	1	—	—	—	—	—	—	1,731	5,544
59	31	141	137	92	18	7	1	1	—	—	—	—	—	—	—	—	428	1,239
60	104	488	664	540	215	74	26	12	3	—	4	1	—	—	—	—	2,131	7,112
61	85	165	145	95	40	24	7	5	—	—	—	—	—	—	—	—	566	1,663
62	7	37	31	19	18	1	—	—	—	—	—	—	—	—	—	—	113	346
63	55	177	142	113	39	28	11	2	—	1	—	—	—	—	—	—	568	1,753
	15,684	36,899	34,970	24,590	12,782	6,044	2,873	1,426	729	365	133	49	30	17	7	8	136,606	437,568

except perhaps by strict estate supervision, of being maintained as a green open space. These dwellings are found to represent a density of 80 persons per acre (net residential density). The condition would be alleviated if these flats had been built in 10 storey blocks instead of three or four storeys for the same number of people thus reducing the number of building blocks and the amount of ground built upon. More ground would have been added to the environment of the place for communal recreation and gardens. Taking these examples into account it is not thought that the maximum density as a criterion should exceed 100 persons per acre. The standard of living conditions so far as they are affected by the density of the development is considered to be unsatisfactory where it is in excess of 100 persons per net residential acre.

The following gives a detailed analysis showing the total population found to be living in these various conditions within the proposed neighbourhood unit boundaries of the plan.

Total City Resident Population : 437,568.

Condition 1.

Property development in excess of 100 persons per acre standard. Population : 262,778 or 60 per cent of the total population. Of this total 47,504 persons or 11 per cent of the total city resident population live in areas not of condition 2 or 3 : 74,567 or 17 per cent live in dwellings of condition 2 and 6,626 or 1.5 per cent live in areas not of condition 2 but of condition 3 and 134,081 or 30.5 per cent live in areas of both condition 2 and 3 as well as condition 1.

Condition 2.

Property that is sanitarily sub-standard and, or, unfit. Population 252,010 or 57 per cent of the total population. Of this total 36,661 persons or 8.4 per cent live in dwellings only of this condition and are not, therefore, also of condition 1 or 3 : 74,567 or 17 per cent live also in dwellings of conditions 1 and 6,701 or 1.5 per cent live in areas also

DISTRIBUTION OF HOUSE SIZES IN DISTRICTS.

TABLE XVI.

Dist. No.	1	2	3	4	5	6	7	8	9	10+	Total.
1	379	706	235	60	22	7	6	3	1	1	1,420
2	143	244	107	56	13	2	4	—	1	1	569
3	106	155	145	81	26	23	15	7	1	3	562
4	231	789	228	42	8	1	2	—	—	—	1,301
5	693	1,964	1,230	577	176	86	14	4	1	—	4,745
6	266	544	471	295	170	90	10	10	6	22	1,884
7	68	189	60	79	69	28	16	8	5	12	534
8	274	1,148	1,162	689	281	118	39	35	12	9	3,767
9	75	153	250	179	173	153	83	65	37	153	1,321
10	395	1,260	1,001	671	224	104	61	44	36	67	3,863
11	234	545	691	493	298	186	68	42	21	52	2,630
12	617	598	494	344	195	114	54	18	13	40	2,487
13	17	623	257	90	20	17	3	8	5	—	1,040
14	—	—	1	4	3	1	—	—	—	—	9
15	2	216	492	319	98	67	38	21	11	20	1,284
16	31	133	370	330	98	146	246	200	140	147	1,841
17	16	195	620	1,421	681	237	79	73	47	38	3,407
18	4	79	88	131	236	187	90	98	61	150	1,124
19	8	50	348	350	139	59	22	24	14	64	1,078
20	10	110	780	690	228	85	54	85	61	84	2,187
21	135	2,932	1,562	548	43	21	8	7	2	1	5,259
22	19	209	218	181	107	71	53	35	41	74	1,008
23	13	123	81	30	20	21	8	11	10	11	328
24	5	143	560	863	394	100	49	42	16	16	2,188
25	9	28	208	241	107	49	53	109	36	68	908
26	35	769	750	436	91	68	16	13	14	19	2,211
27	15	1,471	1,102	479	90	20	3	6	—	4	3,190
28	22	616	881	515	84	54	18	4	—	—	2,194
29	1	35	817	605	214	22	15	3	1	—	1,713
30	9	194	94	552	260	82	43	26	11	13	1,284
31	25	448	1,628	510	12	6	4	6	2	—	2,641
32	1	2	67	256	192	63	25	10	2	—	618
33	2	614	877	1,038	642	413	392	207	150	145	4,480
34	56	2,393	1,283	694	189	36	21	5	—	3	4,680
35	—	94	199	67	28	7	2	2	—	—	399
36	2	14	49	50	55	86	104	118	72	87	637
37	—	2	3	11	103	24	27	6	3	1	180
38	—	22	270	654	307	141	48	15	3	4	1,464
39	—	5	1,961	1,035	23	—	1	3	—	—	3,028
40	17	168	1,750	554	230	23	16	23	10	12	2,803
41	4	125	308	402	401	152	99	107	63	62	1,723
42	107	549	266	124	19	19	34	11	9	9	1,147
43	721	7,470	4,757	1,861	563	378	139	85	47	56	16,077
44	12	491	1,661	108	1	2	—	—	—	1	2,276
45	1	191	1,133	628	245	22	11	4	—	—	2,235
46	65	579	496	453	205	161	103	53	25	30	2,170
47	4	36	227	288	132	148	65	48	16	6	970
48	4	260	50	18	11	—	—	—	—	—	343
49	16	130	148	178	57	18	8	6	3	3	567
50	10	132	152	301	314	134	97	35	10	13	1,198
51	—	11	32	179	278	108	78	47	16	12	761
52	1	1	42	274	249	138	64	25	4	11	809
53	14	449	898	281	100	16	2	6	—	4	1,770
54	4	311	1,571	70	2	1	1	—	—	—	1,960
55	—	2	737	330	162	50	20	13	2	1	1,317
56	8	64	1,561	1,230	583	196	88	35	7	10	3,782
57	9	73	210	122	134	31	37	14	4	14	648
58	—	85	595	626	105	110	57	34	20	25	1,657
59	1	2	54	236	80	35	9	4	2	1	424
60	10	118	1,317	512	39	2	2	2	1	1	2,004
61	2	122	117	129	55	40	24	9	3	5	506
62	1	21	50	27	6	2	1	2	3	—	113
63	4	77	98	94	145	62	31	15	8	8	542
	4,933	31,282	39,870	24,691	10,235	4,843	2,780	1,951	1,088	1,592	123,265

of condition 3 and 134,081 or 30.5 per cent live in areas of both condition 1 and 3 as well as condition 2.

Condition 3.

Property mixed with various industries. Population: 151,300 or 35 per cent of the total population. Of this total 3.892 or 0.9 per cent live in areas only of this condition and are not, therefore, of condition 1 or 2: 6,626 or 1.5 per cent live in areas also of condition 1 and 6,701 or 1.5 per cent live in areas also of condition 2 while 134,081 or 30.5 per cent live in areas of both conditions 1 and 2 as well as condition 3.

From these investigations into the existing state of living conditions it was considered that the population having the worst environment might well be assessed in the following order :—

A. Those living in areas of all three conditions total ... 134,081

B. Those living in areas of conditions 1 and 3 above
total 6,626

C. Those living in areas of conditions 2 and 3 above
total 6,701

Total requiring urgent redevelopment 147,408

Though redevelopment for this population would relieve the worst, there will still be the next worst to deal with which are those living in one only of the above conditions.

CONDITION OF DWELLINGS.

TABLE XVII.

Dist. No.	Name	Total Dwellings	Fit	Sub-Standard	Unfit	Total Defective	Int. vented bath room	No Bathroom	No ind. W. C.	No ind. Sink
a	b	c	d	e	f	g	h	j	k	l
1	High Street	1,420	138	789	493	1,282	1	1,281	814	234
2	Grassmarket	569	93	356	120	476	9	467	297	24
3	Princes Street	562	172	358	32	390	8	382	158	75
4	Canongate	1,301	107	647	547	1,194	3	1,191	747	188
5	Pleasance & St. Leonards	4,745	624	2,906	1,215	4,121	163	3,958	2,463	1,677
6	George Square	1,884	397	1,202	285	1,487	176	1,311	623	246
7	Lauriston	534	171	286	77	363	80	283	154	23
8	Fountainbridge & Tollcross	3,767	805	2,715	247	2,962	519	2,443	870	88
9	West End	1,321	1,030	247	44	291	51	240	103	65
10	Stockbridge	3,863	1,398	1,996	469	2,465	115	2,350	977	75
11	Northside	2,630	1,356	1,016	258	1,274	153	1,121	349	188
12	East End	2,487	742	908	837	1,745	136	1,609	1,165	248
13	Abbeyhill	1,040	303	731	6	737	76	661	167	—
14	Kings Park	9	9	—		—		—		—
15	Prestonfield	1,284	1,239	44	1	45	34	11	4	—
16	Newington	1,841	1,337	483	21	504	55	449	65	9
17	Marchmont	3,407	2,271	1,107	29	1,136	631	505	30	48
18	Grange	1,124	996	126	2	128	—	128	41	41
19	Bruntsfield	1,078	913	147	18	165	94	71	28	5
20	Merchiston	2,187	1,940	247	—	247	51	196	31	—
21	Dalry	5,259	1,051	4,159	49	4,208	455	3,753	191	24
22	Haymarket	1,008	603	399	6	405	36	369	165	6
23	Belford	328	142	127	59	186	4	182	96	24
24	Craigleith	2,188	2,060	128	—	128	2	126	6	6
25	Goldenacre	908	810	98	—	98	50	48	3	—
26	Broughton	2,211	1,388	823	—	823	105	718	22	1
27	Easter Road	3,190	1,517	1,547	126	1,673	29	1,644	203	—
28	Meadowbank	2,194	1,210	975	9	984	113	871	36	3
29	Piershill & Willowbrae	1,713	1,675	33	5	38	20	18	6	—
30	Duddingston	1,284	1,181	22	81	103	2	101	—	—
31	Craigmillar	2,641	2,476	162	3	165	—	165	—	—
32	Blackford	618	612	6	—	6	1	5	—	—
33	Morningside	4,480	3,991	489	—	489	245	244	10	—
34	Gorgie	4,680	2,566	2,114	—	2,114	115	1,999	175	—
35	Roseburn	399	362	37	—	37	18	19	—	—
36	Murrayfield	637	601	35	1	36	7	29	—	—
37	Ravelston	180	174	6	—	6	—	6	—	—
38	Blackhall	1,464	1,390	74	—	74	19	55	4	—
39	Pilton	3,028	3,013	15	—	15	3	12	—	—
40	Granton	2,803	2,524	279	—	279	9	270	31	15
41	Trinity	1,723	1,606	116	1	117	9	108	3	—
42	Newhaven	1,147	357	386	404	790	24	766	275	15
43	Leith	16,077	5,221	9,576	1,280	10,856	321	10,535	2,844	66
44	Lochend	2,276	2,252	23	1	24	1	23	3	1
45	Craigentinny	2,235	2,169	65	1	66	1	65	—	—
46	Portobello	2,170	1,051	1,010	109	1,119	67	1,052	229	17
47	Joppa & Eastfield	970	904	48	18	66	1	65	26	7
48	Newcraighall	343	46	297	—	297	2	295	2	3
49	Gilmerton	567	399	150	18	168	—	168	56	1
50	Liberton	1,198	969	226	3	229	2	227	19	4
51	Braids & Fairmilehead	761	742	18	1	19	—	19	7	5
52	Craiglockhart	809	809	—	—	—	—	—	—	—
53	Slateford	1,770	1,353	399	18	417	157	260	121	16
54	Stenhouse	1,960	1,909	51	—	51	24	27	26	2
55	Saughtonhall	1,317	1,272	45	—	45	42	3	—	—
56	Corstorphine	3,782	3,625	157	—	157	7	150	65	1
57	Davidson's Mains	648	528	120	—	120	3	117	49	5
58	Colinton	1,657	1,563	93	1	94	1	93	25	4
59	Kingsknowe	424	414	9	1	10	—	10	—	—
60	Sighthill	2,004	1,766	228	10	238	94	144	76	11
61	Juniper Green	506	333	173	—	173	3	170	81	8
62	Turnhouse & Maybury	120	95	24	1	25	—	25	1	—
63	Barnton & Cramond	535	446	72	17	89	—	89	21	13
	Totals	**123,265**	**75,216**	**41,125**	**6,924**	**48,049**	**4,347**	**43,702**	**13,963**	**3,492**

Note :—

Figures in column (d) are those dwellings not containing defects detailed in columns (g)—(l) inclusive. The details of these defects do not include all those in the standards prescribed by the Chief Sanitary Inspector, e.g. structural defects such as dampness. Therefore, these figures should not be confused with those quoted as being 'fit' in the Chief Sanitary Inspector's category.

Figures in columns (e) and (f) include all the defective dwellings of Column (g).

Figures in column (f) include all dwellings scheduled as 'Unfit' in the Chief Sanitary Inspector's estimates.

TABLE XVIII.

A S
OF

POPULATION AREA	HOUSES I	HOUSES II	FAM I
EXISTING (Including Residential Property Retained) a	4,933	31,282	15,684
b		36,215	52,5
EXCESS OR DEFICIENCY OF HOUSES c		—16,368	
PROPOSED CITY TOTAL a			16,237
b		54,439	54,4
REDEVELOPMENT AREAS ...		17,612	17,6
DEVELOPMENT AREAS ...		18,359	18,3
CENTRAL SHOPPING AREAS...		267	2
RESIDENTIAL PROPERTY ...		—	—
RETAINED...		—	—

The Accommodation Standard.

Line ' a ' above gives the actual numb

Line ' b ' above gives the total house
shews the standard graphical

 1 & 2 apt Houses Accommod

  3 ,, ,,   ,,

 4 & 5 ,, ,,   ,,

TABLE XIX.

WARDS WHOLLY OR PARTLY	NEIGHBOURHOOD AREA NUMBER		NET RESIDENTIAL AREA	NET RESIDENTIAL DENSITY (AVERAGE)	POPUL
23		1	96·35	7·56	
23		2	47·55	17·0	
23		3	242·99	18·7	4,5
23, 7	A	4	228·17	34·2	7,8
23, 7		5	315·72	23·7	7,4
8, 23, 7		6	307·87	19·6	6,0
23		7	179·18	43·6	7,8
			1417·83	24·9	35,2
23, 8		1	268·16	70·7	18,9
23, 7, 8	B	2	185·62	24·2	4,4
8, 10, 11		3	212·43	11·5	24,4
7, 11		4	61·17	71·5	4,3
			727·38	71·9	52,2
18, 19		1	262·24	51·7	13,6
9, 20	C	2	151·42	115·9	17,5
1,17		3	190·88	147·5	28,3
			604·54	98·6	59,5
17, 2, 16		1	327·83	56·3	18,4
2, 16	D	2	177·39	58·2	10,3
16, 21		3	154·85	16·8	2,8
16, 21		4	223·97	47·2	10,5
			884·04	47·8	42,2
3		1	278·83	41·0	11,4
21		2	106·05	130·5	13,8
21	E	3	107·51	20·9	2,2
21		4	67·93	31·1	2,1
21		5	52·16	20·6	1,07
			612·48	50·2	30,71
5, 13, 14		1	294·97	46·8	13,80
3, 4, 14	F	2	359·68	45·7	16,41
4, 5		3	378·86	35·5	13,43
21, 22		4	200·21	23·8	4,78
			1233·72	39·3	48,44
23		1	106·11	52·9	5,62
6, 23		2	241·32	69·9	16,87
5, 6, 22	G	3	234·08	22·7	5,33
22		4	236·59	11·7	2,78
22		5	70·31	22·2	1,56
			888·41	36·4	32,18
2, 12, 15		X	40·16	382·2	15,43
8, 23		Y	48·18	17·4	84
14, 12, 7		Z	31·75	228·0	7,27
			114·09	206·1	23,55
	NON POP. AREAS GREEN BELT AREAS }		489·00 216·31	217·5 29·7	106,99 6,37
			7187·8	61·0	437,56

APPENDIX No. 1

PLACE OF WORK/PLACE OF RESIDENCE.
PRINCIPAL WAGE EARNERS — IN WORKING DISTRICTS.

TABLE XX.

Combined Residential Districts	Total Workers	WORKING DISTRICTS.						
		A	B	C	D	E	F	G
1	213	7	28	—	147	20	11	—
2	370	22	72	1	231	28	15	1
3	1,612	189	849	7	495	28	41	3
4	5,504	101	2,021	368	2,611	186	181	36
5	29	1	3	—	15	7	3	—
6	816	49	173	3	527	39	24	1
7	1,445	62	249	5	999	83	45	2
8	2,915	166	807	32	1,623	169	115	3
9	1,929	31	273	16	1,187	323	98	1
10	1,176	9	118	5	755	237	51	1
11	834	7	142	188	410	20	32	35
12	518	5	91	112	261	13	24	12
13	2,467	21	73	21	1,347	904	94	7
14	3,691	46	304	26	2,643	398	255	19
15	2,558	19	237	14	1,712	128	427	21
16	800	8	82	25	399	37	194	55
17	394	3	39	4	254	57	37	—
18	404	6	55	—	272	15	40	16
19	382	5	34	—	240	78	24	1
20	746	11	91	6	510	76	50	2
21	303	1	30	—	221	17	31	3
22	170	2	26	2	107	5	26	2
A	4,600	1,240	1,699	33	1,338	201	79	10
B	15,878	637	10,398	244	3,887	354	322	36
C	1,688	25	211	923	428	23	32	46
D	8,620	177	1,210	111	5,979	651	452	40
E	9,538	187	706	67	4,471	3,797	276	34
F	6,009	120	644	68	2,592	309	2,222	54
G	1,684	44	226	148	498	128	142	498
	77,293	3,201	20,891	2,429	36,159	8,331	5,343	939

Place. This represents 28 per cent increase and is mostly made up from the traffic coming from Colinton Road at Churchill. This traffic is again increased to 470 vehicles per average peak hour at the junction with Melville Drive and again to 522 vehicles per average peak hour at the West End where 475 vehicles per hour show a loss due to the intersection with Morrison Street.

Shandwick Place Route. This route is fed by three main routes, Corstorphine Road, Lanark Road and Calder Road, serving the western suburbs including Corstorphine, Murrayfield, Gorgie, Haymarket, Sighthill, Slateford and Juniper Green. Some 56 per cent of the traffic converging at Haymarket from Corstorphine Road appears to be using Morrison Street as a bye-pass of the West End.

This bye-pass traffic, if added to that already estimated for the Princes Street bye-pass scheme, would account for the east going traffic of a similar amount to the estimated west going traffic approximating to 600 vehicles per average peak hour. It should be remembered in this connection that these figures are, of course, based upon the 1946 Census which represents approximately 67 per cent of the peak pre-war year of 1938. In addition it is estimated that in ten or fifteen years time this peak pre-war year traffic is likely to double itself when this bye-pass of Princes Street will have become an acute necessity having to cope with some 1,800 vehicles per peak hour in one direction, apart from local traffic which would also be on the increase but would be using the present Princes Street.

Queensferry Street Route. The area served by this route covers roughly the north west suburban area of the city as well as providing an important outlet for Queensferry and the north. The traffic flow at Craigleith Station as it proceeds in the direction of the city centre amounts to 218 vehicles per average peak hour which is increased to 357 vehicles at the junction of Dean Park Crescent. Traffic travelling in a westerly direction as it approaches the West End amounts to some 523 vehicles per average peak hour if the Queen Street traffic is included with that in Queensferry Street. Of this total 301 vehicles are found approaching the West End in Queensferry Street and 222 going into Queen Street via Randolph Place. Thus the two flows are made up of 358 vehicles going across the Dean Bridge, 55 via Belford Road, 76 via Melville Street and a balance of some 15 or 20 vehicles per average peak hour are found to use the short cut from Queensferry Street to Haymarket via Melville Street.

The table below gives a comparison of the traffic flows over a 16 hour period between the three years, 1935, 1938 and 1946. From these figures it will be seen that the 1946 census presents figures substantially similar in quantity to the peak pre-war year of 1938 with certain exceptions : the average of the 1946 traffic being approximately 64 per cent of the 1938 traffic.

PERCENTAGE DIFFERENCES IN THE TRAFFIC FLOW ON PRINCIPAL ROADS LEADING TO AND FROM THE CENTRE OF THE CITY.

AVERAGE FLOW PER HOUR OVER 16 HOUR PERIOD.

TABLE XXI.

ROUTE	1935 Class and Flow	1935 Class as % of all Vehs. Wednesday	1935 All Vehicles	1938 Class and Flow	1938 Class as % of all Vehs. Wednesday	1938 All Vehicles	1946 Class and Flow	1946 Class as % of all Vehs. Wednesday	1946 All Vehicles	Average Flow All Vehicles as % of 1935 Wed.	Average Flow All Vehicles as % of 1938 Wed.	Average Flow All Vehicles over 6 hour peak period Wed.	Fri.
Queensferry Road (Craigleith Station)	H 52, L 299	14·8, 85·2	351	H 78, L 369	17·4, 82·6	447	H 73, L 259	21·9, 78·1	332	94·6	74·3	421	401
Corstorphine Road (Pinkhill Station)	H 97, L 408	19·2, 80·8	505	H 131, L 466	21·9, 78·1	597	H 162, L 277	36·9, 63·1	439	87·0	73·5	512	434
Calder Road (Gorgie Mills)	H 66, L 192	25·6, 74·4	258	H 88, L 249	26·1, 73·9	337	H 87, L 138	38·7, 61·3	225	87·3	66·8	242	229
Lanark Road (Slateford Road)	H 92, L 251	26·9, 73·1	343	H 104, L 275	27·4, 72·6	379	H 95, L 168	36·1, 63·9	263	76·7	69·5	316	294
Biggar Road (Newbattle Ter.)	H 107, L 307	25·9, 74·1	414	H 118, L 380	23·7, 76·3	498	H 136, L 170	44·4, 55·6	306	74·0	61·5	391	474
Peebles Road (C'millar Park)	H 83, L 224	27·0, 73·0	307	H 97, L 229	29·7, 70·3	326	H 119, L 159	42·9, 57·1	278	90·5	85·3	330	298
Dalkeith Road (Cameron Toll)	H 83, L 184	31·0, 69·0	267	H 56, L 188	23·0, 77·0	244	H 67, L 118	36·2, 63·8	185	69·2	75·8	222	220
Regent Road (Calton Hill)	H 104, L 334	23·7, 76·3	438	H 68, L 300	18·5, 81·5	368	H 88, L 197	30·9, 69·1	283	64·6	76·9	354	278
Constitution Street Leith	H 66, L 117	36·1, 63·9	183	H 72, L 99	42·1, 57·9	171	H 77, L 93	45·3, 54·7	170	93·0	99·5	216	192
East Coast Road (Magdalene Br.)	H 128, L 521	19·8, 80·2	649	H 97, L 350	21·6, 78·4	447	H 87, L 159	35·3, 64·7	246	37·9	55·0	303	273

TRAFFIC ACCIDENT ANALYSIS.

TABLE XXII.

YEAR 1937
ESTIMATED TOTAL POPULATION 466,817
AREA OF CITY, 32,526 ACRES

TYPE OF ACCIDENT—	TOTALS
Non Injurious	2,195
Injurious	1,130
Fatal	63

CLASSIFICATION OF ACCIDENTS—
(Persons involved)

	Killed.	Injured.
Pedestrians	38	589
Passengers (all types)	6	201
Pedal Cyclists	7	232
Motor Cyclists	7	47
Pillion Cyclists	—	12
Drivers	5	49

YEAR 1946
ESTIMATED TOTAL POPULATION 478,769
AREA OF CITY, 32,526 ACRES

TYPE OF ACCIDENT —	TOTALS
Non Injurious	997
Injurious	975
Fatal	52

CLASSIFICATION OF ACCIDENTS—
(Persons involved)

	Killed.	Injured.
Pedestrians	39	498
Passengers (all types)	7	265
Pedal Cyclists	4	107
Motor Cyclists	1	44
Pillion Cyclists	—	10
Drivers	1	51

TABLE XXII—*continued.*

TYPE and NUMBER of VEHICLES
INVOLVED in FATAL or INJURIOUS
ACCIDENTS—

Private Cars	406
Taxis	23
Goods Vehicles	173
Omnibuses	79
Tramcars	101
Motor Cycles (all types)	96
Pedal Cycles	301
Horse-drawn Vehicles	14

TYPE and NUMBER of VEHICLES
INVOLVED in FATAL or INJURIOUS
ACCIDENTS—

Private Cars	257
Taxis	28
Goods Vehicles	192
Omnibuses	105
Tramcars	187
Motor Cycles (all types)	78
Pedal Cycles	148
Horse-drawn Vehicles	32

	FATAL and INJURIOUS ACCIDENTS		
	1937	Average	1946
WEST END AREA— Principal City Shopping Centre. Location of Main Line Railway Station (L.M.S.) and Five Main Road Traffic Routes	13	17	21
EAST END AREA— Commercial and Popular Shopping Centre. Location of Main Line Railway Station (L.N.E.R.). Intersection of Four Main Road Traffic Routes	22	24	26
SOUTH BRIDGE AREA— Extensive Shopping and Entertainment Area. Adjacent High Density Residential Area of St. Leonards and Pleasance Narrow Main Road Traffic Route	26	32	38

	FATAL and INJURIOUS ACCIDENTS		
	1937	Average	1946
FOUNTAINBRIDGE AREA— Industrial and Residential Area. Main Omnibus Route. Heavy Goods and Horsedrawn Vehicles using narrow thoroughfare	12	13	14
LOTHIAN ROAD—TOLLCROSS— Commercial, Shopping and Entertainment Centre. Congestion created by the bottleneck of Earl Grey Street. Main Road Traffic Route	42	35	28
NIDDRIE MAINS AREA— Extensive New Residential Area of High Density with large Child Population. District served entirely by Omnibuses	12	13	14

APPENDIX No. 3

INDUSTRY

This Appendix is in two main sections—Survey and Proposals—and provides details of the studies upon which chapters 1 and 6 are based. It contains :—

A. THE SURVEY.
1. Present distribution of Industry.
2. Extent of industrialisation in terms of site area.
3. Trends in industrial installations.

B. THE PROPOSALS.
1. Conclusions from the Survey of Trends.
2. General proposals.
3. An estimate of the future industrial population.

A. THE SURVEY.

1. *Present Distribution of Industry.* The map on plate no. IX entitled "General Distribution of Industry" shows the location of factories and other undertakings of a gross annual value greater than £49 per annum. Areas occupied by workshops and local industries of a value less than £49 per annum are shown as "unclassified." To give a simple overall geographical picture these are classified broadly and in detail as they are found in existing localities or zones of the city where industry predominates. These classifications of industry are based upon those used by the Ministry of Labour and National Service whose code number is quoted below :—

Extractive : All mining and quarrying industries and those whose products are directly dependant upon mining or quarrying.

Type	Products	M. of L. Code
Coal mining	... ...	SA.
Quarrying	Stone, clay, sand, etc.	SE. SP. SH.
Clay products	Bricks, tiles, pottery, etc.	MA. MB.
Concrete	Pre-cast concrete, artifical stone, abrasives, etc.	MF.

Not represented :

Iron ore and ironstone mining etc. ...	SB.
Lead, tin and copper mining etc. ...	SD.
Slate Quarrying and Mining	SF.
Cement, lime kilns and Whiting... ...	MD.

Productive : All manufacturing industries.

I. *Food, Drink and Tobacco.*

Type	Products	M. of L. Code
Baking	Bread, Biscuits, cakes	XA.
Grain milling	... ...	XD.
Confectionery	Cocoa, chocolate and sugar	XE.
Other foods	Essences, preserves, curing and fish curing	XH.
Drink	Brewing, distilling and aerated waters ...	XK.
Fishing	... ...	RP
Tobacco	Snuff	XB.

II. *Textiles and Textile Clothing.*

Type	Products	M. of L. Code
	Wool and worsted, rayon, jute	VB. VD.
	misc., textiles, bleaching and printing etc.	VM. VX.
Hosiery	... ...	VR.
Wearing apparel	Tailoring, dressmaking, hats and caps, suits and misc. dress	WS. WX. WA.
	Industries	WB. WE. WH.
Footwear	... ...	WX.
Hemp & ropes	Ropes, nets, etc.	VP

Not represented :

Silk spinning and Manufacture	VE
Linen, lace, carpets	VH. VS. VT.
Cotton	VA.

III. *Metalwork Founding and Engineering.*

Type	Products	M. of L. Code
	Light castings iron and steel founding: non-ferrous casting and refining ...	CE. GC. GF.
Metalworking	Tools and cutlery, brass and brass finishing, general metal working ...	GM. GX. CW.
General Engineering	Engineer's iron and steel founding: railway wagon building and repair ...	CD. DE.
Electrical Engineering	Manufacture of Plant	CN.
Ship building	Ship repairing, boat building	BC
Marine Engineering	... ...	CT
Wire Working	Wire ropes, etc.	GR

Not represented :

Pig iron (Blast furnaces)	GA
Tin plates	GH
Bolts, nuts, screws, etc.	GS.
Iron and Steel tubes	GP.

IV. *Chemicals.*

Type	Products	M. of L. Code
Chemicals	Including explosives	FB. FA.
Oils & Fats	Oil, glue, soap, seed-cake, etc.	FD.
Paint and colours	... ...	FH.

Not represented :

Coke ovens and by-products works ...	FE.

V. *Paper and Printing.*

Type	Products	M. of L. Code
Paper	Paper board, etc.	TA.
Stationery	Cardboard boxes, wallpaper, etc. ...	TB. TH. TK.
Printing	Publishing and Bookbinding	TE.

VI. *Miscellaneous.*

Type	Products	M. of L. Code
Furniture	Upholstering, etc.	EB.
Light Manufactures	Clocks, musical instruments	HA. HB.
	scientific apparatus, sports goods ...	HD. HE.
Electrical Apparatus	Cable, Lamps, etc....	GK.
Rubber	... ...	KA.
Leather	Tanning, curing, etc.	KB.
	Leather Goods manufacture	KF.
Glass	Manufacture (excl. bottles), Lenses, etc....	MP.
	Bottles, etc.	MT
Other Industries	Linoleum, brushes, etc.	ZB. ZD. ZS.

Distributive : Warehousing and wholesale distribution.

Type	Product	M. of L. Code
Warehousing	Wholesale, cold storage, etc.	RX

Service : Transport, public utilities and non-manufacturing industries.

I. *Constructional.*

Type	Products	M. of L. Code
Building	... ...	AB.
Public Works Contracting	... ...	AC.
Building Engineering	Electrical Installation, structural, Heating and ventilating (including installing)	AP. CZ. GV.
Sawmilling	Machine joinery works	EA.
Coopering & Joinery	Jobbing joinery	EP.
Box-making	Wood boxes and packing cases	EM.

NATURE

N[...]

TABLE XXIII

EXISTING INDUSTRIAL GROUPS.	TOTALS (classified)	EXTRACTIVE.			PRODUCTIVE.	I. FOOD			
		Coal Mining.	Quarrying.	Clay Products.	Concrete.	Baking.	Grain Milling.	Confectionery.	Other Foods.
1 Central	10·1	—	—	—	—	—	—	0·3	0·3
2 Market Street	4·3	—	—	—	—	0·2	—	—	1·5
3 West End	4·6	—	—	—	—	0·2	—	—	0·2
4 Leith Street & Broughton Road	15·0	—	—	—	—	0·2	—	—	0·5
5 Canongate & Holyrood	33·9	—	—	—	—	—	—	—	0·4
6 High Street	12·1	—	—	—	—	—	—	0·7	—
7 East Fountainbridge & King's Stables Road	10·7	—	—	—	—	0·8	—	—	—
8 Belford	4·3	—	—	—	—	—	—	—	—
9 Stockbridge	0·2	—	—	—	—	—	—	—	—
10 Silvermills	10·3	—	—	—	—	—	—	—	1·8
11 Tanfield	10·8	—	—	—	—	—	—	—	—
12 Canonmills & Logie Green Road	7·8	—	—	0·5	0·5	—	—	0·2	—
13 Beaverhall	12·4	—	—	—	—	—	—	3·3	1·8
14 McDonald Road & Annandale Street	39·0	—	—	0·4	0·4	—	—	—	0·4
15 Albert Street & Brunswick Road	9·4	—	—	—	—	—	—	0·5	1·0
16 Easter Road & Meadowbank	20·4	—	—	—	—	—	—	—	—
17 London Road & Abbeyhill	4·8	—	—	—	—	—	—	—	0·5
18 St. Leonard's & Nicolson Street	17·3	—	—	—	—	—	—	—	—
19 University & Royal Infirmary Precinct	0·2	—	—	—	—	—	—	—	—
20 Causewayside & Sciennes	11·5	—	—	0·2	—	0·7	—	0·5	1·4
21 West Fountainbridge and Viewforth	29·0	—	—	—	—	0·7	—	1·2	3·0
22 Dalry	39·0	—	—	—	—	0·9	—	—	—
Bryson Road (33)	3·7	—	—	—	—	0·2	—	—	1·6
Gorgie (34)	68·0	—	—	—	1·8	10·2	0·5	0·2	—
23 Haymarket	3·2	—	—	—	—	—	1·2	—	—
24 Craigleith	0·9	—	—	—	0·2	—	—	—	—
25 Easter Drylaw	—	—	—	—	—	—	—	—	—
26 East Pilton	22·2	—	—	—	—	—	—	—	—
27 Trinity	3·9	—	—	—	—	—	—	—	—
28 Leith	189·0	—	—	0·7	—	5·5	12·2	0·2	9·2
Newhaven (38)	4·4	—	—	—	—	—	—	—	—
29 Willowbrae & Piershill	7·3	—	—	—	—	0·2	—	—	0·5
30 Craigmillar	27·1	—	—	—	—	—	—	—	5·9
31 West Savile Terrace	10·6	—	—	—	—	—	—	—	0·7
32 Balcarres Street	7·8	—	—	—	—	0·2	—	—	—
33 Bryson Road } (See No. 22)	—	—	—	—	—	—	—	—	—
34 Gorgie	—	—	—	—	—	—	—	—	—
35 Roseburn	21·4	—	—	—	0·2	—	—	0·5	—
36 Coltbridge	1·4	—	—	—	—	—	—	—	—
37 Granton	69·7	—	—	—	—	—	—	—	1·0
38 Newhaven (See No. 28)	—	—	—	—	—	—	—	—	—
39 Seafield	9·2	—	—	—	—	—	—	—	0·7
40 King's Road & Baileyfield	50·0	—	—	1·6	—	0·4	—	—	—
41 Portobello	9·0	—	—	—	—	—	—	—	—
42 Newcraighall & Niddrie	11·0	—	—	10·1	—	—	—	—	—
43 Liberton	0·2	—	—	—	—	—	—	—	—
44 Slateford	21·0	—	—	—	—	—	—	—	13·3
44a Slateford Mill	7·0	—	—	—	—	—	—	—	—
45 Stenhouse	4·8	—	—	—	—	—	—	—	0·2
46 Pinkhill	2·1	—	—	—	—	—	—	—	—
47 Corstorphine	6·6	—	—	—	—	—	—	—	—
48 Davidson's Mains	—	—	—	—	—	—	—	—	—
49 Gilmerton	2·0	—	—	—	—	—	—	—	—
50 Straiton	4·1	—	4·1	—	—	—	—	—	—
51 Colinton	6·0	—	—	—	—	—	3·5	—	—
52 Hailes	4·1	—	—	—	—	—	—	—	—
53 Sighthill *	—	—	—	—	—	—	—	—	—
54 Maybury	11·4	—	—	—	—	—	—	—	—
55 Turnhouse	—	—	—	—	—	—	—	—	—
Unallocated to Groups	45·0	—	—	—	1·5	4·1	2·8	0·7	—
TOTALS CLASSIFIED	**941·2**	—	—	16·5	4·8	25·4	20·2	8·1	46·1

* Undeveloped at date of survey.

II. *Transport.*			III. *Supplies and Services.*		
Type	Products	M. of L. Code	Type	Products	M. of L. Code
Railways		RE.	Gas, Electricity and Water Supplies		ZA.
Trams and Bus Services		RH	Laundering Dyeing and Cleaning		NXL. NXO.
Road Transport (Goods and Passenger)		RMF. RMG.	Motor Vehicle Coachbuilding and Repair		DA. DB.
Shipping and Docks		RS. RT.			

EXTENT OF INDUSTRIALISATION IN TERMS OF SITE AREA

2. While the map shows how the location of industry falls into 56 localities or zones throughout the city with a scattering of unclassified industries over the whole, table XXIV gives the extent occupied in these predominating industrial localities :—

ANALYSIS OF GROSS ANNUAL VALUE OF INDUSTRIES & NUMBERS EMPLOYED.

TABLE XXIV.

INDUSTRY		Gross Annual Value (£) £ Thousands			Insured Workers (Edinburgh) Thousands			Insured Workers (Region) Thousands	Insured Workers (Gt. Britain) Thousands		
		1929	1939	1945	1929	1939	1946	1946	1929	1939	1946
EXTRACTIVE	Coal Mining	2·8	2·5	2·0	2·4	2·4	1·7	18·2	1074·7	868·0	733·2
	Quarrying	6·0	7·9	4·3	0·3	0·4	0·3	2·9	75·5	81·6	54·5
	Clay Products	0·7	0·9	0·8	0·2	0·3	0·2	1·7	155·9	185·4	114·9
	Concrete	0·6	0·9	1·0	—	0·1	0·1	0·2	17·4	32·5	34·8
PRODUCTIVE I FOODS, ETC.	Baking	15·2	21·7	24·1	5·4	6·8	4·2	5·2	144·7	197·8	143·3
	Grain Milling	16·2	18·8	18·4	0·6	0·7	1·0	1·2	29·5	34·5	32·2
	Confectionery	4·0	4·4	4·7	1·0	1·6	1·1	1·2	72·5	89·0	42·9
	Other Foods	27·0	34·4	35·1	0·6	1·2	1·5	1·8	111·1	147·9	136·1
	Fishing	0·8	1·2	1·3	0·6	0·8	0·3	0·4	27·5	31·9	19·9
	Drink	87·3	86·8	97·9	4·0	5·1	5·2	5·9	108·5	125·5	118·4
	Tobacco	1·8	1·8	1·8	0·1	0·3	0·3	0·3	46·0	47·1	44·7
II TEXTILES	Textiles	3·8	5·5	4·4	0·6	0·8	0·3	6·9	1110·0	896·1	556·0
	Hosiery	2·3	3·3	3·3	1·1	1·0	0·6	3·7	105·7	134·0	72·7
	Wearing Apparel	5·8	6·1	7·1	1·7	2·2	1·8	2·4	446·0	554·3	360·9
	Footwear	1·9	1·3	1·3	0·6	0·4	0·4	0·5	135·2	148·2	107·6
	Hemp and Rope	5·0	4·3	6·5	0·5	0·7	0·5	0·8	19·0	20·8	15·7
III FOUNDING ETC.	Founding	2·9	2·7	2·7	0·6	0·6	0·3	0·9	361·3	397·0	354·5
	Metal Working	10·0	11·8	13·2	1·5	1·8	2·0	2·2	254·0	371·9	376·1
	General Engineering	15·1	17·7	27·3	3·0	2·0	3·7	6·5	640·0	751·5	979·2
	Electrical Engineering ...	3·2	4·5	5·2	0·1	1·2	1·3	1·3	84·0	132·0	153·3
	Ship Building	8·6	5·7	6·6	2·1	1·7	3·3	3·4	204·4	180·2	234·9
	Marine Engineering ...	1·5	1·5	1·8	0·1	0·1	1·1	1·0	58·4	61·2	75·3
	Wire Works	1·6	1·9	2·7	0·2	0·4	0·7	2·2	47·6	59·9	60·0
IV CHEMICALS	Chemicals ...	16·1	15·2	16·5	1·1	1·1	1·6	2·2	124·2	160·9	238·8
	Oils and Fats ...	12·6	13·2	13·3	0·6	0·6	0·6	2·6	75·1	83·2	80·0
	Paint and Colour ...	3·0	2·8	2·7	0·1	0·1	0·2	0·2	18·9	26·5	27·4
V Paper	Paper	1·8	3·2	3·4	0·6	0·7	0·6	3·4	55·2	72·0	59·0
	Stationery	10·5	11·7	12·7	2·3	2·2	1·9	1·9	70·4	106·3	63·6
	Printing	36·5	38·7	37·4	6·7	6·3	5·1	5·5	261·1	316·5	227·5
VI MISCELLANEOUS	Furniture	4·4	7·5	7·9	1·5	1·8	1·3	1·4	120·3	155·9	98·7
	Light Manufactures ...	2·7	2·8	2·7	0·9	0·7	0·6	0·7	108·7	118·9	106·8
	Electrical Apparatus ...	0·6	1·2	3·1	0·1	0·1	0·6	1·0	93·9	198·3	240·7
	Rubber	16·4	15·9	17·4	5·4	5·4	4·1	4·3	65·3	72·6	70·2
	Leather	2·9	2·9	3·1	0·5	0·5	0·4	0·7	67·4	78·8	60·4
	Glass	1·3	1·8	1·9	0·5	0·4	0·5	0·6	45·0	53·2	54·0
	Other Industries ...	0·4	0·7	1·1	2·0	2·2	2·3	6·9	149·3	198·0	202·6
DISTRIBUTIVE	... ...	5·1	6·1	6·5	0·1	0·2	0·2	0·3	18·5	22·2	32·8
SERVICE I CONSTRUCTIONAL	Building	7·8	10·6	12·4	10·6	13·0	9·1	14·2	824·0	1067·1	852·1
	Contracting	0·3	0·3	0·9	2·2	1·7	2·8	5·0	164·4	366·2	183·7
	Building Engineering ...	2·8	3·9	4·2	1·4	3·8	1·9	2·3	53·6	120·5	135·2
	Sawmilling	7·2	7·7	7·4	0·5	0·6	0·9	2·3	58·3	71·7	84·3
	Coopering and Joinery ...	7·3	7·9	7·2	0·6	0·5	0·3	0·4	23·2	26·6	24·3
	Boxmaking	0·8	0·8	1·1	0·3	0·3	0·3	0·3	12·8	12·9	17·5
II TRANSPORT	Railways	80·0	81·5	54·6	2·1	2·0	4·0	5·2	138·4	168·8	318·1
	Tram and Bus Transport	83·0	111·5	196·5	1·0	3·8	4·9	5·0	154·0	213·0	238·5
	Road Transport ...	3·3	5·2	7·0	3·8	2·3	2·1	3·5	181·6	206·7	191·7
	Shipping and Docks ...	106·7	130·0	80·2	4·4	4·1	3·3	3·4	311·6	295·4	249·6
III SUPPLIES	Gas and Electric Supplies	176·4	207·6	205·2	1·0	1·7	1·9	} 2·6	170·1	225·7	208·2
	Water Supplies ...	3·5	2·8	2·5	0·1	0·1	0·1				
	Laundering ...	6·3	7·9	7·6	1·8	3·0	2·4	3·2	135·0	208·9	151·0
	Motor Vehicle Repairing	22·2	30·4	32·4	1·5	3·0	4·5	5·6	264·3	497·5	596·4
	Total	846·0	979·4	1022·4	81·0	94·8	90·4	155·5	9093·8	10,692·6	9634·2

ANALYSIS OF TRENDS IN INDIVIDUAL INDUSTRIES

TABLE XXV

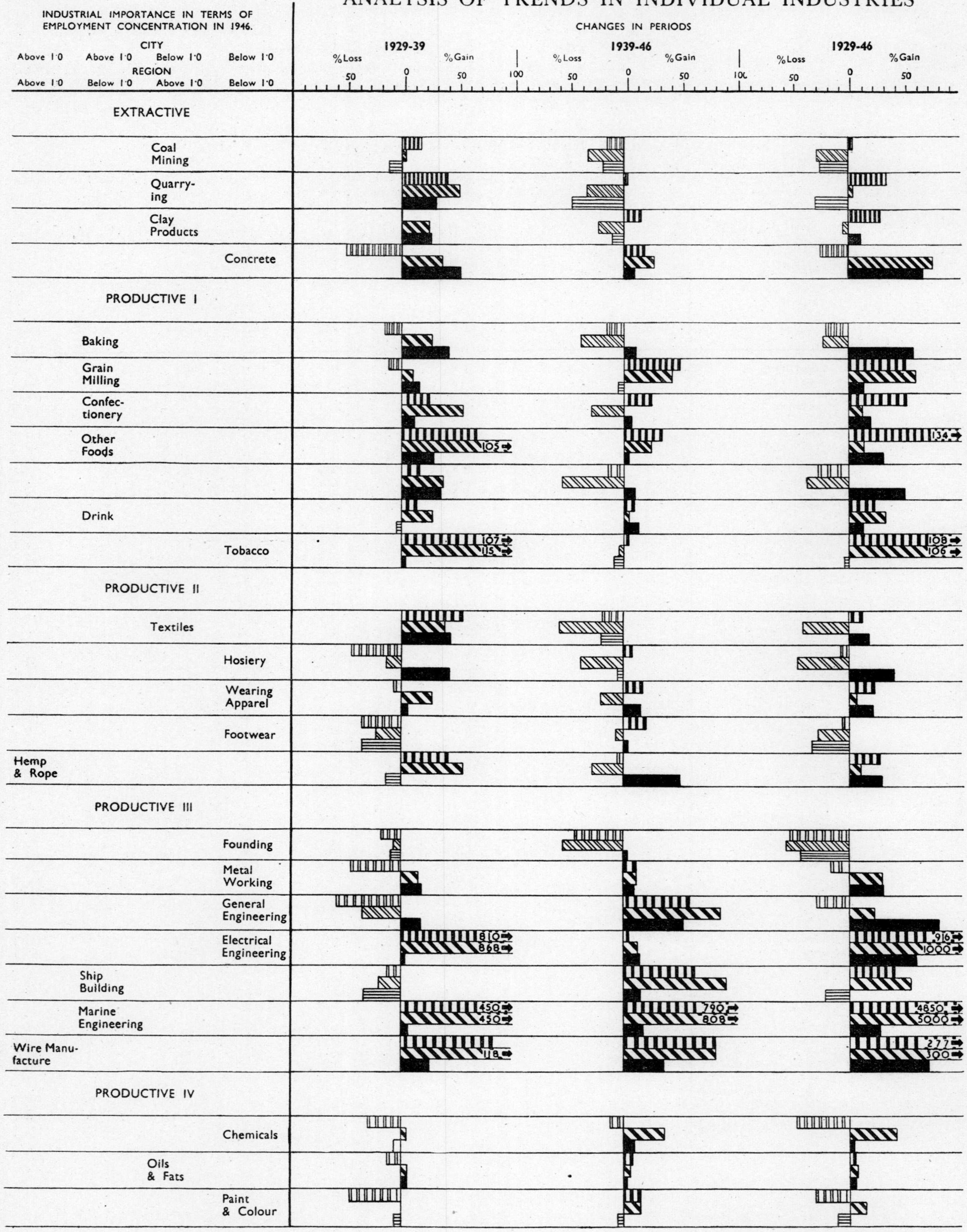

INDUSTRIAL IMPORTANCE IN TERMS OF
EMPLOYMENT CONCENTRATION IN 1946.

	CITY		
Above 1·0	Above 1·0	Below 1·0	Below 1·0
	REGION		
Above 1·0	Below 1·0	Above 1·0	Below 1·0

CHANGES IN PERIODS

1929-39	1939-46	1929-46
%Loss %Gain	%Loss %Gain	%Loss %Gain
50 0 50 100	50 0 50 100	50 0 50

EXTRACTIVE

Coal Mining

Quarrying

Clay Products

Concrete

PRODUCTIVE I

Baking

Grain Milling

Confectionery

Other Foods   105 →   1034 →

Drink

Tobacco   107 → 105 →   108 → 106 →

PRODUCTIVE II

Textiles

Hosiery

Wearing Apparel

Footwear

Hemp & Rope

PRODUCTIVE III

Founding

Metal Working

General Engineering

Electrical Engineering   816 → 868 →   916 → 1000 →

Ship Building

Marine Engineering   450 → 450 →   790 → 808 →   4850 → 5000 →

Wire Manufacture   118 →   277 → 300 →

PRODUCTIVE IV

Chemicals

Oils & Fats

Paint & Colour

ANALYSIS OF TRENDS IN INDIVIDUAL INDUSTRIES

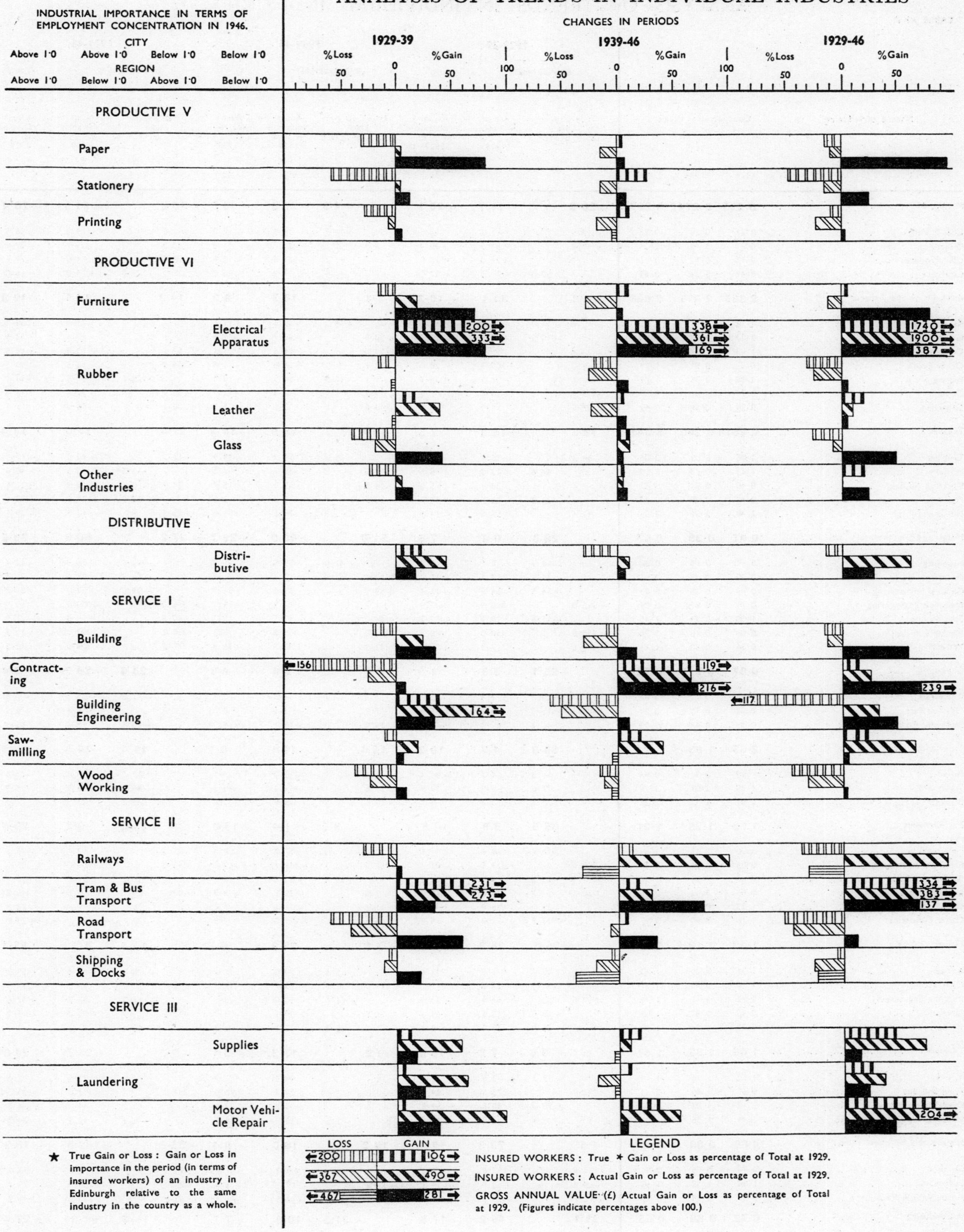

INDUSTRIAL IMPORTANCE IN TERMS OF
EMPLOYMENT CONCENTRATION IN 1946.

CHANGES IN PERIODS

CITY

Above 1·0	Above 1·0	Below 1·0	Below 1·0

REGION

Above 1·0	Below 1·0	Above 1·0	Below 1·0

1929-39   1939-46   1929-46

%Loss %Gain   %Loss %Gain   %Loss %Gain

50 0 50 100   50 0 50 100   50 0 50

PRODUCTIVE V

Paper

Stationery

Printing

PRODUCTIVE VI

Furniture

Electrical Apparatus — 200, 333 / 338, 361, 169 / 1740, 1900, 387

Rubber

Leather

Glass

Other Industries

DISTRIBUTIVE

Distributive

SERVICE I

Building

Contracting — 156 / 119, 216, 117 / 239

Building Engineering — 164

Saw-milling

Wood Working

SERVICE II

Railways

Tram & Bus Transport — 231, 273 / 334, 383, 137

Road Transport

Shipping & Docks

SERVICE III

Supplies

Laundering

Motor Vehicle Repair — 204

★ True Gain or Loss : Gain or Loss in importance in the period (in terms of insured workers) of an industry in Edinburgh relative to the same industry in the country as a whole.

LEGEND

LOSS   GAIN

— 200 / 106   INSURED WORKERS : True ★ Gain or Loss as percentage of Total at 1929.

— 367 / 490   INSURED WORKERS : Actual Gain or Loss as percentage of Total at 1929.

— 467 / 281   GROSS ANNUAL VALUE (£) Actual Gain or Loss as percentage of Total at 1929. (Figures indicate percentages above 100.)

ANALYSIS OF TRENDS IN INDIVIDUAL INDUSTRIES.

TABLE XXVI.

Nature of Industry	Concentration Index			1929-39 EMPLOYMENT 1 True Gain or Loss as % of 1929 +	−	1929-39 EMPLOYMENT 2 Actual Variation as % of 1929	1929-39 G.A.V. 3 Actual Variation as % of 1929	1939-46 EMPLOYMENT 1 True Gain or Loss as % of 1939 +	−	1939-46 EMPLOYMENT 2 Actual Variation as % of 1939	1939-46 G.A.V. 3 Actual Variation as % of 1939	1929-46 EMPLOYMENT 1 True Gain or Loss as % of 1929 +	−	1929-46 EMPLOYMENT 2 Actual Variation as % of 1929	1929-46 G.A.V. 3 Actual Variation as % of 1929
	1929	1939	1946	% +	% −	%	%	% +	% −	%	%	% +	% −	%	%
Mining, &c.	**0·225**	**0·2747**	**0·2591**	+20·2		+11·7	+20·1		−4·3	−27·9	−33·8	+10·3		−19·5	−20·4
Coal Mining	0·23	0·28	0·24	+17·5		+1·2	−10·5		−14·2	−31·4	−17·8	+2·9		−29·2	−26·5
Quarrying	0·37	0·49	0·54	+40·8		+51·9	+30·4	+2·4		−31·7	−46·3	+33·4		+3·7	−29·9
Clay Products	0·17	0·17	0·21	Nil.		+24·0	+25·0	+16·1		−22·6	−10·6	+28·0		−4·0	+11·75
Concrete	0·47	0·34	0·40		−50·0	+37·5	+52·5	+18·2		+27·2	+10·0		−25·0	+75·0	+68·0
Food, Drink and Tobacco	**2·335**	**2·411**	**2·668**	+4·3		+34·1	+10·7	+7·1		−13·3	+8·3	+14·9		+14·1	+19·9
Baking	3·78	3·4	3·02		−14·0	+27·4	+42·8		−14·2	−38·6	+11·1		−19·8	−21·8	+58·7
Grainmilling	2·21	2·03	3·25		−10·9	+10·9	+16·4	+50·8		+43·7	−2·4	+51·6		+59·4	+13·6
Confectionery	1·44	1·74	2·71	+28·4		+55·9	+10·9	+24·0		−28·6	+7·1	+52·0		+10·8	+18·8
Other Foods	0·55	0·81	1·14	+68·0		+105·3	+28·0	+33·1		+24·8	+1·89	+134·0		+13·6	+30·3
Fishing	2·08	2·36	1·79	+16·1		+37·5	+35·7		−16·9	−54·5	+10·5		−28·6	−37·5	+50·0
Drink	3·74	4·01	4·57	+13·1		+28·7	−1·2	+9·2		+2·6	+12·75	+23·9		+32·0	+11·4
Tobacco	0·29	0·58	0·62	+107·5		+115·2	+3·3	+3·6		−3·6	−5·91	+108·0		+106·0	−1·1
Textiles and Clothing	**0·2518**	**0·290**	**3·341**	+18·3		+15·4	+7·5	+10·4		−28·9	+10·4	+21·4		−17·9	+19·4
Textiles	0·05	0·09	0·06	+54·4		+38·6	+44·1		−17·7	−56·9	−18·9	+12·3		−40·0	+17·4
Hosiery	1·13	0·73	0·90		−44·8	−13·2	+43·1	+8·1		−38·4	−1·54		−2·64	−46·5	+40·8
Wearing Apparel	0·40	0·39	0·52		−1·1	+28·1	+5·0	+16·5		−19·3	+15·7	+22·9		+3·4	+21·5
Footwear	0·43	0·29	0·39		−36·8	−22·7	−34·7	+20·5		−6·8	+2·34		−7·0	−28·0	−33·1
Hemp and Rope	2·48	3·36	3·35	+41·4		+54·5	−14·5		−2·81	−28·1	+51·0	+28·2		+10·9	+29·1
Metals and Engineering	**0·47**	**0·39**	**0·57**		−22·3	+0·4	+7·6	+51·0		+60·0	+29·7	+27·2		+60·6	+39·5
Founding	0·17	0·14	0·08		−18·6	−5·1	−5·3		−41·0	−53·5	+1·12		−52·6	−56·0	−42·4
Metalworking	0·62	0·47	0·55		−44·6	+14·1	+17·8	+13·6		+13·6	+11·85		−16·8	+29·6	+31·7
General Engineering	0·48	0·26	0·39		−56·5	−34·9	+17·4	+59·0		+87·6	+54·3		−29·6	+22·0	+81·6
Electrical Engineering	0·15	0·87	0·89	+810·0		+868·0	+3·9	+1·7		+13·9	+15·5	+916·0		+1000·0	+60·5
Ship Building	1·08	0·94	1·45		−11·6	−20·0	−32·2	+64·0		+92·5	+15·7	+40·6		+54·0	−21·7
Marine Engineering	0·04	0·18	1·36	+450·0		+450·0	+6·9	+790·0		+808·2	+18·7	+4850·0		+5000·0	+26·9
Wire Manufacturers	0·36	0·60	1·16	+82·5		+117·8	+25·0	+83·9		+83·9	+36·4	+277·0		+300·0	+70·5
Chemicals	**0·87**	**0·71**	**0·72**		−25·1	+3·8	−1·6	+2·6		+2·4	+4·0		−28·4	+28·9	+2·4
Chemicals	0·93	0·72	0·69		−29·2	+4·4	−5·8		−11·1	+36·0	+8·61		−47·8	+41·5	+2·4
Oils and Fats	0·82	0·75	0·84		−11·5	+3·3	+5·0	+7·9		+3·1	+0·05	+1·6		+6·6	+5·5
Paint and Colour	0·70	0·48	0·58		−46·2	nil	−6·27	+15·4		+15·4	−4·58		−30·8	+15·4	−10·5
Paper and Printing	**2·53**	**1·83**	**2·24**		−36·9	−4·3	+10·2	+15·4		−17·1	−0·1		−11·4	−10·3	+10·1
Paper	1·18	0·92	0·99		−31·3	+4·7	+81·4	+4·5		−15·0	+7·2		−15·6	−10·9	+9·4
Stationery	3·30	2·07	3·12		−57·6	+0·9	+12·9	+28·5		−14·2	+8·8		−48·5	−15·0	+8·8
Printing	2·61	1·95	2·32		−27·1	−5·9	+6·1	+10·5		−18·6	−3·4		−9·3	−23·3	+2·3
Miscellaneous	**1·69**	**1·26**	**1·21**		−35·5	+3·8	+14·8		−3·5	−1·4	+13·0		−35·8	−9·2	+29·8
Furniture	1·30	1·15	1·39		−14·4	+19·6	+71·6	+10·0		−27·2	+4·4	+5·9		−13·1	+79·3
Electrical Apparatus	0·03	0·06	0·26	+200·0		+333·5	+81·3	+338·0		+361·1	+169·0	+1740·0		+1900·0	+387·0
Rubber	8·40	7·31	5·97		−15·2	nil	−2·5		−20·6	−24·8	+9·1		−31·1	−24·8	+6·4
Leather	0·53	0·62	0·65	+17·2		+40·0	−0·3	+2·0		−22·5	+5·86	+20·0		+8·6	+5·5
Glass	1·23	0·83	0·94		−39·0	−16·8	+42·7	+11·1		+11·1	+4·35		−25·9	−7·4	+48·8
Other Industries	1·16	0·90	0·97		−23·9	+1·0	+14·8	+4·5		+1·0	+7·8		−20·1	nil	+23·7
Constructional	**1·42**	**1·18**	**1·22**		−25·8	+26·3	+18·8	+3·1		−22·9	+6·7		−15·4	−2·7	+27·1
Building	1·31	1·20	1·10		−20·3	+23·3	+35·6		−9·1	−30·0	+17·43		−16·2	−13·8	+59·0
Contracting	1·40	0·45	1·57		−156·0	−25·0	+7·1	+119·0		+65·7	+216·0	+13·8		+24·5	+239·0
Building Engineering	2·75	3·11	1·45	+39·6		+164·4	+34·8		−61·0	−50·0	+9·6		−117·0	+32·7	+47·8
Sawmilling	0·95	0·87	1·08		−9·3	+18·5	+65·6	+21·9		+39·1	−3·0	+22·2		+65·0	+3·3
Woodworking	2·72	1·84	1·60		−36·4	−22·8	+8·29		−16·2	−12·1	−4·8		−46·9	−32·3	+3·1
Transport	**1·46**	**1·35**	**1·47**		−9·3	+7·2	+16·6	+9·2		+17·3	+3·1	+2·3		+25·7	+24·0
Railways	1·52	1·16	1·28		−29·3	−2·9	+1·8	+12·1		+98·6	−32·9		−37·1	+93·0	−31·6
Tram and Bus	0·67	1·75	2·33	+231·0		+273·6	+34·4	+18·6		+29·2	+76·0	+334·0		+383·0	+137·0
Road Transport	2·12	1·07	1·13		−58·0	−40·5	+59·8	+1·8		−6·6	+33·4		−43·2	−44·4	+114·0
Shipping and Docks	1·45	1·36	1·34		−5·9	−7·9	+21·8		−3·6	−20·0	−38·2		−5·2	−26·4	−24·7
Supplies and Services	**0·80**	**0·80**	**0·95**	+1·6		+73·9	+19·4	+18·2		+16·0	−0·4	+33·5		+102·0	+18·9
Supplies	0·70	0·76	0·94	+12·6		+57·6	+17·0	+18·4		+9·2	−1·28	+45·1		+72·0	+15·6
Laundering	1·36	1·38	1·66	+3·4		+63·8	+24·2	+11·6		−17·1	−3·4	+25·2		+36·9	+20·1
Motor Vehicle Repair	0·57	0·58	0·78	+2·7		+98·1	+37·4	+35·1		+53·5	+6·48	+80·5		+204·0	+46·2
Warehousing	0·72	0·86	0·65	+23·1		+46·2	+17·6		−31·5	+10·5	+7·7		−15·4	+61·6	+27·4
City Industry	0·91	0·87	0·97		−11·1	+16·5	+15·5	+9·33		−3·88	+4·4	+6·7		+11·9	+20·8

TRENDS IN INDUSTRIAL INSTALLATIONS IN THE CITY.

3. Changes in Industry have been analysed as :—
  a. changes in the concentration of individual industries.
  b. changes in the employment level.
  c. changes in the gross annual value.

(a) *Changes in the concentration of individual industries.* "Concentration" of industry, measured in terms of insured workers, may be appreciated in extent by visualising Edinburgh containing a certain share of the "global" distribution of insured workers over the whole country. That share is represented by comparing the number of Edinburgh's insured workers (engaged in industry generally or in a particular trade) as a proportion of her total population with the same proportion for the whole country given as an average distribution. The "concentration" index is obtained by dividing one proportion into the other. Thus an industry having a concentration index of 1·0 can be said to exist in average national distribution in a locality.

(b) *Changes in employment level.* This is shown in table XXVI as a variation in the actual numbers engaged, and expressed as a percentage of the total employment figure for 1929.

(c) *Changes in the gross annual value.* This is shown in table XXVI as a variation in the actual values and expressed as a percentage of the total value of a given industry in 1929.

Changes in concentration for all the trade classifications in Edinburgh are tabulated in Table XXVI and show, not only the actual increases or decreases between the numbers of insured workers engaged in 1929 and say 1946, but, the difference required to maintain the same industrial importance in terms of employed workers that Edinburgh held (relative to the whole country) in 1929. There are two tables XXV and XXVI in which XXV gives the graphical interpretation of this survey and XXVI the actual figures. In both the facts are given for three different periods— 1929 to 1939, 1939 to 1946 (war period) and 1929 to 1946— in which the true gain or loss relative to the country is given in column 1 and the actual gain or loss unrelated to the country is given in column 2 and for gross annual value in column 3. In some cases the results show that Edinburgh has gained in national importance over the whole period of 1929 to 1946 though it had lost in importance up to the outbreak of war as in the case of the grainmilling trade. A summary of some of the results that may be read from the Tables XXV and XXVI are given below but the story of progress of each industry or trade may be read in the manner of the following sample.

The metalworking Industry : Period 1929-39 : the number of persons engaged increased by 14·1% and the gross annual value of buildings, heritable plant, etc., increased by 17·8% over 1929. But the growth of this Industry in other parts of the country was such that Edinburgh actually lost ground in spite of the local increase in employment. In order to maintain her position at the 1929 level in the metalworking industry, Edinburgh should have shown an increase in the numbers engaged of 14·1% plus a further 44·6% making 58·7% in all.

Period 1939-46 : During the war there was a further increase in numbers engaged of 13·6% over the terminal figure in column 1 of the first period, together with a further increase of 11·9% in gross annual value.

The numbers engaged in this industry in other parts of the country declined during the war to a greater extent than in Edinburgh. The concentration index, therefore, rises and it is found that the increase in workers of 13·6% is sufficient to raise the concentration index to 0·55.

Period 1929-46 : Summarising the changes in the separate periods it is found that in 1946 the industry had gained in numbers employed by 29·6% and in gross annual value by 31·7% but, as shown by the concentration index it had still not regained the position it held in 1929. This drop, however, is so little as to be of no significance.

The exact figures on which Table XXV is based are to be found in Table XXVI.

Categories of Importance.

In order to assess the importance of changes in individual industries it is necessary to place those industries in their various categories of importance. The 'concentration' of a given industry in a locality, for example, may be said to show whether that locality contains a sufficient amount of that industry as to create a "centre."

To interpret the extent of importance of an industry in the city or region (excluding the city) a 'concentration' index relationship has been compiled for each industrial group based upon the numbers of workers in those industries in 1946. From these indices it is possible to derive some indication of the extent to which certain industries are suppliers to the population in the region and to those in the rest of the country and that certain others are mainly local industries. Though it may be a matter for conjecture whether the extent of a trade's importance nationally (as represented by its index) is also a measure of the proportion of its total production that is exported, it is assumed that an industry having a 'concentration' index of 1·0 or about 1·0 is theoretically meeting the needs of the population; and that an industry having a 'concentration' index of, say, 1·5 produces an exportable surplus and is, therefore, of regional or national importance.

In Table XXV, industries in the city are placed in four categories of importance taking an industry having a 'concentration' index of 1·0 as of average 'concentration' nationally.
These categories are :—

(1) Industries having a concentration greater than 1·0 in both city and region (excluding the city). These would be the exporting industries contributing to the needs of the nation, and are, therefore, national industries.

(2) Industries having a 'concentration' greater than 1·0 in the city and less than 1·0 in the region (excluding the city). These are the city industries that may be assumed partly to help fill the gap between the producing capacity of the local industries in the region and the consumption of the local regional population and partly to contribute to the needs of the rest of the country.

(3) Industries having a 'concentration' of 1·0 or less than 1·0 in the city and more than 1·0 in the regional area (excluding the city). The city industries in this case are assumed to be either meeting the requirements of the city population for those products where the concentration is 1·0 or not supporting the population requirements if less than 1·0. The population then looks to the regional industries or alternatively to those elsewhere in the country for the balance of its requirements. Such industries would not be considered as of regional or national importance.

(4) Industries having a 'concentration' of less than 1·0 in both the city and the region. Where this condition prevails the population's requirements may be assumed to be insufficiently met by their own industries and the balance of their needs must be sought from the rest of the country or from abroad.

On this basis the various groups in order of importance are :—

		Concentration Index 1946.
1.	Food, Drink and Tobacco	1·27
2.	Paper and Printing ...	1·22
3.	Transport	1·15
4.	Miscellaneous	1·12
	Constructional	1·12
5.	Supplies and Services ...	0·95
6.	Chemicals	0·72
7.	Warehousing	0·65
8.	Metals and Engineering	0·56
9.	Textiles and Clothing ...	0·34
10.	Mining, etc. ...	0·26

Food, Drink and Tobacco.

Baking. Baking is of national importance as indicated by its concentration index of 3·02 for the city and 2·15 including the capacity of the city and regional industries. That is to say that the employment concentration is higher than it need be to meet the requirements of the population of the city and region taken together. In fact it provides substantially for the rest of the country and Scotland in particular. It has increased its equipment by 58·7% gross annual value mostly before the war. Subject to normal consumption and employment returning the industry is, therefore, well set for development.

Milling. Grain milling is of national importance on account of its concentration index of 3·25 in the city and 2·29 taking the city and the region together. It may be assumed, therefore, that the products of this industrial group contribute to the country's needs generally. There was a large increase of employment in the war period indicating a probable need for future expansion of installations. This has already appeared at the Leith Dock Extensions.

Confectionery. Confectionery is of national importance having a city concentration index of 2·71 and a regional and city concentration of 1·8. The industry is developing ahead of the country as a whole and a further increase of equipment may be anticipated.

Other Food Industries. Occupy a similar position as for confectionery.

Fishing. In spite of a heavy war time drop in man-power expansion of equipment has continued. Prosperity and increasing importance nationally may be anticipated.

Drink. The drink industry is of national importance having a city concentration index of 4·57 and a combined one with the region of 2·96. This may be assumed to indicate that these industries in Edinburgh not only support the region for its requirements but also the rest of the country. These installations expanded by 12·75% during the war period together with a very small increase in employment. This industrial group has improved its national position since 1929 and appears to be very prosperous.

Tobacco. Tobacco is not a nationally important industry having a city concentration index of 0·62 and a combined one for the region of 0·36. In fact it may be assumed that Edinburgh's population requirements are not met by its own local industry. Its importance was more than doubled before the war but without a corresponding increase in equipment. Further expansion in this industrial group seems probable.

2. *Paper and Printing.*

Paper. Paper making so far as the city is concerned has a concentration index of 0·99 and may be said just about to satisfy local requirements but as the combined city and regional index is 3·35 there is probably an exportable surplus being manufactured to supply other parts of the country. Therefore, in the regional sense only the industry is of national importance. It is also reasonable to conclude from this that paper making is essentially a regional industry and that further expansion should probably take place in the region rather than in the city.

Stationery. This industrial group is of national importance owing to its city concentration index of 3·12 and its combined concentration index with the region of 1·82 suggests that this industrial group has an exportable surplus to contribute to the needs of the rest of the country. Its trends of development indicate that in spite of small increases both before and during the war period the industry is lagging behind the country as a whole. An increase in space requirements is, therefore, likely.

Printing. This industrial group is also of national importance having a concentration index of 2·32 and a combined regional and city concentration index of 1·4. This suggests that the city's printing industry supplies not only the region for its requirements but contributes to the rest of the country as well. Its trends indicate a tendency to remain more or less static though with a slight tendency to decline in Edinburgh.

3. *Transport.* This industry is of national importance having a concentration index of approximately 1·3 for the city and of 1·0 for the combined region and city. The trends of development indicate the Docks and Railways reflecting a general shrinkage of trade in the port of Leith. Railways, however, showed an increase of employment of nearly 100% during the war and this appears to be lasting into the post war period. Road passenger transport shows enormous increases all round but goods transport, though showing a steady increase in equipment, lost 58% of its employment before the war. During the war this decline almost ceased and the industry is now probably on the upgrade. Further expansion of installations should not be needed for the present.

4. *Miscellaneous and Constructional.*

Rubber. This is the most important industry in the city having the highest concentration index relative to the country as a whole of 5·97. The region concentration index excluding the city is ·13 and brings the combined concentration index for the city and region down to 3·49 which suggests that both the region and the rest of the country benefit considerably from the production capacity of this industry. Its trends over the survey period indicate a static condition but with a tendency to decline before the war. There was, however, an increase of 9·1% gross annual value during the war period indicating an increase of equipment. There was also a decrease in its employment of 24·8%, a decline relative to the rest of the country of 20·8%, indicating probably modernisation and economy of man power. There is, therefore, room for some expansion of trade within the limits of the present installed equipment.

Furniture. This industry is of national importance having a concentration index for the city of 1·39 and a concentration index of 0·85 for both the region and the city which indicates that the bulk of its exportable surplus probably contributes to the requirements of the region mainly. The fruits of a pre-war increase in equipment of 71·6% gross annual value are seen in the war time increase in concentration. Actual loss of employment during the war shows that further expansion of equipment will not be needed for the present.

Glass. This is not an industry of national importance having a concentration index for the city of 0·94 and of 0·55 for both the region and the city together. In fact it may be assumed that it appears to meet the needs of the city while the region requires to import these products considerably. During the war the industry remained at a higher level than in the rest of the country and in fact slightly increased its employment. A pre-war increase of equipment of 42·7% gross annual value which did not decrease during the war period will probably be sufficient to render further expansion unnecessary.

Electrical Apparatus is not a nationally important industry since, for the city, it has a concentration index of 0·26 and 0·23 for the combined city and regional area. It may be assumed from this that population requirements are met mainly by imports of this product from elsewhere. Trends during the war period indicated a very large increase which was mainly due to the presence of an evacuated firm which has now left Edinburgh.

Leather is not of national importance having a city concentration index of 0·65 and a similar index for the combined city and regional area. Trends have indicated more or less static conditions, which, if they continue, will probably show a decline for both employment and gross annual value.

Building is of regional importance rather than national having 1·0 concentration index for the city and 0·98 for the combined area of the region and the city. There was a pre-war expansion of equipment amounting to 35·6% gross annual value accompanied by an increase in employment of 23·3%. The industry nevertheless lagged in relation to the rest of the country by 20·3%. Development of equipment continued during the war period at a slower rate than other similar industries in the rest of the country.

Contracting is a nationally important industry having a concentration index for the city of 1·57 and for the combined city and region of 1·68. Trends in this industry indicate a lag before the war but it more than doubled itself during the war period so that the city can be regarded as a 'public works' centre. A final nett increase of 239% gross annual value against a nett employment increase of only 24·5% indicates that further space requirements need not be considered urgent for the present.

Building Engineering is of regional importance having a city concentration index of 1·45 and a combined index of 0·96 for the city and region. The most important installation in this group is the structural engineering group which expanded considerably before the war and in advance of the country for average concentration. It has lost ground, however, and further expansion of installations should be looked for in the future.

Sawmilling is not really nationally important within the city as it contributes very slightly in its production capacity to the requirements of the rest of the country. It has a city concentration index of 1·08 and a combined one for the city and region of 1·69. It is indicated that the regional industries have an exportable surplus to contribute to the rest of the country. Trends in the city industries indicate an increase in equipment before the war of 65·6% gross annual value though its employment total did not immediately increase. A war time increase of employment, however, rectified this position. It finally concluded its trend of expansion in 1946 as compared with 1929 with a 3·3% increase in equipment and an employment increase of 65%. As this industry is more highly concentrated in the region (2·57) than in the city further development in Edinburgh may not be necessary.

5. *Supplies and Services.* This industrial group is of regional importance having a city concentration index of 0·95 and may be said to contribute to the requirements of the region as well as those of the city. The concentration of motor vehicle repair (which includes a fair representation of body building) is low relative to the country as a whole and expansion in this industry might well be appropriate in view of the low concentration index of 0·26 for the region excluding the city. The trends in the "supplies" industries before the war relative to those over the whole country were not very great despite its increase in gross annual value of 17·0%. This tendency to lag was more than made up during the war period and the total overall increase between 1929 and 1946 was 15·6% in its equipment as represented by gross annual value and 72·0% in its employment figures. Its true gain as compared with its relationship with industries in other parts of the country in 1929 may be represented by 45·1% increase in employment.

6. *Chemicals*. This group is not found to be represented extensively in Edinburgh as it is not a national centre for chemical products. Its national concentration index for the city is 0·69 and for the combined city and regional area is 0·55. The chemical industry lost ground to the extent of 29·2% of its manpower compared with the average for the country during 1929-39. There was also a reduction of equipment amounting to 5·8% gross annual value. These reductions prevented the industry from being adequately represented in Edinburgh in the years following 1929. War time increase in manpower if maintained may require future expansion of installations.

Oils and Fats. With a national concentration index of 0·83 for the city and 3·37 for the region excluding the city this industry group is not a production centre for the nation though it is highly developed in the region. It is more or less static in the city and is a very suitable industry for the neighbourhood of the Port of Leith. Its further development in the region could equally benefit the port and avoid the necessity for further development of a noxious industry within the city area.

Paint and Colour. A very small industry in Edinburgh which has shown a continuous decline in gross annual value. It has a low national concentration index for the city.

7. *Distributive*. Rather surprisingly this industry has a national concentration below the average in Edinburgh in spite of the Port of Leith. A net increase in employment by 1946 of 61·6 % would indicate a tendency for further expansion of warehouses and installations.

8. *Metals and Engineering*. The general industries in this group are of low national concentration in the city and have shown comparatively little tendency to expand. On the other hand those producing a finished product show great vitality, though increases in equipment appear to be reasonably in step with increases in manpower. Allotment of space for expansion in the near future would appear, therefore, to be unnecessary.

9. *Textiles and Clothing*. With the exception of the Hosiery trade all the " clothing " industries are of very low national concentration in the city. A demand for increased space on account of expansion does not seem likely in any of the industries in this group.

10. *Extractive*. Except in the case of concrete there is no case for further development in this group. Equipment in the concrete industry appears to have increased in step with employment but the industry is still well below the average national concentration. With a return to general building development using modern techniques, the demand for pre-cast and artificial stone products will probably lead to a demand for increased space for this industry.

To summarise, demands for increased space may be anticipated in the Food, Drink and Tobacco Industries; Supplies and Services (especially motor vehicle repair and body building), Distributive and Extractive (Concrete and artificial stone). In most other industries existing installations would appear to be adequate to allow for some increase of output.

PROPOSALS.

1. Conclusions from the Survey of Trends in Industry.
Analysis of the period 1929-39 has shown that Edinburgh was not tending to become an Industrial City. Though there was industrial development it was less than the average for the country as a whole. As a result of war-time developments, however, there is in 1945-46 evidence of increased and possibly increasing industrial equipment and potential employment in the city. This trend, if allowed to continue would eventually alter the balance of industry and other occupations so as to change the character of Edinburgh as primarily an administrative and cultural centre.

2. General Proposals.
The proposals assume roughly a continuance of the present industrial insured population total with an addition of approximately 21% over the 1929 employment figure to meet the estimated number required to operate the industrial equipment existing at 1946.

The reason for the extent of industrialisation cannot solely be measured on this basis if for no other reason than that production and ground space requirements may vary as efficiency of modern equipment varies with or without employment fluctuation.

If too great a proportion of Edinburgh's total population became engaged in industrial production a change to an industrial character could be anticipated and would probably lead to increased industrial use of land.

VARIATIONS IN G.A.V. AND NUMBER OF PERSONS ENGAGED IN INDUSTRY IN EDINBURGH

TABLE XXVII.

	1929	1932	1934	1936	1938	1939	1945	1946
1. G.A.V. (Thous.)	930·6	(987·0)	1022·9	(1050·0)	—	1077·3	1124·5	—
2. % Variation in Do. cf 1929	—	+6·1	+10·0	+12·8	—	+15·8	+20·8	—
3. Indl. Pop. (Thous.)	80·5	84·5	(87·3)	90·5	(94·3)	94·0	75·7	90·1
4. % Variation in Do. cf 1929	—	+5·0	+8·4	+12·4	+17·1	+16·8	—6·0	+12·0

(NOTE—Figures in Brackets are Estimated.)

3. An estimate of the Future Industrial Population.
Owing to the war-time disturbance of population and the present state of industry, the number of persons at present engaged in industry cannot be taken as the number which existing equipment could absorb given conditions of full production and employment.

It is found, that, over a period, changes in the gross annual value of undertakings reflect proportionately changes in both the production capacity (not actual production necessarily) of those undertakings and the numbers of workers. Temporary fluctuations in employment are not reflected. Table XXVII and the accompanying graph show the relationship between gross annual value and the number of workers. The graph line of each is seen to have an almost constant relationship from the two lines running parallel to each other except during the abnormal conditions of war.

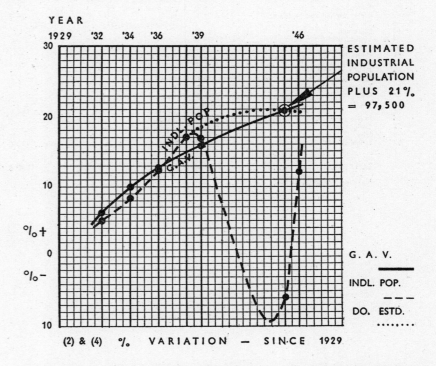

Assuming that the conditions of production and employment existing before the war were applied to the Industrial Equipment installed in 1945 (represented by an increase in gross annual value of 21% over 1929), then it can be stated broadly, that the number of workers needed to man that equipment up to the pre-war standard would be 21% greater than the number engaged in 1929, viz., 98,000 persons as compared with 81,000 persons.

In the Plan it is recommended that the Industrial Population may be assumed to be stabilised at 98,000 or 20·7% of the total population, i.e., 471,900.

This industrial increase in production capacity over the maximum pre-war figure measured in terms of gross annual value should not necessarily commit a corresponding increase in the total population considered in the Plan as a desirable maximum. Instead the extra employment required to man this increased capacity could be found in this total population.

APPENDIX No. 3

TABLE XXVIII SHOWING HOW INCREASE of INDUSTRIAL LAND USE is OBTAINED and HOW HOUSING and OTHER USES are AFFECTED

No.	Existing Industrial Group (See Plate No. 000)	Nett Area Acres	Proposed Industrial Zone (See Folding Map No. 19) Name or Type	Nett Area Acres	Industry Gain	Industry Loss	Housing Gain	Housing Loss (incl. % Sub-Standard)	Other Uses Gain	Other Uses Loss	Nature
1	Central	10.1	Service	9.0	—	1.1	—	—	1.1	—	Commercial.
2	Market Street	4.3	Service	2.9	—	1.4	—	—	1.4	—	Do.
3	West End	4.6	—	—	—	4.6	—	—	4.6	—	Do.
4	Leith Street and Broughton Road	15.0	Service	1.0	—	14.0	—	—	14.0	—	Commercial and Residential.
5	Canongate and Holyrood	33.9	Service	4.0	—	29.9	29.9	—	—	—	
6	High Street	12.1	Service	4.0	—	8.1	—	—	8.1	—	Shopping and Commercial
7	East Fountainbridge and King's Stables Road	10.7	Service	2.5	—	8.2	8.2	—	—	—	
8	Belford	4.3	Service	1.5	—	2.8	—	—	2.8	—	Open Space
9	Stockbridge	0.2	Neighbourhood Service	—	—	0.2	—	—	0.2	—	Neighbourhood Centre.
10	Silvermills	10.3	Silvermills	10.3	2.0	2.0	—	2.0 (25%)	2.0	—	Open Space.
11	Tanfield	10.8	—	—	—	10.8	—	—	10.8	—	Do.
12	Canonmills and Logie Green Road	7.8	—	—	—	7.8	—	—	7.8	—	Neighbourhood Centre and Open Space
13	Beaverhall	12.4	—	—	—	12.4	—	—	12.4	—	Neighbourhood Centre.
14	M'Donald Road and Annandale Street	39.0	Annandale Street	27.0	—	12.0	12.0	—	—	—	
15	Albert Street and Brunswick Road	9.4	—	—	—	9.4	5.0	—	4.4	—	Open Space.
16	Easter Road and Meadowbank	20.4	Meadowbank	77.0	51.8	—	—	31.0 (60%)	—	20.8	Do.
17	London Road and Abbeyhill	4.8									
18	St. Leonards and Nicolson Street	17.3	St. Leonards	25.0	} 13.1	—	—	13.1 (75%)	—	—	
			Service	5.4							
19	University and Royal Infirmary Precinct	0.2	Service	0.2	—	—	—	—	—	—	
20	Causewayside and Sciennes	11.5	—	—	—	11.5	—	—	11.5	—	Open Space and Sub-Arterial Road.
21	West Fountainbridge and Viewforth	29.0									
22	Dalry	39.0	Dalry	271.0	131.3	—	—	131.3 (60%)	—	—	
	Bryson Road (33)	3.7									
	Gorgie (34)	68.0									
23	Haymarket	3.2	—	—	—	3.2	—	—	3.2	—	Railway Yards.
24	Craigleith	0.9	Craigleith	8.0	7.1	—	—	—	—	7.1	Unused Land.
25	Easter Drylaw	—	—	—	—	—	—	—	—	—	
26	East Pilton	22.2	East Pilton	22.2	—	—	—	—	—	—	
27	Trinity	3.9	—	—	—	3.9	—	—	3.9	—	Neighbourhood Centre.
28	Leith	189.0	Leith	278.0	84.6	—	—	44.2 (100%)	—	40.4	Reclamation Dock area and Open Space
	Newhaven (38)	4.4									
29	Willowbrae and Piershill	7.3	—	—	—	7.3	—	—	7.3	—	Open Space and School.
30	Craigmillar	27.1	Craigmillar	44.0	16.9	—	—	—	—	16.9	Open Space.
31	West Savile Terrace	10.6	West Savile Terrace	22.0	11.4	—	—	—	—	11.4	Railway Yard.
32	Balcarres Street	7.8	Balcarres Street	16.0	8.2	—	—	—	—	8.2	Do.
33	Bryson Road	—	See Dalry (No. 22)	—	—	—	—	—	—	—	
34	Gorgie	—	—	—	—	—	—	—	—	—	
35	Roseburn	21.4	Roseburn	13.4	—	8.0	—	—	8.0	—	Railway.
36	Coltbridge	1.4	Included in No. 57	—	—	1.4	—	—	1.4	—	Neighbourhood Centre.
37	Granton	69.7	Granton	156.4	86.7	—	—	—	—	86.7	Open Space, unused Land and Reclamation.
38	Newhaven	—	See Leith (No. 28)	—	—	—	—	—	—	—	
39	Seafield	9.2	Seafield	40.0	30.8	—	—	10.6 (0%)	—	20.2	Open Space and Unused Land.
40	King's Road and Baileyfield	50.0	King's Road	58.0	8.0	—	—	2.0 (90%)	—	6.0	Unused Land.
41	Portobello	9.0	Included in No. 57	*7.5	—	1.5	1.5	—	—	—	*On Railway Property.
42	Newcraighall and Niddrie	11.0	Niddrie	26.7	15.7	—	—	—	—	15.7	Agricultural and Old Pit Land.
43	Liberton	0.2	Included in No. 57	—	—	0.2	0.2	—	—	—	
44	Slateford	21.0	—	—	—	21.0	—	—	21.0	—	Open Space.
44 A	Slateford Mill	7.0	—	—	—	7.0	—	—	7.0	—	Neighbourhood Centre.
45	Stenhouse	4.8	—	—	—	4.8	—	—	4.8	—	Open Space.
46	Pinkhill	2.1	Service	2.1	—	—	—	—	—	—	
47	Corstorphine	6.6	Gylemuir	13.4	6.8	—	—	3.0 (0%)	—	3.8	Agricultural and Open Space.
48	Davidson's Mains	—	—	—	—	—	—	—	—	—	
49	Gilmerton	2.0	Gilmerton	2.0	—	—	—	—	—	—	
50	Straiton	4.1	Straiton	4.1	—	—	—	—	—	—	
51	Colinton	6.0	Colinton	6.0	—	—	—	—	—	—	
52	Hailes	4.1	—	—	—	4.1	—	—	4.1	—	Open Space.
53			Sighthill	144.0	144.0	—	—	—	—	144.0	Agricultural.
54	Maybury	11.4	Maybury	11.4	—	—	—	—	—	—	
55	Turnhouse	—	—	—	—	—	—	—	—	—	
56	Unallocated	45.0	—	—	—	45.0	45.0	—	—	—	
57	Unclassified	166.6	Neighbourhood Service Industries	192.0	25.4	—	—	12.7	—	12.7	Approx. equal from Open Space and Housing.
	TOTALS	**1107.8**		**1508.0**	**643.8**	**243.6**	**101.8**	**249.9**	**141.8**	**393.9**	
	Nett Industrial Gains	—		—	**400.2**						

TABLE XXIX.

1 DISTRIBUTION WITHI[N] NEIGHBOURHOODS.

Wards Wholly or partly included	Neighbourhood Unit Area Number	
23		1
23		2
23		3
23, 7	A	4
23, 7		5
8, 23, 7		6
23		7
23, 8		1
23, 7, 8	B	2
8, 10, 11		3
7, 11		4
18, 19		1
9, 20	C	2
1, 17		3
17, 2, 16		1
2, 16	D	2
16, 21		3
16, 21		4
3		1
21		2
21	E	3
21		4
21		5
5, 13, 14		1
3, 4, 14	F	2
4, 5		3
21, 22		4
23		1
6, 23		2
5, 6, 22	G	3
22		4
22		5
2, 12, 15	X	
8, 23	Y	
14, 12, 7	Z	

TOTALS IN N.U.'s
Areas Not in N.U.'s

TOTALS IN CITY {

2 DISTRIBUTION OF BALA[NCE] OUTSIDE NEIGHBOURHO[ODS]

TOTALS IN CITY

(1) Proposed Resident Population. {
(2) Proposed Total Population.
(3) Existing Total Population (1946). {

APPENDIX No. 5

THE ST. JAMES' SQUARE FESTIVAL CENTRE.

INTRODUCTION.

The need for a Festival Centre situated in the St. James' Square area has already been explained in Chapter 7. The purpose here is to give by illustration the details showing the potentialities of the site situated between St. James' Square and Broughton Street for such a Centre as part of a larger scheme for comprehensive re-development under the 1947 Act.

The site plan below shows how conveniently the Centre could be placed to the East end of Princes Street and to Leith Walk.

The Centre occupies the most important part of the larger scheme for the locality at a point where the sharply contrasting contours offer an opportunity to obtain the maximum of accommodation and to enjoy the magnificent views of the Firth of Forth on clear-weather days.

The scheme depends for its architectural success mainly upon the removal of the Theatre Royal from its present site where it is 'jammed' up against St. Mary's Roman Catholic Cathedral. The burning down of the theatre in 1946 and the subsequent application for planning consent for re-instatement, expedited consideration of the proper re-development of this locality and necessitated a sketch design being prepared in advance of this Report for the guidance of the Town Council. The details illustrated below elaborate the original conception for this north east side of St. James' Square and the ideas are projected in the third dimension to complete the architectural expression. It is from these and other details that the model illustrated on Plates XXVII and XXXVIII was prepared.

The Theatre Royal. The importance of removing this theatre from its old site is obvious : not only is it necessary to separate for reasons of appearance, two important public buildings—St. Mary's Roman Catholic Cathedral Church and the Theatre Royal—and to provide them, together with the Concert Hall with a proper foreground, but to make possible adequate emergency escapes for the theatre and suitable daylight for the church. To achieve this, the resulting composition in the design for the north eastern front consists of the dominant group of concert hall buildings on the highest part of the ground, flanked by a new Theatre Royal on one side and a new Roman Catholic Cathedral

Church on the other, with the site of the existing burnt-out shell of the Theatre Royal turned into garden terraces. In addition, such a scheme would permit a start to be made with the proposed tunnel section of the Princes Street by-pass scheme (which in any case should be constructed section by section) when re-construction begins for the new Theatre Royal.

The purpose of the Centre. The purpose of this festival group of buildings is not only to provide for the diversity of entertainment during the festival, but to give accommodation for one of the main purposes which lie behind the idea of the festival : that is the development of an active interest in the arts of music and drama throughout the year, of which the festival itself, as an annual event, is only the culminating feature of expression. It is therefore thought desirable to incorporate in the scheme facilities for teaching and practice of these two arts. To this end there are provided music practice rooms, dramatic club rooms, refectory and lecture halls, in addition to the Concert Halls, theatre and cinema. The Centre, therefore, will be used throughout the year for concerts, theatrical and film productions, together with courses of lecturing and opportunities for music practice. That was the aim of those intimately concerned in inaugurating the festival in 1947, under the leadership of the Lord Provost at that time—Sir John Falconer.

THE LARGER SCHEME.

This extends between Calton Hill and Greenside, Leith Street, Broughton Street, York Place, St. James' Square, Elder Street and Clyde Street, as may be seen on the site plan Fig. (1). The present use of the property in this locality is of a very mixed nature, consisting of tall tenements, hotels, shops and a heterogenous collection of small industries. The property is in an extremely poor condition, much of which consists of the original buildings constructed at the time of the new town extension in the 18th Century. There has been little change in the living conditions provided by these tenements in St. James' Square since they were first constructed. The lay-out of the road system is awkward and contains steep gradients. The erstwhile back gardens, have now for the most part been entirely built over with one or two storey structures which are completely alien to the original residential character of the neighbourhood. A typical example may be seen on Plate XXVII.

The use proposed for the new buildings in the re-development scheme is commercial rather than residential, for reasons already explained in Chapter 7. Leith Street for example, remains as a shopping street, with commercial offices rather than tenement dwellings above. Broughton Street is re-orientated and widened as the only link between Leith Street and Leith Walk via York Place. The present link between Leith Street direct with Leith Walk is then stopped-up and built over for the purpose of creating a shopping precinct for Leith Street and to encourage 'through' traffic to use the new by-pass roads.

THE CONCERT HALL GROUP.

This group of buildings is situated upon the highest part of the ground at an existing ordnance level of approximately 237, as compared with 157 at the top of Leith Walk. The fine prospect that this change in levels offers, is easily seen from the longitudinal section X—X illustrated in Fig (2). There are two main entrances, one from St. James' Square at the new reduced ordnance level of 232 (one part of the Square is already at 232 O.D.) and the other from Broughton Street, by means of the steps or ramps up to the topmost terrace. Following contemporary practice, provision is made for those arriving by car or bus and garaging space is found beneath the halls with a lift service as direct communication. Entering from St. James' Square, the main foyer connects with the principal concert hall, or opera house and with a small concert hall and lecture hall—all more or less on the same level. Above is the Grand Foyer giving access to the Circle and restaurant and an additional lecture hall. Above again are situated the music practice and drama club rooms. In the first basement level, entrance is gained to the large cinema, ballroom and restaurant. Beneath again to the second and third basements are the principal garaging facilities. The opera house or concert hall as shown, could accommodate 2,500, the smaller hall 1,600, and the two lecture halls 575 each. The structure would be of re-inforced concrete design, with suitable facing material which might be of stone or some suitable form of colourcrete finish, similar to that which should be prescribed for the new Theatre Royal and St. Mary's Roman Catholic Cathedral.

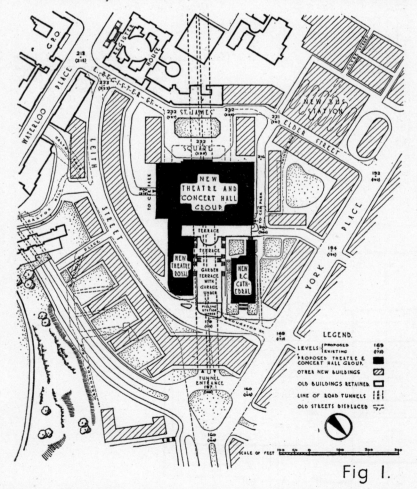

Fig.(1) This is the site plan referred to above, showing the extent of the re-development scheme, including the Festival Centre. This scheme should be one of the first to be started within the next ten years.

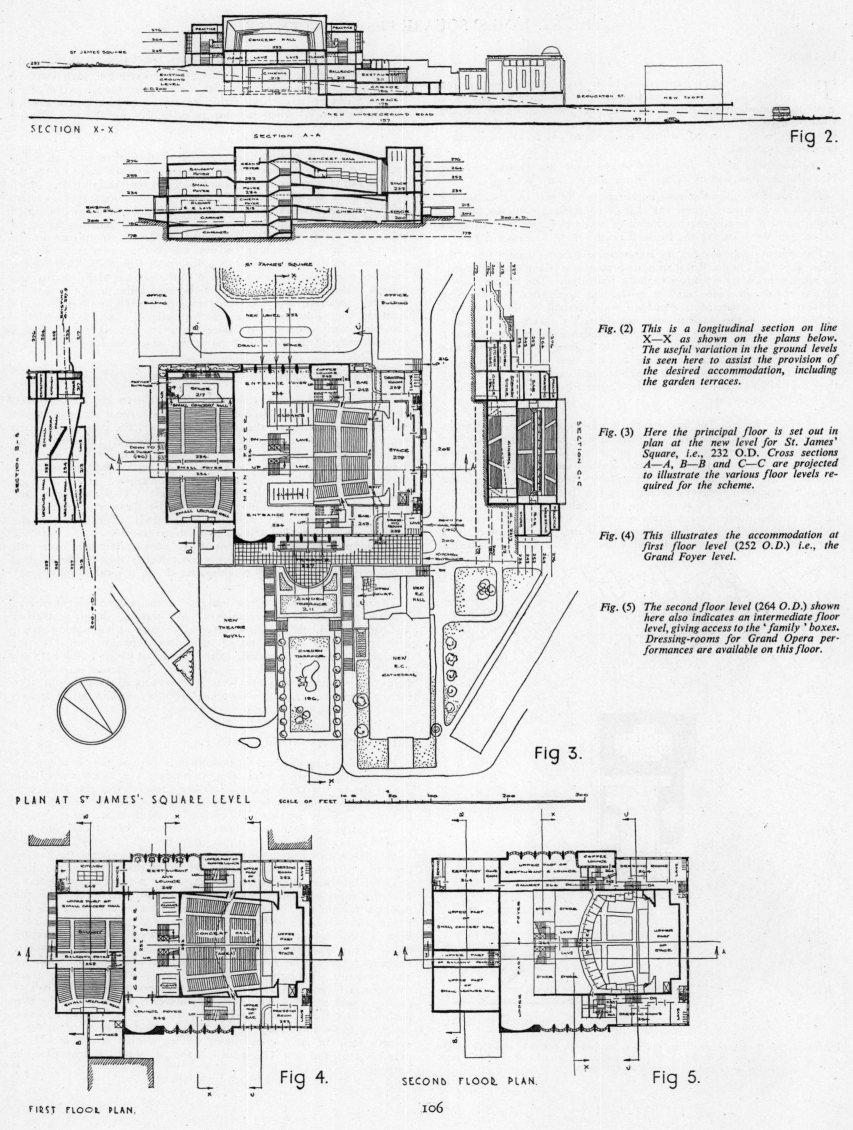

Fig 2.

Fig. (2) *This is a longitudinal section on line X—X as shown on the plans below. The useful variation in the ground levels is seen here to assist the provision of the desired accommodation, including the garden terraces.*

Fig. (3) *Here the principal floor is set out in plan at the new level for St. James' Square, i.e., 232 O.D. Cross sections A—A, B—B and C—C are projected to illustrate the various floor levels required for the scheme.*

Fig. (4) *This illustrates the accommodation at first floor level (252 O.D.) i.e., the Grand Foyer level.*

Fig. (5) *The second floor level (264 O.D.) shown here also indicates an intermediate floor level, giving access to the 'family' boxes. Dressing-rooms for Grand Opera performances are available on this floor.*

Fig 3.

PLAN AT St JAMES' SQUARE LEVEL

SCALE OF FEET

Fig 4.

FIRST FLOOR PLAN.

SECOND FLOOR PLAN.

Fig 5.

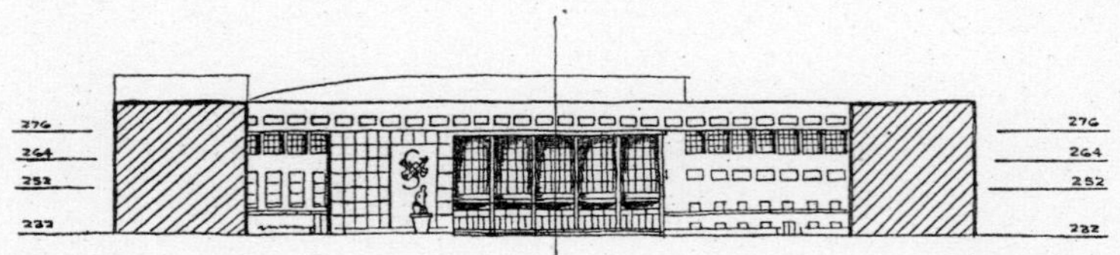

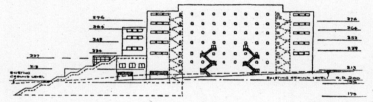

ELEVATION TO ST JAMES' SQUARE.

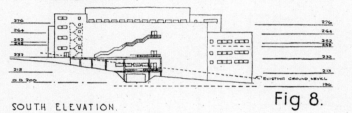

Fig 6.

Fig. (6) The principal elevation to St. James' Square is seen here designed to express, in steel, glass and stone dressed concrete walls, the character of a Festival Centre for music and drama. Gay informality is the mode and the aim.

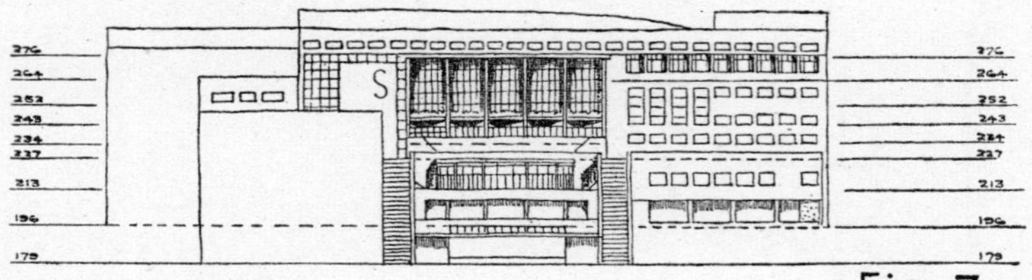

ELEVATION TO BROUGHTON STREET.

Fig 7.

Fig. (7) This elevation to Broughton Street carries on the same mode as that suggested in Fig. (6), the main entrance provides the dominant feature to the terraced gardens on the lower levels in the foreground.

SOUTH ELEVATION.

Fig 8.

ELEVATION TO NORTH ST JAMES STREET

Fig 9.

Fig. (8) These are the north and south elevations which incorporate the and (9) principal emergency ' escapes ' and service entrances.

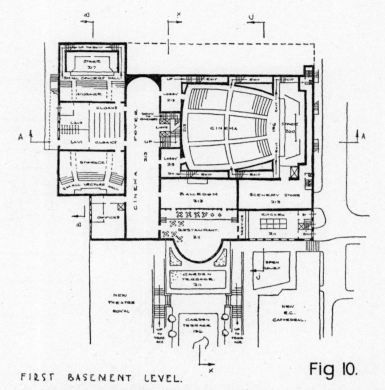

FIRST BASEMENT LEVEL.

Fig 10.

Fig. (10) Here the first basement floor level (213 O.D.) shows the accommodation for a large cinema and ballroom with restaurant, which gives access on to one of the garden terraces.

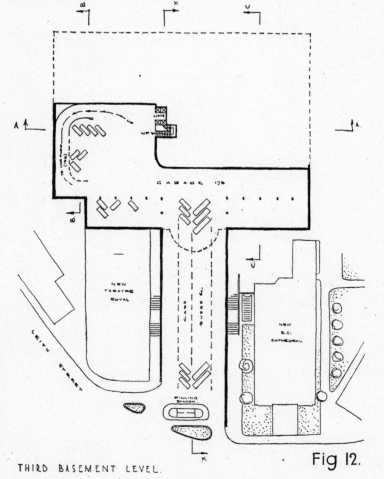

THIRD BASEMENT LEVEL.

Fig 12.

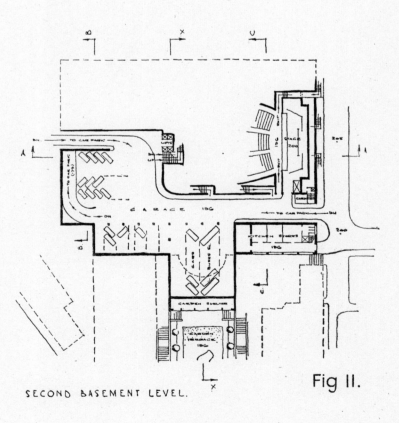

SECOND BASEMENT LEVEL.

Fig 11.

Fig. (11) The second basement floor level (196 O.D. and 159 O.D.) and (12) shown here, indicates garaging accommodation for buses or motor cars.

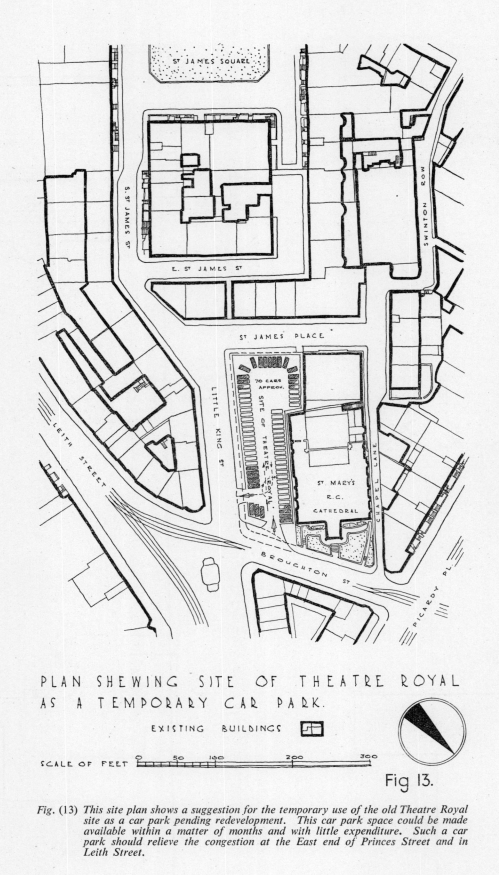

PLAN SHEWING SITE OF THEATRE ROYAL
AS A TEMPORARY CAR PARK.

EXISTING BUILDINGS

SCALE OF FEET

Fig 13.

Fig. (13) This site plan shows a suggestion for the temporary use of the old Theatre Royal site as a car park pending redevelopment. This car park space could be made available within a matter of months and with little expenditure. Such a car park should relieve the congestion at the East end of Princes Street and in Leith Street.

INDEX

References are to pages where not otherwise stated